Catholic Missionaries in Early Modern Asia

Over recent decades, historians have become increasingly interested in early modern Catholic missions in Asia as laboratories of cultural contact. This book builds on recent groundbreaking research on early modern Catholic missions, which has shown that missionaries in Asia cooperated with and accommodated the needs of local agents rather than being uncompromising promoters of post-Tridentine doctrine and devotion.

Bringing together some of the most renowned and innovative researchers from Anglophone countries and continental Europe, this volume investigates how missionaries' entanglements with local societies across Asia contributed to processes of localization within the early modern Catholic church. The focus of the volume is on missionaries' adaptation to four ideal-typical social settings that played an eminent role in early modern Asian missions: (1) the symbolically loaded princely court; (2) the city as a space of especially dense communication; (3) the countryside, where missionary presence was only rarely permanent; (4) and the household – a central arena of conversion in early modern Asian societies.

Shining a fresh light onto the history of early modern Catholic missions and the early modern Eurasian cultural exchange, this will be an important book for any scholar of religious history, history of cultural contact, global history and early modern history in Asia.

Nadine Amsler is Postdoctoral Fellow at the Department for Early Modern History at the Goethe University Frankfurt. She is the author of *Jesuits and Matriarchs: Domestic Worship in Early Modern China* (Seattle 2018). She is also one of the editors of a special issue of the *International History Review* entitled *Transformations of Intercultural Diplomacies. Comparative Views on Asia and Europe (1700 to 1850)* (2019).

Andreea Badea is a researcher at the Department for Early Modern History at the Goethe University Frankfurt. She is the author of *Kurfürstliche Präeminenz, Landesherrschaft und Reform: Das Scheitern der Kölner Reformation unter Hermann von Wied* (Münster 2009). She is also one of the editors of *Establishing Credibility in Early Modern Catholicism: Making and Administering Truth* (forthcoming, Amsterdam 2020).

Bernard Heyberger is Directeur d'Études at the École des Hautes Études des Sciences Sociales and at the École Pratique des Hautes Études in Paris. He is the author of *Les chrétiens du Proche-Orient au temps de la Réforme catholique* (Rome 1994) and, more recently, *Les chrétiens au Proche-Orient: De la compassion à la compréhension* (Paris 2013).

Christian Windler is Professor of Early Modern History at the Department of History of the University of Bern. He is the author of *La diplomatie comme expérience de l'Autre. Consuls français au Maghreb (1700–1840)* (Geneva 2002) and *Missionare in Persien: Kulturelle Diversität und Normenkonkurrenz im globalen Katholizismus (17.–18. Jahrhundert)* (Cologne 2019).

Religious Cultures in the Early Modern World

The Renaissance Ethics of Music
Singing, Contemplation and Musica Humana
Hyun-Ah Kim

Calvinism, Reform and the Absolutist State in Elizabethan Ireland
Mark A. Hutchinson

Indulgences after Luther
Pardons in Counter-Reformation France, 1520–1720
Elizabeth C Tingle

Conversion to Catholicism in Early Modern Italy
Peter A. Mazur

Missionary Strategies in the New World, 1610–1690
An Intellectual History
Catherine Ballériaux

Food and Religious Identities in Spain, 1400–1600
Jillian Williams

John Owen and the Civil War Apocalypse
Preaching, Prophecy and Politics
Martyn Calvin Cowan

Medicine and Religion in the Life of an Ottoman Sheikh
Al-Damanhuri's "Clear Statement" on Anatomy
Ahmed Ragab

Catholic Missionaries in Early Modern Asia
Patterns of Localization
Nadine Amsler, Andreea Badea, Bernard Heyberger and Christian Windler

For more information about this series, please visit: www.routledge.com/Religious-Cultures-in-the-Early-Modern-World/book-series/RCEMW

Catholic Missionaries in Early Modern Asia

Patterns of Localization

Edited by Nadine Amsler, Andreea Badea, Bernard Heyberger, and Christian Windler

Routledge
Taylor & Francis Group
LONDON AND NEW YORK

First published 2020
by Routledge
2 Park Square, Milton Park, Abingdon, Oxon OX14 4RN

and by Routledge
52 Vanderbilt Avenue, New York, NY 10017

Routledge is an imprint of the Taylor & Francis Group, an informa business

British Library Cataloguing-in-Publication Data
A catalogue record for this book is available from the British Library

Library of Congress Cataloging-in-Publication Data
A catalog record for this book has been requested

ISBN: 978-0-367-02881-7 (hbk)
ISBN: 978-0-429-00124-6 (ebk)

Typeset in Sabon
by Apex CoVantage, LLC

Contents

Contributors

Nadine Amsler, Postdoctoral Fellow, Department for Early Modern History, Goethe University Frankfurt

Andreea Badea, Researcher, Department for Early Modern History, Goethe University Frankfurt

Birgit Emich, Professor, Department for Early Modern History, Goethe University Frankfurt

Bernard Heyberger, Directeur d'Études, EHESS and EPHE, both in Paris

Ronnie Po-chia Hsia, Edwin Erle Sparks Professor of History, Pennsylvania State University

Eugenio Menegon, Associate Professor, Department of History, Boston University

Cesare Santus, Postdoctoral Researcher, Université Catholique de Louvain

Nicolas Standaert, Professor of Sinology, KU Leuven

Hélène Vu Thanh, Maître de conférences, Université de Bretagne-Sud, Lorient

Felicita Tramontana, Associate Researcher, University of Warwick

Carla Tronu, Associate Researcher, Kyoto University

Haruko Nawata Ward, Professor of Church History, Columbia Theological Seminary, Decatur, Georgia

Christian Windler, Professor, Department of History, University of Bern

Ines G. Županov, Directrice de Recherche, CNRS, Paris

Introduction

Localizing Catholic missions in Asia

Nadine Amsler, Andreea Badea, Bernard Heyberger, and Christian Windler

Since the sixteenth century, the narratives of mission history have been shaped by the Catholic Church's claims to universality and have been connected with the history of European expansion. It was at that time that the Latin term *missio* gained its double meaning of spreading faith among non-Christians and intensifying faith among Christians.[1] The missions became a central motif in the self-fashioning of the papacy, religious orders, and secular Catholic rulers, as they facilitated a demarcation from the churches that emerged from the Protestant Reformation, which were less active in this field.[2] Members of religious orders wrote the histories of the missions of their communities, in order to legitimate their claims to a well-respected position within church and society. The Jesuits were especially successful in this, but less well-known orders, such as the Discalced Carmelites, also tried to emulate their example.[3]

The varying levels of self-promotion of missionary orders make their effects felt even today in the one-sided focus of research on the Jesuits. However, it has been research on this very order, which has fundamentally changed our view of the Catholic missions in recent times. During the last decades, scholars have increasingly read the mission orders' self-representations against the grain and started to question their universalist-expansionist framework. As a result, the trajectory of the history of religious missions has moved away from the Eurocentric history of religious orders, and toward broader questions of cultural history. These questions are facilitating a renewal of the research on the Catholic missions of the early modern period, which, in turn, offers stimulating impulses for the investigation of intercultural communication.[4]

Research on early modern Catholic missions in China has been a case in point. The controversies about the admissibility of local ritual practices – specifically in the Chinese rites controversies – had already found broad resonance with European contemporaries in the seventeenth century, whose interest in the Chinese missions increased steadily. In the course of the twentieth century the practices of accommodation to local sociocultural contexts associated with the Jesuits have become a central line of historical inquiry. While this research was still mainly focused on missionaries, research from the 1990s onwards has become increasingly focused on the study of the local Christian communities. Their practices are now being redefined as expressions of specific forms of Christianity, which took shape through the interactions between missionaries and locals.[5] Linked with this development is the broadening of the research perspective beyond the urban, courtly milieu of the male literati, to include rural Christian communities,[6] as well as the domestic sphere associated with femininity.[7]

We can observe a similar development toward an increased focus on local forms of Christianity in research on other regions of Asia. In her work on Southern India, Ines G. Županov identifies a "tropical Catholicism" as a locally specific practice of appropriating post-Tridentine Catholicism.[8] Bernard Heyberger's work on Eastern Christians in the Syrian provinces of the Ottoman Empire demonstrates that in the Middle Eastern context a similar development is taking place, whereby research is increasingly focusing on local Christianities.[9] This is accompanied by the insight that the regular clerics working in the context of the Catholic missions were "more than just missionaries of the Christian faith," since they adopted a variety of social roles on the ground.[10] The history of the Catholic missions is thus becoming an actor-centered history of transcultural relations between Europe and Asia. Narratives of European expansion are ceding their place to a decentered view of clerics as mediators of various normative systems.

Such a decentered approach, which focuses on questions of social and cultural history, facilitates a reconceptualization of the history of early modern Catholicism. Combined with the research interest in Western European forms of local religion,[11] a polycentric image emerges of early modern Catholicisms.[12] This image is furthermore complemented by new research on the Roman institutions responsible for overseas missions. This research has brought to light a variety of actors in Rome and beyond who claimed to act on behalf of the reform of the Catholic Church, of the defense of its position against the Protestant churches, and of the expansion of the Christian faith. The Roman congregations of the Holy Office and *Propaganda Fide* stood for a form of administration that legitimized its decisions on the basis of the formalization and standardization of its procedures.[13] In practice, these procedures were determined by the interactions between institution building and the development of interpersonal networks.[14] As rulers in an elective monarchy, the popes remained dependent on the families from which they descended.[15] The secular rulers with whom these families were connected sought in turn to influence the papal election, as well as the Roman practices of governance.[16] In this way, different European Catholicisms extended their influence as far as the Roman Curia. Simultaneously, Iberian and French missions competed with the Curia, invoking their rights of patronate or protection. Shifting configurations of relationships emerged on the ground in Asia, which at times even created the need for cooperation with English and Dutch "heretics" against the Portuguese.[17]

Since the pontificate of Clement VIII, the efforts to establish a congregation for the propagation of the faith were combined with attempts to concentrate church governance on the pope and to curtail the Iberian patronate rights. These enterprises progressed in anything but a straightforward manner.[18] Despite the early modern papacy's claims to universality in jurisdiction and administration, the *Propaganda Fide* founded in 1622 remained an overwhelmingly Italian institution that spent 40 to 50 percent of its extremely tight budget on promoting the missions as an enterprise of the papacy within the city of Rome, while only small sums were allocated to the missions abroad.[19] However, this financial imbalance was not a special characteristic of the missions of the *Propaganda Fide*. Rather, it was a common point of all missions that the money assigned to them was far from sufficient, and that they found themselves forced to generate additional revenue on the ground. As a consequence, missionaries became engaged with local societies not only due to evangelization but also due to economic necessity.[20]

It is both the research conducted on local Catholicisms in Asia as well as research that has pointed toward the limited power of European institutions, especially the Roman Curia, over the missions that form the starting point of this volume and its focus on patterns of localization: the ways in which, and extent to which, Catholic missionaries adapted to and integrated into local societies in Asia. Without denying the larger – and sometimes truly global – framework within which missionaries operated, the contributions are particularly interested into how they acted and saw themselves as local agents.[21] The volume thus inscribes itself into the recent research on local Christianities outlined earlier, but has a sharper focus on the figure of the missionary and his interactions with local societies. Furthermore, it also sheds light on the tensions between missionaries and their sending institutions and shows that localization, as much as it was a necessity, also generated such tensions.[22] These tensions often resulted in the emergence of new cultural and religious phenomena characterized by "in-betweenness," as Nicolas Standaert has observed for Chinese Christianity.[23]

The actor-centered approach connects this volume with the research on cultural brokers and intermediaries, where this approach has a long tradition.[24] Whereas scholars have often described intermediaries as people who "moved between cultures," more recently Nathalie Rothman has put forward the idea that intermediaries played an important role "in fixing the boundaries of the objects they are purported to mediate."[25] This perspective can be fruitfully employed in an analysis of the ways in which missionaries adapted to and integrated into local societies in Asia. Missionaries of different backgrounds described the same societies in strikingly different ways and developed divergent strategies to gain access for evangelization. Thus some members of missionary orders (and, as Cesare Santus and Christian Windler show in this volume, not always the Jesuits) opted for an adaptation of their lifestyle and their teachings to the social group at whose conversion they aimed, whereas others kept more in accordance with the standards set by the Roman Curia and the superiors of the orders. These divergences show that the cultural boundaries drawn by missionaries should be analyzed not only as messages about the societies observed by the missionaries but also as messages about these men's understanding of their own religion and cultures of origin. They also show that the cultural boundaries that missionaries – as intermediaries between Catholic European and non-Christian Asian societies – transgressed were all but rigid and fixed lines but rather were negotiated.

An analysis of patterns of localization necessarily places the attention on the spatial dimension of missionaries' activities. This is why the four sections of this volume do not discuss different geographical regions (such as the Near East, South, or East Asia), but different localities: the court, the city, the countryside, and the household. As Doreen Massey has proposed, localities are best understood as places that are "constructed out of a particular constellation of social relations, meeting and weaving together at a particular locus."[26] They are thus the result of human interaction in a concrete geographical space. The processes during which missionaries inserted themselves into these webs of interaction is what we might call their processes of localization. The four localities that are taken into focus by the four sections of this book are, of course, ideal-typical places and therefore need further clarification. In what respect is rural Palestine comparable to rural mission areas in Japan? Is the Qing court in China comparable to the Safavid court in Persia? In short, can the localities discussed in this volume be used as generic categories under which phenomena from different corners of the Asian continent may be subsumed?

Although work with ideal-typical categories has to take seriously the warnings of comparative research that terms often "suggest equivalence where there is little or none,"[27] the present volume benefits from the recent work of comparative historians who have begun to shed more light on several of these categories. Thus, Jeroen Duindam's global comparisons from 1300 to 1800 have shown that even if courts considerably varied with respect to their mobility, the accessibility of rulers, and the modalities of staff recruitment, they can nevertheless be defined as both "[a ruler's] abode as well as his retinue of kin, consort, guards, domestics, advisors, purveyors." A third defining characteristic of the court is that it "also stands for sovereignty and government."[28] Similarly, Peter Clark has suggested a "kind of catholic definitional matrix" for global comparisons of cities, whom "we might expect . . . usually, but not invariably to have a relatively dense population concentration; a range of economic functions; complex social and political structures (but not necessarily institutional ones); a cultural influence extending beyond community borders; and a distinctive built environment."[29]

Definitions for the categories "countryside" and "household" that are appropriate for broad comparisons are more difficult to find. While scholars of rural history have initiated a dialogue about rural history in the Western world, global comparative studies are still missing.[30] Nevertheless, there is a consensus that early modern rural areas are, as compared with contemporary cities, characterized by comparatively low population density and by a predominantly agrarian economy. Households, on the other hand, have been the focus of studies situated in fields as varied as Islamic studies,[31] Chinese studies,[32] and European history,[33] all of which have pointed to the variety and historicity of "households" and the "families" inhabiting them. In the absence of studies aiming at global comparison, the contributions of this volume are interested in households as material dwellings of "families," using a broad and open definition of "family" that may include various forms of affiliation (cohabitation of generations, parallel families, cohabitation with slaves).[34]

The contributions analyze the four localities through the lens of the missionaries, asking how the localities provided them with different opportunities for interaction and communication. The court, with its pondering figure of the prince, provided missionaries with different communicative options than the city, which was not only a space for dense communication in itself but usually also served as a nodal point for larger regions. In comparison to cities and courts, furthermore, the communicative conditions of rural areas, which were frequently – albeit, as Felicita Tramontana shows for the semi-rural Palestine, not exclusively – visited by itinerant missionaries, were more restrained.[35] Finally, empirical evidence shows that the household was the preferred space for communication between missionaries and women in many Asian societies.[36] This is why women figure prominently in the section about households, although researchers on women's history have repeatedly, and rightly so, reminded us to challenge views that associate women exclusively with the domestic realm.[37]

Mobility is inherent to apostolic life and is part of Christian spirituality. This is evidenced by medieval missions, which were conceived as pilgrimages (*peregrinationes*). Although early modern missions developed the idea of stable residences, early modern missionaries continued to be highly mobile.[38] Missionaries not only traveled from Catholic Europe to Asia, but often circulated between different mission stations. As a consequence, the contributions also analyze the importance of movement between localities. They highlight the importance of general patterns that determined missionaries' movements (Ronnie Po-chia Hsia) but also turn our attention to the fact that some missionaries found it difficult to switch communication modes between different settings (Ines G. Županov).

Why is this volume's focus on Asia, and in what respect did Catholic missions in early modern Asia differ from missions in other parts of the world? First, the Catholic Church's internal organization of missions provides a reason for this focus. As Giovanni Pizzorusso has shown, the Roman Curia defined as missionary territories those in which the common canonical law of the church was not the norm.[39] This is the case for Asia, as described in this volume. In contrast with the Spanish and Portuguese Americas or New

France, the church had only an incipient institutional structure formed by dioceses, seminaries, and local synods. Asian societies were not pervaded by the post-Tridentine norms concerning public space occupation, dress codes, and religious and social practices around birth, marriage, or death, and Christian priests were not considered to be legitimate producers and monitors of the dominant norms. Even if big parts of Asia theoretically belonged to the Portuguese Patronate, it became obvious starting around the end of the sixteenth century that the Portuguese crown was unable to set or manage a Catholic-ruled order over the majority of Asian territories and societies.

A second feature of those parts of early modern Asia studied in this volume is that they were parts of countries with comparatively differentiated political structures. At least in the cities and in their central regions, all these countries possessed a highly developed social system and a sophisticated culture based on writing, quite different from what Europeans encountered in America or Africa, placing them on the highest step of the scale of civilizations conceived by José de Acosta in his *De procuranda Indorum Salute* (1580), comparable with the Greeks and the Romans.[40] Furthermore, European colonial powers were only a minor and, in many places, negligible force. As a consequence, missionaries had to find ways to insert themselves into Asian societies without the backing of European states that they had in the Americas. Under these circumstances, localization also meant coming to grips with local political authorities.

European missionaries were fascinated by the cultural achievements in China, Japan, India, and Persia (and to a lesser extent in the Ottoman Empire), and they tried to become associated with the local educated elites who staffed the courts and administrations. This was possible under specific conditions, like lavishly dressing, practicing the official language, and making compromises with local "civic" rituals. However, Asian empires were not compact homogeneous states. Institutions and society offered interstices where populations with another social organization, and different systems of believing, were segregated, yet tolerated. Within these subordinated segments of society, Western missionaries could frequently find shelter and support, and could experience alternative, bottom-up methods of conversion.

The volume begins with a section on missionaries as actors at court. It is introduced by Christian Windler's chapter on missionaries' attendance at the Safavid court. He compares the various patterns of accommodation observable among the different orders – both in their missionary activities and in their performance of worldly duties vis-à-vis the shah. The shah's inclusive form of government afforded the missionaries not only rapid access to the court but – through their functions as interpreters and intermediaries and their solid relations of trust with local actors – also opportunities for integration which, however, only rarely resulted in conversion to Islam. The Jesuits who attended the Chinese court pursued fewer personal strategies of accommodation: to establish themselves at court, they adopted the manners and thus implicitly the dress code of the literati, thus diverting attention from their identity as European clerics. In his chapter, Eugenio Menegon shows that not only the Jesuits but also all the other orders were thus able to obtain access to the court's inner circles during the late Ming and early Qing dynasties. The Jesuit and Neapolitan nobleman Rodolfo Acquaviva was also especially skilled in communication at court; as both a Portuguese envoy and Jesuit scholar he had a firm place in the structure of the Mughal court. Ines G. Županov uses his example to demonstrate the importance of communicative adaptation to a specific setting for the success, or lack thereof, of missions.

The Jesuits in late imperial China were more successful in shifting between geographical, and thus social and cultural, spheres. Their activities reveal differences between patterns of evangelization in urban and rural areas. Ronnie Po-chia Hsia discusses these patterns in his contribution, examining the significance of patronage in city and village. His chapter introduces the second section, that turns to the city as locality in China, Japan, and the Ottoman Empire. Carla Tronu focuses resolutely on the city. Using the example of Nagasaki, sometimes referred to as Japan's "Christian city," she traces in detail the important role played by the laity in establishing congregations after the post-Tridentine model. The Christian population of Nagasaki was deeply involved in the economic support and development of a functioning infrastructure for the mission. But as congregations and through their priests, they also played a pivotal role in the outcome of the dispute between the Jesuits and the mendicant orders. Cesare Santus also examines disputes between the various orders in the course of the seventeenth and eighteenth centuries, taking his examples from Ottoman cities, where the officials of the Sublime Porte and representatives of the Crown of France and the Roman Curia were also involved in the rivalry between the orders. In deciding between rigorous enforcement of their demands and adapting to circumstances, the missionaries' choice was always determined by their local economic and social interests.

Felicita Tramontana introduces the third section, which focuses on missionary work in the countryside. The Franciscans of the Custody of the Holy Land could look back on many years of in-country experience that nevertheless only extended to missionary work from the late sixteenth century onwards. Established in the rural and semi-urban areas of the district of Jerusalem, they were able to employ a broad strategy of interaction with variously positioned local actors, while at the same time adapting their tactics to each specific setting. Trent Pomplun, on the other hand, focuses more on the missionaries as observers: he analyzes the travel journals of António de Andrade (1580–1634) and Ippolito Desideri (1684–1733), showing how little attention they paid to rural districts, even though the two missionaries spent most of their time traveling in precisely such areas. The local population appears in their accounts in just a few summary sketches. The rural population plays a very different role in Hélène Vu Thanh's chapter.

She examines the interaction between the Jesuits and Japanese peasants, focusing on the substantial practical support that the latter provided to the missionaries. The degree to which the Jesuits were integrated into local economic networks was on the one hand a subject of debates within the order, and on the other a major cause of the Japanese elite's increasing hostility toward the Christians.

The last section takes a look at the household as a sphere of missionary activities and pays special attention to the relationship between missionaries and women, which was often situated in households rather than in the public sphere. Nadine Amsler demonstrates how, in adapting the lifestyle of the Confucian literati elite, Jesuit missionaries in the seventeenth century were also forced to accept its customs regarding gender separation. This meant that Christian women mainly assembled in house oratories established in rich Catholic families' homes. Nevertheless, the missionaries managed to maintain close contact with them via a range of intermediaries, including male relatives, children, servants, and lay brothers. Haruko Nawata Ward, on the other hand, draws attention to women as creators of Kirishitan (Christian) literature, postulating that many of these texts were written through a collaborative process, in which European and Japanese Jesuits worked with Japanese women. Using different examples, Ward examines the role of women translators for the gender-nuanced structuring of the Kirishitan faith. Bernard Heyberger rounds off the section with a chapter on the close collaboration between missionaries and Eastern Christian women in Ottoman cities. Islamic law, local administrative traditions, and the Eastern Christian clergy forced the missionaries to work under conditions of secrecy. Simultaneously, this special relationship with Catholic priests allowed women to develop, through education, alternatives to their traditional roles in the household. The case study once again offers evidence for the double implication of the missionaries' practices of localization: on the one hand, their efforts at adaptation ignited controversies within the orders, with other clerics present in place, and in their relations with the Roman Curia and secular patrons. On the other hand, while the missionaries' actions opened up more opportunities for them to act within the local context, they also, in very different measure, had a transformational effect on the host societies themselves.

The volume closes with two afterwords that look at the contributions from two different perspectives. Nicolas Standaert focuses on the encounter between missionaries and the "other," highlighting the fruitfulness of a focus on "in-betweenness" and on the ways missionaries and local agents were shaped by each other. Birgit Emich situates the local encounters within larger political and economic frameworks, highlighting the importance of both the European and Asian political and economic relations that structured missionaries' options for action. Both authors stress the fact that localization needs to be understood as an ongoing process, one that is continuously negotiated and re-negotiated between missionaries and local societies.

At the origin of this volume was a workshop on missionaries as local agents in Asia held in June 2017 in Rome. We would like to thank the Deutsches Historisches Institut Rom, the École Française de Rome, the Istituto Svizzero di Roma, the University of Bern, the Fritz Thyssen Foundation, and the Swiss National Science Foundation, all of whom generously supported this meeting. Furthermore, many people supported us during the publication process: Joshua Wells from Routledge helped with practical advice, and two anonymous reviewers provided helpful suggestions. Manuel Näf and Brigitta Matt helped with the formatting of texts and the compilation of the bibliography. Regine Maritz and Samuel Weber translated parts of the manuscript into English, and Allison Adelman carefully copyedited the whole manuscript. We would like to thank all of them for their efforts to make this book an enjoyable and instructive read.

Notes

1 See Prosperi, "L'Europa cristiana e il mondo."
2 In the Netherlands of the seventeenth century there had already been increased discussion of the promotion of Protestant missionary activities (see Gommans and Loots, "Arguing with the Heathens"). Nevertheless, the Protestant churches only began to develop their missions outside of Europe in the eighteenth century.
3 The first volume of the *Istoria della Compagnia di Giesù* by Daniello Bartoli S.J. was published in 1653. Interestingly, the first three volumes of this work published in Italian in 1653, 1660, and 1663 were concerned with the history of the Jesuit mission in Asia. In 1667 a volume with a focus on England followed. Isidore de Saint-Joseph and Pierre de Saint-André treated the missions as an important part of the general history of the Italian congregation of the Discalced Carmelites: Isidore de Saint-Joseph and Pierre de Saint-André, *Historia Generalis Fratrum Discalceatorum Ordinis*. There is also an unpublished history of the missions of the Discalced Carmelites, which was written by the *istorico generale* of the order in the eighteenth century: *Istoria delle missioni de' PP. Carmelitani Scalzi della Congregazione di S. Elia, descritta dal M.R.P. Eusebio di tutt'i Santi, della Provincia Romana, istorico generale della medesima Congregazione*, 5 vols., undated (AGOCD, 285/b and c, 286/a, b, and c).
4 A number of edited volumes on Catholic missions testifies to this development. See Fabre, *Missions religieuses modernes*; Flüchter, *Translating Catechisms, Translating Cultures*; Forrestal and Smith, *The Frontiers of Mission*; Marcocci, de Boer, Maldavsky, and Pavan, *Space and Conversion in Global Perspective*. See also the recent, but somewhat heterogeneous, handbook edited by Ronnie Po-chia Hsia: Hsia, *Companion to Early Modern Catholic Global Missions*.
5 See the exemplary texts by Zürcher, "The Jesuit Mission in Fujian" and Standaert, *The Interweaving of Rituals*.
6 See Harrison, *The Missionary's Curse* and *Menegon, Ancestors, Virgins, and Friars*.
7 See Amsler, *Jesuits and Matriarchs*.
8 See Županov, *Missionary Tropics*, in part. 24–28, 269–270.
9 See Heyberger, *Les Chrétiens du Proche-Orient*. On the new practices of female piety: Heyberger, *Hindiyya*. On the *communicatio in sacris* between Catholics and Eastern Christians: Windler, "Ambiguous Belongings," and, more recently, Santus, *Trasgressioni necessarie*, and Santus, "La *communicatio in sacris*."

10 Hsia, "Translating Christianity," 94. See also, more recently, Windler, *Missionare in Persien*.
11 Pioneer studies in this field include Christian, *Local Religion*, and Forster, *The Counter-Reformation in the Villages*, and more recently Sidler, *Heiligkeit aushandeln*, and Zwyssig, *Täler voller Wunder*.
12 See Ditchfield, "Decentering the Catholic Reformation."
13 In this way, the Roman Curia acted as a model for the state, which was to arise from the processes of institutionalization during the early modern period. See Prodi, *Un corpo e due anime*; id., "Il 'sovrano pontefice.'"
14 See Reinhard, *Paul V. Borghese*, Emich, *Bürokratie und Nepotismus*, and Signorotto and Visceglia, *Court and Politics*.
15 See Ago, *Carriere e clientele*, in part. 157–158, 176–180.
16 On the papal election see Pattenden, *Electing the Pope*; Visceglia, *Morte e elezione*; Wassilowsky, *Die Konklavereform Gregors XV*.
17 See Windler, *Missionare in Persien*, 377–498.
18 On the reorganization of papal governance under Clement VIII, see Fattori, *Clemente VIII e il Sacro Collegio*.
19 On the limited range of the jurisdiction of the curial congregations, see Menniti Ippolito, *Un anno della Chiesa universale*. On the Holy Office compare Siebenhüner, *Bigamie und Inquisition*; Black, *The Italian Inquisition*, 27–53. On *Propaganda Fide*: Pizzorusso, *Roma nei Caraibi*, as well as numerous articles by the same author. On the "short reach of Rome" (congregations of the Curia and superiors of the religious orders) in relation to missionaries: Windler, *Missionare in Persien*, 31–153 (on the finances of the *Propaganda Fide:* 39–49). On the finances of the Holy Office see Maifreda, *I denari dell'inquisitore*.
20 See Windler, *Missionare in Persien*, 44–49, 539–573. See also Alden, *The Making of an Enterprise*, 319–567; Golvers, *François de Rougemont, S.J.*, 553–630; Lederle, *Mission und Ökonomie*, esp. 178–251; Vermote, "Finances of the Mission"; Vu Thanh, *Devenir japonais*, 46–51, 157–159.
21 The global dimension of early modern missionaries has been highlighted by Clossey, *Salvation and Globalization*.
22 On the advantages of describing the Catholic Church as a translocal institution, see Zwyssig, *Täler voller Wunder*, esp. 38.
23 See Standaert, "Don't Mind the Gap." See also the afterword by the same author in this volume.
24 For a short overview of the research on cultural mediation, see Rothman, *Brokering Empire*, 3–7. For actor-centered studies on Eurasian diplomacies, see Amsler, Harrison, and Windler, *Intercultural Diplomacies*. For a broad overview on actors of cultural mediation in the early modern period, see Eibach and Opitz, *Zwischen Kulturen*. Several historians have described missionaries as "cultural brokers." See Oesterle, "Missionaries as Cultural Brokers," and the contributions to part II in Rozbicki and Ndege, *Cross-Cultural History and the Domestication of Otherness*.
25 See Rothman, *Brokering Empire*, 5.
26 Massey, "Global Sense of Place," 28. See also Appadurai, *Modernity at Large*, 178, for another relational approach to "locality." Although some of the present volume's contributions work with the concept of "third space" developed by Homi Bhabha (see Bhabha, *The Location of Culture*), this concept does not take center stage in this volume because it pays comparatively little attention to the physical dimensions of social spaces.
27 See Duindam, *Dynasties*, 157.
28 See Duindam, *Dynasties*, 158. For his discussion of the variables "mobility," "accessibility," and "staff recruitment," see 156–200.

29 See Clark, "Introduction," 5.
30 For an overview of regional historiographical traditions in Medieval rural history, see Alfonso, *The Rural History* and Herr, *Themes in Rural History*.
31 See, e.g., Hathaway, *The Politics of Households in Ottoman Egypt* and Doumani, *Family Life in the Ottoman Mediterranean*.
32 See Bray, *Technology and Gender* for a gendered analysis of Chinese households and Ebrey and Watson, "Introduction" for an overview on notions of "household" and "family" in Chinese history.
33 See Eibach and Schmidt-Voges, *Das Haus in der Geschichte Europas*.
34 For recent discussions, initiated by anthropologists, on non-biological definitions of kinship, see Carsten, *After Kinship*. For an overview of new trends in the history of European families and kinship, see Sabean, Teuscher, and Matthieu, *Kinship in Europe*. For a first attempt of global comparisons of domesticities that suggests paying close attention to the materiality of households, see Faini and Meneghin, "Introduction," 9.
35 Missionaries (and especially Jesuits) conceived the rural setting as a specific world to convert: Châtellier, *La religion des pauvres*, 61–121, 247–268.
36 A strong link between women and domestic religiosity also existed in other parts of the early modern world. See Faini and Meneghin, "Introduction."
37 See the foundational article by Rosaldo, "The Use and Abuse of Anthropology," 399–400.
38 See Prosperi, "L'Europa Cristiana e il mondo."
39 Pizzorusso, *Governare le missioni*, 42.
40 Acosta, *De procuranda Indorum Salute*, vol. 1, 60–63.

Part I

Missionaries at princely courts

1 Between convent and court life

Missionaries in Isfahan and New Julfa

Christian Windler

At the end of his *History of Shah ʿAbbās*, Iskandar Bēg Munshī, a secretary at the court of the shah, included an obituary notice in which, to prove the ruler's exceptional qualities, he pointed out that his "court was rarely without a foreign embassy." The group of Muslim and non-Muslim rulers who, motivated by reports of the shah's "just and beneficent rule," sent their ambassadors to Persia included the Pope, "the greatest of the Christian rulers, the caliph of the Christians, and . . . the exemplar of all Christian sects." As proof of the papacy's ties to the shah, Iskandar Bēg Munshī reproduced verbatim the translation of a brief sent to ʿAbbās I by pope Urban VIII, "so that envious persons . . . realize that [he was] not guilty of artificial elaboration such as secretaries indulge in." The breve had indeed been sent to ʿAbbās I in 1624; however, the Persian translation, which according to Iskandar Bēg Munshī had been prepared by foreigners living in Isfahan, differed significantly from the Latin original written in Rome. Whereas the Roman author described the "protection of the world and of mankind" as a distinctive mark of papal dignity, the authors of the "translation" reproduced by Iskandar Bēg Munshī turned the breve into an ode to the shah whom they described as "the refulgence of the infinite divine grace and the refuge of all mankind" and "the model and source of guidance for people throughout the world, and particularly for the Vicar of Christ Our Lord at Rome." Since ʿAbbās I towered over other princes "in grandeur and majesty and dominion," the pope supposedly argued, all mankind should pray for the perpetuity of his reign, which was why he, Urban VIII, considered it his duty to instruct everyone in his churches to pray that God would bless ʿAbbās I with a long life and his assistance.[1]

It remains unclear whether Urban VIII's breve had really been translated by Europeans residing in Isfahan in the exact form in which it was later quoted by Iskandar Bēg Munshī or whether the chronicler had doctored an existing translation before he included it in his treatise. Also, who exactly were the translators? Was the Discalced Carmelite Juan Thadeo de San Eliseo one of them? His role as an interpreter and translator of diplomatic correspondence from Europe to the Safavid court is well documented in other instances.[2] And if European missionaries possibly had a share in this translation, what does that tell us about Catholic missionaries' position at the Safavid court? This article ventures to clarify this question by analyzing the missionaries' integration into networks at the Safavid court of Persia.

It will likely never be possible to identify the translator of Urban VIII's breve.[3] The juxtaposition of the Latin original and the Persian "translation" nevertheless helps shed light on a number of aspects that are central to the history of Catholic missions to Persia in the seventeenth and eighteenth centuries. The first point to note is that both the Latin original and the Persian version gave voice to conflicting claims to superiority; on the ground in Persia this contradiction was "overcome" thanks to the falsification of the papal breve. Meanwhile, the Persian version is evidence of an inclusive conception of dominion and religion that had been a prerequisite for the admission of Catholic clergymen to the Safavid court in the first place. On the one hand, the wording shows how the Safavids weaponized the reception of envoys from non-Muslim rulers to strengthen the dynasty's claim to imperial superiority. On the other hand, the assumption that Christian prayers for ʿAbbās I could be effective attests to the belief that Christians, too, had received divine revelation, albeit in incomplete form. The cultivation of contacts between shah ʿAbbās I and Christian European courts in the early seventeenth century needs to be considered in the context of the shah's imperial and religious ambitions. The consolidation of monarchical power over a socioculturally and religiously heterogeneous empire through the development of institutions and a mercenary army, as well as the integration of various sections of the population into the networks of the court, on the one hand, and the quest for allies against the Ottomans, on the other.[4]

During this period, news of the exploits of ʿAbbās I's armies against the Ottomans reached European courts, reviving interest in an anti-Ottoman alliance with the shah. Beginning around 1600, the Safavid Empire became the focal point of a broad variety of expectations ranging from political, military, and commercial interests to the hopes of finally finding a Muslim population susceptible to the Christian gospel. At the court of Philip III, king of Castile and Portugal, and in the Roman Curia it was hoped that an alliance with Persia would help realize two dreams at once – military triumph over the Turks and the conversion of numerous Muslims to Christianity.[5]

These hopes led to the dispatch of Portuguese Augustinians from Goa and of Discalced Carmelites from Rome, who arrived in Isfahan in 1602 and 1607, respectively, armed with a double religious and diplomatic mandate. They were joined by a group of Capuchins from the province of Touraine who arrived in 1628 as part of a mission under the protection of the French crown which had previously been primarily interested in the Ottoman Empire. Whereas the political dimension of the pope's instructions to the Discalced Carmelites quickly lost importance, the Augustinians in Isfahan maintained close ties to the viceroy of Portuguese India at Goa and to the court of Madrid (later Lisbon), so much so that the prior of the Augustinian convent in Isfahan acted as their permanent agent in the Safavid court. Up to 1700 the same was true of the guardian of the French Capuchins who had been instructed to defend the interests of his king at the Safavid court. Whereas the Augustinians, the Discalced Carmelites, and the Capuchins chose to settle in Isfahan, the Jesuits, who arrived in the 1660s, and the Dominicans, who followed them in the 1680s, took up residence in the Armenian suburb of New Julfa. This choice was in line with these two orders' strategy that aimed at convincing the Armenian community to enter into union with Rome and at caring for the spiritual needs of the European diaspora who resided there, culminating in the establishment of a school run by the Jesuits. The Discalced Carmelites later also adopted this orientation when father Élie de Saint-Albert settled in New Julfa in 1679 and opened a second house of his order there.[6]

Their religious and diplomatic double mandate forced the Augustinians, the Capuchins, and, initially at least, the Discalced Carmelites to cultivate close ties to the court of the shah. The first part of this contribution compares and contrasts the role of one Augustinian (António de Jesus alias ʿAlī-Qulī Jadīd al-Islām), one Capuchin (Raphaël du Mans), and one Discalced Carmelite (Juan Thadeo de San Eliseo) at the Safavid court, pointing out their different patterns of integration into the local court society. The second part discusses the conflicts within the orders that arose from the missionaries' ties to court society. Outsiders aside, the contradiction between the ideals of detachment from worldly affairs and the papal mandate sparked long and intense debates within the orders themselves, most notably among the Discalced Carmelites, for whom missionary work was sometimes viewed as incompatible with the order's commitment to a contemplative lifestyle detached from the world. Fathers who cultivated ties to the court were accused by their brethren of not taking the norms of the orders seriously. The adoption of signs of social distinction that contravened the vocation of members of religious orders came under criticism. This contribution concludes by questioning this criticism from a local perspective using contemporary Protestant travel accounts.

1 Missionaries at the Safavid court

If the fathers who arrived in Persia starting in 1602 enjoyed direct access to the Safavid court, this can be attributed to a practice of conviviality that set the ceremonial at the Safavid court apart from that of its Ottoman counterpart. At the Safavid court the majesty of the ruler was visualized, among other things, through the invitation of foreign guests to feasts that were presided over by the shah. Unlike at the Ottoman court, Christian emissaries also interacted with the ruler in audiences.[7] The accessibility of the ruler facilitated narrow contacts in the context of the missions of the early seventeenth century but also led to misunderstandings. The conversionary hopes which the Augustinians and Discalced Carmelites initially shared were fueled not least by the fact that the missionaries had been admitted to the ruler and had even been granted permission to argue their position before the assembled court.[8]

At the same time, the high visibility of court activities in Persia resulted in European rulers' preferring to entrust diplomatic exchange with the Safavids to agents who, owing to their position outside the worldly status hierarchies or to their clearly inferior social status, would not be regarded as the alter ego of the sovereign by other members of the European society of princes. This was because emissaries to the Safavid court had to submit to the local ceremonial, which visualized the superiority of the shah. Whereas the Protestant States General and the king of England benefitted from the East India Companies as an exit strategy, Catholic courts entrusted members of religious orders with diplomatic missions. Since members of religious orders were barred from entering the worldly competition over status as a result of their commitment to humility and poverty, reliance on them as diplomatic actors freed European rulers from the burden of defending conflicting status claims. Rulers who dispatched members of religious orders as agents could forego the representational expenses incurred by secular envoys and still preserve their honor.[9]

Whereas, in the case of the Discalced Carmelites, the instruction to cultivate political ties to the Safavid court was of some importance only in the early years of the mission, it continued to be crucially important to the Portuguese Augustinians throughout the existence of their convent in Isfahan and to the French Capuchins up until the replacement of the fathers by secular envoys in the early eighteenth century. It is important to bear in mind that such individual missionaries' ties to the local court were exceptions to the rule. However, just as it would be wrong to make sweeping generalizations about all missionaries on the basis of a limited number of well-documented cases, it would be equally misleading to underestimate the importance of individual missionaries with close ties at court to the survival of the convents as a whole. The central role of individual fathers in building rapport with members of the court was the result of their familiarity with the local language and customs and the relationships they formed during their stay in Persia, which in some cases lasted many years. In the case of the priors of the Augustinians, their role as intermediaries is confirmed by instructions to the commander of the Portuguese flotilla in the Persian Gulf and to secular emissaries who were occasionally dispatched to Persia.[10] To European travelers, too, the prior of the Augustinians stood out from the other missionaries on account of his role as the agent of the Portuguese crown. According to the Englishman John Fryer, the prior of the Augustinians dressed in accordance with his function as the resident of Portugal and lived "in a splendid palace, with noble walks and gardens," whereas the fathers of the other orders "walk[ed] humbly about the Streets and Markets, discalceated, and in their distinct Habits."[11] The costly interiors of the house of the Augustinians and their numerous servants are reminiscent of the lifestyle of Indo-Portuguese elites. The varied origins and religious backgrounds of their servants – in 1694 the group included a Portuguese cook, three "Moors," two Arabs, three Armenians, and four Indians[12] – attest to the fathers' integration into sociocultural systems of reference and an economy that were, at one and the same time, local and characterized by strong ties to South Asia. While the Augustinians initially relied on their close ties to the Portuguese crown and the viceroy of Portuguese India, who funded the mission through the *Padroado*, they reacted to the decline of Portuguese influence in Asia by moving the mission to a self-sufficient footing.

While they appear to have been fairly successful, economic self-sufficiency came at the cost of far-reaching accommodations that culminated in the conversion to Islam of two fathers in the 1690s. As early as 1685 – that is, before the spectacular conversions – the viceroy of Portuguese India wrote that the convent in Isfahan had undoubtedly once been well respected. At the moment of writing, however, the Augustinians in Isfahan, as well as in Bandar-i Kung, Bengal, and Mombasa, were interested in little else than in "acquiring assets, buying carpets and doing similar business deals" ("adquerir fazenda, comprar alcatifas e fazer outros resgates semelhantes").[13] While the two conversions to Islam remained an exception in the history of the missions to Persia, the apostasy of prior António de Jesus in 1697 induced the Augustinians to address the forms of integration into local society, which can otherwise only be read between the lines, in their internal communication. These ranged from practices of social interaction with Muslims and "heretics," such as mutual invitations to dinner, games and other forms of entertainment, and celebrations of local holidays, including specifically Muslim holidays, to economic integration into, and dependence on, local society.[14]

News of the prior's apostasy reached Goa at a time when the viceroy of Portuguese India received orders from the king to thank António de Jesus for his assistance in negotiating an alliance with the Safavids.[15] Following his conversion and his wedding to a Muslim woman, António de Jesus alias ʿAlī-Qulī Jadīd al-Islām sided with the Shiite clergy in the religious controversies with the Sufis and missionaries[16] and worked for the shah as a translator and interpreter of European languages. By dint of this position he was seen as a knowledgeable and influential broker who was wooed by secular and clerical emissaries to Persia, including his successor as prior of the Augustinians.[17]

In his capacity as translator and interpreter of European languages at the shah's court, father António alias ʿAlī-Qulī Jadīd al-Islām took up the position of a Capuchin, Raphaël du Mans. From the 1650s until his death in 1696, father Raphaël had an ambivalent role as confidante of a succession of shahs and a point of contact for Europeans of various origins, including envoys of the king of France and the French East India Company. His function as a translator in the court of the shah was first attested in 1654/1655.[18] By 1665, his ties to the court had deepened to such an extent that he was suspected of favoring the shah over Christian envoys. When a Dominican arrived at Isfahan, carrying letters from the pope and other Catholic rulers, the father was not allowed to use the service of an Armenian dragoman who was traveling with him; instead, he had to accept the Capuchin as an interpreter who welcomed him in the name of the shah and ushered him into the audience chamber.[19] As the Dominican later reported to the Grand Duke of Tuscany, the shah had informed him that he would accept no other interpreter than father Raphaël.[20]

Even though the function of "royal interpreter" never led to a permanent appointment or the awarding of a formal title,[21] Europeans seeking access to the court had to be mindful of the trusted Capuchin. This was also true of the Dutch East India Company who in the face of the tensions between France and the United Provinces in the late seventeenth century was particularly alarmed at the close relationship between the French Capuchin and members of the local court. The director of the Bandar ʿAbbās factory, François de Hase, spared no effort in seeking to preserve the "good friendship" with the father and in casting the offices that the Company continued to provide for him in the best possible light, despite the war between France and the United Provinces.[22] In 1690 Joan van Leene, who in his function as ambassador of the Dutch East Company was tasked with negotiating a new trade treaty with the shah and working out a number of differences, initially negotiated with the Capuchin who filled in for the shah. The longer van Leene stayed at Isfahan, the more aware he became that the father was visiting him not just as a sign of his personal commitment to "good correspondence" but on the explicit instructions of the court.[23]

Turning our attention to one of the founders of the convent of the Discalced Carmelites in Isfahan, Juan Thadeo de San Eliseo, will allow us to grasp the significant differences that arose from the changing circumstances that missionaries faced in Persia. The Capuchin Raphaël du Mans was more integrated into the court of the shah than any other missionary before or after him. The numerous reports on his activity at court penned by members of the clergy and laymen alike focus on his roles as translator and interpreter, as well as broker of knowledge and contacts. The dominance that the Shiite ulama won over the course of the latter half of the seventeenth century, as well as the increasingly sharp lines of demarcation that were being drawn between religious groups at the time,[24] forced the Capuchin friar to adopt an accommodation strategy, which in turn fueled accusations that he had abandoned his original vocation as a member of a religious order and missionary. In 1700 the Jesuit Jacques Tilhac accused him of having spent more than 50 years engaged in learned conversations with the gentlemen and scholars of the court. To Tilhac, father Raphaël's ties to courtiers and Muslim scholars, which had earned him the praise of many lay travelers from Europe, were a glaring example of the unobservant lifestyle of missionaries in Persia.[25]

By contrast, the Discalced Carmelite Juan Thadeo de San Eliseo's work as a translator and interpreter at court in the 1610s and 1620s had been part of a missionary strategy that aimed to establish close ties to Muslim elites with the goal of eventually converting them to Catholicism. Against the backdrop of successful attempts to gain a foothold in the court and among Muslim scholars, beginning in the 1610s father Juan Thadeo promoted a missionary strategy that aimed more at leading by example than at refuting the "errors" and "ignorance" of Muslims. In so doing, he hoped, missionaries might convince Persian Muslims to see the errors of their ways and abandon their faith.[26] The Discalced Carmelite combined attempts at predication and disputation with offices that were of immediate practical use to the shah. This included, among other things, his work as interpreter and translator at court, which is particularly well documented between 1619 and 1621. Father Juan Thadeo was always present when ʿAbbās I received the Spanish ambassador García de Silva y Figueroa. His letters, as well as those of other Christian guests, were passed on by the shah to the Discalced Carmelite who summarized the content orally before producing a written translation of the texts.[27]

However, the prerequisite for the missionaries' presence at court was not just the practical use that the shah could make of their offices as interpreters and translators. What made it possible in the first place was the Islamic conception of salvation, which included Christian revelation, even though the Islamic conception regarded this as incomplete and imperfect. Most importantly, however, the presence of missionaries at court was part of the inclusive strategy that ʿAbbās I used to consolidate his power. Yet the disputations which they were allowed to conduct with members of the Shiite clergy as part of the shah's inclusive strategy also fueled conversionary hopes. It is important to stress that the inclusion of Catholic clergymen in the Muslim practice of disputation was not just the result of opportunistic considerations linked to foreign policy goals. On the contrary, the disputations between people of different points of view ostensibly tolerated by the ruler or even in his presence were, under ʿAbbās I, part of a policy of religious patronage. The disputations visualized the superior role of the shah as arbiter in a system of power that brought together various heterogeneous actors. Enabling this was the culture of knowledge of the Shiite ulama, who recognized the independent quest for truth through the means of human reason, valued mathematical, scientific, and medical knowledge, and promoted the active reception of the canon of knowledge from Antiquity.[28]

In 1616 Juan Thadeo de San Eliseo wrote to the *praepositus generalis* of his order that he was well respected by all learned Persians with whom he had participated in disputations. To the Discalced Carmelite, the disputations with scholars were not only an opportunity to build rapport; they also allowed the fathers to preach at court on a regular basis.[29] At the court of the shah, the Discalced Carmelite Juan Thadeo not only offered his services as a broker well versed in European and local languages but also engaged in scholarship. In addition to translating Biblical texts and theological treatises into Persian, for which he was able to win the support of three mullahs and one rabbi, he was also interested in studying the beliefs and knowledge of his Muslim interlocutors and opponents. One sign of this dual interest is the list of manuscripts which father Juan Thadeo brought back to Europe in 1629 when he returned to Rome after 20 years in Persia. On the one hand, the list includes Persian translations of Biblical texts, the constitutions of the order of the Discalced Carmelites in Arabic and Persian, two works by Jerónimo Javier de Ezpeleta y Goñi in Persian, and other pertinent Christian theological writings translated into Persian or Arabic; on the other hand, the Discalced Carmelite owned a copy of the Koran, a volume of the sayings of ʿAli and a collection of Islamic law, as well as a mirror for princes and a moral treatise with annotations in Persian.[30] During his long stay in Persia the Italian traveler Pietro della Valle was able to rely on the Discalced Carmelite's contacts to cultivate his own ties to Persian scholars. Della Valle described Persian scholars as equal members of the Republic of Letters who had not yet seen the true faith.[31] In his diary we find a note on a visit to a certain "Hhussein-culi Mirza, nostro amico," which he made in 1617 alongside Juan Thadeo de San Eliseo. Della Valle characterized the mullah, with whom he and the Discalced Carmelite shared a commitment to erudition and religious devotion, as "a man of letters" who spent his life "in utmost modesty" and "completely devoted to his studies and all things religious."[32]

In the latter half of the seventeenth century, ties to local scholars no longer had the same importance as they had had in the days of the Discalced Carmelite Juan Thadeo de San Eliseo. Thanks to his knowledge of mathematics and astronomy, the Capuchin Raphaël du Mans was still able to win the respect of courtiers and scholars.[33] Shiite clergymen – even some from outside Isfahan – visited the learned Capuchin in his convent.[34] But these ties no longer fueled conversionary hopes. The writings of the Capuchin also show that, in the latter half of the seventeenth century, the picture of Persian erudition became bleaker as a response to the changes to European cultures of knowledge. In his *État de la Perse* Raphaël du Mans stressed the particular status of scholars in Persia, which differed markedly from the position they had in his native France. However, in the face of the progress made in France especially in the field of mathematics, he now saw the preference of Persian scholars for canonical knowledge from Antiquity as a deficit.[35]

2 Local entanglement and observance: The missions as a parallel world

Even at a time when hopes of converting Muslims and forming an anti-Ottoman alliance had long been dispelled, some missionaries continued to act as brokers in the court until the fall of the Safavid dynasty in 1722 and, in some cases, even beyond that year. This gave rise to a number of conflicts over competing norms. Whereas criticism of the role of members of religious orders at court was a staple of anti-Jesuit polemics elsewhere, in Persia it was a member of the Society of Jesus, Jacques Tilhac, who became one of the most vocal critics of the missionaries who allegedly fashioned themselves as courtiers and scholars rather than as members of the regular clergy. To the Jesuit Tilhac, the Capuchins Raphaël du Mans and Felice Maria da Sellano, who traveled to the Safavid court as a papal envoy in 1700, were prime examples of the transformation of members of mendicant orders into courtiers and gentlemen as a result of their presence at court. Tilhac criticized the violations of the vow of poverty of the religious orders which were the inevitable result of the instructions missionaries had received from European courts. One particularly glaring example of this was Felice Maria da Sellano who, after arriving in Persia, wore gold- and silver-threaded clothes. The diplomatic missions, Tilhac argued, led missionaries to dress up as gentlemen and mimic the manners of nobles and knights so much that they ended up adopting the feelings associated with these manners.[36]

In the case of the Discalced Carmelites, conflicts over competing norms had given rise to serious controversies within the order itself as early as the first years of the mission. Their dispatch as missionaries by the pope in 1604 meant a fundamental departure from the order's origins as a contemplative community whose institutional structures and rules provided a framework for a life detached from the world behind the walls of the convent rather than for overseas missions. The question as to whether missionary activities were compatible with the order's rule gave rise to debates within the Italian congregation of the Discalced Carmelites which lasted for several decades and elicited different answers from the order's leaders depending on the current composition of the *definitorium generale* and the general chapter.[37]

It is interesting to note that there was no clear-cut opposition between the order's superiors and the missionaries, between Rome and Persia, on these issues. Instead, differences in opinion cut across all levels of the order's internal hierarchy. Those fathers who cultivated ties to the court were accused by their brethren on the ground of not taking the norms of the order seriously. As early as 1609, Juan Thadeo de San Eliseo reported that fellow members of his order had disapproved of his decision to follow the army of the shah.[38] In 1616 the accusation of following the shah and his army in pursuit of worldly affairs led to a decision taken by the *definitorium* which invited the fathers to refrain from this practice whenever possible.[39]

The adoption of signs of social distinction that were at odds with the vocation of members of religious orders also became a target of criticism. Citing the need to preserve their "honor," Discalced Carmelites reportedly rode across the city on horseback instead of settling for a donkey or, better still, walking. Similarly, some fathers, in a bid to enhance their status, carried arms, abandoned the practice of moving around in bare, sandal-clad feet, to which the order owed its name, and traded in the traditional religious habit for more costly attire. Another controversial status symbol was the purchase of slaves or the employment of wage-earning domestic servants. Given the frequency of these reprimands and prohibitions it is safe to assume that, in light of specific social obligations in the missionary area, rules and regulations were often disregarded.[40]

Those who justified these deviations from the norms of the order often cited cultural differences which required missionaries to adopt a code of conduct that departed from allegedly fixed norms. Describing the missionary area as an antithesis to Catholic Europe, they questioned the applicability of universal normative orders and the authority of distant decision makers and demanded more autonomy from the center. Just as a physician would have difficulties diagnosing illnesses and their causes from a distance and administering the right remedies and medicine, the definitors in Rome were unable to solve individual problems that required familiarity with the situation on the ground. Given this, argued Juan Thadeo de San Eliseo in 1624, the missions in Persia should be elevated to form an individual province of the order.[41]

In response to accusations of a lack of observance, the Discalced Carmelite Ange de Saint-Joseph, who was forced to resign from his post as prior of the convent of Isfahan by a visitor of his order in 1674, wrote numerous letters to one of the definitors, who later became *praepositus generalis*, in which he stressed the inadequacy of the norms of his order in the local context: "All general principles of conscience, politics, economics, and observance," such as they were laid down in books, could simply not be applied in Persia. Christians and other non-Muslims were deemed impure. Only if members of the Catholic clergy were known as learned and well-mannered individuals were they well accepted: "Poverty, simple clothing, bare feet and other things which contribute to edification in Europe" would give "occasion for scandal and indignation" in Persia. Missionaries did not acquire authority on account of the vow of poverty or penance, as was the case in Europe, but only once they could demonstrate, after years of practice, that they were able to enter into disputations on a wide range of issues "with the most sophisticated men of the world."[42]

This criticism of the strict enforcement of norms that he deemed inadequate to local conditions was linked by Ange de Saint-Joseph to criticism of the clerics who had hitherto been selected for the mission. Since they were expected to enter into contact with Muslim scholars, he argued, much more attention needed to be paid to their overall education and language skills. According to the father, newly arrived missionaries with no knowledge of the local language, who had no other choice than to retire behind the walls of the convent, were using observance as a pretext to inconvenience those who were familiar with local customs and languages and who, therefore, left the convent to pursue missionary and other interests.[43]

The correspondence of Ange de Saint-Joseph shows how local knowledge could be weaponized to empower subaltern actors and to question the authority of the order's superiors. The father cited the otherness of local circumstances to justify various deviations from the constitutions of his order. While he relativized norms pertaining to everyday practices that were seen as particularly devout in Europe, he was still willing, with the notable exception of religion, to recognize local culture – especially in the field of erudition – as equal to his own. In his view, the Persian scholars he met were not "barbarians" but well-educated men and sophisticated interlocutors who were crucial to the teaching of the Christian gospel. In the prologue to his *Gazophylacium linguae Persarum*, which was printed in 1684, the father conceded that Persian authors possessed just as much eloquence and erudition as European scholars. Persian medicine in particular was on par with its European counterpart.[44]

***

Based on instructions to cultivate relations to the highest echelons of power, members of the religious orders performed various functions outside the convent which led them away from their religious mission. However, as in other missionary areas, these deviations could be justified by arguing that it was these members who made the missions possible in the first place. The Discalced Carmelites, who had initially honored the pope's instruction to build rapport with the Safavid court, continued to be embedded in local networks long after the diplomatic aspect of their mission had become irrelevant. Besides the dependence on the ruler's protection, the main reason for this was insufficient funding from Italy, which forced the fathers to seek local funding for the convents in Persia. When their missions survived, this was due to successful attempts of the fathers to put the missions on a modest but viable economic footing.[45] The widespread practices of accommodation nevertheless gave rise to tensions that were only heightened by the fact that the orders present in Persia did not allow for the Jesuit exemption from certain rules in everyday life.

As a result of the missionaries' presence at the Safavid court, some parallels to other Asian Empires emerged; given the religious and linguistic proximity – Persian was the shared language – and the shared practice of disputations under the patronage of the ruler, comparisons with the court of the Indian Mughals seem particularly promising.[46] Meanwhile, the ways in which some missionaries won prestige by embracing local role models is reminiscent of the Jesuit missionaries to China. Just like the latter, the fathers in Persia were "more than just missionaries of the Christian Faith."[47] Unlike some Jesuits in China, however, none of them ever held a formal position at court, although in the latter half of the seventeenth century Raphaël du Mans attained a position of trust which led European travelers who dealt with the Capuchin to describe him as a "royal translator." For several decades European visitors to the court of Persia could simply not avoid him even if some, such as the representatives of the Dutch East India Company, would have wished to.

In cultivating their ties to the court, missionaries to Persia embraced local role models who promised social recognition and seemed more or less equivalent to their position as clerics. The high esteem in which Persian erudition was held led to a targeting of Shiite scholars (ulama) who became the missionaries' most important interlocutors and adversaries after the first contacts to the court had been brokered. The fathers realized that these scholars were an influential and respected elite with whom they shared a form of knowledge and a cultural practice: the familiarity with authors of ancient Greece and the practice of disputation and controversy as a way of finding truth.

The horizon of reference of those who criticized the fathers' practices of social distinction as unbecoming of members of the regular clergy was the strict normative orders of reformed mendicants. This was not peculiar to Persia: The image of the missions within the orders was overall ambiguous. Even in the case of the Jesuits, whose constitutions gave a central place to the apostolate, missionary activities would be seen not only as the fulfillment of an essential duty of the order but also as a potential danger for regular observance.[48] If the Congregation for the Propagation of the Faith heavily criticized their lifestyle and the supposed lack of willingness or the inability of superiors to course-correct, this should be seen in the context of broader efforts to impose this body's particular frame of references on the regular clergy.[49] The descriptions of members of religious orders in local society that can be found in contemporary Protestant travel accounts are, therefore, probably far more accurate depictions of missionary life on the ground. Recounting that missionaries in Persia continued to wear their religious habit, the Calvinist Jean Chardin claimed that they generally affirmed their reputation "as men detached from the world and devoted to the worship of God and Christian service" through "a fairly pure and orderly lifestyle," which earned them the respect of Muslims.[50] John Fryer, who worked as a physician for the English East India Company and arrived in Isfahan in 1677, also attributed the prestige of the fathers to their specific lifestyle as members of religious orders. As Fryer reported, they cultivated gardens in their convents "with their own Hands" and lived in accordance with "the Rules of the Poverty prescribed them," which earned them "a Reputation and Reverence not only from the Emperor, but the well inclined Subjects."[51] In short, members of the orders were entangled in relations of "good correspondence" and "friendship" with Christians of various denominations and Muslims, whose expectations they were able to meet in many ways. Thousands of "baptisms" of terminally ill children show the expectations which Muslim parents placed on them, not just due to their medical knowledge but because they attributed them supernatural powers as men of God.[52]

If the centrality of Rome as a norm-setting authority was called into question in the missionaries' day-to-day lives, this cannot be ascribed solely to the conditions in which missionaries, the superiors of religious orders, and the Roman Curia communicated with each other in the seventeenth century. Far more decisive were the circumstances in which Europeans entered into contact with Asian societies in the period: the relations they fostered had little in common with the asymmetries of colonial relations of the nineteenth century. For the Safavid Empire the political and economic ties to South Asia were far more important than links to Southern and Western Europe. With the exception of religion, most clerics and laymen of European origin continued to perceive the cultures of the Asian empires as equal to their own. This fostered a readiness to relativize the norms of the society of origin for more than pragmatic reasons. When they entered into contact with the princely courts of Asia, clerics and laymen subordinated themselves to local ceremonial practices which supported local princes' centrality. Missionaries became part of non-European centers of power when they put themselves at the service of rulers in whose view Rome was not the center of the world but, at best, that of a distant European periphery. This was as true of the court Jesuits in Beijing as it was of the Discalced Carmelite Juan Thadeo de Eliseo and the Capuchin Raphaël du Mans in Isfahan. The papacy's claim to universal validity and the universal aspirations of the religious orders active in the missions clashed with the integration of missionaries into the host societies which turned them into local actors.

English translation: Samuel Weber (Bern)

Notes

1 Iskandar Bēg Munshī, *History*, vol. 2, 1305–1307. Also see the edition of the breve of Urban VIII of 9 March 1624 in: [Chick], *Chronicle*, vol. 2, 1294.
2 See further down.
3 At least, many years of research for my book on missionaries in Persia have not provided any answers. See Windler, *Missionare in Persien*.
4 On inclusiveness as a distinct mark of the Safavid imperial system, see Matthee, "Politics of Protection," 245–271; idem, *Persia in Crisis*, in part. 10, 21, 27–31, 146–147, 173–181; Mitchell, *Practice of Politics*, 12, 176–197, 202.
5 On the anti-Ottoman orientation of papal diplomacy under Clement VIII, see Fattori, *Clemente VIII*, 116–127; Ó hAnnracháin, *Catholic Europe*, 138–172. On the Roman Curia's ties to the court of ʿAbbās I, see also Piemontese, "I due ambasciatori," 357–425. On the ties of the Spanish-Portuguese monarchy to the court of ʿAbbās I, see Gil Fernández, *El imperio*. On the negotiations between ʿAbbās I and the European courts, see Steensgaard, *Trade Revolution*, 211–304.
6 In comparison with other missions, the Catholic missions to Persia have long been rather neglected by historians. For a bibliographical overview, see Windler, *Missionare in Persien*, 17–27.
7 See Babaie, *Isfahan*, in part. 7–8, 65–69, 99–103, 143–149. On the ceremonial of the Ottoman court: Necipoğlu, *Topkapi Palace*.
8 See Windler, *Missionare in Persien*, 186–192.
9 Windler, *Missionare in Persien*, 165, 201–212.
10 Windler, *Missionare in Persien*, 204–205.
11 Fryer, *A New Account*, 247.
12 Gemelli Careri, *Giro del mondo*, 60.
13 Francisco de Távora, Viceroy of Portuguese India, to the king, Goa, 20 January 1685 (DAAG, Signature 56 – Monções do Reino, vol. 49, fol. 230r).
14 *Informacione do convento de Santo Agostino em a cidade de Aspan pera o Rev[mo] e dignissimo Padre Geral de toda la Ordem Agustiniana*, 1700, edited in: Alonso, "El convento agustiniano," 178–180. See Windler, *Missionare in Persien*, 276–278.
15 Pedro António de Noronha de Albuquerque, Conde de Vila Verde, Viceroy of Portuguese India, to king Peter II, Goa, 28 December 1697 (DAAG, Signature 70 – Monções do Reino, vol. 61, fol. 196r).

16 Richard, "Un Augustin portugais," 73–85; Urquiola, "Convert Literature," 45–51, 67–190; idem, "Muslim-Christian polemics," 247–269.

17 See Windler, *Missionare in Persien*, 274–276.

18 Richard, *Raphaël du Mans*, vol. 1, 38–39. In 1654 ʿAbbās II sent a letter from Charles II of England, which had been given to him by Henry Bard, 1st Viscount Bellomont, from Qazvīn to Isfahan in order to have it translated by the Capuchin. The envoy was invited to a banquet only when the translation had been sent back from India. See Manucci, *Mogul India*, 22–23.

19 *Relation de ce qui s'est passé dans les missions du Levant l'an 1665, écrite par F. Martial de Thorigné* (APF, SOCG, vol. 239, fol. 57r–80v, here: 71v), edited in: Richard, *Raphaël du Mans*, vol. 1, 157–158.

20 *Relazione della Persia di un ambasciatore a Ferdinando II granduca di Toscana*, Isfahan, 23 May 1665 (Biblioteca Nazionale Centrale, Florence, Panciatichiano 219, 150–151).

21 Richard, *Raphaël du Mans*, vol. 1, 62.

22 The issue at hand was the liquidation of the legacy of the French bishop of Babylon and the distribution of the proceeds to his heirs. See François de Hase to Raphaël du Mans, O.F.M.Cap., Gombroon [Bandar ʿAbbās], 31 October 1672 (NA, 1285, fol. 8r).

23 On van Leene's mission to the court in Isfahan, see Matthee, "Negotiating," 50–63. On the role of the Capuchin: *Notulen off corte aanteijkening van de principale en voornaemste saecken en belangen van d'edele Compagnie in de ambassade aan't hoff van den koning van Persia, van den 13e Julij anno 1690 tot 22 October 1690* (NA, 1476, fol. 376–395, here: 378r/v, 382r–383r, 389v); *Vervolg van de notulen off korte aentekening*, 26 October 1690 to 6 January 1691 (NA, 1476, fol. 596–598, here: 596r/v).

24 Matthee, *Persia*, in part. 182–193, 200.

25 Memorandum by Jacques Tilhac S.J., attached to a letter to Tirso González, general of the order, Isfahan, 27 December 1700 (ARSI, Gallia, 97 II, fol. 395r).

26 Juan Thadeo de San Eliseo O.C.D. to Benigno di San Michele O.C.D, Isfahan, 26 March 1616 (AOCD, 237/m/9).

27 See Pietro della Valle to Mario Schipano, Isfahan, 24 August, 1619, in: della Valle, *Viaggi*, vol. 2, 23; also see 49–50; idem to idem, Isfahan, 21 October 1619, in: ibidem, 62–63, 65; idem to idem, Isfahan, 4 April 1620, in: ibidem, 72–74, 109–110; idem to idem, Isfahan, 24 September 1621, in: ibidem, 239–240. Also see the sources on the mission of García de Silva y Figueroa in the spring of 1619: Silva y Figueroa, *Comentarios*, 533.

28 On disputations between Shiite scholars and missionaries, see Halft, "Schiitische Polemik," 273–334; idem, "Arabic Vulgate"; Richard, "Catholicisme et Islam," 339–403; Urquiola, "Convert Literature"; idem, "Muslim-Christian polemics," 247–269; Windler, *Missionare in Persien*, 220–248.

29 Juan Thadeo de San Eliseo O.C.D. to Fernando de Santa María, *praepositus generalis* O.C.D., Isfahan, 12 February, 1616 (AOCD, 237/m/8).

30 *Nota delli libri portati di Persia dal Padre Giovanni [Juan Thadeo de San Eliseo O.C.D.] per servitio della Sacra Congregatione de Propaganda fide e della sua religione, e missione* (APF, SOCG, vol. 209, fol. 355r/v).

31 Brentjes, "Western European Travellers," 406–412. On della Valle's contacts to scholars in Lār, which focused on a shared interest in astronomy and included debates on heliocentrism, see Ben-Zaken, *Scientific Exchanges*, 46–75; Lee, "A Printing Press for Shah ʿAbbas," 202–236, 250–261.

32 Pietro della Valle, *[Diario di viaggio]*, 1614–1626 (BAV, Ott. Lat. 3382, fol. 1r–260r, here: 77v–78v, quote: 78r).

33 Richard, *Raphaël du Mans*, vol. 1, 7, 37–39, 62–68, 97–98. On the culture of mathematical knowledge in the Safavid Empire see Brentjes, "Mathematical Sciences," 325–402.

34 See Raphaël du Mans O.F.M.Cap. to Engelbert Kaempfer, Isfahan, 19 September [1685], edited in: Kaempfer, *Briefe*, 218–219.
35 Brentjes, "Republic of Letters," 457–460. See Raphaël du Mans to Engelbert Kaempfer, [Isfahan], 19.9.[1685], edited in: Kaempfer, *Briefe*, 218–219. See also the negative view of the Capuchin toward the end of his *État de la Perse* from 1660: Raphaël du Mans, *Estat de la Perse 1660*, edited in: Richard, *Raphaël du Mans*, vol. 2, 1–199, here: 194–199.
36 Memorandum by Jacques Tilhac S.J., attached to a letter to Tirso González, general of the order, Isfahan, 27 December 1700 (ARSI, Gallia, 97 II, fol. 395r).
37 See Windler, *Missionare in Persien*, 502–511.
38 Juan Thadeo de San Eliseo O.C.D. to Vicente de San Francisco O.C.D., Isfahan, 14 May 1609 (AOCD, 237/m/4).
39 *Definitorium generale* of 4 January 1616, confirmed by *definitorium* of 30 May, 1617 (Fortes, *Acta*, 30, 42).
40 See Windler, *Missionare in Persien*, 519–531.
41 Juan Thadeo de San Eliseo O.C.D. to Paolo Simone di Gesù Maria, *praepositus generalis* O.C.D., Isfahan, 31 August 1624 (AOCD, 237/m/22).
42 Ange de Saint-Joseph O.C.D. to Jean Chrysostome de Saint-Paul, *definitor* O.C.D., Isfahan, 1 October 1672 (AOCD, 236/i/19 and 20).
43 Idem to idem, *praepositus generalis* O.C.D., Isfahan, 8 September (AGOCD, 236/b/19) and 22 December 1675 (AGOCD, 236/b/18). Other fathers before Ange de Saint-Joseph had demanded that the missionaries dispatched to Persia have the same level of erudition as the Muslim scholars with whom they would interact. See, for example, Felice di Sant'Antonio O.C.D. to the general chapter of his order, Rome, 15 October 1649 (AGOCD, 261/m/1).
44 Angelus a Sancto Ioseph [Ange de Saint-Joseph] O.C.D., *Gazophylacium linguae Persarum, triplici linguarum clavi Italicae, Latinae, Gallicae [. . .], Amsterdam, ex officina Jansonio-Waesbergiana*, 1684 (partial edition and french translation in: Bastiaensen, *Souvenirs*, 38–41, 120–121).
45 Windler, *Missionare in Persien*, 548–567. These findings on the Discalced Carmelites in Persia fit into the broader picture of predominantly local missionary economies that has been painted of Jesuit missions in other parts of Asia. On the funding for the Japanese mission: Boxer, *Christian Century*, 91–121. Also see Vu Thanh, *Devenir japonais*, 46–51, 157–159; Rodrigues, "Japanese mission," 115–137. On the funding of the Society of Jesus: Alden, *The Making of an Enterprise*, 319–567. On the local economy of the Jesuits in China: Golvers, *François de Rougemont*, 553–630, and Vermote, "Jesuit Finances and Networks."
46 See, for example, Muzaffar and Subrahmanyam, "Catholics and Muslims."
47 Hsia, "Translating Christianity," 94.
48 Brockey, *The Visitor*; Dompnier, "Tensions et conflits"; Turley, *Franciscan Spirituality*.
49 See, for instance, the draft of a general instruction for the nuncios and the prefects of the missions, which was probably penned sometime in the 1640s and should have helped end "many abuses": *Istruttione generale*, n.d. (APF, Istruzioni diverse, 1639–1648, fol. 162r–167v).
50 Chardin, *Voyages*, vol. 7, 438.
51 Fryer, *A New Account*, 246.
52 What the missionaries considered as baptism was interpreted by Muslim parents as a ritual that would cure their children physically. Compare Windler, *Missionare in Persien*, 263–269.

2 "The habit that hides the monk"

Missionary fashion strategies in late imperial Chinese society and court culture

Eugenio Menegon

On 3 June 1711, Matteo Ripa, a young Italian Catholic missionary and artist at the Chinese imperial court in Beijing, took up his pen to write a report to his superiors in Rome. Unlike most missionary-artists in China at the time, who were Jesuits, Ripa was an "apostolic missionary" of the papal Congregation for the Propagation of the Faith (*Propaganda Fide*). Ripa was no friend of the Jesuits. In his letter to Cardinal Giuseppe Sacripante, Prefect of *Propaganda Fide* in Rome, he reported details about his recent arrival in Beijing and his experience of inserting himself at court as a painter and print-maker. This was a common way for Catholic priests at the time to remain in China and try to obtain state patronage in the imperial capital for their confrères across the provinces of the empire. Ripa offered a scathing review of the lifestyle of the court Jesuits, criticizing them for their lavish Chinese-style clothes and comfortable life, in these terms:

> They say that poverty cannot be practiced [here], but that a missionary who wants to come here has to dress richly, and similar arguments. They say that otherwise the [Chinese] will despise the missionaries and hold them in no esteem. To this I reply: 'Are we here to be held in high esteem and to be honored by the Chinese?' . . . In fact, my experience has been quite the opposite. In Canton I was dressed with cotton cloth, and no gentile among the many I met was scandalized. Actually, once they learned why [I was dressed in that manner], they felt edified.[1]

In his ascetic yearning, and very much in the Catholic tradition prizing the clerical habit, Ripa saw clothing as one of the central markers of religious life. "Dressing richly" with silk gowns and owning multiple sets of robes for official purposes and for use at home, as the Jesuits did in Beijing, seemed to him to completely undermine the very essence of priestly and missionary vocation, and the vow of poverty.

Yet his zeal was soon tempered by the intervention of his own superiors. Even before he set foot at court, Ripa's spiritual director in Macao had commanded him to wear silk robes according to Chinese custom.[2] This was excessive for Ripa's sense of religious poverty, so much so that he commented that "clothes here are of so many kinds that they provoke much confusion."[3] He felt pressure to conform, a pressure that came not just from the Jesuits but also from members of the imperial court, and, most significantly, from the Bishop of Beijing and Vicar Apostolic of *Propaganda Fide*, the Italian Reformed Franciscan Bernardino della Chiesa. In 1715, four years after Ripa's arrival at court, Della Chiesa scolded him for his stubborn sartorial resistance:

> I say to Your Lordship that in dressing you should comply with the others not only because of your singularity among so many Europeans, but also for the lack of respect that you show His Majesty and his courtiers, going to his presence and being with each other without the propriety [= *decenza*] in dressing required by the place and status. It would also be unusual in Europe if the prelates and domestics of His Holiness did not go dressed according to their statuses. The same would be the case in any court of European princes, if one of his courtiers were to dress as a plebeian. *We are here as if on a stage.* Your Lordship holds the position of courtier, and thus should comply with courtly dress. . . . It is my will that you dress in silk and comply with the others the best way you can.[4]

This conflict reveals in the clearest possible terms the importance of clothing not only in religious life, where the use of the habit to proclaim an order's identity, as well as the social boundaries surrounding consecrated individuals, was so prominent; it also demonstrates clothing's importance in society at large and at the court in particular. Clothes were a tangible way to construct a hierarchy, to mark distinctions, and to affirm social status, in early modern Europe and late imperial China alike. Sumptuary laws prescribed what one could and could not wear or consume, precisely to maintain social order, and rising classes often challenged that order through their sartorial choices. China had a system of sumptuary laws and rituals that was even more intricate and stringent than those established across Europe, and it is not surprising that Ripa found the complexity of Chinese clothing bewildering.[5] By the late Ming, when missionaries arrived in China, a veritable "confusion of pleasure" had scrambled the clothing hierarchy, and urban rich merchants in particular challenged dress and consumption legal restrictions at every turn.[6]

For the Jesuits the matter was complicated by their religious status, which required yet another set of clerical dress rules. Reports and letters, lists of accounts, inventories, and similar materials reveal that clothing was one of the first concerns that missionaries encountered in China, and it was not a trivial one. Clothing and bodily practices can be viewed as a gauge of broader issues in the history of the encounter between China and the West, and in the history of Jesuit and Christian presence there and demonstrate how "going local" was an inevitable outcome in China.

1 The Jesuits and their approach to clothing: The foundational years in Europe

Over a century before Ripa had to face his sartorial choices in Beijing, the first Jesuit missionaries arrived in China on Portuguese ships. Europeans in East Asia had to play by the rules of native powers, and that included the adoption of local diplomatic ceremonial, and respect for the social and cultural order of those countries.

By the time the Jesuits were founded in the mid-sixteenth century, ecclesiastical clothing had already accumulated over a millennium of historical development, from the simple tunics of the first monks in the Middle Eastern deserts, to the variety of male and female habits of the medieval and early modern monastic and mendicant orders.[7] The Protestant Reformation, however, provoked a deep reflection on religious life within Catholicism, and one of the consequences was the emergence of a new category of religious men, the "Clerics Regular."[8] The Jesuits belonged to this new wave of priests, who followed rules adapted to more intense social interactions, entailing freedom of movement and inconspicuous appearance for the purpose of apostolic work. Their habit had to be functional for works of charity, education, and religious duties among the laity, and while clearly inspired to "ecclesiastical dress," it had no strict requirements. Like other Clerics Regular, Jesuits dressed in a generic cassock, which simply imitated that of "reputable priests," as mentioned in the founding Formulas of the Society of Jesus.[9] The Latin word used there for "reputable" was *honestus*, a word that appears again in the original Spanish text of the Jesuit constitutions drafted by Ignatius of Loyola and his early Jesuit companions.[10] The habit had to be locally "accommodated" to the place where one lived, following church tradition. Last, the habit had to be modest and inexpensive, in compliance with the vow of poverty. Generally speaking, the vagueness of Loyola's prescriptions encouraged some variety in clothing in the early history of the Society, and even produced some controversy.[11]

Even after uniformity was reached, the habit continued to remain a signifier of internal hierarchy between the priests and the lay brothers ("temporal coadjutors"). The brothers were Jesuits as well, but received limited education, so that they would remain humble and within their professional niche as manual laborers.[12] Their difference in rank also took visual form in their clothing, with their cassocks and cloaks shorter than those of the priests. They were also encouraged to wear a round hat instead of the square biretta, a symbol of the priestly educational and spiritual position. The brothers, however, fought for almost a century to maintain the use of the biretta, resorting to petitioning more than one pope, and finally losing that privilege in 1645. These apparently cosmetic sartorial choices had, in fact, important consequences, and some brothers lost their vocation and left the Society after feeling humiliated by the changes.[13]

This situation seems to reveal a contradiction: on the one hand, clothing was "indifferent" and adaptable. On the other hand, however, it also was increasingly uniform, subtly hierarchical, and thus laden with power and meaning. The habit had to conceal the shape of the body, conferring a second protective skin, even a halo of supernatural aloofness, while avoiding any sexual innuendo. It also represented poverty and penance, and thus often had the shape of sackcloth. Yet its main function was to distinguish the priests and nuns from the laity, and to affirm an established societal and spiritual order.

2 Missionary clothes and bodily practices in Ming China

European expansion in the sixteenth century confronted the church with non-Christian societies and their customs and clothing across the globe, including in East Asia.[14] After their arrival in Japan in the late 1540s, the Jesuits wore the silk robes of the Buddhist monks, to earn the same kind of respect they enjoyed in local society.[15] Following some soul searching and controversy within the Japan mission, the famous Jesuit Visitor Alessandro Valignano then initiated the policy of accommodation that was also applied in China in the 1580s, when Michele Ruggieri and Matteo Ricci started their efforts to settle within the Ming empire.[16] At first, local officials in Guangdong province asked Ruggieri to adopt the identity and the clothes of Buddhist monks.[17] Valignano swiftly approved the move. This entailed shaving any facial hair, wearing very short hair, and donning Buddhist robes. Ricci characterized this attire, adopted by the fathers and all their servants between 1582 and 1595, as *honesta* – the same word used by Loyola – specifying that the robe was "modest and long, with long sleeves, not very different from our [Jesuit robe]."[18] At the suggestion of the Chinese literatus Qu Taisu 瞿太素, Ricci and his companions started shedding the identity of Buddhist monks, considered a disreputable group by many in the Confucian elite. Soon Valignano approved the use of "proper silk garments for visiting magistrates and other important persons who, on visits, wear ceremonial dress and hats."[19] Ricci and his companion Lazzaro Cattaneo grew long beards and hair in the second half of 1594, and in May 1595 Ricci paid a visit to an official dressed for the first time as a Chinese scholar.[20] Ricci described his new wardrobe as including at least two silk gowns, one for public visits, and the other to wear at home.[21] The earliest known oil portrait of Ricci, still kept in Rome, only gives us an idea of the robe worn at home.[22] The one used for visits, sketched in an early xylograph of Ricci, was far richer and not for practical use, and was known as a "ceremonial robe" or *lifu* (禮服) (see Figure 2.1). Actually, Ricci's robe differed from those authorized by Ming sumptuary laws for degree-holders and officials, as he said himself: "Those who have neither office nor grade but are persons of importance also have appropriate visiting-dress, different from that of the ordinary people, and which we have adopted in this kingdom."[23] From then on, this became the accepted wardrobe for Jesuits in Ming China.

Figure 2.1 Portrait of Matteo Ricci in *Life of Master Li Xitai from the Great West* (Daxi Xitai Li xiansheng xingji 大西西泰利先生行蹟). Manuscript copy made in 1636 [original printed edition 1630]

Source: Courtesy of the Bibliothèque nationale de France, Paris, Chinois 996

One of the great masters of European painting, Rubens, drew an almost photographic reproduction of a Jesuit *lifu*. That famous image portrays the Procurator of the China mission Nicolas Trigault, who returned from China with important business in 1616–17.[24] One remarkable feature in the new garb was the hat, which in the early portraits of Ricci appears, as he put it, "somewhat like a bishop's miter."[25] This was called a "Dongpo hat," from the name of the famous Song-dynasty poet and scholar Su Shi 蘇軾, also known as Su Dongpo 蘇東坡, who allegedly popularized it. In the late Ming, this hat, prized for its association with antiquity, was worn by literati who had not attained an official degree, by those who were no longer in an official position, or by officials who did not wear their insignia of rank in private life.[26] Trigault's portrait, however, reproduced a different kind of hat, as did the portrait of another procurator to Europe, Álvaro Semedo, 30 years later (see Figure 2.2). This was a "square hat" (*fangjin* 方巾) worn by students and literati without a degree but also by officials of lower rank whenever they were not wearing insignia.

Last, the China Jesuits followed a new bodily practice, adopting a long beard and growing their hair long, as was the norm in Ming China. Their hair was collected in a knot and hidden under a hat. Long beards, however, were difficult to grow for most Chinese, and they were usually an attribute of old age that symbolized wisdom. Ricci observed that "the men have sparse beards or none at all; what little facial hair they have is completely straight and it is so late in growing that a man of thirty might be taken among us for twenty."[27] He also mentioned that men, except for children and Buddhist monks, would let their hair and beards grow without ever shaving during their lifetime. The decision of the missionaries to adopt the persona of the literatus and to abandon that of the Buddhist monk by growing their beards to the longest possible length, was made together with Valignano. Ricci wrote in 1595 that he let his facial hair grow "because in China a long beard is a rare thing [*è cosa rara*]."[28] A seventeenth-century Chinese source described Ricci's physical appearance in this way: "A curly beard, green eyes, and a voice like a great bell."[29] The curly, long beard was obviously one of the physical traits that stood out in Chinese eyes. Long hair and beards signaled age, and age in China meant authority and gravitas. Another possible reason for the Jesuits' adoption of long beards was that they were attempting to put a greater distance between themselves and women, who had contacts with priests for confession, holy mass, and other sacraments. The mature and distinguished looks of long-bearded and robed Jesuits, together with the presence of male chaperons from the women's families, made such encounters even more detached, establishing a clear gender demarcation.[30]

The apparently uncontroversial adoption of the literati robes during Ricci's lifetime, with the blessing of Visitor Valignano, however, did not completely silence criticism on the use of silk, both within the Society and from other missionary orders, as it was considered a breach of the poverty vow and was a decision that directly contravened the constitutions and Loyola's opinion.

Figure 2.2 Álvaro Semedo's portrait, published in his *Historica relatione del Gran Regno della Cina* (Rome 1653)

Source: Public domain, CC BY-SA 4.0

During the late 1620s, another Jesuit Visitor, André Palmeiro (1569–1635), had to face some tensions over the use of the silk robe between the members of the Japanese Province, by then mostly exiled to Macao after the prohibition of Christianity in Japan, and the members of the inland Chinese mission. In his final report on the visitation to the General in Rome, he regarded this matter as one of the most important reasons for the inspection, dedicating a separate report to clothing alone.[31]

Palmeiro also made an important statement on the meaning of the religious habit, and its relationship to the special identity of the Jesuits as a new order of men working in the world:

> There is no doubt that it is not yet the time nor the timely conjunction for our men residing within China *to wear a particular habit or an identifiable mark on their external attire by which to be recognized by all as a specific family or congregation. We must all be one, but without being known as such.* Nor should we declare this fact to the simple folks, but we do explain it to those who are more intelligent, who understand it perfectly.[32]

Here the Visitor formulated the Jesuit strategic intention of maintaining a hidden identity and using the garments of the Chinese literati to blend into society, while hiding – at least to the non-initiated – their true religious identity. After consultation with veterans of the mission, however, the Visitor also ordered members of the Chinese vice-province to discontinue the use of silk gowns for daily use, as he had noted excesses. For example, Trigault alone owned five sets of personal silk garments. In more established Christian communities, the abolition of silk robes in daily use was a feasible expectation, as Chinese elites had become familiar with the Jesuits' emphasis on the austerity of religious life, and would understand their modesty, especially if some members of the local gentry had converted. However, Palmeiro also gave special powers to the vice-provincial to grant exemptions and still allow silk for courtesy robes to meet officials. Given this latitude, there were still silken domestic robes depicted in portraits, such as that of Semedo in 1642.

More research is needed to clarify what truly happened beyond prescriptive regulations. The 1630s and 1640s were times of great upheaval in China. The Ming dynasty had plunged into a great internal crisis, beset by famine, peasant rebellions, and military collapse, while the rising power of the Manchus in the north represented a challenge that would eventually engulf the empire and lead to dynastic change. Starting in the 1630s, the number of high members of the elites interested in Jesuit teachings in matters of science as well as morality and religion dramatically decreased, while the solidity of grassroots Christian communities increased. The need for contacts with elites and especially with officials to obtain patronage diminished as well.

The growth of native Christian communities allowed for the dispensing with personal silk gowns but also for the acceptance of sumptuous liturgical

Figure 2.3 Portrait of Giulio Aleni wearing the *jijin*, from *Life of Master Ai Siji from the Great West* (Taixi Siji Ai xiansheng xingshu 泰西思及艾先生行述). Manuscript copy made in 1689 [originally composed ca. 1650]

Source: Courtesy of the Bibliothèque nationale de France, Paris, Chinois 1017

vestments for communitarian worship. A late Ming Chinese text on the mass by the Italian Jesuit Giulio Aleni explains that the garments must be magnificent in order to offer sacrifice to God. The most peculiar vestment he described was a special hat invented for the celebration of the mass in China, called a "sacrificial hat" (*jijin* 祭巾) (see Figure 2.3).[33] This bonnet became necessary because, unlike in Europe, in China meeting a superior with a bare head was considered extremely disrespectful.

3 Missionary clothes and bodily practices in Qing China

The Ming-Qing transition was an immensely traumatic event. Untold numbers of people died in fighting, famines, and sieges between the mid-1640s and the 1650s. Many men committed suicide to avoid serving the Manchu invaders, who were the founders of the new Qing dynasty, and many women did the same to avoid rape and family disgrace. One of the new Manchu laws that traumatized Ming men like no other was the infamous order to cut their hair according to Manchu fashion, and to change their style of clothing. This shows how central hairstyles and clothing were to Ming Chinese masculinity.[34] The explosive issue of men's hair led to rebellions in 1645 in the lower Yangzi regions. The Chinese believed that the crown of the head was medically sensitive, that it was unfilial to shave one's hair, and that doing so signaled a renunciation of sexuality. Most significantly, the new hairdo represented submission to the barbarians.[35]

The Jesuits, who had chosen to be seen as members of the literati elite, rather than as Buddhist or Daoist clergy – the only subjects exempted from the hair cutting decrees – had no choice but to follow the Manchu directives. They also did so because their loyalty was not to a specific dynasty – or even to an ethnic or cultural order – but rather to a timeless divine plan for the conversion of the Chinese empire. Most missionaries became instant turncoats once the triumphant Manchu troops reached their locales.

The new Manchu rulers immediately coopted the Jesuits for their technical knowledge, and after occupying Beijing in 1644 they named the Jesuit Adam Schall von Bell as co-director of the Imperial Astronomical Directorate, a post that Catholic missionaries kept almost without interruption until 1838. Schall did not describe in detail his adoption of the Manchu hairstyle or clothing at the time of the Manchu entry into the capital. He only mentioned that when he surrendered wearing commoner's clothes (probably still in Ming style), he petitioned the Manchu authorities on his knees to allow him to remain in his residence in the "Tartar City" – thus avoiding forced eviction with the Han population, all transferred outside the walls into the new and makeshift "Chinese City." In his later reports, Schall mentioned that, once he received a bureaucratic appointment, he agreed to wear Qing official robes with insignia corresponding to his rank (see Figure 2.4).[36]

Figure 2.4 Adam Schall in Qing official robe, from Athanasius Kircher, *China monumentis illustrata* (Amsterdam 1670)

Source: Courtesy of the Universitätsbibliothek Bern

The surrender of Schall's confrère Martino Martini in Southern China is described in much greater detail. During the summer of 1646 in Yanping, Fujian, Martini first accepted the orders of the Southern Ming Longwu Emperor to wear Ming official robes, after apparently turning down a position offered to him to facilitate a military alliance with the Portuguese in Macao against the Manchus. Within four months, however, Martini submitted to the triumphant Qing troops in the region of Wenzhou, in southern Zhejiang province.[37] In his best-seller "On the Tartar War" (*De bello Tartarico*, Antwerp, 1654), Martini described his shift in dynastic loyalty in the presence of a Manchu military commander. The highly symbolic act of surrender and declaration of allegiance pivoted around the shaving of his hair and the shifting of his clothes to the new style:

> The Tartar commander . . . asked me if I was ready to change by my own accord *my hair style and Chinese clothes*. I agreed, and he ordered me to shave my hair in his presence. I then gestured to him that that kind of shaven head did not fit with Chinese clothes any longer, and he took off his leggings, gave them to me to wear, and put his Tartar hat on my head.[38]

Martini commended the new Manchu hat as "a comfortable and elegant ornament," and this positive reaction contrasted with his assessment of the care shown by Ming men for their long hair, in a language that implied a condemnation of the practice, which he probably deemed unmanly.[39] He added elsewhere a commentary on the beauty, straightforwardness, and human touch of the Manchus, which left no doubt as to his preference for them over the "effete" Han Chinese.[40] He ridiculed the Chinese for putting up a mighty resistance to the hair-cutting edict, "preoccupied more with their own hair than their own native land."[41]

Under Manchu rule the diatribes on the use of silk continued to simmer, especially because members of the newly arrived Dominican and Franciscan orders started to criticize the ways of the Jesuits.[42] Martini, therefore, while in Rome as Procurator in 1655, wrote a memorial to the General, mentioning the need for the China Jesuits to wear common (*suté*, i.e., *sude*, simple 素的) kinds of silk, reiterating as well that silk was not a particularly prestigious fabric in China, and that even farmers used it.[43] By this time, it appears, the Jesuits had developed a protocol that simply followed a general principle of adapting to the clothing of the literati, whatever the style was in accordance with dynastic sumptuary laws and current practices. New regime, new clothes: no big deal.

4 Missionaries at the Qing court

The Jesuits had no qualms about adopting the new attire and wearing official Qing robes when some of them attained positions within the Chinese bureaucracy. Once the German astronomer Adam Schall became an official, and for some time a favorite of the young Shunzhi Emperor, he wore sumptuous official robes in the new style, including Qing official hats with rank buttons. In his 1661 apologetic *Historica Relatio*, Schall mentions how he tried to turn down bureaucratic posts, but finally had to give in and wear Qing official robes with insignia corresponding to his rank, obeying orders from Vice-Provincial Francisco Furtado.[44]

Schall soon became a controversial figure not only for his work in astronomy, which some in the church considered tainted by Chinese calendrical superstition, but also because of his extravagant lifestyle and arrogant behavior toward other Jesuits. His confrère in Beijing Gabriel de Magalhães started a veritable war against him, writing long reports to the Visitor of China and Japan, Manuel de Azevedo, in 1649, denouncing Schall's great expenses for an excessive number of personal fine clothes and hats, as well as for official robes decorated with dragons.[45] His best-known portrait in official garb shows the sumptuousness of his attire; the robe sports an embroidered "mandarin square" on his chest with a white crane, symbol of the first rank (see Figure 2.4).[46] The complaints against Schall required the creation of two special disciplinary commissions in Rome in the 1660s to decide whether he was guilty of superstitious practice and "excessive extravagance." He was finally exonerated because of the great advantages of his position for the church and the mission in China and the possible dangers had he refused his official position.[47] The early internal arguments among Jesuits on clothing, silk, and poverty in China increasingly became the weapons of enemies outside the Society of Jesus – Dominicans, Franciscans, Foreign Missions of Paris – to attack them for breaking the rules of religious life, especially at court.

Over the course of the late seventeenth and eighteenth centuries the wardrobe for attending ceremonies at the palace or work in the imperial workshops became codified in sumptuary laws following court etiquette. After the attacks on Schall's extravagance and his high rank at court, his successor at the Directorate of Astronomy, Ferdinand Verbiest, also had to face opposition within the Society of Jesus concerning his acceptance of high office in the Qing administration.[48] In 1681, he defended the Jesuit policy of wearing Chinese silk robes according to the current literati fashion from the attacks of the Dominican Domingo Fernández Navarrete, simply noting that all successors of Ricci followed his wise policy of sartorial adaptation, avoiding splendor, and showing religious gravity in their dress.[49]

While the missionaries' daily wardrobe in the provinces also became standardized according to the new Qing fashion and was gradually accepted by all orders, requirements for those working at the palace were much more stringent.[50] Only very few missionaries who occupied official posts in the Astronomical Directorate wore special robes with embroidered chest squares according to their ranking, and only when called for ceremonial audiences at the palace. Their normal "work" attire was that of well-dressed elites. By the eighteenth century, a consensus had been reached and controversies over the use of silk were no longer center-stage, but formal silk robes had become part and parcel of the identity of any China missionary, especially for those serving at the court.

However, due to the extreme continental climate of the capital, swinging from torrid summers to freezing and windy winters, the wardrobe had to be varied according to the season. Ripa observed that in Beijing in winter even commoners wore

> over a long cotton shirt, a jacket padded with lambskin or other fur. On top, they wear an external shirt padded with cotton, long to the knees, and over that, the *paozi* (袍子), i.e., a robe reaching the feet, lined with fox or ermine. Over the *paozi*, they wear a *waitao* (外套), a kind of short tunic, also lined with fox or ermine. Moreover, when it snows they wear a mantel, long almost all the way to the ground, lined on the outside with otter skins (*cane marino*).[51]

In summer it was necessary to wear light garments: a refreshing shirt made of kudzu vine fiber (*gepu* 葛布), covered by a *paozi* of the same light fabric, and on top a *waitao* made of *sha* (沙) silk gauze. Ripa added that a great variety of other garments were necessary for the mid-seasons as well; these garments were increasingly lighter when nearing summer, and, inversely, heavier when progressing toward winter. Almost exasperated by this complexity, he concluded: "This is something that is not practiced anywhere in any other part of the world, no matter how cultivated and delicate such place might be."[52]

All these garments cost dearly. Teodorico Pedrini commented in 1742 about the high expenses for clothes to attend functions or simply work at the imperial palaces, especially since they had to be varied according to seasons and type of ceremony, "now of one kind of fur, now of another; now of a certain color, now of another." On one occasion, he even borrowed a robe from the Chief Eunuch, as his own *waitao* was black, a color forbidden at court that day.[53] The Discalced Augustinian Sigismondo Meinardi da San Nicola, a court clockmaker, in 1752 confirmed the high expense needed to appear at the palace, "where one has to be neatly dressed from head to toe. I spent in one year for such clothing more than in the twelve years I lived in Beijing before being called to the palace."[54] Elsewhere he added that he had to spend much in "proper, albeit ordinary, clothes, which have always to be according to propriety as we see the emperor every day."[55] His confrère Anselmo da Santa Margherita confirmed in 1793 that the Beijing missionaries needed a multi-seasonal "honest" wardrobe (*vestire onestamente*), especially because of their courtly roles. Even those who had no technical functions at the palace, in fact had to participate in ceremonies of greetings to the emperor four times a year: on the Chinese New Year; at the return of the emperor from the Yuanmingyuan suburban villa after winter; at his departure for the hunting resort of Chengde in the spring; and at his return from the hunts in the fall.[56]

Church authorities in Rome suggested that "that both in their clothing and their general outside appearance [missionaries] show a certain dignity and decency," to make clear to their Chinese audience that they were serving the court not out of any economic need or personal greed, but only to support their religion.[57] While the Jesuits spent generously on their attire, the meager subsidies of *Propaganda Fide* could often reduce their men to a look that conjured "not religious poverty, but rather vile sordidness."[58]

The imperial bestowal of silk bolts as payment for services, and the occasional free tailoring of robes and fur coats under imperial order for the missionaries, underlined the central preoccupation with clothing in courtly life in Beijing and how the gifting of clothes was considered a common form of compensation for court missionaries. In 1738, the Discalced Augustinian miniature painter Serafino da San Giovanni Battista, for example, reported that upon his and Meinardi's arrival in the capital from Europe, the emperor had ordered that they "measure our sizes for a *waitao* and a *paozi*, one to be lined with ermine, and the other with sable" and that "the lining was of high quality, and the cloth on top quite beautiful."[59] Practices changed with time, possibly also linked to the declining imperial favor toward the missionaries. In 1764, for example, the court artisan and Discalced Carmelite Arcangelo Maria di Sant'Anna observed that in the past the emperor had generously ordered the court tailors to take the Europeans' measurements during the summer months and prepare a complete fur coat for the coming winter. That practice, however, had more recently been abandoned in favor of the cheaper bestowal of bolts of ordinary silk "barely sufficient to clothe us for a few years, [and, moreover, for robes to be worn] only at home."[60] During the latter part of the eighteenth century, especially after the dissolution of the Society of Jesus in China in 1775, the Beijing mission entered into a long phase of decline, and the number of court missionaries dwindled. The last lone survivor, the Portuguese Lazarist Cayetano Pires Pereira, Apostolic Administrator of Beijing, died on the eve of the Opium Wars in 1838. He was still formally charged with the position of Co-Director of the Astronomical Directorate and thus wore and was portrayed with official robes.

5 Conclusion: Accommodation, dissimulation, or necessity?

On his way back to his Beijing mission, the French Jesuit Jean de Fontaney wrote from London in 1704 to a Jesuit correspondent in France on the matter of silk clothing. Referring to his recent tour of France as procurator of the China French Jesuit mission, he reported the criticism of someone who had asked him:

> You go around dressed in silk in China and you do not walk about the cities, but you use sedan chairs. Did the apostles preach the Gospel in this manner? And how can one respect religious poverty while dressing with silken gowns?

He replied:

> Our China missionaries are the brothers of those who go barefoot with penitential clothes and who fast austerely in the missions of Madurai [in India]; and of those who follow in the snow the savages of the forests of Canada, suffering cold and hunger. . . . Is it a relaxation of rules that the Jesuits in Canada can eat meat, while those in India never eat it? . . . *What is good and sufficient in one country to have the Gospel accepted, in some cases does not work at all or is insufficient in another country.*[61]

This was the ultimate rationale for proclaiming the Ignatian "indifference" to material accidents in the pursuit of souls and for defending the importance of a "habit that hid the monk," allowing the missionaries to move stealthily in Chinese society, both in the provinces – especially after 1724 when they all became clandestine following the imperial prohibition of Christian proselytization – and in the capital, where they continued to occupy official and technical positions to protect the illegal activities of their confrères across the empire. The words by de Fontaney reflect a clear Jesuit strategy surrounding clothing and the body. As long as the aim of conversion and the religious message were kept central, the means remained indifferent. There were, however, limits in the adoption of extravagant or luxurious attires, and restraints had to be put in place to avoid the corrosion of ethical standards and religious discipline, which in turn would endanger the entire edifice of the mission.

Scholars have used various intellectual frameworks to understand missionary adaptability. Many have espoused the concept of accommodation, also called the *modo suave* ("soft method"), especially in non-European contexts. The word *accomodare* ("to accommodate") is often found in primary sources in relation to missions.[62] Others have explored the culture of "dissimulation" so typical of the Baroque era, an age of religious conflicts and rhetorical masking, as a possible source of Jesuit flexibility. Contemporary critics, both Catholic and Protestant, actually accused the Jesuits of duplicity, travesty, and simulation, including in their Asian missions.[63]

Communication of Catholic and European ideas and practices occurred at different levels in China: through the "apostolate of the book" written in Chinese; through scientific propaganda; through the proxy of native catechists and their oral ministry; through priestly rituality enacted in the liturgy and the sacraments; and through the materiality of objects (pictures, amulets, luxury items for the court, etc.) that mediated concepts, channeled spiritual forces, and facilitated relationships. Clothes were yet another powerful way to communicate. In this case, Chinese-style apparel communicated to the Chinese public and the imperial court that the missionaries had been readily assimilated to the native culture of China, and that the alterity of the "Western Ocean men" (*Xiyang ren* 西洋人), as Europeans were called, had been neutralized and domesticated, in the time-honored Confucian process of *jiaohua* 教化, i.e., "transformation through teaching" of Chinese ethics, language, literature, and customs.

Here I have approached the topic of clothing and bodily practices from the classic point of view of accommodation, and the European missionaries themselves have been the actors at the center of the historical stage, literally clothed in Chinese costumes. The Chinese evolving material circumstances in the Ming-Qing period, however, powerfully influenced missionary accommodation from the outside. Dressing like the natives was absolutely necessary for the survival of the missionary enterprise. It allowed the foreign missioners to be inconspicuous and to become culturally acceptable, even before becoming culturally proficient. This was doubly important at the court, as missionaries were closely observed "as if on a stage" by the imperial family and the metropolitan bureaucracy. They needed to show respect for courtly etiquette and sumptuary laws, and visibly fit within the hierarchies of power; this included using their bodies and attire. Wearing European clothes was thus never a possibility. Selecting the best social image that certain local clothes conveyed – the attire of the literati elite rather than that of the Buddhist or Daoist clergy – was, to an extent, a choice. That choice, nevertheless, was not made independently but rather at the suggestion of Chinese interlocutors, both literati and officials. Indeed, a new path away from Buddhist clerical identity emerged only after native informants offered their crucial input, a fact that confirms how the actions of missionaries in China were shaped by the Chinese social and material context, as much as they were by the missionaries' own spiritual tradition and modus operandi.[64] Li Zhizao 李之藻, one of the most prominent literati converts of the late Ming period, put it quite clearly: "After Ricci entered China, for several years he followed a confused path (*hunji* 混跡). Then he met Qu Taisu, who deemed that it was not appropriate to behave like a Buddhist monk. Following this, Ricci let his hair grow and started identifying himself as a Confucian who had come to China to admire its superior civilization."[65] In this Chinese rendering of the story, Ricci hardly seems to have been the one in charge.

The tension within the missionary community between the uniformity of religious rules and attire, on the one hand, and the need to adapt to a diversity of places and cultures, on the other, never completely disappeared but certainly became attenuated over time. Our scholarly interpretation of how this tension played out depends on how we read the sources and what perspective, Chinese or missionary, we privilege in our reading of those sources. In this chapter we have mainly heard the words of the missionaries themselves, grappling with the repercussions of their "going local." Yet, the voices of their Chinese counterparts – the Confucian literati, the provincial and court officials, the eunuchs, the emperor, and the common men and women of the Ming and Qing empires – were never too far off in the background to become inaudible.

Notes

1 APF, SOCP Indie Orientali e Cina, vol. 26, fol. 313r.
2 APF, SOCP Indie Orientali e Cina, vol. 26, fol. 313r.
3 APF, SOCP Indie Orientali e Cina, vol. 26, fol. 313r.
4 Van den Wyngaert and Mensaert eds., *Sinica Franciscana*, vol. 5, 626. Italics mine.
5 "Sumptuary Laws and Changing Styles," in Wilkinson, *Chinese History*, 182–183.
6 Brook, *The Confusions of Pleasure*, 130–136.
7 Rocca, *La sostanza dell'effimero*.
8 Rocca, *La sostanza dell'effimero*, 103.
9 Padberg, *The Constitutions*, 12; for a general discussion of clothing and identity among the early Jesuits, see Levy, "Jesuit Identity, Identifiable Jesuits?"
10 Spanish original in Loyola, *Constitutiones*, vol. 2, 543; English version in Padberg, *The Constitutions*, 12; compare "Kleidung," in Koch, *Jesuiten-Lexikon*, 986–988.
11 On the discussions surrounding Jesuit clothing in Spain in the 1560s, see Borràs, "En torno a la indumentaria."
12 Ganss, "Toward Understanding the Jesuit Brothers' Vocation," 35.
13 "Bonete de los Hermanos Coadiutores," in Astrain, *Historia*, 289–290.
14 For a global treatment of missionary clothing, see, e.g., Sanfilippo, "Travestimento o tradimento?"; Sanfilippo, "L'abito fa il missionario?"; Sanfilippo, "Adattamento e travestimento."
15 Valignano, *Il cerimoniale*, 152–153; compare Schütte, *Valignano's Mission Principles*, vol. 2, 245.
16 Hoey, "Alessandro Valignano"; Zampol D'Ortia, "Purple Silk and Black Cotton."
17 Ruggieri to Acquaviva, Zhaoqing, 7 February 1583, in OS, vol. 2, 416.
18 FR, vol. 1, 192. On Jesuit clothing in this phase, see also Bettray, *Die Akkomodationsmethode*, 4–10; Peterson, "What to Wear?"; Hsia, "From Buddhist Garb to Literati Silk"; Hsia, *A Jesuit in the Forbidden City*, 138.
19 FR, vol. 1, 337; compare Harris, "The Mission," 89.
20 OS, vol. 2, 136.
21 OS, vol. 2, 199; translated in Harris, "The Mission," 90.
22 On 24 August 1617, Girolamo Alaleoni SJ so described the famous portrait at the Professed House of the College of the Gesù in Rome: "The portrait of our Fr. Matteo has been hanging for several weeks in the entrance hall of this house with those of our other Blessed Jesuits. But the image does not depict the Father as he would go outside . . . but rather *as he dresses at home, without fan and solemn dress*"; see OS, vol. 2, p. 497 (italics mine). On this portrait see also Guillen-Nuñez, "The Portrait."
23 Harris, "The Mission," 90.
24 Logan and Brockey, "Nicolas Trigault," 157; compare also Alsteens, "A Note."
25 OS, vol. 2, 199; translated in Harris, "The Mission," 90.
26 Cortes, *Le voyage en Chine*, 374; Ricci calls the hat *sutumpo*, see FR, vol. 1, 358.
27 FR, vol. I, 88; compare also OS, vol. 2, 157.
28 OS, vol. 2, 173.
29 *Kangxi Renhe xianzhi*, *juan* 22, 22–23.
30 Menegon, "Deliver Us from Evil," 39–40; Menegon, *Ancestors, Virgins, and Friars*, 230–236; Amsler, *Jesuits and Matriarchs*, 26–27.
31 Brockey, *The Visitor*, 302–306.
32 Brockey, *The Visitor*, 303; original Portuguese in ARSI, JS 161-II, fol. 114r. Italics mine.
33 On the *jijin*, see Anonymous, "Une pratique liturgique propre à la Chine," 376–377, 404–406; Dudink, "The Holy Mass," 219; Philippi Collection Online

(private collection of religious hats, Kirkel, Saarland, Germany) http://philippi-collection.blogspot.com/2011/07/chinese-jijin-tsikin-tsikim-tsi-kim.html. The Chinese text on the *jijin* is in Giulio Aleni's *Misa jiyi* 彌撒祭義 (The meaning of the sacrifice of the mass), *juan* 1, fol. 15a6–15b7, reprinted in CCT BNF, vol. 16, 513–514, compare Bontinck, *La lutte*, 58, note 122; for the 1615 request to Rome of permission to celebrate the Mass with the head covered, see Ibid., 36–37, 40–41.

34 Wilkinson, *Chinese History*, 187; Spence, *The Search*, "Two edicts," 26–28.

35 Wilkinson, *Chinese History*, 183, 187.

36 Schall, *Relation historique*, 157.

37 On the murky circumstances of Martini's whereabouts just before his surrender and his shifting loyalties, see Menegon, "I movimenti." A description of the Ming robe bestowed on Martini in Biermann, "War Martin Martini," 223; a 1654 portrait of Martini in Qing attire by Michaelina Woutiers is discussed in Golvers, "Note."

38 Martini, *Opera Omnia*, vol. 5, 280 (Martini, *De bello*, 100) (italics mine).

39 Martini, 226–227 (Martini, *De bello*, 38–39).

40 Martini, 227 (Martini, *De bello*, 40).

41 Martini, 275 (Martini, *De bello*, 95).

42 Biermann, "War Martin Martini"; Menegon, "I movimenti."

43 Martini, *Opera Omnia*, vol. 1, 309.

44 Schall, *Relation historique*, 157.

45 Passages from Magalhães, *Apontamentos do modo de viver e proceder do Padre João Adão nesta Corte . . .*, Letter to the Visitor and Vice-Provincial of China, 1649 ? (ARSI, JS 142, no. 32, fol. 3r), edited in Pih, *Le P. Gabriel de Magalhães*, 256, 328, 330.

46 Schall's color portrait was originally painted by his confrère Johannes Grueber in 1659–1660 in Beijing: see Pih, *Le P. Gabriel de Magalhães*, 362; Väth, *Johann Adam Schall*, 238, 351–352; Chang, "Das Porträt von Johann Adam Schall." On the insignia of rank, see Cammann, "The Development of the Mandarin Square."

47 Pih, *Le P. Gabriel de Magalhães*; Romano, *Impressions de Chine*.

48 On the diatribes against Verbiest within the Society of Jesus, see Malatesta and Rouleau, "The 'Excommunication' of Ferdinand Verbiest," 485–494; on his Qing ranks and his attempts to turn them down but also his politicking to obtain the position of Director, see Vande Walle, "Ferdinand Verbiest and the Chinese Bureaucracy," 501.

49 Verbiest, *Correspondance*, 307; Golvers, *Letters*, 362.

50 Lucas Tomás, circular letter to the fathers of the Seraphic Mission, Canton, 21 January 1705, in *Sinica Franciscana*, vol. 8, ed. Margiotti, 779–780.

51 Ripa, *Giornale*, vol. 2, 4–5.

52 Ripa, *Giornale*, vol. 2, 4–5.

53 Pedrini to Procurator Miralta, Beijing, 2 November 1742 (APF, Procura Cina, Box 1, fol. 1v).

54 Meinardi to Procurator Guglielmi, Beijing, 10 September 1752 (APF, Procura Cina, Box 15, fol. 1r).

55 Meinardi to Prefect of Propaganda, 30 November 1752 (APF, SOCP Indie Orientali e Cina, vol. 50, fol. 207v).

56 Anselmo da Santa Margherita to Prefect of Propaganda, Beijing, 25 October 1793 (APF, SOCP Indie Orientali e Cina, vol. 68, fol. 647r–653r).

57 Ex-Jesuits Ventavon and Poirot to Propaganda, 1779 (APF, Acta CP Indie Orientali e Cina, vol. 14, fol. 45v).

58 Ex-Jesuits Ventavon and Poirot to Propaganda, 1779 (APF, Acta CP Indie Orientali e Cina, vol. 14, fol. 45v).

59 Serafino da San Giovanni Battista to Procurator Miralta, Beijing, 11 May 1738 (APF, Procura Cina, Box 30, fol. 3r).
60 Arcangelo Maria di Santa Anna to Procurator Palladini, Haidian, 30 September 1764 (APF, Procura Cina, Box 14, fol. 1r).
61 LEC, vol. 3, 136 and 138. Italics mine.
62 Muller, "The Jesuit Strategy of Accommodation."
63 See, e.g., Hsia, "From Buddhist Garb"; Levy, "Jesuit Identity"; Sabina Pavone, "Spie, mandarini, bramini."
64 Standaert, "Jesuit Corporate Culture."
65 FR, vol. 1, 336, note 1; Chinese original text in Li, *Tianxue*, *juan* 1, 13a.

3 Between Mogor and Salsete

Rodolfo Acquaviva's error

Ines G. Županov

In 1591, Antoni de Monserrat, a Catalan Jesuit, completed a massive manuscript in which he provided a portrait of the Neapolitan Jesuit Rodolfo Acquaviva, his companion at the Mughal court of the Emperor Akbar in Fatehpur Sikri between 1580 and 1583. Upon returning to Goa, Acquaviva was killed in a village disturbance in the province of Salsete, where he was about to take up the position of the Rector of Margão college, and subsequently became a beatified martyr of the Society of Jesus.[1] Monserrat's discursive brush was large enough to encompass the stereotypical signs attributed to saintliness, but certain perceptive details betray his empirical penchant and touch of humor. Acquaviva emerges as someone distracted by his own religious zeal. "He was entirely forgetful of himself (*sui uero immemor*), frequently sleeping the whole night in his clothes (*indutus*)."[2] He also had a habit of talking to himself or singing "ejaculatory prayers (*jaculatorias*)." He wore a hair shirt, flogged himself regularly, and frequently fasted. With his eyes fixed on God he would frequently misplace his hat, spectacles, and books. In addition to these endearing human qualities, Monserrat focused on Acquaviva's talent for learning Persian that enabled him to argue against the Qur'an, and most importantly, to build a deep connection with Akbar, who openly spoke about his love for Rodolfo.

To this image of noble, courtly affection between a Muslim king and a vassal-cum-ambassador-cum-spiritual-teacher, Acquaviva, Monserrat juxtaposed the dangerous side of the encounter. Since Acquaviva burnt with the desire to die a martyr, he reportedly asked: "Whether these will make us martyrs"? But, as Monserrat wrote, it was "in his own country [Goa]" that he was "slain by the tributaries and subjects of his own king."[3] Even if Acquaviva indeed desired martyrdom, this extreme form of missionary zeal was discouraged because losing an able worker was costly for the Society of Jesus.[4] This was especially the case in the 1580s when the Order was still in the process of establishing "missions" in the overseas territories. The fact that Monserrat included his remark about Acquaviva being killed in his "own country" by the vassals of the Habsburg king, was probably how the matter had been viewed in Goa. The event was also used by the Estado da Índia to impose punitive measures against the rebel village in the Salsete province.[5] It became (or was, in fact, from the start) a political problem.

This is why nobody wanted to notice Acquaviva's error in judgment. Just as he used to misplace his glasses or his hat, he blindly stumbled into a situation of social unrest in a rural region with which he was unfamiliar with. His aristocratic origin was a disadvantage, but most importantly his early missionary experience was marked by a very different communication setting at the Mughal court. Another remark by Monserrat confirms Acquaviva's inability to accommodate himself to others: "He was so gentle and simple, and thought all others to be like himself in these respects."[6] Not taking into account complexities and differences meant not engaging in them, and was a prescription for communication failure, as the Jesuits learnt in the village of Cuncolim the hard(est) way.

In this article I want to understand how a noble, well-educated, Italian Jesuit missionary, Rodolfo Acquaviva, failed to understand the coordinates and the limits of his strategic position among the people who were the targets of his proselytizing. He failed two times, and the second put an end to his missionary career but precipitated his career as a blessed martyr. The first mission he had been elected to lead was to the Mughal court in 1580. The second was in the Salsete peninsula, south of Goa's administrative center, among the neophytes and the "gentile" rural population. Since the mission to the Mughal court was the first, it is safe to say that he and his two companions were responsible for constructing the model of courtly communication with the Muslim kings in India. Acquaviva's error was to think that by targeting the head, the Mughal emperor Akbar himself, and by establishing a deep personal "friendship," he would be able to seize him "from within." This Jesuit strategy had been formulated in a cryptic Ignatian piece of advice: "entrar con el otro y salir con sigo," often translated as "entering through the door of the other and making him come out through the same door."[7] In a word, Acquaviva put all his efforts toward teaching Akbar to feel "love" and to become attached to the Jesuits, as a convert and a Christian would feel attached to his confessor. Akbar's interest and good will were interpreted by Acquaviva, in a fit of wishful thinking, as much more than expressions of the bonds of vassalage. He thought, at least for a while, that he had "caught" Akbar and was making him enter the new "emotional community" that the Jesuits promoted though their *Spiritual Exercises* and other pedagogical tools.[8] In the rural Salsete a slightly different model, for ministering to and administering rural populations, was already in place through the Portuguese territorial extension of the Estado da Índia in 1543, but had been put under Jesuit missionary pressure. Each model was, of course, a work in progress and constantly renegotiated, but they were also based on certain imported traditions and evolving mutual expectations. Acquaviva's error was simple carelessness and failure to inform himself and to understand the sociopolitical and economic situation in the Salsete region.

1 Courtly discussions

At the Mughal court, the Jesuits were not the sole actors who had to improvise an *ad hoc* communication style with the king and other military and literati elites. Scholars and divines whom Akbar – the third in line of the Timurid kings in India – gathered around him in his newly built court at Fatehpur Sikri shared the same space and anxiety as the Jesuits. Akbar had his own goals and oversized dreams of which the Jesuits were unaware when they arrived. By the end of the 1570s, after a period of conquests and imperial expansion, Akbar set out to establish his own political ideology in order to contain and assimilate diverse populations and religious or theological traditions. A policy called *ṣulḥ-i kull* ("universal peace" or "peace for all"), often interpreted (though with a stretch) as identical to the concept of "toleration," was a strategy to ensure the civility and diversity of opinions, and to block those that the emperor found unacceptable.[9] In order to introduce and coordinate new knowledge sources, Akbar organized a debating club *ʿibādatkhāna* (*House of Worship*) which at first only accepted Muslim scholars before opening the door to Brahmans, Jains, Christians, and others. According to Abū l-Fażl ibn Mubārak, official chronicler of Akbar's reign and his contemporary, the House of Worship was meant to "establish a feast of truth."[10] Jesuit presence was, therefore, sought and cherished at the court, since Akbar and Abū l-Fażl were impressed with Jesuit symbolic, cultural, and visual tools that appeared useful for shoring up Mughal political sovereignty.

In Acquaviva's eight letters written from Agra and Fatehpur Sikri, he emphasized his capacity to engage the king and to inspirit his desire to maintain a permanent dialogue with the missionaries. It was an effort to create a relation of intimacy and empathy in which Akbar and the Jesuits would share a sufficient common ground to build upon. This strategy had already been framed, tested, and expounded in a long literary tradition of dialogues between Christians and Muslims going back to the first centuries of Islam up to the medieval period. It was practiced and shared by both Islamic and Oriental Christian authors.[11] The European tradition of the sixteenth century focused in particular on refuting the Qurʾan and Islamic institutions in general. One such work, *Desengano de perdidos* (*The Disillusion of the Lost*), a combination of catechetical and doctrinal teaching directed primarily at Christians and neophytes, was published in Goa in 1573 by the Archbishop Dom Gaspar Jorge de Leão de Pereira, evoking earlier treatises written for Iberian Moriscos such as João de Soares's *Libro de la verdade de la fe* (1543) and Bernardo Pérez de Chinchón's *Alcorano* (1535).[12] The whole set of topoi was developed to counter Islam, Muhammad, and the Qurʾan. One of them was that Islam was a carnal religion, that Muhammad was a false prophet, and that he inserted into the Qurʾan ideas and customs that went against reason, such as: that Jesus was not the son of God, that Mary's conception was not immaculate, that the Sacred Trinity was nonsense, and that polygamy was not a sin.[13] These and similar "refutations" were the object of fiery Jesuit debates and conversations at the Mughal court in the sixteenth and early seventeenth centuries.

During the third Jesuit mission headed by another famous Jesuit, Jerome Xavier (alias Jerónimo de Ezpeleta y Goñi), these debates were public events and the target was the king (Jahangir) and his courtiers. Earlier Acquaviva had focused exclusively on building a personal and affective relationship with Akbar. While Xavier produced or coauthored a huge amount of literature in Persian for the Mughal court, Acquaviva tried to work his authority through "oral" and personal enchantment. Every encounter with Akbar was recorded by Acquaviva, who tried to detect not just what Akbar thought but also what he felt. "The king showed great contentment in seeing us" after impatiently waiting for the Jesuits who arrived on 28 February 1580. On another occasion, just a week later on 3 March, upon receiving the Plantin Polyglotte Bible in seven volumes, he turned the pages of the books "with great reverence and happiness." The same day in the evening, the Jesuits were invited to debate with the "molás" (*mullahs*) whom Akbar had warned to tread carefully with the missionaries. One particular argument or proposition surfaced early on and followed as a thread through all other discussions, according to Acquaviva. It was the question of miracles, which prompted the mullahs to challenge the Jesuits to trial by fire. "They started to say that we should enter fire with the Bible, and they would enter with the Qur'an." To which the Jesuits responded that they do not need miracles when they can reason according to their law.[14]

Acquaviva's capacity to turn what would seem to be a minor failure or a glitch into a sign of favor stands out in the first letter written from the mission. His text captures all kinds of clues and cues that he left without clarification but hinted at a possible triumphalist explanation. The Jesuits were told by Akbar that he wanted them to build churches just as the Turk (Ottoman sultan) did in his country but that "there are also gentiles who have their temples (*pagodas*) and ceremonies, and that nobody should be surprised [at that fact]." And again, he showed his "great love and payed them many compliments." The remarks about the gentile temples also being supported by Akbar and the king's "tolerant" attitude to all religious cults are recorded without comment.

Another character trait of the Neapolitan missionary was impatience. Such was Acquaviva's restlessness when Akbar again failed to summon the Jesuits to the court that he wrote another letter reminding the king that "Your Majesty wrote a *formão* (*farmān* or "order") to our Father Provincial in which you asked for fathers to declare the law of God." The response from Akbar was ambiguous, as Acquaviva explained in his letter to the Provincial in Goa.

> His Majesty [wrote] that all this was in the hands of God who is powerful for providing means and that that is what he wants in this world; . . .

> and he pretended (*fingiria*) that he would like to go to Mecca and would make himself Christian.[15]

Did Akbar distinguish the Christian law and Christian holy places from the Muslim? Acquaviva again provided no comment. The reader of the letter could interpret the meaning on his own.

The ups and downs of the relationship were recorded in Acquaviva's letters in detail. After the Easter in April of 1580, Akbar resumed showing interest in the Jesuits and their celebrations and prayers. He even started visiting them, completely on his own, in their residence, usually on Saturdays. His intimacy with the Jesuits made them hopeful, even more than before, that his conversion was imminent. What seemed to have attracted him, however, were religious objects and paintings, in particular, an image of the Virgin Mary and Child Jesus (*Salus Populi Romani*), a copy of a copy painted by Manuel Godinho de Heredia in Goa.[16] For three months – during which Akbar in fact had to deal with political unrest in Bengal – the missionaries waited for his call, and when it did not come, they wrote another letter.[17]

In the first letter, Acquaviva had already declared that

> we are like a physician who cures somebody of a very serious illness and says that if he does not get better, he will die from it, but he will not leave him [the sick person] until he loses all hope for (or trust in) him.[18]

In another letter to the Provincial in Goa, he uses a standard Biblical medical metaphor, popular in missionary literature: "Curavimus Babiloniam, et non est sanata: dereliquimus eam."[19] The principal cure was a dialogue, which was of course difficult to establish, especially on Jesuit terms.

2 Language

Investing in a personal, affective relationship with Akbar required learning vernacular languages. Like most of the "foreign" Jesuits working under the Portuguese *padroado*, Acquaviva had to learn Portuguese first and then whatever language was necessary for the particular mission. "Excuse me for the way I write," he wrote to Everard Mercurian, the Superior General in Rome, "because with the Portuguese language I forgot a lot of Italian, and now with Persian (*Parsia*) I mix up everything." This became a missionary topos, evoked by each new missionary, as if a "sacrifice" of mother tongue was the first "martyrdom" and a proof of the divine election. Even in this letter the question of learning languages is associated with martyrdom. Acquaviva, thus, pointed out in the very next paragraph that he feels "the greatest happiness in these parts for being near martyrdom," since according to the Qur'an those who deny that Muhammad is God's prophet, which he does loud and clear, are to be put to death. With martyrdom in the back of their mind, in the meantime, both Acquaviva and Monserrat focused on learning Persian. "I am learning a lot of this language," wrote Acquaviva, "because the king and his (subjects, elites) use it and by the grace of God I have advanced so well that I started speaking with the king."[20]

Another way of "helping" the king except by personal example (*idificar com a vida*) was to put into writing in Persian a short instruction "about our faith." If this did not work, then, Acquaviva thought, they would have to start a hospital. In fact, it was Akbar who demanded the translation of the New Testament (*Evangelho*) into Persian, but it was also important to get a translation into Arabic, from Portugal, as this would be of great service, just as was the translation of the Qur'an into Portuguese.[21] According to Monserrat, the missionaries were already working on piecemeal translations. Thus on 6 August 1580, in the *'ibādatkhāna*, Rodolfo Acquaviva presented Akbar with "a paper written in Persian, which contained the story of the birth of Jesus Christ, our Lord, taken from the New Testament (*Evangilho*)."[22] What the Jesuits did not know is that the whole purpose of these discussions and the institution of the *'ibādatkhāna* was to help discredit the ulama who were considered the men of knowledge. The architect of this strategy of Akbar's imperial consolidation or "Akbari dispensation of power," as Muzaffar Alam calls it, was in good part Abū l-Fażl.[23]

Akbar's apparent doubts and flexibility in the matters of the "law" – which the Jesuits wanted to exploit – had interesting parallels in matters of language. While the Jesuits identified Persian as the key to their missionary success in winning the rational debate, they nevertheless remarked on the existence of other languages. Monserrat wrote in his 1582 *Relacão* that Akbar belonged to the *Chaquata* ("Chagatai") nation who were Turks. "The popular language of the nation is *turquesca*," although very different from the one spoken by Turks. The court language, on the other hand, was Persian (*parse*), "but although the vocabulary and phrases were the same, the pronunciation and sound is different from the language that they speak at the court and in the lands of the king of Persia."[24] In his *Commentary* ten years later, Monserrat wrote that Acquaviva's "quickness in learning [Persian] not only gave him a great reputation for cleverness and wisdom but that even his foreign accent (*ipso peregrine vocis sono*) pleased them."[25]

The Jesuits feared, nevertheless, that they would provoke public suspicion if Akbar showed them excessive favor by "granting them too many confidential conversations."[26] And these conversations were in Persian, yet even the Jesuits realized that the private language used with family and outside of the court was something else. The Jesuits referred to it as "língua da terra" or "língua industana." Thus, in September 1582, already torn by doubts about the mission, Acquaviva wrote to the Jesuit Goan headquarters insisting that Akbar "loves" them. The proof was that Akbar proposed himself to be a Jesuit *língua* or translator when he crashed a wedding service taking place in the Jesuit "house" for a bride who spoke only the *língua da terra*.[27] Focusing exclusively on Persian and for the minority of the Persianized elite had been identified as short-sighted during the third Jesuit mission since it neglected a vast majority of the non-Muslim and Hindavi-speaking population.

Monserrat might have been right in claiming that Acquaviva's "foreign accent" was pleasing to the Mughal elites, but it can be inferred from his earlier statement that most of the courtiers had some kind of "foreign" accent compared to the Safavid standard. The spread of Persian as a language of power, kingship, and culture in South Asia took a couple of centuries, from its beginning in the ninth century when Sindh became part of the Saffarid kingdom of Ya῾qūb ibn al-Layth.[28] When the Timurids came to rule India, Persian had grown deep roots into North Indian language and literary traditions from the time of the Ghaznavids (tenth–eleventh centuries), under the Delhi sultanates (thirteenth century), to the Afghan Lodi dynasty, whom the Timurids displaced in the early sixteenth century. While the first Mughal emperors, Babur and Humayun, spoke Chagatai Turkish at home, they were all patrons of the Persian literati and it was under the Mughals that the New Persian literary style that was in the making, through the encounter between Persian and Indian literary concepts, matured into the *tāza-gū'ī* ("fresh speech") of the Mughal poets.[29] Finally, Akbar made Persian into the official language of the administration which also meant that all the local scribal experts and secretaries (*munshīs*), coming from Hindu lineages such as Kayasthas and Khatris, had to learn Persian in order to pursue their careers in the Mughal service. Except for the Iranian literati who were cherished by Akbar, all other Persian speakers must have had some kind of "foreign" accent.

However, if the initial status of "foreigner" played to Jesuit advantage on different levels, it was short lived when it came to excellence in Persian. For a proper *munshī*, learning Persian meant erudition in a rich literary tradition.[30] By the middle of the seventeenth century the Hindu *munshīs* had produced a whole literature on how to learn Persian properly for different purposes or imperial services, but had also started producing literary works and translations from Sanskrit and other Indian languages.[31]

One can only speculate about what Acquaviva's project for the mission at the Mughal court was; it was probably the tolerance (*ṣulḥ-i kull*) of religious diversity that inspired Acquaviva to devise a "trick" to introduce his own (intolerant) law to compete with other laws. In fact, his assessment of Akbar as uninterested in the "truth" but keen on introducing "novelties" was a double-edged sword. Thus Akbar was seen as easily mixing up elements of all the "laws." The danger, in Acquaviva's mind was that Akbar would choose what he wanted from the Sacred Scriptures for some other purpose or that he did not quite grasp the point of certain, crucial Christian rites.[32] Or was Akbar speaking ironically when he asked after attending a "divine Mystery celebrated with a lot of tears by Father Rodolfo. . . . You ate and drank and did not invite me?"[33]

In spite of the intentional tricks on which both Acquaviva and Akbar built their relationship, the "love" and "friendship" rhetoric was employed by both sides. For the two of them this was part of the standard vocabulary of courtly vassalage, but for the Jesuits it was, in fact, considered more than that. This type of language was supposed to transcend human relationships and build spiritual bridges, thus reflecting the divine will. Of course, the interpretation or discernment of the divine will was tied to Jesuit spiritual tools. Acquaviva's error, as he himself may have started to understand, was that he tried to build a new type of relationship of love with Akbar based on the type of obedience required by the *Spiritual Exercises* in the wrong language. It is possible that Acquaviva realized that although Persian was the key for proselytizing among the Mughal elites, especially the native speakers of Persian, Hindustani had been a "mother tongue" to most others, Akbar included. For the deep spiritual regeneration the Jesuits were promoting, the target of proselytism was the mother tongue first, as the vehicle through which conversion could be made. In Acquaviva's last letter from the mission (in the last paragraph) he included a plan: to organize a seminary in Goa in the Persian language for the Muslims and in "Hindustani . . . for the gentiles, or at least of the sons of gentiles and Muslims, those who can be found there (in Goa) and who can be sent from here." However, it was Acquaviva's doubts, ever since he was left alone in the mission, that prompted him to ask for consultation with the Provincial in Daman, promising to reveal things that cannot be put in writing: "I have many things to communicate to you that I discovered ever since I learned the language."[34]

Unfortunately, Akbar proved to be unpredictable, although he also responded to Jesuit love with love: in his letter (of *farmān*) to the Jesuit Provincial in 1583, Akbar insisted that he had "much love for the Father (Acquaviva)." This is how he explained his permission to let Acquaviva return to Goa.[35] In the annual report on the "mission del Mogor" that Rui Vincente sent to Rome in October 1582, he concluded that "no other fruit can be expected except a glorious crown of martyrdom for which Our Lord equipped Father Rodolfo for his great virtue."[36]

3 Village disturbance

It was not at the court but in the Cuncolim village that the well-known martyrdom scene took place and propelled Acquaviva to sainthood, a particular spiritual nobility. Between his return from the Mughal court to Goa in May of 1583 and his death on 15 July (Julian calendar) in the same year, Acquaviva left no written traces from his own hand. Letters and reports closest to the event by Thomas Stephens, Duarte de Sande, and Alessandro Valignano mention at least briefly that the situation in the southern Salsete region had been tense for at least the past two decades since this territory had been incorporated into the Estado da Índia in 1543.[37]

Rodolfo Acquaviva stumbled into the Cuncolim's providential trap accompanied by four Jesuits, Pietro Berno, Francisco Aranha, Alfonso Pacheco, and Antonio Francisco, and a retinue of some 60 Christians, mostly from a local village (Orlim), four of whom would also be killed, on 15 July 1583. The story is well known and retold with embellishments and variations in the hagiographical literature, based on Jesuit reports and histories written in Goa, all of which were celebratory but attentive to "facts."[38] In order to establish the case for beatification and canonization of the martyrs, the event had to be properly recorded and narrativized. It required a core story line, and a fine balancing act between crude facts, descriptive embroideries, and emotional intelligibility.[39]

What transpires from the first relatively detailed accounts by Valignano and Sebastião Gonçalves is that the Portuguese acquired the region around Cuncolim from the Bijapur sultanate (*tierras de Dialcón* or *Idalkhan*) in the war and that it was imperfectly Christianized.

> There are sixty-six [Sahāsaṣṭha in Marathi = Salsete] villages (*aldeas*) of the natives of the land with a lot of people; and because there are many Brahmans on this land, it is prone to the abominable cult of idolatry, and all the gentile wickedness and superstitions. And it was subjected to this Estado years ago and so close to Goa, [but] they were always obstinate and hard [=adamant] in their idolatries so that for a long time it was impossible to enter it for conversion and Christianity (christiandad).[40]

According to Valignano, in 1574 the population of Salsete was 80,000, with only 4,000 to 5,000 Christians, all of them converted by the Jesuits who lived and worked as parish priests in the six churches (Margão, Verna, Cortalim, Mormugão, Orlim, and Rachol).[41] In 1576, a document compiled by Diogo Velho, a revenue official (*veador da fazenda*), contained an intricate financial plan of how to divide money – according to Portuguese official property and revenue rules – acquired from the revenues of the former temples in Salsete and Bardez in favor of various churches, colleges, and their employees.[42] What is clear from the document is that this money from the temples was crucial for the upkeep of all ecclesiastical institutions and that there was a lot of tension between various actors.

Another census, the *Foral de Salcete* (Charter of Salsete), was compiled in 1567 and was important to the Jesuits who were given the task of Christianizing the population because it listed the lands and goods that the villages of Salsete allocated to temples.[43] Since temple revenues became church revenues, the information about the properties, types of fields, palm or coconut orchards, livestock, and so forth was precious. In the 1576 document *Salsete de Goa*, the Jesuits recorded how the money had been and should have been distributed or spent in order to support the growth of a Christian population. The intrusion of the Portuguese "inquisitive" revenue officials and their scribes and accountants went hand in hand with Jesuit agents such as *línguas* ("interpreters") and local priests who were able to translate and even decipher (or simply interpret) agricultural relations that the villages and the *gauncars* ("village landlords and administrators") tried to explain or dissimulate.[44]

The village of Cuncolim, the biggest of the villages that became infamous for the 1583 disturbance leading to the killing of the five Jesuit priests was, in addition, located at the very border with the non-Portuguese territory belonging to the Bijapur sultanate and had a history of resisting Portuguese efforts at control. Moreover, during the Bijapur's control, the local *gauncars* were turned into armed tax collectors (*tandar-mor*). The Portuguese suspected its "Hindu" inhabitants of siding with the Bijapuri armies that managed to besiege Goa on a few occasions in 1570–1571. According to the Jesuit reports, all five villages involved in the disturbance of 1583 (Cuncolim, Veroda, Assolna, Velim, and Ambelim) continuously negotiated through rebellions, burning churches, and even bribing Portuguese officials for the right to continue their "idolatrous" ceremonies.

It seems that the immediate reason for the Viceroy Dom Francisco Mascarenhas to send his nephew Gil Eanes Mascarenhas, the captain-major of the Malabar Coast, to intervene in the region was that for years these five villages refused to pay *foros* ("quit-rents") and disrupted the postal service passing through the village between Cochin and Goa.[45] After entering the Sal river in April of 1583, the army of Gil Eanes Mascarenhas burnt and destroyed the paddy fields, orchards, and all agricultural land although, according to Valignano, the main goal of this punitive expedition was, to destroy "idols."

Sebastião Gonçalves, another prolific Jesuit writer, provided more gory details. It seems that after the first round of temple destruction, "the blacks (*os negros*)" rebuilt the big temple and four of five small ones around it.[46] The soldiers burnt them again while the two fathers, Manoel Teixeira and Pietro Berna "destroyed a big anthill (*formigueiro*)," killed a cow, and stuffed it on top by which they desecrated the place in order to make it impossible to be rebuilt. The army then destroyed orchards and paddy fields in Cuncolim again, and erected palisades (*tranqueiras*) around their fort for the protection of the soldiers.[47]

Both Valignano and Gonçalves, and later on Francisco de Sousa, introduced into their narratives these sporadic insurrections and the violence used against the rebels in order to set the stage for the scene of martyrdom. Rodolfo Acquaviva had recently come from the *corte del Gran Mogor* where he was said to have been kept for three years as a "captive" and under death menace, although showing "great virtue and sanctity." He joined the fathers in Salsete, taking up the job of a Rector of the college (in Margão) and thus found himself present in the mission to pacify Cuncolim.[48] It was after the Jesuit party crossed the river Sal that the situation suddenly worsened. They were on the enemy territory, where even nature was inimical. The fathers' companions from Orlim entered Cuncolim in search of a "fresh and pleasant place" to build a church but found none. In the meantime because it was monsoon season, the fathers took refuge in the "*ramada*," a shelter made of palm leaves, but all the signs of hospitality were wrong. Nobody came to meet them while they heard a "wizard" (*feiticeiro*) screaming on the road: "War, war . . . it is time!

You have them moored here. And another voice saying: This is a good gift and of many heads."[49] The local Christians explained to the fathers that the "devils ran away from the village" because of their presence. At their leisure, the fathers then ate and had some rest and finally met with two important men from the village who warned them that there was a strife in the village and that the "wizard" was calling people to hurt the fathers.

What happened next has been welded by Catholic hagiographers and historians in an endless repetition of the basic plot with picturesque variations: The Jesuits were attacked by a mob of villagers after having failed to "leave," prevented by a sudden rain shower and other delays.[50] Then the villagers, preceded by the howling "wizard," charged toward the Jesuit shelter with swords and arrows. They also shouted: "Kill, kill these wizards who disturb the land, enemies of gods (*pagodes*) and destroy their temples (*templos*) and ceremonies."[51]

The mayhem started when more "blacks" (*negros*) joined in. They first slashed the legs of Rodolfo Acquaviva, who then fell on his knees "looked up to the sky, unbuttoned the collar of his habit [and] expected the second blow." His shoulder was also slashed, and they cut off four or five fingers before piercing him with an arrow. The second was Brother Francisco Aranha whose half-dead body was thrown into the paddy field. The third, Pietro Berno, was stripped and mutilated starting with gauging an eye out with a *zarguncho*[52] and cutting off his genitals which they then stuffed in his mouth. He was then thrown next to Aranha into the paddy field "as a true wheat that, falling on the earth and dying, brings a lot of fruit." The fourth was Alfonso Pacheco who had his head cut off; the fifth, Antonio Francisco, was also subjected to various wounds of which he immediately died. The worst torture was saved for Aranha whom they fetched from the paddy field and brought in front of the "*pagode*"; they made him stand on one leg and forced him to pay his respects to the god. When he refused they pumped arrows into him.[53] As he was dying, women and children pounded him into a pulp with stones and lances and smeared his blood over the idols (*pagoda*). Two Brahman boys, Domingos, a native of Cuncolim, and Alfonso, were also killed in addition to other "honorable" native Christians, Francisco Rodrigues and Paulo da Costa, and a Portuguese man Gonçalo Fernandes. Only Domingo de Aguilar, helped by a "gentile" friend, managed to escape.

The Portuguese retaliation was just as violent. A few days later a Portuguese official in the fort of Assolna, on the other side of the river Sal, invited in, under the pretext of negotiation, 16 *gauncars* or "principal heads" from Cuncolim. They were then killed (except for one), and their heads were cut off and impaled on the walls of the fortress.[54] The move was a clear effort at "decapitating" the old regime elites who were forced to either convert or flee outside to the neighboring "Muslim" lands. Moreover, the Portuguese Crown expropriated the lands of the *gauncars*.

An ex-Jesuit historian, Teotónio de Souza, has offered an economic and social explanation for the event. Cuncolim was a temple village and a bazaar, located on the important north-south caravan route. Local social elites – the *ganvkars* (*gauncars*) – perceived the Christianization carried out by the Jesuits as a direct menace to their economic privileges linked to the Mahadeva (Śiva) temple which was at the heart of the trade activities taking place under its auspices.[55] Rowena Robinson, a sociologist, has extended the discussion to the post-conversion history of Cuncolim in which the converted *ganvkars* resumed both economic and cultural (cultic) control in spite of the Portuguese "punishment." They did so by investing in confraternities and replacing the temple with the church from which the earlier system of distinctions (honors) could be re-inscribed. A more recent interpretation by Ângela Barreto Xavier, focusing on the very moments of the crisis and violence, suggests that the trigger (if not the cause) was a ritual of possession that got out of hand.[56] Thus the Jesuit demonization of local deities mirrored the way the Cuncolim religious specialists demonized the Jesuits.

Just as in the Mughal court, Rodolfo Acquaviva – who somewhat undeservedly plays a major role in the hagiographies of the Cuncolim martyrdom – had been drawn into the logics of local practices. From fragmentary details provided by Valignano and Gonçalves, Acquaviva was not, in fact, the leader of the Jesuit party. He did not know the local language, it was his first visit to the region, and the complexity of the rural setting was most probably still beyond his understanding. Acquaviva's error was that he went into the field completely uninformed and careless in assessing the situation. Just before the event he had been peacefully reading canonical hours instead of listening carefully to the menacing voices.

The martyrdom of the five Jesuits was, in fact, a huge loss in terms of missionary personnel since there were never more than 12 to 14 Jesuits at a time in the entire Salsete region.[57] However each missionary loss or "error" could be narrativized into hailing the advantages of such "pious deaths."[58] Even more than in the Mughal mission, in Cuncolim Acquaviva was disoriented and shortsighted (with or without his glasses), and perhaps aware of that, so that offering his throat to be cut was an extreme solution, which preserved and confirmed his noble ambitions. Acquaviva's missionary life, if viewed from outside the narrative arc constructed around it – filled with the desperate gestures of a young, noble, and impatient Italian Jesuit – had a logical (and happy) end in martyrdom, a kind of failure at finding a better solution. However, if the Jesuits failed to communicate their message (of "love"), the *gauncars* of Cuncolim made a mistake as well, which cost them their lives and the ownership of their land for another 400 years.

Notes

1 Banerjee and Hoyland, *Commentary of Father Monserrate*, 192–196. For the Latin text established by Hosten, "*Mongolicae Legationis, Commentarius*," 513–704. For a recent Catalan version see Monserrat and Alay, *Ambaixador a la cort del Gran Mogol*. I am quoting from both translated and Latin text. I have corrected embellishments or "explanations" in the English translation.

2 All quotations in this paragraph are from Banerjee and Hoyland, *Commentary of Father Monserrate*, 192–193; Hosten, "*Mongolicae Legationis Commentarius*," 638.

3 Banerjee and Hoyland, *Commentary of Father Monserrate*, 194–195; Hosten, "*Mongolicae Legationis Commentarius*," 639. The English translation embellishes the text as "Will these Musulmans never martyr us."

4 See Županov, *Missionary Tropics*, 147–170. However, as Bruna Soalheiro has pointed out, the Conselho do Arcebispo de Goa approved the mission and even believed that if the missionaries had been killed it would have been a legal pretext for attacking the Mughal empire. Soalheiro, *Política e Retórica*, 49. "Conselho do Arcebispo de Goa e mais bispos da Índia sobre o que se faria acerca da embaixada do Grão Mogor" Goa, 20 November 1579, published in Rego, *Documentação*, vol. 12, 455–457.

5 Today this province is written as Salcete or Sashti in Konkani.

6 Banerjee and Hoyland, *Commentary of Father Monserrate*, 192; Hosten, "*Mongolicae Legationis Commentarius*," 638.

7 Fabre, "'Entrar con el otro y salir con sigo'." See also Mostaccio, "Spiritual Exercises."

8 The new emotional community of the Jesuits was based on the idea of uniformizing the feelings of belonging. Each one had to learn to feel like all the others in the community. On emotional communities, see Rosenwein, *Emotional Communities*.

9 Truschke, *Culture of Encounter*.

10 Rezavi, "Religious Disputations," 197. He quotes Abū l-Fażl ʿAllāmī, *Akbarnāma*, 112.

11 See articles in Thomas and Mallet, *Christian-Muslim Relations*, and in Heyberger et al., *L'Islam visto da Occidente*. See also Bernard Heyberger, "Polemic Dialogues," 495–516.

12 Pérez de Chinchón, *Libro Llamado Antialcoran*. See also Županov, "'The Wheel of Torments'."

13 On the way Islamic theology engaged with Christian ideas from the ninth century onwards, see Thomas, *Christian Doctrines*.

14 Rodolfo Acquaviva, Antonio de Monserrate and Francisco Rodrigues to Rui Vicente, Agra, 13 July 1580, in DI, vol. 12, 38.

15 Rodolfo Acquaviva, Antonio de Monserrate and Francisco Rodrigues to Rui Vicente, Agra, 13 July 1580, in DI, vol. 12, 39.

16 On this important Byzantine icon in the church of the Santa Maria Maggiore in Rome and its reproductions in the early modern period, see Mochizuki, "Sacred Art," 129–143. See also Dekoninck, "*Propagatio Imaginum*."

17 Dekoninck, "*Propagatio Imaginum*," 41.

18 Dekoninck, "*Propagatio Imaginum*," 41.

19 Rodolfo Acquaviva to Rui Vicente, Fatehpur Sikri, 20 July 1580, in DI, vol. 12, 56.

20 Rodolfo Acquaviva to Everard Mercurian, Fatehpur Sikri, 18 July 1580, in DI, vol. 12, 51.

21 MacLagen, *The Jesuits and the Great Mogul*, 200.

22 Antoni Monserrat to Rui Vicente, Fatehpur Sikri, 9 September 1589, in DI, vol. 12, 66.

23 Alam, "The Mughals," 124–163.

24 Antoni Monserrat, *Relaçam do Equebar, rei dos mogores*, Goa, 26 November 1582, in DI, vol. 12, 647.

25 Banerjee and Hoyland, *The Commentary of Father Monserrate*, 50; Hosten, *Mongolicae Legationis Commentaries*, 569.

26 Banerjee and Hoyland, *The Commentary of Father Monserrate*, 50; Hosten, *Mongolicae Legationis Commentaries*, 569.

27 Rodolfo Acquaviva to Rui Vicente, Fatehpur Sikri, 27 September 1582, in DI, vol. 12, 598.
28 Alam, *The Languages*, 115.
29 Alam, *The Languages*, 121. See also Alam, "The Culture and Politics," 131–198; Dudney, "Sabk-e Hendi and the Crisis of Authority," 60–82.
30 Munshī was a secretary or a language teacher.
31 Alam, *The Languages*, 130–131.
32 Alam, *The Languages*, 130–131.
33 Sousa, *Oriente conquistado a Jesu Christo*, 957.
34 Rodolfo Acquaviva, 27 September 1582, in DI, vol. 12, 598–599.
35 Flores and Saldanha, *Os Firangis na Chancelaria Mogol*, 69–70.
36 Rui Vicente to Claudio Acquaviva, Goa, 25 October 1582, in DI, vol. 12, 626.
37 Thomas Stephens to Richard Stephens, Goa, 24 October 1583, in DI, vol. 12, 817–826. English translation in Schurhammer, *Orientalia*. Duarte de Sande to Claudio Acquaviva, Goa, 4 December 1583, in DI, vol. 12, 891–910; Alessandro Valignano to Rui Vicente, Goa, 18 December 1583, in DI, vol. 12, 916–933.
38 See the recent translation and edition by Paul Gwynne of the first Jesuit epic written by a rhetoric professor at the Collegium Romanum, Francesco Benci about Rodolfo Acquaviva and his companions in martyrdom and published in Venice in 1591; a corrected version then appeared in Rome in 1592. Gwynne, *Francesco Benci's, 'Quinque Martyres'*.
39 For the reconstruction of this event see Xavier, *A Invenção de Goa*, 333–379. See also Xavier, "Power, Religion and Violence," 27–50 and Robinson, "Cuncolim," 334–340.
40 Valignano, 18 December, 1583, in DI, vol. 12, 918.
41 Alessandro Valignano to Everard Mercurian, Goa, 25 December 1574, in DI, vol. 9, 507 and [Rui Lopez,] *Documenta de usus redituum templorum olim ethnicorum*, Goa, 9 November 1573, in DI, vol. 9, 273–281.
42 "Regimentos da fortalezas (Goa em 1576), Arquivo Histórico do Estado da Índia, 5–13v," published in Rego, *Documentação*, 12: 343–368. The full *Regimento (Rule)* for Goa in 1576 was printed by Pissurlenkar, *Regimentos das Fortalezas*, 15–163.
43 Xavier and Županov, *Catholic Orientalism*, 63. There is a huge and well-known scholarship on the function of the Hindu temple (especially in Southern India). See Talbot, "Temples, Donors, and Gifts," 308–340; Appadurai, "Kings, Sects and Temples," 47–73.
44 For an introduction to Goan collective ownership of land by shareholders, also known as *gaunkaria* or *communidades*, see Axelrod and Fuerch, "Portuguese Orientalism," 439–476.
45 Sebastião Gonçalves, *Da gloriosa morte de cinco religiosos da Companhia de Jesus que forão martirizados nas terras de Salcete no anno de 1583*, Goa, December 1609, in DI, vol. 12, 976.
46 These five small temples were dedicated to five guardian gods – *panchadevata*, attested in other sources and typical in some Goan villages. See Trinidade, *Conquista Espiritual*, 1: 339; Xavier, "Power, Religion and Violence," 24.
47 Gonçalves, *Da gloriosa morte de cinco religiosos*, in DI, vol. 12, 78.
48 Alessandro Valignano, 18 December 1583, in DI, vol. 13, 920.
49 Gonçalves, *Da gloriosa morte de cinco religiosos*, in DI, vol. 12, 980.
50 Gonçalves, *Da gloriosa morte de cinco religiosos*, in DI, vol. 12, 982.
51 Gonçalves, *Da gloriosa morte de cinco religiosos*, in DI, vol. 12, 982, and Alessandro Valignano, 18 December 1583, DI, vol. 12, 926 (in the Spanish text – *pagodas* are *dioses*).
52 *Zarguncho*, a weapon of African origin, similar to a short lance or *chuzo*. In the backlands of Brazil a *jagunço* (the same etymology) became an armed hand usually hired by big farmers and "colonels" especially in the northern region.

53 Gonçalves, *Da gloriosa morte de cinco religiosos*, in DI, vol. 12, 983–984.
54 Gonçalves, *Da gloriosa morte de cinco religiosos*, in DI, vol. 12, 993. *Admirable Vida y Virtudes del Santo Martyr Rodulfo Aquaviva*, no place, no date (eighteenth century), 223. See also ANTT, Armário Jesuitico, Ms. 89, No. 21.
55 Souza, "Why Cuncolim Martyrs," 37–47. It was this very temple that was destroyed by the missionaries-cum-soldiers' assault in 1567, but it was rebuilt in 1579 by a local resident, Vittaldas Vittoji.
56 Xavier, "Power, Religion and Violence," 27.
57 Rui Vicente to Claudio Acquaviva, Goa, 8 November 1581, in DI, vol. 12, 421; Rui Vicente to Claudio Acquaviva, Goa, 21 October 1582, in DI, vol. 12, 616.
58 Manoel Teixiera and Giovanni Pietro Crasso (or Grasso) to Giovanni Pietro Maffei, *Respostas aas pregontas che V. R. mandou preguntar à India per'a Historia che faz da India*, Goa, December 1583, in DI, vol. 12, 960.

Part II

Missionaries in cities

4 Urban residences and rural missions

Patronage and Catholic evangelization in late imperial China

Ronnie Po-chia Hsia

The geographic patterns of Catholic missions in late imperial China, defined for this chapter as the period from the late Ming to the mid-Qing dynasty (1600–1800), were determined by one overriding factor: patronage. More than in any other mission, Catholic missionaries in late imperial China depended on their patrons for their social positions, and hence they appeared in the most diverse garments, reflecting the different fortunes of their missionary stations, from blue silk robes embroidered with a mandarin square and caps with feather and jade, to the worn and common cotton jackets and trousers of a commoner. Patronage was also the single most important factor in determining the urban/rural location of missionary work. Using patronage as the central concept, we can think of the Catholic mission in late imperial China as falling into two distinct spatial periods, with the 1705 imperial prohibition of evangelization as a watershed between them.[1]

First, it may be useful to summarize the urban history of late imperial China that is relevant to the Catholic mission.[2] The delineation of macroregions and the theory of central place urban hierarchies, developed by G. William Skinner in 1977, is still useful as a heuristic device for us to map the urban/rural patterns of Catholic missions.[3] Briefly stated, there were two systems that defined the urban hierarchy in Ming-Qing China. The first was administrative with the imperial capital(s) at the top, descending to sites of governorships, and provincial, district, and county administrations. While the nomenclature may have differed between the Ming and Qing dynasties, the basic fact remains that both dynasties consistently used a three-tier system (capital, district, county), as the offices of supra-provincial and provincial administrations were almost invariably located in district-ranked cities (*fu* 府), which were also the locales for lower level county magistracies (*xian* 縣). The few exceptions to this pattern pertained to frontier military regions and need not be considered here. The second system was defined by geography and economy, the two naturally overlapping in determining the density and size of urban networks and the accessibility of transport routes. To a large extent, the administrative and geographic/economic urban systems coincided; the capital cities and the provincial capitals also represented the largest urban centers and economic hubs, but that was not always the case. Urban history followed the overlapping but different types of logic of politics and economy; and the Catholic mission in late imperial China oscillated between the urban and the rural. The key word is patronage, or, as Nicolas Standaert formulates it, *guanxi* 關系: "They [the missionaries] also became aware that in the Chinese art of relations management, that is the establishment and the maintenance of *guanxi*, human feelings or human obligations (*renqing* 人情) play an important role."[4] Using Skinner's central place theory, Standaert adapts the data collected by Joseph Dehergne in mapping the contours and periodization of the growth of the Chinese Christian community. Standaert also uses Dehergne's concept of *chrétienté* to define the Christian community, investing it with perhaps more of a parochial/spatial connotation than the actual historical reality on the ground in Ming and Qing China. Dehergne's *chrétienté* was heavily influenced by the religious sociology of Gabriel Le Bras, whose idea about a church-centered village parish, characteristic of rural society in the medieval West, and about the importance of ecclesiastical institutions, had influenced a whole generation of religious historians in Europe.[5] However, late imperial China was very different from medieval Europe. Although Christian communities succeeded in developing strong spatial and institutional structures in some places in Shanxi, Jiangsu, and Fujian, it was just as likely that the contingencies of *guanxi* and historical change rendered the contours of Christianity in China much less stable and more amorphous in shape. The geographical shape of the mission was determined by the patronage of mandarins, retired officials, local gentry, small town merchants, and rural farmers, who provided protection and support for the many generations of European missionaries. The changing shape of the mission in China reflected the rise and decline in the political fortunes of the mission and mapped the geography of Christianity onto that of the urban map of China.

1 Missionary motions

The purpose of this article is to demonstrate that the directions of these missionary movements depended on two major factors: the patterns of patronage and the urban-rural structures of late imperial China. While the Society of Jesus was founded as a religious order that focused on evangelical missions in urban centers, in the course of the later seventeenth and eighteenth centuries it extended its work into rural areas in Europe in the form of sermon tours by famous preachers.[6] However, that historical movement of expansion in Europe, from the cities to the countryside, was absent in late imperial China. Religious movements of this period did not so much follow the logic of central place and network but rather the loci of patronage. When missionaries were dependent on mandarin patronage, from officials who sat in urban magistracies, the Jesuit mission assumed a strong urban pattern; when retired officials in their country homes became the main patrons of Jesuits, the Catholic mission took on a distinctively rural character.

In fact, all directions of urban-rural movements that would come to characterize the Catholic mission in China in later history had been demonstrated by its first decades. These movements can be described as ascending, horizontal, and descending across the system of urban hierarchy and macro-regions, as the following cases will illustrate (see Map 4.1).

Ascent

The location of the first Catholic mission, that initiated by the Jesuits Michele Ruggieri and Matteo Ricci, was determined by its mandarin patrons. It was Chen Rui 陳瑞, the Supreme Commander of Guangdong and Guangxi, who invited Ruggieri in 1582 to come to Zhaoqing, the charming but small district town that lay halfway between Guangzhou, the provincial capital of Guangdong, and the border of Guangxi province. It was Liu Jiezhai 劉節齋, a successor of Chen, who forced the Jesuits to leave Zhaoqing in 1589 and resettle in Shaozhou, another district town in the north of Guangdong province. And it was yet another mandarin, Wang Zongming 王忠銘, who enabled Ricci to escape the tropical frontier province that had been the bane of his existence for 13 years by relocating in 1594 to Nanchang, the provincial capital of Jiangxi.[7]

Ricci's own career reflected this ascent in the system of urban hierarchy as he slowly but successfully climbed the ladder of social success in late Ming society. While his move from Zhaoqing to Shaozhou in 1588 represented a setback, since the density of political patronage was much lower in the latter district city (*fu* 府) than in Zhaoqing, the two urban centers were comparable in size and economic importance. Overcoming this temporary setback, in 1594 Ricci tried to establish himself in Nanjing, the southern capital of the Ming. However, this attempt failed, and with this overreach, he was forced to return to the south. Poignant was the dream that came to our exhausted and depressed missionary returning to Nanchang, where he stayed briefly en route to the southern capital. In the dream, an unknown man, who turned out to be God, promises Ricci that he would "be propitious to him in the two capitals."[8] Ricci's goal was the apex of the political hierarchy, the imperial capital. Instead, for the time being, he compromised by settling in Nanchang, which nonetheless represented a significant ascent, since the provincial capital of Jiangxi was a site for Ming feudal principalities and the imperial civil service examination system. The political, cultural, and economic importance of Nanchang enabled Ricci to construct a social network much higher up in the Ming social hierarchy than he could have done in Guangdong. Moreover, as a center for publishing, Nanchang also enabled Ricci to publish his first books in Chinese to wide reception and positive acclaim. Its function as a cultural capital, in addition to an administrative one, provided Ricci with the opportunity to engage extensively with Confucian scholars in addition to the mandarin elites, thus furnishing the intellectual content for the persona he had created under mandarin patronage.

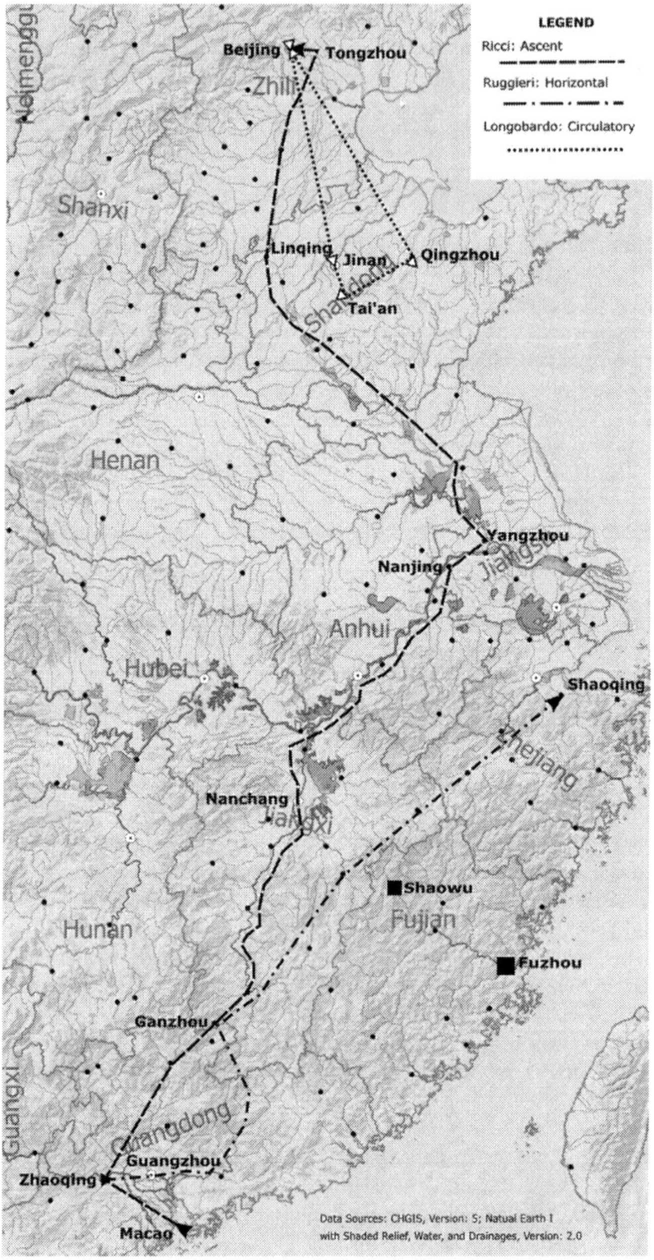

Map 4.1 Movements of Jesuits in late Ming China

Source: © Ronnie Po-chia Hsia

In Nanchang, Ricci got his next break. In 1598, a mandarin acquaintance from his Guangdong days agreed to take him to Beijing. Ricci traveled to Nanjing before sailing on the Grand Canal to the imperial capital. For the second time, Ricci had overreached. He lacked the political and social networks to establish residency. Forced to return to Nanjing, Ricci profited greatly from the two years it took him to become a recognizable name in society, thanks to his reputation in mathematics, astronomy, and Confucian learning. In 1600, Ricci made the final journey of his life; despite initial setbacks, he succeeded in establishing a permanent position in the imperial capital, Beijing. The last decade of his life marked the pinnacle of Ricci's personal success as well as that of the China mission. His journey traversed four of the nine macro-regions identified by Skinner (Lingnan, Middle Yangzi, Lower Yangzi, and North China), although economic factors had hardly played a role in Ricci's ascent.

Horizontal (transregional)

Less successful in his missionary career, Michele Ruggieri, Ricci's senior colleague, undertook an interesting journey between November 1585 and August 1586.[9] Patronage played a factor, but it was an economic impetus that propelled his attempt to break free of Guangdong. The patron of the Jesuits in Zhaoqing, the district magistrate (*zhifu* 知府) Wang Pan 王泮, was a native of Shaoxing, a prosperous city in Zhejiang, which was part of the densest urban macro-region, the Lower Yangzi, according to Skinner. Wang Pan had a brother who was a merchant. In November 1585, he came to trade in Guangzhou. Playing the middleman, Wang Pan established a connection between his brother and Ruggieri. Through the Jesuit, Merchant Wang connected with the Portuguese in Macao to whom he quickly sold the silk that he had brought from Zhejiang. This transaction linked the transregional trade in China with the international trade between Portugal, China, and Japan. The Lower Yangzi macro-region, center of the silk industry, provided raw silk and brocades for the Japanese, Southeast Asian, and European markets through Portuguese middlemen, who imported Japanese silver to pay for the goods.[10] Two auxiliary commodities also passed through this transregional trade network in China: tea, harvested in Zhejiang and neighboring Fujian, and porcelain, fired in Jingdezheng, the industrial metropolis of Ming China in Jiangxi province. With their transactions completed, Ruggieri and the Portuguese Jesuit Almeida traveled in Merchant Wang's entourage to return to Zhejiang. They used the excellent river transport network provided by the Pearl River and its tributary (the Beijiang) and crossed the low-lying Meiling range that separated the macro-region of Lingnan from the Middle Yangzi (and Guangdong from Jiangxi) before reverting to river transport on the Gan River. Notably, Merchant Wang's party transacted further business in Jiangxi en route, no doubt buying porcelain for the home market in Zhejiang.

I have written about the missionary activities of Ruggieri and Almeida in more detail elsewhere.[11] But this episode in Ruggieri's career is a reminder that Ricci's ascent (his dependence on mandarin and scholarly patronage, and emphasis on scientific and cultural exchange) was a subsequent invention. The first Jesuits missionaries, of whom Ruggieri was the pioneer, succeeded in entering China due to the trade network between Portuguese Macao and Guangzhou. It was silver that made possible the Gospels, as Luis de Camões would write in *Os Lusíadas*, much in the way that sixteenth-century Japan became open to the Gospels.[12]

Descent

A third Jesuit, the Sicilian Nicolas Longobardo, broke with the pattern of urban missions established by Ricci. Longobardo joined the China mission in 1597 and was first stationed in Shaozhou, where Ricci had spent the unhappiest years of his career. Seeing little interest for the Christian message within the city, Longobardo traveled to the surrounding villages, preaching the Gospels with the help of a catechist, and found warm and enthusiastic reception. These episodes indicated the great demand for religious services in the countryside, which was only sparsely endowed with the temples and monasteries that dotted the urban spaces in late imperial China. Rural missions, carried out from urban residences, would become a pattern of evangelization in China, as they would also characterize the work of the Jesuits and Lazarists in seventeenth-century Southern Italy, France, and Spain.[13]

After the death of Ricci in 1610, Longobardo was named as his successor as the superior of the Jesuit China Mission. From the south he traveled to Beijing, the imperial capital, a city with incomparable size, splendor, and importance, in contrast to the provincial district backwater town of Shaozhou. Between 1611 and 1655, Beijing served as the base for Longobardo, the longest serving missionary in China. His duties as a superior kept the Sicilian immobile most of the time, but Longobardo undertook several journeys to Shaanxi, Zhejiang, and Shandong, of which the last turned out to be the most significant. In the same macro-region of North China as the imperial capital, Shangdong was easily accessible from Beijing. In 1637 and 1640 Longobardo undertook two long missions to that province.[14] Patronage and social networks again played a role. Longobardo's first journey to Jinan, the provincial capital, was due to a previous connection: the Jesuits had been recommended to serve in the Calendar Office at court by Xu Guangqi 徐光啓, a high mandarin and friend of Ricci. Li Tianqing 李天經, a student of Xu's, and a convert like his master, was appointed as the director of the Calendar Office. Li had previously served in Jinan and wrote recommendations to former mandarin colleagues to facilitate Longobardo's visit. On this trip, Longobardo also visited Tai'an, which was designated a *zhou* 州, a smaller town than Jinan and lower on the administrative hierarchy because it was the native place of his servant in Beijing and Longobardo could tap into his servant's kinship network.

The 1640 missionary journey took Longobardo to Jinan and further to Qingzhou 青州, a mid-size district-level town, significant for being the location of a Ming feudatory branch. Several of the Ming princes played host to Longobardo, repeating an earlier patronage pattern seen in Ricci's career in Nanchang. One of the cadet princes converted to Christianity because of his interest in monotheism. Longobardo recorded the first Christian-Muslim dialogue in China that took place in the palace, as the prince wanted to hear arguments from the two different advocates for monotheism. It was also in Qingzhou that the leader of a secret religious society came to visit Longobardo. The sect leader had learned fragments of the Christian message from a fellow villager who had heard Longobardo's sermons in Jinan three years earlier. Eager for more profound religious knowledge, the sect leader traveled to Qingzhou to seek out the great master. After several days of intense catechizing, Longobardo baptized the sect leader and his companion and sent them on their return journey.

These descending movements, radiating out from a higher-ranking central place to lower-ranking urban centers, enabled the spread of Christianity to rural areas, as district and county capitals also served as market towns for their rural hinterlands. The Christian mission's first recorded encounter with secret popular religion in China was mediated through this line of transmission.

Circulatory

Descending missionary movements from higher order central places to lower order urban centers did not necessarily move down the social ladder in late imperial China, as exemplified by Longobardo's journeys; they could also represent horizontal social movements. When mandarins retired from office and returned to their native places, they provided patronage that shaped missionary movements that may be described as circulatory. The best example is provided by the Italian Giulio Aleni. Entering China in 1610, the year of Ricci's death, Aleni imitated Ricci's missionary strategy and acquired the sobriquet of "Confucius of the West" for his Confucian learning.[15] His extensive missions took him to Beijing, Shanxi, and the Jiangnan region of Southern Zhili and Zhejiang province. In 1625, the Grand Secretary Ye Xianggao 葉向高 (1562–1627), who had first met Ricci in 1599, retired from office in Beijing. He invited Aleni to accompany him on his return to Fuzhou, his native place, and the provincial capital of Fujian. Although Ye never converted, he provided the patronage and social network for the foundation and expansion of the Jesuit mission in Fujian. As the provincial capital, Fuzhou was the site for imperial civil service examinations. In 1628 two brothers from the garrison town of Haikou 海口, Li Jiubiao 李九標, and Li Jiugong 李九功, came to Fuzhou to sit for the provincial examination. Catechized by Aleni, the Li brothers converted. In the notes of conversations and teachings, the Li brothers recorded some of the travels of their Christian master. Aleni himself wrote that he had visited seven of the eight prefectures in Fujian province. *The Diary of Oral Admonitions* (*Kouduo richao* 口鐸日抄), compiled by the Li brothers, recorded several movements of the Jesuit between October 1637 and 1638.[16] From Fuzhou, the highest order central place in Fujian province and the southeast coastal macro-region, Aleni undertook preaching missions to ten towns in the four coastal prefectures of Fuzhou, Xinghua, Quanzhou, and Zhangzhou.

A mountainous region with a narrow coastal strip, Fujian had been the foremost maritime province in China since the fourteenth century.[17] The three prefectures of Xinghua, Quanzhou, and Zhangzhou, lying south of Fuzhou, formed the center of maritime China. Quanzhou and Zhangzhou men comprised the overwhelming majority of the merchants, seamen, and pirates who sailed the East and South China seas; traveling to the Philippines, Vietnam, Malacca, and Siam, they formed the backbone of the Chinese diaspora in Southeast Asia. A young woman from Putian County in Xinghua prefecture, Lin Moliang 林默娘, who lived in the Song dynasty, came to be deified as Mazu 媽祖, honored as the Consort and Empress of Heaven, and as the universal protector of Chinese seamen in the Ming and Qing dynasties.[18]

The activities of Aleni represented the patterns of mission foundation at a provincial level. Patronage, central place, and descending mission movements all played their part in the circulatory consolidation of mission territory.[19] In the special case of Fujian, which coincides with the southeast coastal macro-region, the Hokkien (Southern Fujianese) maritime diaspora would connect this mission territory with another Catholic land, the Spanish Philippines. The towns of the four coastal prefectures visited by Aleni would later become residences for the Spanish friars who sailed from Manila in an enterprise that would challenge the Jesuit domination of Catholic China.

Before this section concludes, it may be useful to recapitulate the findings thus far: established in urban areas, largely in the administrative centers of late imperial China, the Jesuit mission moved in a motion of ascent up the hierarchy of urban places until it had established itself in the imperial capital, Beijing. Having accomplished this after 1600, the mission expanded in descending and circulatory motions from higher to lower-order central places and into the countryside. This was the general pattern; it was patronage that determined the motions of missionary movements.

2 Missionary structures

This section will strengthen the argument that patronage was decisive for the locations of Jesuit residences in the first century of Catholic evangelization in late imperial China, in other words during the first period of evangelization. I will aggregate data from missionary reports in order to construct three synchronic views of the Catholic mission. These three views concern three locales, those of Jiangzhou in Shanxi province; Shanghai, which was a minor and insignificant town in the late Ming; and Fuzhou, the provincial capital of Fujian. These three Christian communities occupied very different places in the hierarchy of urban rank-size, and yet they all demonstrate the decisive factor of local families that acted as patrons for the Jesuit missions.

The first synchronic view is that of the year 1636, when the Jesuit mission was flourishing just eight years before the collapse of the Ming dynasty; the second represents the period from the 1690s to 1705, on the eve of the prohibition of Christian evangelization by the Kangxi emperor; and the third dates from approximately the year 1750, the year of the last extant reports from the two Jesuit missions in China, less than two decades before the dissolution of the Society. The sources consist of annual reports sent by different missionary orders. For the Jesuits, these consisted of reports compiled by the vice-province of China and, after the 1680s, the independent French Mission, submitted to the Curia of the Society in Rome; for the most part, there are manuscripts in the Roman Archive of the Society of Jesus and in the Ajuda library in Lisbon. For the mendicant orders, I draw on letters and reports sent by the Spanish friars in China to their superiors in Manila, collected and published in the multi-volume *Sinica Franciscana* and on documents from the China Dominican mission. I supplement this data with additional information from the records of the Missions Étrangères de Paris and the Archive of the Congregation for the Propagation of the Faith in Rome.[20]

Jesuit mission in 1636

Up to the end of the Ming dynasty in 1644, with the exception of two mendicant friars from Manila, the China Mission was entirely staffed by Jesuits. At the time of Ricci's death in 1610, there were four Jesuit residences in the two imperial capitals, in the provincial capital of Nanchang, and in the district city of Shaozhou. Twenty-six years later, the number increased to nine. While Shaozhou was abandoned, the Jesuit mission opened new residences in Hangzhou, Xi'an, Kaifeng, Fuzhou, Jiangzhou, Shanghai, and in other lower-ordered administrative centers. Although the Jesuits preferred central places and major administrative centers for their missionary work, as pointed out by Standaert, in many cases the new communities began because a mandarin/literati convert lived or worked in a place on a lower administrative level.[21] Four of the new residences were established in provincial capitals, following the pattern observed in the first section. Jiangzhou and Shanghai seemed to be anomalies, as they were county towns, or *xian*, which was the lowest in the three-tier central place system. Jesuit residences were established there because of patronage: Jiangzhou and Shanghai were respectively the native places of Han Lin 韓霖 and Xu Guangqi. Han Lin and his brothers, Han Yun 韓雲 and Han Xia 韓霞, belonged to a prominent gentry family in Jiangzhou. In their youth, Han Yun and Han Lin followed their father who sojourned in Qingpu county in Songjiang district during 1607–8. The neighboring county, Shanghai, was the native place of Xu Guangqi, who became a teacher to the Han boys. Under Xu's influence, the Han brothers later converted to Christianity and sponsored the first Jesuit missions to their native place in Shanxi, which endured as a center for the Catholic mission thanks to the patronage of the Han lineage.[22]

Xu Guangqi played a similar role for the Jesuit mission in Shanghai.[23] A close collaborator of Ricci, Xu would rise to the highest position in the imperial bureaucracy, serving briefly as the Grand Secretary before his death in 1633. As the most prominent Chinese convert, Xu made his native place into a Catholic center. Practically all descendants in the extensive Xu lineage were baptized; and the Xu family compound served as a Jesuit residence over the centuries. In the 1685 Annual Report from the Jesuit vice-province of China, Shanghai is described as the most important Christian community in all of China.[24] In the same year, the Franciscan Bernardino della Chiesa reported that half of all Christians in China lived in Shanghai.[25] The 1691 *Litterae Annuae* describes Shanghai as the largest Christian community in China, with 70,000 converts.[26] These reports are all the more remarkable not only because Shanghai was considered merely a county town, but it was also one of little distinction for most of the Ming dynasty, acquiring its city walls only in 1553.

The Xu family compound, Xujiahui 徐家匯 (Zikawei in the Shanghai dialect), lying to the southwest of the walled city, became the central place for Catholic missions in the Lower Yangzi macro-region. From there, Jesuit missionaries and Chinese catechists went on missions to Suzhou, Songjiang, Changshu, Wuxi, Taichong, and Zhongming Island.[27] The first two cities were district centers, the others county towns similar in status to Shanghai. This is a remarkable reversal of the pattern of movement from higher-order to lower-order central places, observed in the political, economic, and cultural structures of late imperial China, and also manifested in the peregrinations of Giulio Aleni in Fujian, as described in the first section. It demonstrates that patronage played a more important function than central place, economy, or geography in explaining the location and size of Christian communities.

On the eve of prohibition

The composite picture I have reconstructed comes from four sources: the 1685, 1691, 1697, and 1700 Litterae Annuae of the vice-province of China.[28] In this period, the Catholic Mission had extended to six of the nine macro-regions of China, notably adding the middle Yangzi region. With the exception of the Lower Yangzi region and Shanghai, the highest order central places also functioned as nodes for the network of Christianization. In North China, Beijing served this function and Jesuits from both the Portuguese vice-province and later the French mission undertook visits up to a 90-mile radius of the imperial capital. For example, to the east, missions were sent to Tongzhou, the terminus of the Grand Canal 12 miles away; and to the south, in Zhili province (today Hebei), Baoding, a provincial- and district-level city, was a missionary destination that stood at the extreme limits of the Beijing node.[29]

In the central Yangzi, a macro-region opened to Christianization in the Qing dynasty, a Jesuit mission was established in Wuchang, the largest city of the region, which functioned as the administrative capital of the large transregional governorship of Hubei, Hunan, Guangdong, and Guangxi, additionally functioning as the capital for the province of Hubei and the district of Wuchang. Some Jesuit missions from this central place took up to eight days of travel and reached De'an 德安, Xinzhou 新州, and Yunmeng 雲夢. To the south of Wuchang, the provincial capital of Changsha (for Hunan) functioned as another missionary node. From there Jesuit missions were sent to Yongzhou 永州, to the east near the border with Jiangxi, and to the south at Xiangtan 湘潭, as well as to Hengzhou 衡州 and Qiyang 祁陽. This pattern can also be seen in Jiangxi and Guangdong (the Lingnan macro-region), where the provincial capitals of Nanchang and Guangzhou, the highest-order provincial administrative central places in the Qing empire, also functioned as missionary nodes. It should be noted that while the mountainous features of Jiangxi limited the scope and radius of missions to rural areas, the Catholic missions in Guangdong benefited from its maritime location. During the Qing dynasty, Guangzhou was the only port open to maritime trade; its proximity to Portuguese Macao also facilitated communications with Europe and the Catholic world beyond China. Both the Jesuits and the Franciscans maintained residences in Guangzhou as well as in district-level cities along coastal Guangdong.

As noted the Lower Yangzi macro-region was anomalous in that the largest administrative city (Nanjing) and the largest manufacturing center (Suzhou) did not function as nodes for the Christian mission, a function which was performed by Shanghai. There was another anomaly to the general pattern of most of the macro-regions with a central place and node: the province of Fujian or the macro-region of the Southeast coast.[30] Christianity had been introduced to this macro-region by the Jesuit Aleni in the late Ming, as already mentioned. It followed the pattern of mandarin/retired official patronage that established the provincial capital of Fuzhou as the node of evangelization. However, the economic development of the Southeast coast diverged from the logic and movement of central administrative control; maritime trade, which shaped the economy and character of Fujian, was oriented away from Beijing and China to Southeast Asia, the Indian, and the Pacific Oceans. Through the Hokkien trade network, Spanish missionaries (Dominicans, Franciscans, and Augustinians) traveled to this region from the Philippines. While the first friars began by depending on the missionary network established by Jesuits, they soon struck out on their own. Rivalries between religious orders, differences over methods of conversion, and the national rivalry between Spain and Portugal all played a part. This resulted in a polycentric map of partially overlapping Christian networks, in which missionary movements between urban and rural areas did not obey the general rule of central place hierarchy, as patronage and protection for the mendicant friars came from their Hokkien converts. The importance of lineage in South China, both in Fujian and in Guangdong, would play a major role in missionary movements there. Hokkien merchants and seamen had extensive family ties in Luzon as well as in their native places in Southern Fujian, where the ancestral halls in each eponymous village functioned as nodes for social networks. As the research of Eugenio Menegon and Zhang Xianqing has shown, the location of Christian communities and mission stations in eastern Fujian depended on the settlement patterns of the lineages that patronized Christianity.[31]

After prohibition

The prohibition of evangelization in 1705 radically changed the geographical patterns and the urban/rural balance of the Catholic mission.[32] First, the number of urban residences declined as Western missionaries left China. They were tolerated, however, in three cities. First, in the imperial capital of Beijing, where the Jesuits and later some missionaries from the *Propaganda Fide* served as artists, technicians, physicians, and musicians in the imperial court. This imperial patronage in turn allowed the Jesuits to extend patronage and protection to the Chinese convert community, who were legally barred from church services but were tolerated de facto in congregating in the four churches of the capital. The second was Shanghai, the native place of Xu Guangqi and his lineage and the most important Catholic center, as mentioned earlier. Here, two factors allowed Christianity to flourish despite the imperial prohibition. In Shanghai the Xu lineage exerted strong local patronage, and the low administrative and political status of the city allowed the community to remain in low profile without attracting political intervention. Third, the provincial capital of Guangdong, Guangzhou, was the site of two Franciscan residences and the center for the economic operations of the Catholic mission. Both the Portuguese vice-province and the French Jesuit Mission stationed their procurators in Guangzhou, as did agents of the Franciscans and the *Propaganda Fide*. Responsible for the financial operations of the missions, procurators relied on the proximity of Portuguese Macao as well as the presence of Western merchants in Guangzhou to conduct their business: cashing in letters of exchange, converting currencies, receiving news and letters from Europe, and forwarding correspondence from the missionaries stationed in China. The procurators were also on hand to receive the Jesuit missionaries appointed as envoys of the Qing Emperor Kangxi to Europe during the fruitless negotiations with the Papacy on resolving the Rites Controversy.

Outside of these three central places, the Catholic mission assumed a more strongly rural and clandestine nature, especially in the aftermath of local persecutions, such as the 1746 arrest and execution of five Spanish Dominicans

Chart 4.1 Numerical strengths of the Portuguese vice-province and the French Jesuit mission, mid-eighteenth century

French Mission, 1754	
Total	25
French Jesuits	18
Chinese Jesuits	7
Vice Province, 1755	
Total	45
Portuguese Jesuits	24
German & Bohemian Jesuits	6
Italian Jesuits	4
Chinese Jesuits	11

Source: © Ronnie Po-chia Hsia

in Fujian and the martyrdom of two Jesuits in Jiangsu two years later. The prohibition also had the effect of increasing the proportion of Jesuits among all Catholic missionaries in China. After their voluntary exit from China in 1707, the mendicant orders kept a tenuous foothold: the Dominicans maintained a low-profile in Southern Fujian, relying on the contact of the Hokkien communities in Fujian and the Philippines; the Franciscans were present in small numbers as missionaries sent by the *Propaganda Fide*; the MEP had yet to reach its numerical maximum of the late nineteenth century; and for a couple of decades before its suppression, the Society of Jesus recaptured their domination of the China Mission as it was at the beginning. The Annual Reports of the French Jesuit Mission (1754) and the Portuguese vice-province (1755) give us these figures, as illustrated by Chart 4.1.[33]

New religious orders were more strongly oriented toward rural areas. Priests from the Missions Étrangères de Paris (MEP) created missions in two new macro-regions – Upper Yangzi and Yungui – consisting of the provinces of Sichuan, Yunnan, and Guizhou in Southwest China. These initial attempts at evangelization would expand rapidly after 1842, when the Qing state rescinded the prohibition of evangelization. Outside of the provincial capitals of Chengdu and Kunming, the Catholic mission was highly rural, both due to the mountainous and remote geography of large regions in these provinces and to the MEP missionaries' preference of focusing their work among non-Han minorities who inhabited the more inaccessible parts of these regions.

3 Conclusion

In reflecting on Catholic missionaries as local agents in late imperial China, it is difficult to differentiate between their urban and rural functions. The image of Catholic missionaries in late nineteenth-century rural China belies the urban origins of the Catholic China Mission. With dense urban networks and well-developed macro-regions, most people of late imperial China had access to urban central places. The towns were central places where farmers sold their produce, bought manufactured goods, and picked up news; there, the Christian missionary was first seen, his sermon heard, and perhaps his religious tracts distributed. The urban central places in late imperial China functioned as nodal points in networks that distributed cash, goods, ideas, and culture to the countryside. This intense urban-rural exchange was reinforced by the residence of local elites, who often resided in ancestral rural family homes, where the lineage halls and clan schools were located. It was the social and spatial differentiation of late imperial Chinese society that determined the geographic contours of the Catholic mission; and it was Chinese patronage – from the emperor on high, to mandarins and scholars who honored Western missionaries, down to the poor Christian farmers who sheltered them during times of persecution – that shaped the patterns of Christian evangelization.

Notes

1 For a first orientation to the periodization of the China mission, see Hsia, "Imperial China," 344–364. For the period up to the Chinese Rites Controversy, the most comprehensive study to date is Huang, *Liang tou she*. This collection of essays, based on an exhaustive study of Chinese sources, offers the best prosopography of the leading Chinese Catholic converts, who played a pivotal role in patronizing the Jesuit Mission in the late Ming and early Qing dynasty. This study should be supplemented by Brockey's *Journey to the East*, which uses extensive records in Portuguese collections, although it does not deal with the initial French Jesuit mission. For the period after 1705, when Christianity was officially prohibited, there is no single synthesis. For exemplary studies see Krahl, *China Missions in Crisis*. On the role of patronage in Christian conversion, the importance of local lineage is stressed by Menegon, *Ancestors, Virgins, and Friars*, ch. 5. On the interesting question of female patronage of the Jesuit mission in China, see Amsler, *Jesuits and Matriarchs*, ch. 9, and Hsia, *Noble Patronage and Jesuit Missions*.
2 See Standaert, "The Creation of Christian Communities."
3 See Skinner, "Regional Urbanization in Nineteenth-Century China," and Skinner, "Cities and Local Hierarchy of Local Systems." See especially the maps on 214–215 and the figure on 291.
4 See Standaert, "The Creation of Christian Communities," 541.
5 See, for example, the testimony of Paolo Prodi: "I was greatly influenced by Gabriel Le Bras's long-term institutional and legal coordinates embracing institutions and canon law," in Prodi, "Europe in the Age of Reformations," 57.
6 See Chatellier, *The Europe of the Devout*.
7 See Hsia, *A Jesuit in the Forbidden City*, chs. 4–7; Criveller, "Matteo Ricci's Ascent to Beijing."
8 See Hsia, *A Jesuit in the Forbidden City*, 146, and sources cited.
9 For this journey see the memoirs of Ruggieri in ARSI, JS 101 I, fol. 44–152.
10 See Boxer, *The Great Ship from Amacon*.
11 See Hsia, *A Jesuit in the Forbidden City*, 99–102.
12 Luiz Camões, *Os Lusiadas*, Canto X, stanza 131.
13 See Forrestal, *Vincent de Paul*, 87–108, and Hsia, *The World of Catholic Renewal*, 200–201.

14 Longobardo's reports in his own handwriting are found in APF, SC Indie Orientali e Cina, vol. 1, fol. 49–55. For an analysis see Hsia, "Tianzhu jiao yu Mingmo shehui," and Hsia, "Christian Conversion in Late Ming China."
15 For studies on Aleni, see Lippiello and Malek, "*Scholar from the West,*" and Menegon, *Un solo cielo.*
16 See Zürcher, *Kouduo richao.*
17 See Vermeer, *Development and Decline*, and Chang, "Chinese Maritime Trade."
18 See Hsia, "Convergence and Conversion."
19 For the importance of local patronage in shaping Catholic missions in Fujian, see Menegon, *Ancestors, Virgins, and Friars.*
20 It would also be useful to consult the following works for estimates of the numbers of missionaries and converts: Standaert, "Numbers of Missionaries," and Standaert, "The Creation of Christian Communities," and the following articles by Dehergne: "La mission de Pékin vers 1700"; "Les missions de la Chine du Nord vers 1700"; "La Chine centrale vers 1700"; "La Chine centrale vers 1700 II"; "La Chine centrale vers 1700 III"; "La Chine du Sud-Ouest"; and "La Chine du Sud-Est."
21 Standaert, "The Creation of Christian Communities," 549.
22 See Huang, *Liang tou she*, 231.
23 See Jami, Engelfriet, and Blue, *Statecraft and Intellectual Renewal in Late Ming China.*
24 BA, JA 49-V-18, fol. 671v.
25 Wyngaert and Mensaert, *Sinica Franciscana*, 93.
26 BA, JA 49-V 22, fol. 612r–613v.
27 Missions from Shanghai to these urban centers and rural Zhongming are reported in BA, JA 49-V-18, fol. 627r; BA, JA 49-V-22, fol. 612r–613v.
28 BA, JA 49-V-19, fol. 627; BA, JA 49-V-18, fol. 657v–689r; BA, JA 49-V-22, fol. 612r–650v; BA, JA 49-V-23, fol. 504r.
29 BA, JA 48-V-22, fol. 612r–613v.
30 There is a vast literature on maritime China, especially on Fujian and Hokkien trade. See, for example, Vermeer, *Development and Decline*, especially the article by Blusse, "Minnan-jen or Cosmopolitan?" 245–264; Wei-chung, *War, Trade and Piracy*; Chang, "Chinese Maritime Trade"; and Olle, *La invención de China.*
31 See Menegon, *Ancestors, Virgins, and Friars*, and Zhang, *Guanfu, zongzu yu Tianzhujiao.*
32 For a brief account of the Christian mission after prohibition and the scholarship on this period, see Hsia, "Imperial China," esp. 359–364; see also Hsia, "Christianity and Empire," esp. 216–219.
33 ARSI, JS 134, fol. 436v ff.

5 The post-Tridentine parish system in the port city of Nagasaki

Carla Tronu

Most of the early modern urban missions in Japan, where evangelization started in 1549, were located in Western and Southern Japan, mainly on the island of Kyushu, where missionaries depended on the authorization and protection of the local military lords. Missionaries established residences in the castle-towns (*joka-machi*) or residential towns of the lords that favored them, such as Yamaguchi and Funai, which missionaries abandoned soon due to local warfare. In the castle-town cities of Omura and Arima, both in Kyushu, whose lords embraced Christianity and ordered their subjects to do so as well, a large proportion of the population became Christian. In contrast, in central Japan, the Christians remained a minority in most of the cities targeted and the missionary presence was short-lived or interrupted, especially in political centers, like Miyako (presently called Kyoto), where the emperor resided, or in the cities where the Japanese unifiers had set up their strongholds, such as Azuchi, Osaka, and Fushimi. The same applied to Edo (presently called Tokyo), in Eastern Japan, which became the political center in the seventeenth century. The case of the Nagasaki port city stands out because it was not a castle-town but a self-governed city (*machi-shu*, literally a confederation of wards), newly founded in 1571 as the port city for the Portuguese silk trade with Macao. The Jesuits and the Portuguese were involved in the founding and planning of the city and almost all of its citizens where Christian. It became the center of the Jesuit mission and the Japanese diocese, and the only city in Japan where the bishop implemented the parish system.

Nagasaki is often referred to as "the Christian city" in early modern Japan, although that assumption is not always thoroughly justified beyond the fact that it had a high number of churches, while in most mission posts there was only one church. I argue that what made Nagasaki a Christian city was the fact that its citizens actively engaged with Christian ritual and charity practice and supported the Catholic post-Tridentine parish system. Here, in order to understand how was this possible, I first present its historical development in the sixteenth century, looking at the complex interactions between the Japanese authorities (central and local), Nagasaki's citizens' representatives, the European merchants, and both the Jesuit missionaries under Portuguese patronage and the Franciscans, Dominicans, and Augustinians under Spanish patronage.[1] Then I analyze the factors that allowed the process by which 11 parishes were erected in Nagasaki by 1614, the year Christianity was banned from Japan. I then focus on the question of the funding for the parish churches and the stipends of its clergy, and finally I explore what specific practices in the building of churches in Nagasaki tell us about the Jesuit and Mendicant approach to cultural adaptation in Japan.

1 The founding of Nagasaki and its development in the sixteenth century

Starting in 1550 a Portuguese ship (*nao*) from Macao came to Kyushu annually to sell Chinese silk, and the Jesuits became the middlemen between the Portuguese and the local merchant families. After the ship had anchored in several ports in Kyushu, the need for a port that was easy to protect from enemies and suited for the large Portuguese ships to anchor during the typhoon season led the Jesuits and the Portuguese to examine the coastal line of the Omura territory. As a result, a port city was founded in the Nagasaki bay in 1571, as an independent urban unit from the inland Nagasaki village.[2] Nagasaki was a self-governed city (*machi-shu*). Initially the city was formed by six streets or wards (*machi*), although with the trade revenue the city would expand dramatically to 70 wards by 1664. Each ward had elected a head among the citizens who owned a house in the ward (those who rented were excluded), and among the street heads, four men were elected as leaders of the city (*otona*). All of them belonged to powerful local merchant families and from the beginning established good relations with the Jesuits. When the first six wards were designed and distributed, Jesuits were given a plot of land at the end of the Morisaki cape, and they built a residence and a small church dedicated to Our Lady of the Assumption (*Santa Maria*). For one decade it remained a rather peripheral mission post, but when the local lord Omura Sumitada donated Nagasaki port city to the Jesuits in 1580, the vice-provincial father moved to Nagasaki.[3] The decade that followed was one of intense warfare in Kyushu, and in 1582 the city was fortified, but it continued expanding and new streets developed outside the city wall. Since the area outside the wall remained Omura territory, its inhabitants paid an annual land tax to Sumitada, from which the inhabitants of the original port city were exempted.[4] The wards inside the wall exempted from land tax were called *uchimachi* ("inner wards") and the streets subject to the Omura jurisdiction and land tax, *sotomachi* ("outer wards").

A relevant local agent in Nagasaki was the confraternity of the *Misericordia*, officialized in 1583, when its members built their headquarters and an adjacent church dedicated to Saint Elizabeth (*Santa Isabel*) in *uchimachi*, as well as a hospice for lepers outside the city, on the Nishizaka hill. Its members were mainly rich merchants and included the four elected representatives who administered the city (*otona*). Its main purpose was to carry out works of charity, taking care of the ill and collecting alms for the poor, as well as mutual assistance, like securing funerals for members and posthumous care for their families. The Jesuits fostered its creation, providing the Japanese with the rules of the *Misericordia* of Macao, which followed the pattern of the Lisbon *Misericordia*, but its leaders were laymen, elected annually among its members. While in Macao the members were only Portuguese, in Nagasaki all were Japanese. The official members were men only, but according to missionary records their wives also carried out similar activities; for example, they took care of a hospice for female lepers.[5] The *Misericordia* was crucial as a model for the other confraternities that appeared later, as we will see below.

In 1587, Toyotomi Hideyoshi, the second of the three military leaders who unified Japan, put all the Kyushu lords under his control. He also issued an edict expelling the missionaries from Japan and appropriated the Nagasaki port city, putting it under the direct control of the central authorities. The administration of the city remained in the hands of the *otona*, but a magistrate (*bugyo*) appointed by Hideyoshi took care of judicial matters, and a bailiff (*daikan*) was appointed to take care of the collection of land tax in *sotomachi*. Hideyoshi also forbade the Jesuits to mediate in the Nagasaki trade between the Portuguese and the Japanese and sent his representatives to deal directly with the Portuguese, but the new arrangement did not work out. In 1591, Hideyoshi allowed ten Jesuits to stay in Nagasaki to mediate in the Macao trade and to cater to the religious needs of the Portuguese. Many churches were destroyed all over the country, but the Jesuits were determined not to leave Japan. They moved to the Kyushu countryside, away from the political centers, and refrained from public preaching and processions. When all Jesuit land in the Nagasaki port city was confiscated in 1592, the Jesuits of the port city house moved to the *Misericordia* headquarters and the Jesuit residence in the Nagasaki village. Two years later through negotiations with the Nagasaki magistrate, Jesuits managed to recover two thirds of their confiscated lands and built a college named after Saint Paul and a larger church, with funds granted by the Portuguese Captain Major.[6]

During this period of instability, two small churches were built anew in the outskirts of Nagasaki, in Omura territory, a small hermitage dedicated to Saint John the Baptist in Nishizaka next to a lepers' hospice, built in 1591 thanks to a donation from the Portuguese Captain Major,[7] and a small hermitage dedicated to Saint Mary at the foot of Mount Tateyama. We do not know exactly when Saint Mary was built, but it became quite popular for processions, especially among Portuguese merchants and sailors, to show gratefulness to Our Lady for having reached Nagasaki safely, so much so that in 1594, the Nagasaki magistrate forbade all processions to Saint Mary.[8] In times of difficulties, the Jesuits went underground and fostered evangelization through the circulation of doctrinal and devotional works translated into Japanese.[9] Nevertheless, the demand for mass celebrations and confessions in private houses, as well as the processions to the small churches outside Nagasaki organized by the Portuguese, attest to deep engagement with Christianity by both Japanese and Portuguese citizens.

In this context Hideyoshi developed diplomatic relations with the General Governor of the Philippines in 1590, asking him to consolidate the trade from Manila. This prompted Spanish embassies from the Philippines to Japan, for which Mendicant friars were chosen as ambassadors. In 1593, Franciscan missionaries were allowed to stay in Japan as ambassadors and built a convent and a church in Kyoto.[10] This was strongly opposed by the Jesuits, who had obtained a bull from the Pope in 1585, legitimizing them as the only missionary order in charge of the evangelization of Japan.[11] Moreover, in 1588, the Pope had established the Japanese diocese, and it was agreed that all bishops would be Jesuits, appointed by the Portuguese king, which reinforced the Jesuit power in the Japanese mission.[12] The first appointed bishop never made it to Japan, but the second, Pedro Martins, arrived in Nagasaki in 1596. Although he was criticized by his fellow Jesuits, he protected the Jesuits' interests and fiercely opposed the Mendicant missionaries.[13] The Franciscans, however, refused to abandon Japan and tried to establish a mission base in Nagasaki, but they found strong opposition from both the Jesuits and the local administrators, so that in spite of the economic support of Portuguese merchants, they were not able to secure stable accommodations.[14] When the Spanish galleon San Felipe bound to Acapulco shipwrecked in Japanese waters, disputes between the Japanese authorities and the Spanish captain regarding the confiscation of the cargo escalated and brought attention to the Franciscans' preaching activities. Hideyoshi executed all the friars active in Kyoto and Osaka, and several Japanese Christians who helped them run their hospitals and forced the friars in Nagasaki to return to Manila.[15] In sum, the first Franciscan attempt to settle in Nagasaki ended quite abruptly.

The 1597 execution was a reminder that the expulsion edict had not been revoked, so when the third Bishop of Japan Luis Cerqueira arrived in Nagasaki in March 1598, the Jesuits did not present him as such to the Nagasaki magistrate and the central authorities. However, Hideyoshi's death in September of the same year would change the situation for Christians in Japan in general and specifically in Nagasaki. In 1601, Tokugawa Ieyasu, the military lord who de facto assumed control after Hideyoshi's death and completed Japan's political unification, welcomed all missionary orders. This opened a flourishing decade for the Japanese mission but also intensified the confrontations between the Jesuits and Mendicants.

2 The revival of the mission in the early seventeenth century

In a series of sessions celebrated between 1545 and 1563, the Council of Trent put forth a series of reforms aimed not only at the elimination of abuses but also at a renewed pastoral program that placed the bishops and the parish priests at the center of the Church's mission.[16] Although the Council did not discuss missionary activity, some of the reforms, like that of the parish system, were applied to the Japanese mission. Parishes first appeared in Europe at the end of the eleventh century due to the need to serve large urban Christian communities, but at that early stage, territorial limits were not clearly defined, and baptism had to be administered in the cathedrals. The Council of Trent defined parishes as territorial units under the authority of a parish priest, legitimately appointed by the bishop to provide religious services to the faithful dwelling within its boundaries.[17] Parishioners had to receive the sacraments of baptism, mass, and marriage at their parish church, and were meant to provide fixed or occasional financial contributions. The Trent decrees also established that each diocese should have a seminary to train its own diocesan priesthood, and while this took decades to become a reality in the whole of Catholic Europe, in Nagasaki, Bishop Cerqueira set up a seminary to train diocesan priests in 1601, as soon as the ban on Christianity was revoked. He counted on the best students and teachers from the Jesuit *colegio*, and as early as 1604, he ordained the first diocesan priest. Another post-Tridentine element was the publication, in 1605, of a liturgy manual with a liturgical calendar following the Roman *Rituale*.[18]

Until diocesan priests were ordained, the bishop made the most of the particularities of Nagasaki, namely the presence of a large mass of population who had embraced Christianity for several decades, with local administrators strongly engaged with Christian values, a high concentration of Jesuit priests, and several churches. He divided the city into areas, "in the fashion of parishes," assigning one particular Jesuit priest to each church to say mass every week and on holidays and to take pastoral care of its acolytes.[19] In 1603, when the church of the hospital of Santiago was built, in addition to the cathedral there were four churches providing mass regularly with a designed priest.[20] In 1606, after the bishop had ordained the first local diocesan priest, the parish system was officially implemented, and with it a new kind of church emerged in Nagasaki, the diocesan parish churches.[21]

Diocesan priests trained in Japan, who were mostly Japanese, served at the diocesan parish churches, and were not sustained by any missionary order. This model was probably inspired in the church of the *Misericordia*, which was not a property of the Jesuits, but of the members of the confraternity, and which was also economically self-sufficient. Examples are the new churches built in 1606 and 1607 in *sotomachi*, in the sites of the small hermitages of Saint John the Baptist in Nishizaka and Saint Mary in Tateyama, and a new church dedicated to Saint Anthony in Cruz-machi of *sotomachi*. In 1609, yet a new diocesan church, the church of Saint Peter, was built from scratch in *uchimachi*, not far from the Jesuit compound.[22] This added four more churches to the parish system and challenged the Jesuit control of *uchimachi*.

Ieyasu was interested in establishing regular trade with the Spanish in the Philippines and New Mexico, and allowed Spanish Franciscans, Dominicans, and Augustinians to open mission bases in Kyushu, Central Japan, and Northern Japan.[23] In spite of the Jesuit opposition, all of the Mendicant orders targeted Nagasaki, which was the center of the mission. In 1607 the Franciscans moved into a small lodge in *sotomachi*, and in the following year the Spanish merchant José de Aduna bought a plot of land and a house for them in *uchimachi*, challenging the Jesuit hegemony in the most prestigious and powerful part of the city.[24] After official bulls, by which the Pope opened the Japanese mission to all missionary orders in 1608, reached Japan in 1611, the bishop accepted the presence of the Mendicants in Japan and even integrated their three churches in Nagasaki into the city's parish system. In 1610, the Dominicans arrived in Nagasaki and established a convent and a church in *sotomachi*, but very close to *uchimachi*, practically on the same street of the Franciscan convent.[25] The Augustinians, after a first attempt in 1607, settled in Nagasaki in 1612, building a monastery and a church in the poorest area of *sotomachi*.[26] In sum, by the time the prohibition edict was issued in 1614, Nagasaki had 11 parishes, four in the charge of Jesuits, four in the charge of diocesan priests, and three in the charge of Mendicant missionaries. This was a remarkable achievement for a mission in a non-colonial setting, but who funded the parish churches and the stipends of their parish priests?

3 Economic support of the churches and priesthood

While initially Jesuit churches were built relying mainly on Portuguese and Spanish merchants, as explained earlier, starting in 1592 the Jesuits had instructions to ask the local Christians to collaborate with funds or labor on the building of their churches.[27] By the seventeenth century most new churches were built with local funds. For example, in 1603, in Nagasaki and villages nearby, the locals were providing support for some of their local priests, as well as for the enlargement of the churches and the building of a new hospital in Nagasaki.[28] Bishop Cerqueira used funds from the Spanish Crown to establish the seminary for diocesan priests, but he relied on the local population to support the diocesan clergy, either as individual donors or lay brotherhoods. For example, the bailiff of *sotomachi*, Murayama Toan, provided the funds to build the church of Saint Anthony in 1607, which was probably named after his Christian name "Antonio," and was curated by his son Francisco Murayama Tokuan. Toan also sponsored the building of the church of Saint Peter in 1611, and the expansion of the churches of Saint Anthony and Saint John the Baptist in 1612.[29] On the other side, the renovation of the church of Saint Mary in Tateyama in 1606 and the maintenance stipend for its parish priest were covered by the lay confraternity of Saint Mary, founded when it became a parish church.[30] While Jesuits were never members, and neither took leading roles in the *Misericordia* nor in other confraternities they founded in Japan, the top leader of the confraternities founded by Mendicants was usually a missionary, and diocesan Japanese parish priests assumed the leadership of the confraternities that sustained their parish churches.[31]

The Mendicants mainly lived on charity, as their order's rules encouraged. They were not allowed to carry money with them to Japan, but they did not have to sustain a community as large as that of the Jesuits. While, in 1604, there were 34 Jesuits and 60 *dojuku* in the College of Saint Paul, there were initially only two Franciscans residing in Nagasaki, and this only increased to seven in 1613, when missionaries expelled from other areas gathered in Nagasaki. We do not have details regarding the funding of the church of Saint Francis in Nagasaki, but we know that the house they made into their monastery in 1609 was a donation from a Spanish merchant, probably Jose de Aduna, and that in Kyoto they borrowed money from Japanese Christians, later returned with funds from the Spanish civil authorities in Manila.[32] All Mendicant orders established a third order, a devotional organization of lay members, wherever they established a mission base. Sources also mention local confraternities, basically branches of the confraternities they had spread in Europe and the Spanish colonies: the Confraternity of the Cord of Saint Francis, the Confraternity of the Holy Rosary, and the Confraternity of the Cincture of Saint Augustine. Mendicant sources consider all the members of their confraternities to be "tertiaries," that is, as belonging to the third order of their religious family. There are various cases of double membership in different Mendicant confraternities, but there are no such cases of anyone belonging to both a Jesuit and a Mendicant confraternity, which suggests that the antagonism between the Jesuit and Mendicant missionaries was understood and reproduced by the laity. The Mendicant confraternities had a foreign missionary as the top leader, with ward-based sub-groups led by local Christians, a man and a woman in each ward.[33] I have not found explicit references to their economic circumstances so far, but, following the model of the other confraternities in Nagasaki, they probably contributed to sustaining the Mendicant churches and their priests.

The Jesuits had a strong connection with the *Misericordia* brotherhood. From its foundation, Jesuit priests said mass at the *Misericordia* church of Saint Elizabeth, and the *Misericordia* provided logistic support for the Jesuits. For example, when the Jesuit church on the Morisaki cape was closed in 1592, the *Misericordia* headquarters provided accommodation for seven Jesuits.[34] They also took care of the Santiago hospital that the Jesuits established in 1603. The Jesuit hospital mainly depended on alms, and especially on large donations from the Captain Major and the Portuguese merchants that came with the *nao*, so that in years when the *nao* did not come they experienced financial hardship.[35] The Jesuit catalogue and account book for 1609 explicitly says that the Jesuits residing in the churches of the Assumption, All Saints (*Todos os Santos*), Saint Elizabeth, and Saint James (*Santiago*) hospital, worked as parish priests, but there is no mention of any regular external funding for the parish priests. However, the annual letter of 1611 clearly states that the confraternities taking care of the maintenance of the Santiago hospital patients sustained the Jesuits residing there, like the *Misericordia* supported the Jesuits taking care of Saint Elizabeth.[36] Specific sums of money are not given, but it seems that while the Jesuits in Nagasaki initially provided economic support for all their members, relying occasionally on donations from the Portuguese merchants, by 1611, following the pattern of the diocesan clergy, lay Christian associations assumed the role of financially supporting the Jesuit parish priests and their assistant Jesuits.

In 1611, the Jesuits reinstated the Confraternity of the Holy Sacrament based in the church of Saint Mary of the Assumption, which functioned as the cathedral and as the church of the Jesuit College. In that same year a new church dedicated to Saint Michael was built in the cemetery, and although it was not a parish church, the Confraternity of Saint Michael maintained the Jesuit priest in charge of it.[37] In general, the main purpose of confraternities in early modern Catholicism was not to provide economic support for the local priest or church. Instead, they rather aimed at strengthening the devotion of its members, providing support to members in distress, and promoting Christian values and practices, such as charity deeds, scourging, etc. Furthermore, they also promoted specific religious practices that defined their religious identity.[38] The Japanese confraternities did of course pursue these fundamental purposes, but here I have concentrated on the economic factor because it is a rather distinctive characteristic of the confraternities in Japan, and a crucial premise for the establishment of the parish system in Nagasaki.

The fact that there were several confraternities suggests a Nagasaki city that was profoundly and actively Christian but not homogeneous. The existence of several confraternities, each with different organizational structures, purposes, practices and habits, introduced nuances and complexity to the large Christian community of Nagasaki. Through the lay confraternities, the missionaries materialized and reinforced their presence and influence on Nagasaki. The confraternities also speak of the power balance between the Jesuits, the Mendicants, and the diocesan local priests, and of their differences in spirituality and in devotional practices. In this regard it is significant that while the Misericordia founded by the Jesuits was the only confraternity in the city for decades, during the Jesuit monopoly the new confraternities founded in the seventeenth century by the Mendicant orders and the diocesan priests prompted the Jesuits to establish other kinds of confraternities. Another lens that allows for a closer look into the different characteristics of Jesuits and Mendicants are the church buildings themselves, that speak about the missionaries' approaches to cultural adaptation.

4 Japanese churches and cultural accommodation

It is rather well known that the Jesuits in Japan developed a cultural adaptationist discourse that was systematized into specific policies and practices by the Visitor of the Asian missions, Alessandro Valignano. His guidelines for the Japanese mission cultural adaptation practices written in 1581, *Advertimentos e avisos acerca dos costumes e catangues de Jappão*, include a chapter on how to build residences and churches, in which he clearly states that churches should be built in a Japanese style, explicitly prescribing several Japanese elements.[39] Other internal documents of the Japanese mission also stated that churches had to be built "according to the Japanese style," although no further details on what that meant are given, probably because these were provided in the previously mentioned *Advertimentos*.[40] The Council of Trent basically authorized the traditional conceptions and rules for building and decorating churches, giving no specific directives regarding the design of Catholic churches. However, Carlo Borromeo, Archbishop of Milan, summarized the traditional elements of a Catholic church in his book *Instructiones Fabricae et Supellectilis Ecclesiasticae* published in 1577, such as the orientation of the altar toward the east, the Latin cross plan, the number of naves and doors, the windows, the bell towers, etc.[41] The only European element that Valignano stressed profusely was the alignment of the main entrance and the nave with the altar. This he considered essential in order to differentiate the Christian churches from the Japanese Buddhist temples.[42] In general, the Mendicants were more reluctant to adapt to the Japanese culture and there are several episodes in which they neglected or complained about Japanese etiquette, especially when it conflicted with their poverty vows. However, based on a close look at the scattered and scarce references to the churches built in Japan, it seems that they compromised with the local practices to a certain extent. Arimura stresses that although scholarship focuses on Jesuit accommodation, adaptation can be seen in the Mendicant churches as well, since the Mendicants also took into account native people's input when building churches.[43]

Initially, Jesuit churches in Japan, and particularly in Nagasaki, were rather humble. During the first decades of the mission, the Jesuits often reused already existing buildings, often abandoned Buddhist temples. They were built in a Japanese style, in wood, with tatami floors, and Christian elements were mainly to be found inside the churches, in their decoration and furniture (paintings, altars, textiles, liturgical objects, etc.).[44] A clear example of this is the Church of All Saints in Nagasaki, originally a Buddhist temple which was later rebuilt. The first church of the Nagasaki port city, built when the city was founded in 1571, although in a very prestigious and strategic location, was rather simple. The Jesuit Superior at the time was not accommodative and imposed religious poverty, so that there were no specific spaces to entertain visitors and no separate space for the local elites within the church, and in general it looked poor and dirty. Even after the Valignano reform, however, due to Hideyoshi's edict and the need to go "underground," the Jesuit College and the church of Saint Paul built in 1594 were kept rather simple.[45] The Jesuits were dismayed to know that the Franciscans in Kyoto had built a convent and a church in the "Castilian style," namely a church with three naves, a choir separated by a grille, and cloister.[46] After Hideyoshi died in 1598 and Tokugawa Ieyasu showed tolerance to the Christian missionaries, the Jesuits no longer needed to be contained or "underground," and at the beginning of the seventeenth century they started to build larger churches. They introduced Valignano's accommodative elements, and perhaps as a way of keeping up with the Franciscans, also European architectonical elements. A good example is the new building for the cathedral of

Nagasaki in 1601, which incorporated most of the accommodative elements prescribed by Valignano, such as specific rooms to accommodate the elites inside the church (separated by sliding doors from the main nave where the commoners were meant to sit), a surrounding porch, and a garden in front of it. Moreover, special rooms to entertain visitors were built apart from the church, so as not to pollute the church with the consumption of food and drink when entertaining guests in the Japanese way. Cleanliness is a very important element in Japanese Shinto beliefs, where pollution and purity were not symbolical values, but were quite literally understood, so that clean and new materials were required for Shinto shrines; the renewal of the Ise shrine every 20 years serves as a clear example. Valignano insisted that churches should be kept clean and purified through consecration if necessary. In Nagasaki, when two Japanese fought inside the church in 1581, the altar and the image of Our Lady were removed, and after the blood stained tatami mats had been replaced, the altar was sacralized anew with full ceremony.[47] No plans or illustrations of early modern Japanese churches by the missionaries or the local builders are extant, but several Japanese folding screens on the arrival of the Portuguese to Nagasaki depict the cathedral (see Figure 5.1.).[48]

Figure 5.1 Detail of a folding screen showing a Christian church. Namban screens attributed to Kano Naizen (1570–1616). Designated Important Cultural Property. Ikenaga Hajime Collection, Kobe City Museum, Japan

Source: Photograph courtesy of the Kobe City Museum

In addition to accommodative elements, perhaps to compete with the Mendicants, the Jesuits also introduced some European elements like the three naves and multiple altars of Saint Mary of the Assumption, rebuilt in 1601, and the bell and clock towers added to all the churches in Nagasaki in 1604.[49] Mutual influence is also suggested by the fact that although the Franciscans in Kyoto initially received guests inside the church, in spite of the warnings of the Jesuits, they ended up using a separated reception room to entertain elite Christians, although they kept it austere and poor.[50] We know very little about the Franciscan church in Nagasaki, but the Dominican church (Saint Dominic) was also built in the "Castilian style," with a cloister and an inner yard connecting the convent and the church. Some claim that it was built of stone, and although this is unlikely, since they reused the timber of the Kyodomari church, archaeological excavations confirmed the use of stone pavement in front of the church, and along the path leading to it.[51] Yamazaki's comparative study of the Christian tiles unearthed in Nagasaki shows that all the churches in this city used cross-pattern roof-tiles, but Jesuit churches used a flower-shaped cross pattern, while the Mendicant and diocesan churches used a slightly different cross-pattern. This difference might merely be indicative of the construction period of the churches, but the use of the same mold for roof-tiles in Mendicant and diocesan parish churches suggests a strong connection and cooperation between the three Mendicant orders and the diocesan priests.[52]

In sum, we can conclude that although the Jesuits were more intentionally accommodative to Japan customs, all orders built their churches with local manpower and used Japanese building techniques and materials, like wood poles standing on foundation stones, timber for walls, tatami for the interior floors, and wooden or paper sliding doors. This is probably because all of them took into account the locals' input on how to build, and often obtained building materials from local patrons; moreover, the local Christians participated in the construction of their churches. Arimura discusses possible interpretations of the phrase "churches built our way," which was often used by both Jesuits and Franciscans in their letters. In light of Valignano's remark that temples usually placed the main image on the longest side, but that in Christian churches the altar had to be placed on the shortest side, she argues that building "in our way" would mean locating the altar on the shortest side, according to the European tradition, while in the case of the Franciscans, building in "our way" seems to refer to the contiguous disposition of the monastery, the cloister, and the church, like in the conventual complexes of the Discalced friars in Castile.[53]

5 Conclusion

At the beginning of the seventeenth century, three decades after its foundation, Nagasaki became the center of the Japanese diocese, as the bishop established his seat in the main Jesuit church on the Morisaki cape. It was the Japanese city with the highest number of churches and some of the most impressive ones, which attracted both Christian and non-Christian visitors from afar. It was also the only city in Japan where the post-Tridentine parish system was implemented before the persecution of 1614. This was possible because of the initiative of the third Bishop of Japan, Luis Cerqueira, and the particular characteristics and historical background of the Nagasaki port city. Cerqueira found in Nagasaki a large and self-administered Christian community, a large number of Jesuit resident priests and brothers, as well as Japanese postulants educated by the Jesuits, and a local political elite who were engaged deeply with Christianity. More specifically, they engaged with Christian ritual and other religious practices, founded confraternities, gave advice, materials, human labor, and funds for the construction of churches, and provided input which shaped the missionaries' accommodation practices. In this context, Cerqueira made the most of the peculiar situation in Nagasaki and in order to implement the post-Tridentine parish system, established a seminary to train local diocesan priests, published the Roman Calendar and a liturgical manual adapted to the Japanese culture and language, and encouraged local support for the building and maintenance costs of the parish churches, as well as for the stipends of its curates. A large body of faithful, a parish priest, a suitable church with a baptistery, a confessionary, and a cemetery were all prerequisites for the establishment of a parish, introduced by the Council of Trent. According to parochial law, the rights and duties of parishioners and parish priests required that the priest would take pastoral care of the parishioners, and the parishioners would provide adjacent housing and fixed or occasional financial support for the parish priest and the administration of the church.[54] In Nagasaki, the building of churches had first been funded by the Jesuits and the Portuguese merchants, but by the seventeenth century, the building of churches and the maintenance of the parish priests, either regular or diocesan, depended mainly on local funding from the bailiff and the lay confraternities.

Tensions and competition between the Jesuits and the Mendicants fueled the growth of churches and confraternities in Nagasaki but also led to a dramatic internal crisis in the Japanese diocese. Although in 1608 the Pope had sanctioned the activity of the Mendicants in Japan and all missionary orders were integrated into the Nagasaki parish system, the rivalry between the Jesuits and the Mendicants continued and crystalized after the bishop died in early 1614 without a successor. The Jesuit vice-provincial stepped in as the bishops' representative until a new one could be appointed and could reach Japan, but the diocesan priests, encouraged by the Mendicants, revoked their consent and instead appointed a Mendicant. The Archbishop of Goa did not accept this, and the Jesuits managed to revert to the first agreement so that in the end the "Schism of Nagasaki" did not break the Jesuit hegemony in the Japanese mission. The fusion of confraternities initially founded by Mendicant and diocesan priests, as well as the establishment of certain rural areas in Arima and Omura as Jesuit parishes (1615) as a means to keep Mendicant missionaries off limits, account for the continuation of the rivalry between the Jesuits and the Mendicants after 1614. Nevertheless, in spite of their rivalry and their different evangelization methods, not only differences but also some commonalities can be seen in the practices of the Jesuits and Mendicants regarding the building of churches in Nagasaki. While the Jesuits were more intentionally accommodative to Japanese customs, all orders built their churches with Japanese materials in collaboration with the locals.

Although usually accommodation and the promotion of the post-Tridentine doctrines are seen as a dichotomy, this was not the case in Nagasaki. The Jesuits got involved in the foundation of the port city, as well as in its economic activity and political development. Their conscious choice to foster practices that were accommodative to the local customs allowed input from the local Christians and compromised with local political and religious organizations. Precisely, all of this created the conditions that made it possible for Bishop Luis Cerqueira to train diocesan native priests and implement the post-Tridentine parish system and the Roman Calendar.

Notes

1 There is a tendency in previous research on the Japanese mission to focus only on a single order, often the Jesuits, but the present approach suggests the importance of taking into account the Mendicants' activities, and the interaction between the two groups, in line with recent comprehensive studies such as Tronu, "The Rivalry between"; Arimura, "The Catholic Architecture"; Jiang, *Missionary Rivalry.*
2 Pacheco, "The Founding of the Port."
3 Schütte, *Textus catalogorum*, 126.
4 Amaro, *Study on the Christian Facilities*, 107.
5 Annual letter 1585 in CE 2, fol. 130r. On the Nagasaki, *Misericordia*, see Kataoka, "Fundação e organização." On the *Misericordias* in Japan, Costa, "The Misericórdias among Japanese."
6 Pedro Gómez, 8 February 1594 (ARSI, JS 12 – I, fol. 170v).
7 Pacheco, "Iglesias de Nagasaki," 62.
8 *Relación* by Francisco Pasio, 12 February 1585 (ARSI, JS 31, fol. 108r–113v).
9 Apart from the doctrinal handbook *Dochiriina Kirishitan* (1590), the most popular devotional books were the compilation of Saints' lives *Sanctos no Gosagyo* (1591) and the *Contemptus Mundi* (1596), a translation of Luis de Granada's *Guía de Pecadores* (1566). These works circulated in manuscript form before their publication date. On publications by the Jesuit Japan Press, see the Laures Kirishitan Bunko Database, an updated version of the classic catalogue by the Jesuit Johannes Laures.
10 Tronu, "Rivalry."
11 Magnino, *Pontificia Nipponica*, 35.
12 Magnino, *Pontificia Nipponica*, 40.
13 López Gay, "Father Francesco Pasio," 31.
14 Juan Pobre de Zamora, *Historia de la pérdida*, 188.
15 For contemporary reports on the martyrdom, see Fróis, *Relación del martirio*, Tello, *Relación*, and *Dos informaciones*.
16 Bireley, "Redefining Catholicism," 148.
17 Session XXIV of the Council of Trent in Kirsch, "Council of Trent." There are no extant official documents regarding parishes in Nagasaki, but indirect evidence

registers the appointment of parish priests and the approximate erection date and location of parish churches.

18 An important innovation in this area were several elements of adaptation to the Japanese culture, for example adding a holiday of Our Lady on the Japanese New Year's day, which was the most important local holiday, and translating some of the sacramental formulae into Japanese. For a monographic study on the *Manuale*, see López Gay, *La liturgia*.
19 Annual letter 1601 (ARSI, JS 50, fol. 178v).
20 Annual letter 1602 (BL, Add Ms 9859, fol. 194v).
21 Luis Cerqueira, 15 October 1606 (BRAH, Cortes, 9/2665, fol. 45v).
22 Yamazaki, *Nagasaki Kirishitanshi*, 234–235.
23 Juan de Santa María, *Chrónica*; Aduarte, *Historia*; Sicardo, *Christianidad del Japón*.
24 Ávila Girón, *Relación*, in Schilling and Legarza, "Relación," 119.
25 Muñoz, *Los Dominicos* 1965, 27–28; Nagasakishikyōikuiinkai, *Nagasakishi Sakuramachi*.
26 Hartmann, *The Augustinians*, 50–51; Amaro, *Study on the Christian Facilities*, 136.
27 López Gay, *La liturgia*, 27.
28 Costa, "A crise financeira," 246.
29 Álvarez Taladriz, "Fuentes europeas."
30 Luis Cerqueira, 5 March 1612 in Ribeiro, *Bispos portugueses*, 49–50.
31 Gonoi, *Kirishitan no bunka*, 212–226.
32 Willeke, *Kirishitan jidai*, 14. Arimura, "The Catholic Architecture," 68.
33 Gonoi, *Kirishitan no bunka*, 214, 216, 225.
34 *Rol das Casas* in Schütte, *Textus catalogorum*, 286.
35 Gonoi, *Kirishitan shinkōshi*, 190.
36 Annual letter 1611 (ARSI, JS 57, fol. 136v–137r).
37 Annual letter 1611 (ARSI, JS 64, fol. 103r–103v).
38 On confraternities in early modern Catholic Europe, see Dompnier and Vismara, eds., *Confréries et dévotions* and Kawahara and Ikegami, eds., *Yoroppa chukinsei*, which also includes a chapter on Japanese confraternities by Kawamura, 357–401.
39 Valignano, *Advertimentos* in Schutte 1946, 270–281.
40 López Gay, *La liturgia* 26–27.
41 Gallegos, "Charles Borromeo and Catholic Tradition," 14, 17.
42 Valignano, *Advertimentos* in Schütte, *Il cerimoniale*, 270–281.
43 Arimura, "The Catholic Architecture," 71.
44 Arimura, *Iglesias kirishitan*, 19.
45 Amaro, *Study on the Christian Facilities*, 197.
46 Arimura, "The Catholic Architecture," 68.
47 Pacheco, "Iglesias de Nagasaki," 53.
48 Sakamoto, *Nanban byōbu*.
49 Annual letter 1601 (ARSI, JS 50, fol. 180v); Annual letter 1604 (ARSI, JS 55, fol. 97v); Amaro, *Study on the Christian Facilities*, 199–200.
50 Ribadeneira, *Historia*, in Arimura, "The Catholic Architecture," 70.
51 Miyamoto, "Nagasaki Santo Domingo."
52 Yamazaki, *Nagasaki Kirishitanshi*, 246–247.
53 Arimura, "The Catholic Architecture," 64, 71.
54 Boudinhon and William, "Parish."

6 Conflicting views

Catholic missionaries in Ottoman cities between accommodation and Latinization

Cesare Santus

In the last decades, the spread of Catholicism in the Near East has been contextualized as the fruit of the encounter between missionaries trained in the cultural climate of Counter-Reformation Europe and the local dynamics of Ottoman society, while more recent studies aim to integrate the study of the Christian Orient into the connected history of the so-called "Global Catholicism."[1] In this regard, an important paradigm shift in the historiography of the missions has coincided with the refusal to describe the missionary phenomenon as a simple process of diffusion from a center to its periphery, instead trying to consider the peculiar characteristics of the various local "Catholicisms" deriving from the encounter between the European religious and the indigenous faithful.[2] Furthermore, while the study of the agency of the missionaries has shed light on the extent of their compromises and accommodation to local realities, new interpretations have revealed the continuation of behaviors that crossed confessional borders even within Tridentine Europe.[3] In sum, what has become increasingly apparent is that the early modern Catholic Church was characterized by a pronounced internal diversity. This plurality often turned into rivalry, competition, and conflict – not only in the Far East, where missions were shaken by the great missionary controversies concerning the Chinese or Malabar rites but also in the Ottoman Empire and Persia.[4]

In this chapter I address this issue by taking into account the different strategies employed by the religious (especially Capuchins, Jesuits, and Franciscans) in the urban settings of the Ottoman Empire. The focus will be on the missionaries' relations with the local Orthodox and pre-Chalcedonian Christian communities, which constituted the preferential target of Catholic apostolic efforts. I have chosen three main points of inquiry: the adaptation of European missionaries to the local social structures and the different forms of dependence or rivalry they entertained with the European consular network; their approach toward Eastern Christian rites and traditions (respect versus "Latinization"); and, finally, the measure of tolerance or intolerance they displayed toward the practice of sacramental intercommunion between Catholic converts and non-Catholics.

The first decades of the eighteenth century saw the rise of several controversies revolving around these questions. These were motivated not only by ideological rivalry or competition but also by the different social and political conditions specific to each mission. By discussing some examples related to the cities of Jerusalem, Damascus, Constantinople, Aleppo, and Cairo, I will demonstrate how local circumstances influenced the missionaries in their relationship with the Ottoman Christians, with the officials of the Sublime Porte, and with the representatives of the Crown of France and the Roman Church. I thus aim at showing that, contrary to widespread stereotypes, the different strategies of the missionaries did not necessarily depend on their belonging to different orders but were primarily determined by the contexts in which they interacted.

1 Protected by consuls, threatened by pashas – or vice versa?

By perusing the correspondence of European missionaries in the Levant, one can observe how frequently they mention the "protection" granted by the French king through his ambassador to the Sublime Porte and through the consular network. Although there was no institutionally established patronage comparable to the colonial territories of the Iberian monarchies, the successful commercial and diplomatic penetration achieved by France during the sixteenth and seventeenth centuries practically forced Catholic missionaries to rely on its material and human support.[5] Despite the dangers this reliance entailed, especially at times when Gallican tendencies re-emerged, the Congregation of *Propaganda Fide* accepted this situation and even proposed French protection as the primary means of handling the political and economic troubles encountered by the missionaries in their daily activity. In fact, there was no alternative: especially since the second half of the seventeenth century, French mediation was necessary to obtain the authorization required for the installation of new missions from the Ottoman authorities, the *berat* of investiture for the Eastern prelates of Catholic tendencies, and to ensure the naval connection that allowed men and information to circulate between Rome and the Levant.[6] In 1685 and 1690, for example, Ambassadors Guilleragues and Châteauneuf obtained two imperial commands that authorized the Jesuits to settle in any city in which a French consul resided, by also giving them "the faculty of explaining the points of faith to the Greeks and Armenians who would voluntarily come to them."[7] Accordingly, the newly founded but already promising mission of Erzurum, one of the most thriving commercial hubs in the eastern provinces of the empire, was quickly regularized by appointing one of the local Armenian merchants as a consul. Whenever the Jesuits tried to settle in a town without the help of a permanent representative of France, as in the nearby Trabzon, local pashas found it easy to harass them by applying the Capitulations in a strict way.[8]

However, this does not mean that the relations between the missionaries and the diplomatic personnel of the French Crown were idyllic – quite the contrary. The religious active in the Middle East were of different origins and political affiliations (as for example Italian, papal, or imperial subjects), and, in many cases, national rivalries and different priorities fueled the conflicts between them: in this situation, the missionaries had to rely on appeals to Rome or, more frequently, on local solidarity networks built over time. In Jerusalem, for example, the situation was almost the opposite of that of Erzurum and Trabzon. The Franciscans of the Holy Land had settled there since the fourteenth century, while the French attempts to open up a consulate had always met with a strong opposition from the Muslim inhabitants of the city, who claimed that the Caliph ʿUmar, as well as Saladin, had forbidden the installation of European representatives in the third most holy place of Islam.[9] Although the Franciscan Custos (who was also the "Guardian of Mount Zion and of the Holy Sepulchre") had the powers of apostolic prefect for the missions of Palestine, Syria, Egypt, and Cyprus, evangelization was not the main activity of the Friars of the Holy Land, whose main task was rather the preservation of the Latin presence in the "holy places." Moreover, the Custody of the Holy Land was a complex organization with a large budget, mostly funded by the Crown of Spain and through the alms collected in its Iberian and Italian domains, from where the majority of the friars also came. This set of circumstances, which allowed the Franciscans not to rely on the French diplomatic network in the same way as the other religious often needed to, also caused some politically motivated quarrels from time to time, such as one in 1661, when a French pilgrim threatened the Guardian of the Holy Land with a sword because one of the friars had mentioned the King of Spain before the King of France in a public prayer.[10] This also helps to explain why Sebastien de Brémont (or Brémond), who was appointed French consul of Jerusalem in 1700, accused the Franciscans of plotting against him because of his intentions to examine their management of the generous alms sent from Europe. When the pasha asked him either to show the imperial license justifying his presence (for which he had been waiting in vain for three months) or to leave the city, Brémont claimed that this ultimatum was due to the intrigues of the procurator of the Holy Land, the Mallorcan father Rafael Ventayol. To justify himself, the latter mobilized all his acquaintances, providing the French ambassador in Constantinople with memorials in his favor signed by members of all the local Christian communities and even by the Jewish physician of the city, a close friend of the pasha.[11]

Besides proving that the allegations of Brémont were unfounded, these documents show the extent of the network surrounding the Custody of the Holy Land and, above all, the different degree of knowledge of local practices between the newly arrived consul and the experienced procurator. Indeed, Ventayol complained that Brémont had never followed his advice to be cautious, but had, on the contrary, behaved in a haughty manner with the Ottoman authorities, for example by denying them the usual gifts, even when he was explicitly requested to hand them over.[12] Moreover, while aware of his own precarious position until the arrival of the *berat*, he had nonetheless provoked the pasha by demanding the punishment of one of his servants who had been involved in a fight with a French servant. When Ventayol had tried to calm the pasha down, the latter was surprised by the intercession of the friar in favor of the consul: "Do you know he claims that you friars are Spanish and Italian, and that he will drive you out of Jerusalem in six months' time because he has orders from his king to seize your accounts and to take the alms management away from you?," he allegedly asked him.[13] Brémont exaggerated, but his claims were not at all implausible: nine years later, the consul of Sayda put the Guardian of the Holy Land Gaetano da Palermo back on a ship to Europe because of internal frictions with other members of the order but also for political reasons.[14] However, whenever the missionaries could count on solid local support, this would not happen: Ventayol stayed in place for many years, and his confrere Tomás Díaz de Campaya managed to be the principal Catholic authority in Damascus against the will of the French Crown and of the other missionaries, also thanks to his influence on the local pasha, whom he had healed from an illness.[15]

2 Local networks and European rivalries: The "missionary jealousy"

The case of Damascus just mentioned is particularly interesting because it also introduces another fundamental element, namely the complex system of rivalry and competition between the various religious orders present in the Ottoman Levant, as well as the conflicts of jurisdiction between them and the local Eastern Catholic clergy. In the eighteenth century, the Syrian urban landscape hosted the activity of Capuchins, Jesuits, and Friars of the Holy Land: the Capuchins were simple missionaries, the Jesuits were often employed as chaplains of the French consuls, but only the Friars of the Holy Land were officially entrusted the pastoral care of local Catholics, therefore also competing with the local Maronite and Melkite hierarchies, who repeatedly tried to reaffirm their rights over the faithful and to prevent their passage to the Latin rite.[16]

In Damascus, where the Franciscans were in charge of a renowned hospice, for a long time they exercised their parish duties in the only Catholic church, formally owned by the Maronites. In 1718, when the Maronites succeeded in recovering the church, the friars decided to build a small church inside the hospice. As is widely known, it was, in theory, forbidden to build new churches or to expand existing ones in the Ottoman Empire. In practice, however, this was made possible precisely thanks to the good relations between the local Ottoman authorities and the President of the Hospice, the already mentioned friar Tomás Díaz de Campaya, who even managed to obtain an authorization from the qadi.[17] Paradoxically, criticism and resistance to his work were then expressed not by the Muslim population, but by fellow Catholics: Jesuits and Capuchins denounced the risk that such construction would, sooner or later, cause the intervention of the Sublime

Porte and a severe punishment toward the religious, but the main reason for their opposition was actually due to the harsh competition for the control of the faithful. In the area of Greater Syria and Egypt, the missionary orders joined forces against the monopoly of the Holy Land, failing to notify the Guardian of new converts to Catholicism in order to prevent the local parish priests from exerting their parochial rights over them. For, in the words of the Guardian Lorenzo Cozza, Eastern Catholics were like "the beasts of the woods, falling under the dominion of the first who finds them."[18]

This rivalry was also fueled by the different strategies employed by the missionaries in the urban landscape of the empire. The Jesuits, for instance, wore the clothes of Eastern Christian priests in order to secretly visit the houses of their penitents, hearing their confessions and teaching them the catechism; another typical feature was their insistence on the direction of female devotees, completely loyal to the teachings of their spiritual father. This kind of apostolate was criticized by the other missionaries (as well as by the representatives of *Propaganda Fide*) because its secrecy and exclusiveness were deemed suspicious by Ottoman authorities, while the excessive familiarity with women was viewed as scandalous among the most conservative groups of local Christians.[19] Both the Capuchins and the Franciscans of the Holy Land often resorted to their medical knowledge in order to gain converts, but while the former used their ascetic lifestyle to elicit the admiration of the people, the latter preferred to use their wealth and brokerage capabilities to build friendly and cooperative relations with the Ottoman authorities and with the leaders of the Eastern Christian communities. Moreover, in the first half of the eighteenth century the Franciscans proceeded with a gradual work of Latinization of their Eastern faithful, urging them to follow the calendar and fasts according to the Western model, mainly through adhesion to the Third Order of Saint Francis. This is exactly the case of the aforementioned Tomás Díaz de Campaya, who in the 1720s found himself in the middle of a series of strong objections coming from the other missionaries as well as from the Eastern hierarchy. Summoned back to Rome, he was able to clear himself of these accusations by producing a long series of statements in his favor and by emphasizing the high number of conversions he had obtained, particularly among Syrians and Greeks. Rejected by the superiors of his own order and thwarted by the French diplomacy, he was able to come back to Damascus and maintain his authoritarian rule over the local Catholics thanks to a powerful network of protection, both in Syria (the local Melkite community, through the procurator Usṭā Manṣūr, a friend of ʿUthmān Pasha Abū Ṭawq) and inside the Roman Curia (the *minutante* of *Propaganda Fide* Carlo Uslenghi and probably Cardinal Zondadari himself, who, previously, had been nuncio to the court of Spain). When, in 1745, the Discalced Carmelite Emmanuel Ballyet de Saint-Albert was sent to Syria as Apostolic Delegate in order to assure the respect of the encyclical letter *Demandatam*, which urged the Catholic inhabitants of Damascus to respect the Eastern rite, he faced the outright opposition of Campaya: in a letter to

Rome, the Delegate expressed his concern about suffering the same fate as Maillard de Tournon during his unfortunate legation to China.[20]

I did not quote this unexpected reference only to highlight that both cases concerned the question of the authority of the Holy See in a hostile political and religious context, where Catholics could rely on non-Catholic authorities against a representative of Rome. Up until this point we have seen that conflicts among the missionaries were mainly due to issues of jurisdiction, national pride, and what the French Ambassadors called *jalousie de métier*. In the eighteenth century, however, one of the main reasons of debate inside the Ottoman Catholic world was linked to a complex and long-lasting dispute, which in some ways is reminiscent of the contemporary and much better-known "Chinese Rites" controversy. I am referring to the issue of *communicatio in sacris*, an expression with which the Roman Church labeled all kinds of participation of Catholics in the liturgical celebrations and sacraments of non-Catholic worship.[21]

This practice was almost inevitable among Eastern Christian converts to Catholicism: first of all, a complete break with pre-existing personal and family ties between Catholics and Orthodox was perceived as traumatic and very difficult to achieve; secondly, the early missionary strategy of secret conversions did not demand a formal rejection of the original community (even allowing, in some cases, neophytes to continue to attend their old churches); finally, and most importantly, according to the juridical framework of the Ottoman Empire, Greek, Copt, Syriac, and Armenian faithful were forced to resort to their national "schismatic" clergy for all those sacraments and rites that held civil effects, i.e., baptism, marriage, and funerals. Those who refused could also be considered rebels from a political point of view because of their refusal to obey their legitimate patriarchs, appointed by the Sultan. While these were the practical problems of the converts, the Catholic missionaries were also confronted with the conceptual challenges posed by the *communicatio in sacris*: first, the question of the validity and orthodoxy of the sacraments imparted by the Eastern Churches, especially when their form was very different from the one used in the Latin Church; second, the theoretical question of the liceity of the Catholic participation in the liturgy of the "schismatics and heretics," much debated among canonists and theologians; and finally, the crucial question concerning what form of tolerance should be granted to those converts who were forced to resort to the priests and churches of their own nation for fear of violence or persecution.

Constantinople was one of the main centers of this controversy. There, the large Armenian community was the target of both Jesuits and Capuchins. In this case, however, the balance of power and the traditional contraposition between rigorism and accommodation were reversed. Contrary to what happened in Syria and Egypt, in the Ottoman capital city the role of French chaplains belonged not to the Jesuits, but to the Capuchins, and they exerted, right at the core of the empire, a function of mediation and brokerage similar to that of the Franciscans in the Holy Land.[22] Their high degree of integration in the social structure of Constantinople is attested by the large number of notarial records and arbitral decisions concerning the local Greek and Armenian population that were kept in their archives, together with the translations of official acts coming from qadi courts and Ottoman chancellery.[23] On the other hand, if we are accustomed to thinking of the Jesuits as the missionaries more willing to adapt to local cultures and circumstances, in Constantinople they followed a stricter stance and tried in every way to separate the Armenian converts from their original churches and rites, even though this provoked violent clashes and quarrels.[24]

Consequently, the Jesuits opposed all compromises or tentative agreements promoted by the Capuchins between the Catholic and Apostolic Armenian members of the community. In 1701, a truce of this kind was signed by the representatives of both parties under the auspices of the French ambassador Charles de Ferriol and with the consent of all the other missionaries. In the text of the agreement, the Armenian Catholics promised to resume their attendance of national churches and to follow their native rite in its entirety, but the others were not to demand of them a profession of faith and agreed to erase the most evident anti-Catholic parts of the liturgy. The Jesuits were the only ones who refused to sign the agreement. Their local superior, François Braconnier, wrote to Rome that the text had been conceived by the Capuchins in following a political and not a theological criterion, while the support of the French ambassador was even more dangerous, since "it is dangerous that private individuals decide anything in matters of religion."[25] This last statement sounds somewhat ungrateful if one considers that in the first six years of the century the ambassador Charles de Ferriol spent 7,900 *livres* only for religious affairs.[26]

In contrast, the guardian of the Capuchins Hyacinthe-François de Paris denounced the Jesuit attitude as motivated not by doctrinal opinions but rather by material interests. According to him, the members of the Society of Jesus did not want to lose the copious alms given by the Armenian faithful to their church in Galata. Indeed, when some years later someone advanced the idea of obtaining a separate place of worship for Catholic Armenians, the Jesuits were equally opposed, although in this case their concerns about orthodoxy seemed less justified.[27]

3 "From place to place, the status of the dispute may change": The missionaries' attitude toward *communicatio in sacris*

The controversy around *communicatio in sacris* is particularly useful for understanding the different approaches deployed by Catholic missionaries according to local circumstances. During the first 20 years of the eighteenth century, a deluge of questions and doubts about the legality of the practice came to the Holy Office, concerning especially (but not only) the Armenian communities of Anatolia and Syria. In 1720, two years after Abbot Mekhitar (Mxit'ar Sebastac'i) had once more raised the issue, the congregation seized the opportunity and decided to address the problem in a more serious way.[28] First of all, it was necessary to collect more detailed information on the extent and characteristics of the phenomenon, including the opinion of the Latin missionaries but possibly also that of the Eastern Catholic clergy. Such a survey was to be carried out as widely as possible because, depending on the place, the terms of the dispute could change, and what in one country could be seen as scandalous, in another could be acceptable. In other words, the Cardinals recognized that the conditions were not the same everywhere, and so the final judgment about the lawfulness of *communicatio in sacris* could vary. As a consequence, *Propaganda* was asked to submit three questions to the most experienced missionaries active in the East, or recently returned to Italy: (1) whether there was a real need for Catholics to resort to the "schismatic" churches and clergy for the celebration of baptisms, marriages, and funerals; (2) whether they otherwise incurred any serious or life-threatening danger; and (3) whether this form of *communicatio in sacris* could be performed "without making profession of a false sect, without scandal, and without danger of perversion." The 29 replies that were received were collected in a thick dossier of 250 leaves, together with the votes of the consultors and other material related to their bureaucratic examination.[29]

As could be expected, half of the replies came from the three main cities of the Ottoman Empire (Constantinople, Aleppo, and Cairo), but it is interesting to note that soon after those came Venice, where three among the questioned missionaries resided. The inclusion of places where there were no Armenians (like the island of Corfu, for example), might seem surprising but the choice to consult other Eastern Christian communities was made "for greater security of the truth, lest the Armenians do not hide some illicit rite, or defend themselves with false excuses." With regard to the religious affiliation of the missionaries, the most represented groups were the Franciscans of the Holy Land and the pupils of the Urbanian College (directly dependent on the Congregation of *Propaganda Fide*), followed by the Jesuits, Capuchins, and Discalced Carmelites. As already mentioned, what is most interesting is the diversity of their opinions, which often seems to depend on their place of activity. For example, the majority of the missionaries who denied the need to attend the "schismatic" churches was constituted of the religious working in Egypt. According to one of them, the Franciscan Agostino da Morano, the local Ottoman authorities had little interest in regulating Christian religious practices, especially in Cairo, where "the government is almost republican and it is possible to enjoy a certain freedom of religion."[30] Similarly, his confrere Giacomo d'Albano wrote that in the Egyptian capital "the Turkish government is very different, and not as despotic and absolute as it is in Aleppo or Damascus": in many years of mission he had never heard "that any Catholic of any nation had been imprisoned or beaten for coming to our church to hear the mass and receive the sacraments."[31]

This position, however, was not shared by all the missionaries: the Franciscans accused the local Jesuits of allowing Catholic Copts to take communion from the "schismatic" priests, provoking confusion among their faithful. Indeed, the Jesuit superior in Egypt, Claude Sicard, personally wrote that in his opinion Eastern Catholics were always allowed to perform baptisms, weddings, and funerals in their own national churches, *quamquam schismatica*; it was also acceptable to occasionally go "to the mass of the schismatics," but only in terms of physical presence yet without any real participation, as long as the Sunday obligation was then fulfilled in a Catholic church.[32] As we have seen, his ideas were not shared by his confreres in Constantinople, with the partial exception of Jacques Caschod, who – as a personal friend of Abbot Mekhitar – tried to hold a compromise position, which balanced the pastoral needs and the principles of orthodoxy.[33] The Jesuits of Aleppo were even more explicitly opposed to *communicatio in sacris*, claiming that by entering non-Catholic churches there was no way to avoid the danger of scandal. On this point the local Franciscans completely disagreed, and Luigi Antonio di Casalmaggiore admitted that he had allowed his penitents to assist "externally" to the "schismatic mass."[34]

In other words, the rivalry between religious orders could take different forms: as we have seen, in Syria the confrontation was the opposite of the one in Egypt. This variety and divergence of views confused the conscience of the Eastern faithful, who did not know what the true doctrine was to follow. As a layman from Aleppo wrote to Rome,

> we find ourselves in great perplexity in spiritual things, because some missionaries teach us one thing, and others a different one: the Franciscans teach us that it is not a sin to attend the liturgies performed in the Armenian church, if we do not intend to communicate with the heretics . . . the Capuchin fathers neither say 'yes' nor 'no', while the Jesuits and Carmelites absolutely forbid it, so much that they do not even allow us to approach the church door.[35]

This situation was deemed unacceptable by the Roman congregations: after some cautious statements and an *interim* decree in 1723 that only increased the confusion, an instruction which prohibited *communicatio in sacris* in a broader way was finally issued in 1729.[36]

However, even this clear stance was not sufficient to eradicate the phenomenon, which remained widespread in the East for decades. Armenian Catholics were now caught between the Roman prohibition and the Ottoman obligations, finding it impossible to respect both. Throughout the eighteenth century, continuous requests to soften the norm were sent to Rome from the Near East, while, periodically, scandals erupted about the permissiveness shown by some missionaries toward their faithful. At a certain point, the rivalry between missionaries led to a rupture even within the Armenian nation itself, since the religious trained in Rome (the so-called *Collegiani*, pupils of the Urbanian College of *Propaganda Fide*) accused the disciples of Abbot Mekhitar (based in the Venetian island of San Lazzaro) of being too much friendly with the "schismatics." In fact, while the *Collegiani* had introjected a theological and ecclesial system based on Western Scholastic tradition, on the Latin liturgy and on the Counter-Reformation model, the Mekhitarists struggled to remain faithful to both the Catholic Church and the Armenian tradition, convinced as they were of its substantial orthodoxy.[37] Such an approach exposed the order to continuous accusations and controversies, especially when the intransigent pro-Roman missionaries ended up victims of the Ottoman persecutions (often in the aftermath of confessional troubles they had promoted), unlike the more tolerant monks from Venice.[38] On 30 July 1770, *Propaganda Fide* decided that every Mekhitarist about to leave for the Levant was obliged to take an oath not to engage in *communicatio in sacris*.[39]

4 Conclusion

As I have tried to show, the endless competition between the missionaries and their conflicting views on some fundamental topics are not easily explained by traditional or stereotypical contrapositions (such as "Jesuit accommodation" versus "Franciscan rigorism"), which have been increasingly questioned by scholars in different geographical and historical contexts.[40] In fact, despite the real specificities of each order (for example in terms of authority management or information flow), it is not possible to speak of consistent missionary policies, as different opinions could be found within the same religious families, among fellow nationals, and even in the same residency, depending on varying circumstances. Concerning the problem of *communicatio in sacris*, for instance, some missionaries even changed their minds over time, after being put in close contact with the local situation: this was the case for the Franciscan Guardian Lorenzo Cozza and for the Jesuit Provincial of Syria Pierre Fromage, who both switched from a rigid approach to a tolerant one toward the practice of *communicatio in sacris*.[41] If a generalization must be made, we may say that European missionaries were ready to adapt to local customs and power networks whenever they were exposed to economic insecurity or political isolation. In contrast, where the missionaries were able to gain positions of power and a strong control over their followers, they did not feel the need "to go native," maintaining a strict view about the possibility of attending national churches (as the Jesuits did in Aleppo and Constantinople) and even promoting some forms of Latinization: in the case of the Franciscans of the Holy Land, this option was also a result of their being not so much a missionary order as the guardians of Latinity in the Middle East.

As for the missionaries of local origin and the Eastern Catholic clergy, their different stances derived from two opposite strategic choices: on the one hand, a "Latinizing attitude" – embodied here by the pupils of *Propaganda Fide* but also by some Uniate prelates – was perceived both as a greater guarantee of catholicity (against the proclamations of Rome itself, which in theory emphasized the need to respect the Eastern rites) and as a tool to gain the trust of the European political authorities; on the other, the fidelity to one's own ritual tradition served to reaffirm the existence and specificity of an Eastern Catholic identity, while the good relations with the "schismatic" hierarchies also helped to protect Catholic converts from any harassment on the part of Ottoman officials.

Finally, we should also underline the role played by the different urban contexts, either in stimulating rivalry and competition among the missionaries (as in Damascus, "the commercial scale where the diversity of religious orders has produced the greatest troubles," according to a French ambassador)[42] or in allowing greater or lesser freedom of action: such is the case of Cairo, which was deemed different from the other cities of the Near East for its "republican" regime – an allusion to the oligarchic system of government established by the Mamluks, which had somewhat survived the Ottoman conquest of Egypt.[43] While the large urban areas offered greater opportunities for the apostolate, they could also prove to be dangerous places: "persecutions are more easily excited in Aleppo, in Constantinople, and in Damascus than elsewhere; in the case of smaller and less populated places, it is rare that this happens."[44] All the aforementioned distinctions and contradictions made up an extremely complex picture, suggesting that generalizations or oversimplifications should be avoided: only the careful consideration of particular local dynamics and the refusal to follow established patterns can lead to a correct understanding of the missionary activity in the urban settings of the Ottoman Empire.

Notes

1 Heyberger, *Les chrétiens du Proche-Orient*; Clines, "Society of Jesus."
2 Ditchfield, "De-centering the Catholic Reformation," 186–208; Menegon, *Ancestors, Virgins, and Friars*.
3 Luria, *Sacred Boundaries*; Kaplan, *Divided by Faith*; Dixon, Freist, and Greengrass, *Living With Religious Diversity*. These are just a few examples among many.
4 Županov and Fabre, *Rites Controversies*; Windler, *Missionare in Persien*; Santus, *Trasgressioni necessarie*.
5 Since the beginning, this was also due to the explicit will of the French Crown to promote its own interests in the Levant through a network of missionaries of French origin, especially Jesuits and Capuchins (who were soon to become rivals). See Pierre, *Le Père Joseph*; Ruiu, "Missionaries and French Subjects," 181–204.
6 See Girard, "Impossible Independence," 67–94.
7 Châteauneuf to Pontchartrain, 17 June 1692 (AN, AE, B/I, vol. 381, fol. 203v). A French translation of the 1690 text was published by Fleuriau d'Armenonville, *Estat présent*, 98–111.
8 AN, AE, B/I, vol. 381, fol. 204r/v.
9 The first attempt to establish a French consul in Jerusalem dates back to 1621, with the appointment of Jean Lempereur, who actually resided there for only 2 years (1623–1625). He was accused by the Ottoman authorities in Damascus of being a spy and an ally of the Druze Emir Fakhr al-Dīn II; he was imprisoned in Damascus and eventually expelled. See Pietro Verniero di Montepiloso, *Croniche*, vol. 2, 61–69.

10 Lemmens, *Acta S. Congregationis*, vol. 1, 190–191.

11 Ferriol to Pontchartrain, 4 August 1700 (AN, AE, B/I, vol. 383, fol. 190r–199v); letter from 15 April 1700 with attached documents (AN, AE, B/I, vol. 628, fol. 82).

12 Pietro Verniero di Montepeloso, Deputy Custos in the 1630s and first real chronicler of the Franciscan presence in the Holy Land, left an interesting testimony on the vast experience and know-how acquired over the centuries by the friars about how to deal with local Islamic authorities. The first draft of the second book of his *Chronicles* is devoted to detailed listing of all the donations (in cash, clothes, or other goods) that should be offered to the "Turks" according to the occasion and the degree of the officer involved. See Pietro Verniero di Montepiloso, *Croniche*, vol. 4, 18–32, 32 ff.

13 According to Ventayol, part of the responsibility for this lay on the bad advice given to the consul by a French friar, the Vicar François Macé, deemed too young to have real knowledge of the local dynamics. Ventayol to Ferriol, 20 June 1700 (AN, AE, B/I, vol. 383, fol. 200r–205v).

14 See Heyberger, *Les chrétiens du Proche-Orient*, 245–246.

15 Previously, Ventayol had played a key role in obtaining from the Ottoman Porte the victory over the Greeks in the long-running dispute concerning the control of the Holy Sepulchre; he died in Jerusalem on 9 January 1726. On the Castilian Friar Tomás Díaz de Campaya, who graduated as a doctor from the University of Alcalá de Henares, see later in this chapter: The mention of his friendship with the pasha of Damascus is in APF, CP, vol. 77, fol. 107v. It should be noted that there was no French consulate in Damascus; in order to undermine Campaya's power his opponents tried several times to move him to another city where a French representative could keep him under control.

16 See the protests of the Maronite Patriarch Isṭifān al-Duwayhī and of the Melkite Patriarch Cyril Tanas against the "usurpations" of the Friars of the Holy Land: Heyberger, *Les chrétiens du Proche-Orient*, 446–447.

17 Memorial of Campaya, 1724 (APF, SOCG, vol. 648, fol. 192r/v). On the previous situation, see Lemmens, *Acta S. Congregationis*, vol. 1, 401–402 (General Report on the Custody of the Holy Land, 1717–1719). On the pragmatic attitude of Ottoman authorities concerning church renovation, see Gradeva "From the Bottom Up and Back Again," 135–163. On relations between the Ottoman authorities and the Christian community of Damascus, see also Marino, "Le 'Quartier des Chrétiens.'"

18 Letter to the Congregation of Propaganda fide, 28 February 1714, in Castellani, *Atti del Rev.mo Lorenzo Cozza*, 288–296, 294. In another letter, he suggested that this was also due to the exaggerated or false claims of conversions boasted by the Jesuits (14 March 1714, in ibid., 301) See also Heyberger, "Terre Sainte," 127–153.

19 Memorial of a dragoman from Aleppo, 1725 (APCP, Constantinople, series E, doc. 23). On the creation of groups of female devotees and consecrated virgins, see Heyberger, "Individualism and Political Modernity," 71–85; Heyberger, *Hindiyya*.

20 Report of Emmanuel de Saint-Albert from Tripoli, January 1745 (APF, CP, vol. 83, fol. 390v). On the previous accusations against Campaya, see APF, Acta, 1724, fol. 366r; Acta, 1725, fol. 321r ff.; SOCG, vol. 648, fol. 169r–176v; CP, vol. 75, fol. 62v–68v, 106v–113v; CP, vol. 77, *passim*. See also Heyberger, *Les chrétiens du Proche-Orient*, 346, 352, 487–489.

21 Vries, "*Communicatio in Sacris*"; Santus, "*communicatio in sacris*"; Santus, *Trasgressioni necessarie*. The interweaving of this issue with the famous Chinese and Malabar *querelles de rites* is at the core of a research project that I will carry out at the Université Catholique de Louvain. See also Windler, *Missionare in Persien*, 589–607.

22 In 1685, before taking up his post as French Ambassador to the Sublime Porte, Pierre de Girardin resorted to the diplomatic experience of a Capuchin from Constantinople, who instructed him about the right people to approach in order to deal effectively with the Ottoman Court. See Ghobrial, *The Whispers of Cities*, 46–48.

23 See the documents in APCP, Constantinople, especially in the series F, R, S, T, U, V, X, and Z. One of the most stunning examples concerns the request addressed in 1705 by the qadi of the Greek Islands Yūsuf Agha, who asked Fr. Hyacinthe-François to intercede on his behalf with the French ambassador in order to quickly receive from the Kapudan Pasha the passport required to exert his duty; in return, the qadi sent three wheels of cheese to the friar as a gift! (APCP, Constantinople, series P, doc. 46).

24 This negative stance was shared by the Jesuit Curia in Rome, whose theologians explicitly rejected any form of *communicatio in sacris*: ARSI, Gallia 104, fol. 269r–271r, 280r–282v. Not all the Jesuits, however, were of the same mind: while the local superior François Braconnier and Pierre Ricard were hardliners, some years later their confrere Jacques Caschod seemed to have expressed more conciliatory positions (see later in this chapter).

25 ARSI, Gallia 104, fol. 274r–279v. The memorial is not signed, but the handwriting of Braconnier is recognizable. On the 1701 agreement, see De Craon, "Le projet d'union," 47–67; on the historical background, see Kévorkian, "Documents d'archives français," 333–371.

26 *Mémoire des dépenses que j'ay faites pour les affaires de la Religion depuis le premier Janvier 1700 jusqu'au 20 Juin 1706* (AN, AE, B/I, vol. 385, fol. 49r–51v).

27 Letters dated 18 October and 14 November 1714 (APCP, Ms. 1261, 108–117); see Santus, "La comunità armena," 51–59. For a more detailed analysis of the local context, see Santus, *Trasgressioni necessarie*.

28 Nurikhan, *Il servo di Dio abate Mechitar*, 255. See the *Informatione alla Sacra Congregatione del S. Offitio fatta dal Pad. Michitar Petro, Abbate delli Monaci Armeni del titolo di S. Antonio Abbate, circa la questione controversa nell'Oriente, se sia lecito alli Catolici di andare nelle Chiese delli Scismatici* (ACDF, SO, St. St., M 3 a, fols. 338r–352v). See also Mekhitar of Sebastia, *Lettere del Servo*, 396–403.

29 ACDF, SO, St. St., M 3 a, fol. 166r–416v. This dossier is examined in Santus, *Trasgressioni necessarie*.

30 4 May 1721 (ACDF, SO, St. St., M 3 a, fol. 288r). This peculiar condition may also be explained by the rather marginal status of the Coptic Church in the Ottoman Empire: "unlike their Armenian and Greek correlates, who had active patriarchates in Istanbul, [the Copts] were primarily governed by local powerholders in Egypt . . . as such, they scarcely provoked the interest of sultans or their deputies." Armanios, *Coptic Christianity*, 9.

31 27 April 1721 (ACDF, SO, St. St., M 3 a, fol. 259r).

32 The reason behind Sicard's tolerant attitude was not only the idea that the Eastern liturgy and sacraments were valid and substantially devoid of errors, but also the awareness that those Eastern Christians who refused to take part in the social and religious ceremonies of their rite were doomed to be expelled from their communities. Letter from Cairo, 6 April 1721 (ACDF, SO, St. St., M 3 a, fol. 249r–250v). Sicard could publicly express his tolerance toward *communicatio* (in 1725 he even wrote an Arabic and French pamphlet, *Dissertation sur la communication qu'on peut avoir avec les hérétiques et schismatiques dans les prières et les sacrements*: APF, CP, vol. 77, fol. 95r–98v) perhaps thanks to his reputation as a scholar and to his network of patrons, fascinated by the many Egyptological discoveries he had previously made: See Sicard, *Œuvres*. At any rate, he died

in 1726, before any Roman censorship could hit him. The history of the Jesuit mission in Cairo can be studied in detail thanks to the documents published by Libois, *Monumenta Proximi-Orientis*, vols. 5 and 6; more in particular, see Hamilton, *The Copts and the West*, 85–91.

33 On Jacques Caschod (or Gachoud), known for his apostolate both among the galley slaves of Constantinople and the local Armenians, see Jordan, "Le P. Jacques Gachoud." In his reply to Rome he stated that both an absolute ban on attending national churches and widespread tolerance of *communicatio in sacris* would have caused serious problems. However, he pointed out that a distinction was needed between the simple assistance to prayers and psalms (which did not offend anyone), participation in the mass, reception of the sacraments, etc.: 4 July 1721 (ACDF, SO, St. St., M 3 a, fol. 255r–256v).

34 17 April 1721 (ACDF, SO, St. St., M 3 a, fol. 278r–279v).

35 Giorgio Lucas, 1 June 1722 (ACDF, SO, St. St., M 3 a, fol. 284r–285v).

36 5 July 1729 (ACDF, SO, St. St., M 3 a, fol. 476r–483v). See Santus, "*communicatio in sacris*," 330–332. However, even at a later phase some missionaries continued to express resistance and dissenting opinions. See Windler, "Ambiguous Belongings."

37 See Zekiyan, "Armenians and the Vatican," 251–267; Abagian, "La questione della *communicatio in sacris*."

38 In 1721, the Collegian missionary don Giovanni Minas had already attributed the ultimate responsibility of his sufferings not to the "schismatics," but rather to those "coward Catholics" that were stirred up by the Mekhitarists to refuse the rigor of the Roman norms: 17 May 1721 (ACDF, SO, St. St., M 3 a, fol. 274r–275v).

39 APF, Acta, 1770, fol. 321v; APF, SC, Armeni, vol. 19, fol. 395r–397r.

40 On the dissent within the Jesuit order concerning the rites controversy, see for example Županov, *Disputed Mission* and Pavone, "Dentro e fuori la Compagnia," 943–960. One example of how accommodation could also be promoted by other missionary orders is the case of the Discalced Carmelites in Persia, recently studied by Windler, *Missionare in Persien*.

41 Compare Lorenzo Cozza's stance in 1721 (ACDF, SO, St. St., M 3 a, fol. 316v–318v) with that he expressed a decade earlier (Castellani, *Atti del Rev.mo Lorenzo Cozza*, 112–121); in 1727 Pierre Fromage explained that his previous negative stance was due to his lack of awareness about the local circumstances (APF, CP, vol. 77, fol. 9v–10v).

42 See the Memorial of the Ambassador Louis-Sauveur de Villeneuve (1740) in Rabbath, *Documents inédits*, 561–578, 564.

43 See above, footnote 30; Winter, *Egyptian Society*.

44 Letter of Lorenzo Cozza, 10 March 1721 (ACDF, SO, St. St., M 3 a, fol. 319r/v).

Part III

Missionaries in the countryside

7 Funding the mission

The Jesuits' economic integration in the Japanese countryside

Hélène Vu Thanh

During his first stay in Japan (1579–1582), the Visitor to the East Indies, Alessandro Valignano, decided to revitalize the hitherto stagnating Jesuit mission. Unlike the mission's superior, Francisco Cabral, Valignano saw Japan as a highly promising land which could not only be evangelized in full but could also become a stronghold of Catholicism.[1] Central to his strategy was the decision to open colleges, which would train Japanese converts and expand the ranks of the Society of Jesus across the country. In a context where, according to Valignano, the mission mostly subsisted on scarce and intermittent funding in the form of royal or papal donations, his plan meant a new economic model had to be developed. Valignano conceded that, ideally, the mission should have relied on donations alone, but the constraints faced by the mission and the high hopes of securing Japan's evangelization called for unusual if possibly debatable solutions. The Visitor's well-known initiative was to systematize and increase the mission's investment in the Portuguese silk trade, a solution which was to fuel decades of controversy with the mendicant orders. As this article demonstrates, another much less publicized but no less crucial way of supporting the mission was to build on local networks to secure all kinds of funds, supplies, and services. Profit from trade and locally raised resources soon overtook donations from Europe as the missions' main economic sources, allowing for the implementation of Valignano's ambitious plans – much to the dismay of the superior Cabral, whom Valignano promoted out of the country.

This article thus offers a new perspective on the material economy of the Japanese mission in the sixteenth and seventeenth centuries through an examination of an hitherto unexplored aspect, namely the Jesuits' reliance on local networks. It shows how the Jesuits managed to integrate and mobilize their local social and economic environment, chiefly across the countryside of Kyūshū – Japan's southwestern large main island, where Portuguese merchants came once a year to sell Chinese silk, and where the Jesuits won most of their *daimyō* ("local lords") and peasant converts. The article then explores how the missionaries interacted and built relationships with the local population, which was to them a source of expenditures but also a provider of resources, whether in kind or in money. Indeed, not only the *daimyō* but also the peasants contributed decisively to the mission's upkeep. This in turn raises the question of how resources were managed locally and what kind of system the Jesuits devised to share costs and resources across the scattered and relatively autonomous Christian communities. And, as this article purports to show, the integration of the Japanese countryside fueled debates among the Jesuits in Japan, as many were concerned with the spiritual and political implications of the mission's unusual ways of supporting itself.

The ideal and consensual scenario would have been for the mission to rely on the long-term patronage of elite converts. But Japan was still experiencing a highly unstable political environment, where *daimyō* houses quickly rose and fell and alliances were usually short lived. The country had been experiencing disunion and civil wars since the late fifteenth century, when the Ashikaga Shogunate gradually lost its authority to local lords, the *daimyō*. The Kyōto-based emperor, meanwhile, had lost his political authority long before. The second part of the sixteenth century, however, saw the slow accretion of power and territory by three successive warlords, Oda Nobunaga (1534–1582), Toyotomi Hideyoshi (1536–1598), and Tokugawa Ieyasu (1543–1616), a process that effectively led to the political reunification of the country. Meanwhile, the countless wars between *daimyō* had unpredictable and decisive consequences for the Jesuits, who often found themselves in dire need of resources to cope with various crises.

These dynamics of the Jesuits' local networks have generally been overlooked by historians of the Japanese mission.[2] One reason could well be that Valignano's discourse, as we shall see, ruled out the very possibility of securing local funding yet provided a sustained defense of his silk trade investment, which in turn has received much more attention. Or yet another reason may be that the Jesuits did not come to own estates the way they did in America, in India, or in Europe.[3] More generally, there has been more interest in social and cultural rather than economic issues, a trend paralleled in the historiography of other Asian missions.[4] When financial aspects of missions have been examined, it has been mostly from a regional or global perspective, following Dauril Alden's pioneering work in the 1990s, which famously analyzed the Society of Jesus as a capitalist venture.[5] But Alden's model has undergone criticism in recent years.[6] Alden compared the Society to a global corporation, in other words, to an organization aiming to deploy itself rationally across the world, by demonstrating how closely the Jesuits' financial structures came to be intertwined with those of the Portuguese empire. But historians nowadays tend to depict the Society less as a monolithic, unitary system and more as an evolving field where provinces, missions, and individuals of various nationalities cooperated and competed with each other.[7] While Alden's effort to look at the global picture is still valued, there is more interest in horizontal links between missionary fields, in local strategies, and in the diversity of resources mustered by the Jesuits, beyond mere royal patronage. Aliocha Maldavsky for instance has examined the role of laypersons in the funding of evangelization in Peru through an analysis of donations and pious foundations made by the *encomenderos*.[8] In the case of Japan, however, the study of local funding has become synonymous with an interest in the Macao vessel, which linked China with Japan and in whose trade the Jesuits made investments.[9] The question of how the Jesuits tried to find resources within local Japanese society, and especially in the countryside, has yet to be examined, as does the Jesuits' social role in the Japanese countryside.

1 An impossible recourse to local funding? Faces of Japanese Christianity

The country's poverty is a recurring theme in Valignano's writings, when describing the nobility as well as the common people.[10] The Visitor initially counted on the Christian *daimyō* to provide the Society with fixed revenues, but he no longer saw this as a possibility in the 1580s. This would run against the Visitor's design of Japanese Christianity taking care of itself, and also against the way the church traditionally operated in Europe. Valignano thus had to account for this state of affairs, and he produced a certain number of justifications.[11] First, Valignano pointed out that the *daimyō* themselves were not wealthy. According to Valignano, the many wars they fought represented a heavy financial burden, and they also had to provide for their vassals, who were entitled to their lord's income according to their rank. In the end, the *daimyō* could only keep for themselves a small part of their income, which was much needed for their own house's upkeep and in order to sustain the lifestyle that was expected of them. Valignano claimed that the situation of the Christian *daimyō* was made worse by the fact that they were often minor lords, ruling over lands both mountainous and poor, mostly on the southern island of Kyūshū.[12] The income they could rely on was thus particularly limited. Meanwhile, the Jesuits were only foreigners, living in a land that was outside Iberian control, which meant they could only count on the support of a small community of Christians, which had only recently been established.[13] In the Visitor's argument, the mission could not survive and grow without financial help from Europe or investments in the silk trade.

Accordingly, the accounts sent to the Roman Curia make no mention of local resources, with the prominent exception of Ōmura Sumitada's 1580 donation of the port of Nagasaki, whose customs revenues then benefitted the Society, nor do they mention revenues from Indian plantations.[14] Apart from that, the only other types of resources mentioned are papal and royal donations, as well as the income derived from the sale of Chinese silk in Nagasaki.[15] These were deeply needed because Valignano had decided to open several education facilities (colleges and seminars), designed for the training of an indigenous clergy, representing a serious financial burden for the Society. As the Visitor pointed out, the mission's finances were suffering from several issues. First, external funding did not easily find its way to Japan, and when it did, it was only intermittently. One of the difficulties was that the funds changed hands many times and sometimes got lost; they could also be "diverted" to other missions on the way, in particular the Indian ones.[16] The Japanese mission was also entitled to a share of the Malaccan customs, but that did not always materialize. Second, expenditures were often heavier than expected, as political instability meant the Jesuits had to manage many crises. The Society thus had to borrow money from Europe, even though there is no trace of that in the accounts.[17] It also deviated from the regulations overseeing the foundation and funding of educational institutions. The constitutions of the Society indeed prescribed that a college could only be established if its founder endowed it with property and a source of income.[18] Ignatius de Loyola had even made it a condition for the Society to assume responsibility for any such establishment, at a time when the order had not yet explicitly outlined its educational purposes. This concern for material security, which meant that the colleges would own and manage their own property (including productive land in the case of the Salsete and Goa colleges in India), seemed to flout the order's oath of poverty, but was seen as a necessity to make educational projects viable. Conversely, non-educational establishments such as houses, residences, and churches could not be endowed, and had to subsist on alms and donations from the population,[19] a rule that can be verified in the Indian mission's accounting. The 1586 accounts state that the houses in Chaul and on the Pearl Fishery Coast owned neither land nor rent, and only survived on donations from the King or from Christians. In Japan, not only were educational institutions opened without the support of a founder, but, if we accept the Visitor's claims, residences could not rely on local donations. However, there are reasons why we should doubt the Visitor's account.

Japanese Christianity's strongest bases were mostly found in the south of the country, on the island of Kyūshū. The largest communities were concentrated in the regions of Arima and Ōmura (Nagasaki's surroundings) as well as Bungo until 1587.[20] While the Jesuits tended to emphasize their conversion of *daimyō* and noblemen, the vast majority of converts were poor peasants and fishermen scattered in countless villages, a structure that is also reflected in the mission's catalogues with its lists of establishments.[21] Furthermore, residences were the seat of roaming missions that covered a large number of communities, similar to the roaming missions established in Peru or China.[22] One consequence was that communities could wait for months (and sometimes for years in the case of regions with few Christians) before they were visited by a missionary. Consequently, they had to rely on themselves for the organization of religious life and the observance of Christian principles. The missionaries' strategy was to entrust a lay convert with the religious leadership of the community and to interact with him through written correspondence. For instance, when the Jesuits had to abandon the community in Hakata because of war in 1579, they decided to put a convert in charge of the local church.[23] Two official positions were created to fit such supporting roles: that of *kanbō*, for men who had left secular life but had not pronounced their oaths, and that of *jihiyakusha*, who were mostly married men with a lay occupation aside from their work for the mission.[24] Both assisted the missionaries during Sunday liturgical celebrations and could take care of religious education and prepare the faithful for confession on their own. They could also organize funerals and baptize children.[25] Nevertheless, the Society had to devote some of its resources to supporting the Christian communities' religious activities when missionaries were away. The Society took care of purchasing and distributing books and objects of devotion (rosaries, images, calendars) to the Christians.[26] But communities often required little, as few had their own church – converts often had to walk for several hours to reach the nearest one,[27] or would have to wait for the visit of a Jesuit, who would celebrate mass in a villager's house, often the *kanbō*'s.[28] Yet, in any case, they would have to provide for the visiting missionary and for charity activities. Unfortunately, there is no available accounting for the Jesuit institutions in Japan, which makes it difficult to know how resources were managed locally. But a few hypotheses can be formulated. Redistribution may have occurred, but more likely at the level of residences, rather than at that of communities. It would have been the procurator's duty to oversee such a system, considering his role of keeping records of the earnings and expenditures as well as the funds allocated to each residence.[29] These were then managed by the residences' superiors, with instructions as to how much to spend for every father, friar, and *dōjuku* (catechist). The superiors could also autonomously manage small amounts of alms, but decisions relating to more significant amounts needed to be approved at a higher level.[30] But it seems that the funds were not managed satisfactorily at that level and that little control was ever applied to the superiors' expenditures – a situation that was resented by the mission's procurator at the beginning of the seventeenth century, Carlo Spinola.[31] Last but not least, brotherhoods were also allocated funding: in particular the alms received during mass. They were supposed to distribute some of the funds to the neediest, but we have little information on how this was done.[32]

The procurators' regulations, which were in part drafted by Valignano, contradict some of the Visitor's own claims addressed to the Curia. They suggest that the local communities were involved if not in funding the mission then at least in the management of its funds. In practice, lay Japanese Christians contributed significantly to supporting the Society in the country.

2 The significance of local resources: Various types of support

In the absence of any mention in the accounting documents, we must rely on circumstantial evidence found in sources such as letters, chronicles, or procurator regulations in order to identify the nature of the local funding that benefitted the Society. Most of it must have consisted of temporary or one-time donations, and as such was not supposed to be featured in the accounts, which were to keep track only of resources considered to be durable. By design, the accounts thus provide only a limited picture of the mission's resources, leaving out contributions from the Japanese people.

Using other kinds of sources, we can identify several different types of resources. Donations could be made in silver, as in the case of the Arima *daimyō*'s gift in 1603 of 300 *taels* destined to the Jesuits' seminar, in compensation for the suspension of the Macao trade that year, which meant the Society got neither funds from Europe nor its share in the trade's profits.[33] But it seems that in most cases contributions were made in kind, such as small objects (paper, socks),[34] food, lumber for the construction of churches, or offers of accommodation. The Christians also provided their workforce for the edification of local oratories or churches.[35] In some cases, such as in Hakata around 1562, a community could be self-sufficient, covering its priest's upkeep in full.[36] Donations could also come from non-Christian friends of the Society, although Luis Fróis, the official chronicler of the Japanese mission, acknowledged that this was unusual. For instance, one non-Christian contributed to the erection of a church in Miyako by giving some money or sending his servants out to do the work, much to the *bonzos*' displeasure.[37] The social background of donators was quite varied, from noblemen to peasants; they also included craftsmen and merchants.

Contributions were not only made to the Society itself but also more broadly helped support Japanese Christianity and its charitable activities. These activities could be organized by the Jesuits themselves. In such cases there were detailed regulations concerning, for instance, the management of funds and the types of activities they could originate from. The 1612 *Obediencias* drafted by Valignano and his successor Francisco Pasio stated that alms should be collected in the villages of a residence's catchment area, and given in priority to paupers – however, it was recommended that the missionaries negotiate with Christians that a certain part of the alms should be used for the residence's upkeep.[38] Alms were also given during funerals and were the object of specific rules.[39] Among them, the principle of accepting almsgiving during funerals had been a contentious issue among the Jesuits in Japan. Many, including Valignano, were concerned that alms given on such occasions could be construed as offerings to the converts' dead parents, in the hope of improving their chances of escaping hell.[40] This accounts for the limitations on the use of alms in that case. The Jesuits would not accept any money for themselves and all of it was to be distributed among the Christian community, whether to paupers in the area, to the *kanbō*, or to the churches devoid of a permanent priest. Alms could also be spent on hospitals the Jesuits had opened, which mostly cared for the country's many lepers. The hospital in Bungo for instance attracted a significant volume of donations, covering its operating costs entirely.[41] Part of the alms, however, was managed by the Japanese Christians through the brotherhoods, which acted as a relay of the Jesuits' actions and played a key role in charity work and solidarity among the Christian community.[42] One of the first *Misericórdias* was created in 1555, in Funai, and many communities, such as Ōmura's,[43] created informal brotherhoods. Some of these were later granted a formal status, based on the Portuguese model: such was the case of the Nagasaki *Misericórdia*, one of the most powerful brotherhoods which attracted large volumes of donations every year. Members of the *Misericórdia* created a charity fund to collect donations, which were then distributed at the end of the Sunday mass.[44]

Japanese Christians thus contributed significantly to the funding of the mission through donations of money and in kind. Such an organization reflects how well the Jesuits integrated into the local society and the strength of their lay networks, at least in the densely Christianized areas. A more salient case is that of the material relationships with the *daimyō*.

While, according to Valignano, the poor and embattled Christian *daimyō* were unable to support the convert community, the list of the Japanese mission's benefactors attests to the significance of donations by *daimyō* converts, especially in the form of annuities.[45] The *daimyō* are mentioned in the same section as the King of Portugal and the Pope, with no distinction of rank being made.

Four *daimyō* families provided the mission with donations in the form of annuities, with Ōtomo Yoshishige (dom Francisco), Ōmura Sumitada (dom Bartolomeu),[46] Arima Yoshisada (dom André) and his son Harunobu (dom Protasio), and the Amakusa *daimyō* (dom Miguel and his sons). These were the most dedicated Christian lords, all based in Kyūshū. Some of them adopted an aggressive policy against Buddhism, as illustrated by the Arima *daimyō*'s imposition of Christianity onto his entire domain in 1580.[47] The Arima *daimyō* was also the largest contributor to the mission, with yearly contributions of 4,160 *taels*, which covered more than a third of the mission's running cost, estimated between 10,000 and 12,000 *taels* yearly, while the poorer Amakusa *daimyō* provided only 250 *taels*. The regular donations were mostly raised on rice- or wheat-producing lands, whose revenues were transferred to the Jesuits. But they also included services or donations in kind that were valued in monetary terms. Thus, the list of benefactors describes how the small yearly annuities of 250 *taels* provided by the Amakusa family over 30 years in fact consisted of services and donations in kind, which proved vital for the survival of Christianity in the poor, remote domain. In the same token, the Arima domain's subjects were required to donate salt, fish, or fruit to the Society, a contribution valued at 160 *taels* a year, not counting the *corvée* labor they were to provide once a week. Nevertheless, annuities could not always be relied upon, as the contributors could renege on their promises of future payments at any time. Some were given only for a fixed period, such as the revenue from the wheat produced in Mogi (Arima), which provided 500 *taels* for four or five years, and they could be lost as a result of war: the Jesuits only benefitted from a rent raised in Hakata for two years, before the Ōtomos lost the region to a rebellion.

The Jesuits insist on the fact that the money was merely transferred to them, and that they did not own or manage any productive land (they could only own land donated for the erection of a church or a residence). While this insistence was probably intended to deflect the charges leveled by the other orders, it can also be accounted for by the new political context that emerged in the 1580s, with Toyotomi Hideyoshi's rise to power. In 1591, Hideyoshi ordered a national land survey and went on to implement significant reforms, one of which outlawed intermediaries between lords and cultivators. Taxes could only be raised by the *daimyō*, who could then transfer the funds to the Society. Moreover, like many other groups, such as the warrior class, the Society was barred from owning productive land. The *corvée* system (*yaku*), which generally supplemented taxes, was meanwhile managed by the *daimyō*, but could be replaced by a payment in cash or in kind.[48] The Society adapted to the social and economic structures of the Japanese countryside, which meant it was highly dependent on *daimyō*. This situation was troubling to many missionaries.

3 Between local integration and the global framework: The Jesuits' position in Japanese society

At the beginning of the 1580s, the mission's two strongest personalities, namely its superior Francisco Cabral and the Visitor Valignano, clashed over several issues. First and foremost was the question of the evangelical strategy and of the adoption of a policy of accommodation.[49] Cabral held a very negative view of the Japanese and rejected Valignano's idea of training an indigenous clergy. The two also fought over the organization of the mission and its funding by the Japanese. The dispute continued through written exchanges that were submitted to the Society's general, even after Cabral's reassignment to India in 1581.[50]

To Cabral, the Japanese mission was financially self-sufficient, thanks to donations from the King and the Pope but also owing to the annuities provided by the Christian *daimyō*. The superior elaborated his own version of the mission's accounts, which he sent to Rome to refute those that Valignano was producing.[51] In his letter, Cabral lists the residences' expenditures, which amount to a total of 4,455 *taels*. Revenues are estimated at 8,000 *taels*. This includes major donations by *daimyō*, such as the annuities provided by the Ōmura *daimyō* (raised on rice-producing lands and the customs of the Nagasaki port), which on their own were enough to support the Jesuits in the Shimo region. But the superior also stresses that in the Ōmura and Amakusa regions the Jesuits' expenses are entirely covered by the donations of the *daimyō*. Unlike the picture of an underfunded mission reported to the Roman Curia by Valignano, Cabral's accounts portray the mission as financially secure and benefitting from significant local financial support. Even after leaving Japan, Cabral stuck to this view and hoped to convince the general that the Japanese mission should contribute to the Indian one, to which it was administratively subordinated.[52]

The opposition between Valignano and Cabral about local funding derived from two competing visions of how the mission should position itself in Japanese society. To Cabral, annuities granted by the *daimyō* were a good way of avoiding the need to take part in the silk trade between China and Japan.[53] The involvement of the Jesuits in mercantile activities, from the earliest days of the mission, aroused much criticism within the mission. It later became the focus of denunciations by the mendicant orders, as they began settling in Japan in 1580. Such involvement sat uncomfortably with the oath of poverty, and contributed to tarnishing the image of the Society in Europe.[54] While Valignano conceded that the method was not ideal, he saw it as indispensable to his great ambitions for the Japanese mission, and more particularly the development of educational institutions.[55] Above all, the Visitor rejected the reliance on annuities granted by the *daimyō* as long as the Society would be considered a foreign entity in Japan. In his opinion, such reliance would expose the Christian *daimyō* to political risk, unlike their generous support of Buddhist monks, who had family ties with the *daimyō* and who were seen as an integral part of local society.[56] Valignano concluded: "It is a very great grace by our Lord, and we must see it as supernatural that they [the Japanese] tolerate us on their lands."[57]

Eventually, at the heart of the debate between Cabral and Valignano was the position of the order in Japanese society. Cabral wanted the Japanese Christians to support the order while refusing any participation on their behalf in the leadership of the community, which in his view had to remain the preserve of European Jesuits. To Valignano, integrating the order in Japanese society required the training of a native clergy, which would "naturalize" the Christian faith and then allow for its funding by the Japanese, following the same model as the Buddhist monks.[58] It was in this way that the Society could shield itself from being suspected of acting as a fifth column and that the *daimyō* could transfer resources to the Jesuits without being accused of disloyalty.

The Jesuits' strategy of imitating Zen Buddhist monks succeeded at facilitating their integration in the countryside. Like the *bonzos*, the Jesuits provided religious services to the peasants, who were used to assigning particular importance to local shrines.[59] Not only did the Visitor model the hierarchy of the Society of Jesus after that of the Zen monasteries,[60] but residences also followed their organization, modeled on the Pure Land Buddhist monasteries, known collectively as Ikkō-shū, and more particularly on its Shin-shū Honganji branch.[61] Interestingly, when Toyotomi Hideyoshi decreed the expulsion of the missionaries in 1587, he used the word *jinai* (temple precincts) to refer to the Jesuits' residences.[62] In so doing, he explicitly attributed to the Jesuits the same organizational structure as that of the powerful temples owned by the Pure Land sect and coordinated by a main temple (Honganji). To Hideyoshi, the city of Nagasaki was the equivalent of the Honganji, to which the Kyūshū residences scattered across Kyūshū were subordinated. To that must be added that the Shin-shū focused on the countryside to expand its ranks, forming *Ikkō Ikki* bands (rebellious peasant communities organized around temples). The Ikkō sect became a major political force in the Sengoku period before its military suppression by Oda Nobunaga, Hideyoshi's predecessor.

The comparison reveals the mounting distrust on behalf of the Japanese leadership against Christians in the 1580s but also against the position achieved by the Jesuits in the countryside, comparable to the Buddhist sects. The Jesuits were perceived as a new type of Buddhist monks because of the services they provided and of the way they structured the local population around their establishments, creating horizontal solidarities among rural communities, as the Ikkō-shū had done since the fifteenth century. This perception was reinforced by the fact that the Jesuits made sure that their residences closely resembled Buddhist temples (see Figure 5.1). Christian buildings blended into the architectural landscape, and churches were sometimes consecrated out of former Buddhist temples, granted by the *daimyō*.[63] This practice can be traced to the earliest days of the mission and repeated itself afterwards, most visibly in the Arima domain, which adopted Christianity as its only faith in 1580, and converted every one of its temples into a church.[64] Missionaries often entrusted former Buddhist monks with the role of *kanbō*, a layman entrusted with the leadership of the community. Luís Fróis mentions the case of Roque, formerly a high-ranking *bonzo* in the Kiyomizu temple in the capital Miyako, who was given the leadership of the Christians in the region after his conversion.[65] The adoption of the *bonzos*' model facilitated both the Jesuits' integration in the countryside and the willingness of the population to convert. Commoners found in Christianity, as in Pure Land Shin-shū, a way to strengthen ties between communities. In a time when villages needed to cooperate in order to survive, by organizing self-defense militias and maintaining irrigation systems, monotheistic ideologies provided commoners with a significant binding force with their regular reunions in temples and religious meeting halls. But that did not say much about the strength of the new Christians' faith nor about what the population really understood of the new religion. The policy was criticized and faced significant opposition within the order, most notably from the general Acquaviva. While he could understand Valignano's reasoning and choices, he stressed that the Japanese mission was at risk of abandoning the order's soul and called for it to respect its constitutions.[66] More crucially, the strategy proved to be a double-edged sword, as the successful integration of the Jesuits in local society was perceived as a political threat by Hideyoshi and his successor, Tokugawa Ieyasu, who banned Christianity in 1614.[67]

4 Conclusion

There is no denying that the Jesuits succeeded at integrating the Japanese countryside. This can be attributed to the Society's efforts at blending in the local social structures but also to the material support it found among the population. While the Jesuits were forced to rely on the *daimyō*'s financial support in order to raise regular revenues, their direct relationship with the peasantry was just as important, owing to the labor they provided and the material and spiritual services they received from the Jesuits in return. In this regard, the Jesuits' arrival did not significantly alter the social structuring of the Japanese countryside. Instead, to a large extent the Jesuits imitated the Buddhist monks' organization and managed to eclipse their influence on the peasantry. Nonetheless, they did develop, in parallel, new forms of devotion and of circulation of goods through the creation of brotherhoods. The impact of the Society of Jesus at the local level was thus much more significant than what can be inferred from Valignano's statements and accounts submitted to the Roman Curia. As the global structures of the Society could not provide the level of support the Japanese mission needed, its members chose to rely on the local structures, acquiring a high degree of autonomy from the centers of power in India and Europe, and not without generating some tensions within the Society in the process. Ultimately, the success of the Japanese mission can be credited to its capacity to articulate the local and the global in order to obtain the support and resources it needed. But this provoked the suspicion of the rising Japanese leadership, who were as concerned by the Jesuits' weight in the countryside, especially in the south, as with their close links with Portuguese merchants. The beginning of the persecutions in the early seventeenth century paradoxically helps us understand how strong the roots of the Jesuits had grown in the Kyūshū countryside. Despite unrelenting repression, a form of Christianity subsisted clandestinely here until the reopening of the country to the world in the middle of the nineteenth century.[68]

Notes

1 On the Visitor to the East Indies, see Tamburello, Üçerler, and Di Russo, *Alessandro Valignano.*
2 See however Rodrigues, "Local Sources."
3 Mörner, *The Political and Economic Activities*; Cushner, *Lords of the Land*; Negro and Marzal, *Esclavitud, economía y evangelización*; Guasti, *I patrimoni dei Gesuiti.*
4 Charles Borges's work about India or Frederik Vermote's more recent one on China are exceptions. See Borges, *Economics of the Goa Jesuits*, and Vermote, "The Role of Urban Real Estate." See also Windler, *Missionare in Persien*, 539–573.
5 Alden, *The Making of an Enterprise.* On the global funding of the Society, see Clossey, *Salvation and Globalization*, 162–192. On the Chinese case, see Hsia, *Noble Patronage.*
6 See Castelnau-L'Estoile's criticism in *Les ouvriers d'une vigne stérile*, 19.
7 Catto, *La Compagnia divisa.* See also Gay, *Jesuit Civil Wars.*
8 Maldavsky, "Giving for the Mission," 260–284.
9 See Boxer, *Portuguese Merchants*; Cooper, "Macao-Nagasaki Silk Trade," 423–433; Vu Thanh, "Les liens complexes."
10 Valignano, *Les Jésuites au Japon*, 39.
11 Valignano, *Les Jésuites au Japon*, 229–234.

12 On the Kyūshū *daimyō*, see Ribeiro, "Christian Nobility," 45–64.
13 On the beginnings of the evangelization of Japan, see Bourdon, *La Compagnie de Jésus*.
14 The donation only lasted for seven years, until 1587, when Toyotomi Hideyoshi took the city from the Jesuits and named governors to administrate it. See Elison, *Deus Destroyed*, 85–106.
15 On Valignano's accounting, see Vu Thanh, "Un équilibre impossible."
16 *Sumario de todos os colegios e casas, residencias e pessoas, rendas e gastos que tem a provincia da companhia na India feito no anno de 1586*, written by Valignano to Jeronymo Cardoso, procurator of India, in DI, vol. 14, 463.
17 The borrowed money is, however, mentioned in the procurator's regulations. See Frison, "The Office of Procurator," 64. See also Carvalho, *Apologia*, 57.
18 Loyola, *Écrits*, 475.
19 Loyola, *Écrits*, 530.
20 The Japanese mission was for most of its existence divided into three regions: Shimo (Kyūshū's northwest), Bungo (Kyūshū's northeast), and the Miyako region (around the capital, present day Kyoto).
21 Schütte, *Textus catalogorum*.
22 Vu Thanh, *Devenir japonais*, 31. On the flying missions, see the Peruvian example in Maldavsky, *Vocaciones inciertas*, 139–206. For the Chinese case, see Brockey, *Journey to the East*, 170.
23 Annual letter by Francisco Carrión S.J. to the Superior General of the Society of Jesus, written in Japan in 1579, in *Alcune lettere*, 20.
24 Costa, "The Brotherhoods," 73.
25 BA, JA, 49-IV-56, fol. 159v.
26 On this issue see Vu Thanh, *Devenir japonais*, 288.
27 Lucena, *Erinnerungen aus der Christenheit von Ōmura*, 180 and 184.
28 Luís de Almeida to the Jesuits in Europe, Yokoseura, 25 October 1562, in Ruiz de Medina, *Documentos del Japón*, 560.
29 *Regimento do procurador que està em Jappão* (1591), in Frison, "The Office of Procurator," 63.
30 *Obediencias* (BA, JA, 49-IV-56, fol. 154v).
31 Carlo Spinola to Acquavia, Superior General, Nagasaki, 25 March 1615, in Frison, "The Office of Procurator," 60 (original: ARSI, JS 36, fol. 168v).
32 Frison, "The Office of Procurator," 61.
33 Annual letter 1603 (BA, JA, 49-IV-59, fol. 123r).
34 *Obediencias* (BA, JA, 49-IV-56, fol. 154v).
35 Annual letter 1603 (BA, JA, 49-IV-59, fol. 126v–127r).
36 Letter by Luís de Almeida, Yokoseura, 25 October 1562 in CE 1, fol. 108r–109v.
37 Letter by Luís Fróis, Usuki, 9 September 1557 in CE 1, fol. 389r. The term *bonzos* refers to the Buddhist monks.
38 *Obediencias* (BA, JA, 49-IV-56, fol. 155r).
39 *Obediencias* (BA, JA, 49-IV-56, fol. 161v–162r).
40 Vu Thanh, "Between Accommodation and Intransigence."
41 Letter by Luís de Almeida, Bungo, 1559 in CE 1, fol. 62r–62v.
42 On the brotherhoods, see Costa, "*Misericórdias*," 67–79.
43 Lucena, *Erinnerungen aus der Christenheit von Ōmura*, 178.
44 Letter by Baltasar Gago, Bungo, 1 November 1559 in CE 1, fol. 64v.
45 ARSI, JS 23, fol. 5r–6r; Valignano, *Les Jésuites au Japon*, 229–231.
46 Lucena, *Erinnerungen aus der Christenheit von Ômura*, 142.
47 Fróis, *Historia de Japam*, vol. 3, part 2, chap. 20, fol. 65r.
48 Hall, *The Cambridge History of Japan*, 50–53.
49 Valignano to Acquaviva, Goa, 17 December 1585, in DI, vol. 14, 89.

50 Cabral was named Superior of the Japanese mission in 1571, after Cosme de Torres's death.
51 ARSI, Fondo Gesuitico 723; Francisco Cabral to the General, Macao, 5 October 1583 (ARSI, JS 9 II, fol 167r–168v).
52 Francisco Cabral to the General Acquaviva, Cochin, 15 December 1593, in DI, vol. 16, 518–522.
53 Valignano describes the details of the trade in his *Sumario de las cosas que pertencen a la provincial de la India oriental y al govierno della*, written to the Superior General Mercurian in August 1580, in DI, vol. 13, 223.
54 See the many treaties criticizing the Jesuits' involvement in the Macao trade and the alleged enrichment of the Society, such as the *Memorial* by Francisco de Montilla, procurator for the province of San Gregorio de las Filipinas and submitted to the Spanish court (1597), edited by Lorenzo Pérez in *Archivum Franciscanum Historicum*, 476–494.
55 The investment in the silk trade did not prevent the mission from running a deficit at the beginning of the seventeenth century. See Costa, "A crise financiera."
56 Valignano, *Les Jésuites au Japon*, 232.
57 Valignano, *Les Jésuites au Japon*, 233.
58 Valignano, *Les Jésuites au Japon*, 229.
59 Hall, *The Cambridge History of Japan*, 382.
60 Vu Thanh, "'Il nous faut acquérir de l'autorité,'" 471–496.
61 Kawamura, "Communities," 151–166.
62 Elison, *Deus Destroyed*, 119–124.
63 Diniz, "Jesuit Buildings," 107–128.
64 Fróis, *Historia de Japam*, vol. 3, part 2, chap. 20, fol. 65r.
65 Fróis, *Historia de Japam*, vol. 4, part 2, chap. 56, fol. 497v.
66 Acquaviva to Valignano, 24 December 1585 (ARSI, JS 22, fol. 87r–90v).
67 Kouamé, "L'État des Tokugawa," 107–123.
68 Martin Nogueira Ramos, "Religion et identité villageoise"; Costa, "Le jésuite Juan Baeza," 109–130.

8 Trading in spiritual and earthly goods

Franciscans in semi-rural Palestine*

Felicita Tramontana

The spread of Catholicism among the local Christian population in the Syro-Palestinian region has attracted the attention of many scholars. Previous research has described how missionaries' work was facilitated by the patronage of local notables, by the establishment of personal ties with locals, and more generally by a wide range of daily interactions, such as providing medical assistance.[1] In this framework, academic attention has mostly focused on the cities, consistent with the fact that missions were far more numerous in urban areas. An important exception is a pioneering work by Bernard Heyberger. This early study reconstructs how, departing from their houses in cities such as Sayda and Tripoli, Jesuits and Capuchins visited rural villages in Galilee and Lebanon. Inspired by the model of rural missions developed in Europe during the Catholic Reformation, their activities hinged on confession and preaching. In line with the regional framework, missionaries also carefully built ties with locals and offered their medical competencies, which greatly helped their cause.[2] Although the importance of interactions with the locals in the spread of Catholicism in the Middle East has been widely acknowledged, many questions about the nature of these interactions still remain unanswered: How did the administrative and economic system that characterized rural and semi-rural spaces influence missionaries' interactions with the surrounding areas? What was the relationship between missionaries' entanglement with local society and their evangelizing activities? And, finally, to what extent did these interactions turn the missionaries into "localized" protagonists?

I will address these issues, focusing on the Franciscans of the Custody of the Holy Land in semi-rural areas of the Ottoman district of Jerusalem and more specifically in Bethlehem and the surrounding villages Bayt Jālā and Bayt Sāḥūr. At the beginning of the seventeenth century, the friars had hostels and convents in Ramla, Bethlehem, and Jerusalem. They were headed by a Custos elected every three years and their number varied throughout the centuries. In 1620, according to Eugène Roger, they numbered between 90 and 110. Similar figures are attested for the last decades of the century, with 125 friars in 1680.[3] Many of the Franciscans were lay people, occupied with craftwork and economic activities. In the seventeenth century only few of them spoke Arabic, with the number increasing in the following century.[4]

Even though the Franciscans were the main agents for the spread of Catholicism in Jerusalem and the area around it, their "mission" had certain peculiar characteristics that make it especially worthwhile to explore the relationship between the missionaries and local communities. First, the Franciscan minors settled in Jerusalem and Bethlehem in the Middle Ages with the main tasks of offering assistance to foreign Catholics and, primarily, preserving the Holy Sites. It was only from the end of the sixteenth century onwards that – on par with other religious orders that arrived in the Middle East during the sixteenth and seventeenth centuries – they devoted themselves to the "reconciliation" of local Orthodox Christians. Second, as guardians of the Holy Shrines, and contrary to other missionary orders in Asia, the Franciscans had always been able to rely on a stable source of income. The convent of St. Saviour – the friars' residence in Jerusalem – regularly received the alms sent from "Christendom" for the subsistence of the friars and the maintenance of the Holy Sites. This meant in practice not only the arrival of big sums of money but also of precious and daily objects, such as food and all sorts of garments. Third, due to the initial lack of a missionary ethos, Franciscans' relationships with the local actors had not been originally influenced by missionary concerns and strategies but by the friars' daily needs and the role of the convents as productive units. This was also coherent with the organization of a conventual life that until the 1620s pursued neither sacramental nor charitable activities toward the locals. Following a well-established tradition of mendicants' medieval missions in Muslim lands, the friars took care almost exclusively of the Catholics coming from Europe: travelers, pilgrims, merchants, and slaves.

Finally, another peculiar characteristic of the Franciscan "mission" in the area is that the friars fostered the adoption among locals of the Latin rite, contrary to the prescription of the Roman Congregation of *Propaganda Fide*. Whereas in the Middle East those who were reconciled would generally become part of the newly established Catholic Eastern Churches[5] – led by local clergy – this was not the case with those reconciled by the Franciscans. As a consequence of the adoption of the Latin rite, they were instead integrated into the Franciscans' parishes. Some parishes already existed, mainly devoted to the care of foreigners, and others were established as the reconciliations progressed. Because of this, the friars' missionary activity also became a sort of extension of their pastoral duties, as noted by Heyberger.[6]

Departing from these considerations, I will investigate Franciscan integration in Bethlehem from different but interconnected perspectives. The first two sections of the chapter reconstruct the friars' earlier participation in economic and productive networks. In section three, the chapter then goes on to discuss how these patterns of interaction were influenced by the beginning of the missionary activity in the 1620s and influenced it in turn. In this respect the research argues that for a long time after their arrival in the thirteenth century, Franciscans' entanglement with the local society was fundamentally economic in nature. This explains the role economic exchanges would later play in both conversions of the local Christians and in the friars' relationship with new converts, as highlighted by previous works.[7] In fact, the spread of Catholicism in Bethlehem starting in the 1620s was facilitated by these pre-existing ties. The engagement in missionary activity led to some changes but did not alter the fundamental characteristics of the friars' participation in village life. The fourth part of the chapter compares the friars' integration into the framework of the existing power relations in the semi-rural environment of Bethlehem and in the urban setting of Jerusalem. This will entail a broader discussion about how the different settings influenced the role of the friars as local agents. The chapter ends with some remarks on the limits of the friars' integration in the local context and their role as "localized actors."[8]

1 The convent of St. Catherine and the economy of Bethlehem

Bethlehem is located eight kilometers south of Jerusalem; the village and the neighboring Bayt Jālā (two kilometers west of Bethlehem) were the most populous villages of the district, respectively numbering 287 and 239 households at the end of the fifteenth century. The great majority of their inhabitants were Christian. To what extent can these villages be defined as semi-rural? And what is the meaning of the term in this case? Sharing some scholars' doubts about the traditional dichotomy of "urban" versus "rural," this study instead considers the Bethlehem cluster (Bethlehem, Bayt Jālā, and Bayt Sāḥūr) as a stage along a continuum that links the two.[9] This approach more adequately captures the complex and multidimensional reality of early modern Palestine, where borders between towns, cities, and villages were blurred, and the cities, countryside, and desert together constituted an integrated economic and social system.[10] It is also more appropriate for describing an area in which villages were very different from one another, and at the same time shared many features with the cities. This is the case, for example, with some of the parameters that are commonly used to define "ruralness," such as occupational structure. In 1690/91, whereas in Bayt Jālā the majority of the population was employed in agriculture, a high percentage of the population of Bethlehem (94 out of 144 taxpayers) was occupied in crafts and services,[11] a percentage reminiscent of the occupational structure that characterized urban areas. Moreover, since Bethlehem and Bayt Jālā were the most populous villages of the district, in the Ottoman surveys they were both divided into neighborhoods, as was usually the case with cities. However, other characteristics of urban settlements as found in tax registers, such as numerous market taxes and roads tolls, were absent from the Ottoman surveys on Bethlehem and Bayt Jālā.[12]

A distinction between the villages and the city is also suggested when we consider the "way of living," which according to some research should also be a defining characteristic of "ruralness," and the perception of the friars themselves.[13] Indeed, in Franciscans' documents the inhabitants of Bethlehem are usually addressed with the Italian term *villani*, which means dwellers of the countryside, such as peasants.[14] The point is made more explicit in a letter on inter-confessional marriages sent to Propaganda in 1633 by the Guardian Vincenzo Gallicano. Complaining about the lack of Catholic women in Bethlehem, Father Gallicano explains that no Catholic from Jerusalem would willingly give his daughter to a villager from Bethlehem because of the difference in status between them. Women from Jerusalem, moreover, were used to staying at home while the villagers of Bethlehem needed women who would work in the fields.[15]

How did the Franciscans, who had settled in Bethlehem in 1347 in a monastery that had once belonged to the Augustinians, participate in the life of the village? In order to answer this question, we might turn to scholarship on Ottoman history, which has recently acknowledged the importance of monasteries as actors in the Greek countryside. When Greece was conquered by the Ottomans, rural monasteries mostly kept their land assets, and during the following centuries, they acquired more land. In addition to agriculture, they developed various economic activities such as fishing, wood cutting, and trade; they also acted as moneylenders. These activities prompted the monks' participation in rural economic and productive networks, and more generally in a wide range of interactions with the inhabitants of the surrounding countryside.[16]

From a legal point of view, contrary to the Greek monks, the Franciscans were not subjects of the Sultan.[17] They were considered *musta'min*, a legal term that was employed for the non-Muslim foreigners who lived under Muslim rule *via* a safe-conduct (the *amān*).[18] This meant, for example, that they could not purchase properties directly, but only through a nominee. In spite of this difference, similarly to the Greek monks, the Franciscans' acquisition of land, their productive activities, and the activities for covering their daily needs prompted their participation in the local economy in various forms.[19] First, the Franciscans in Bethlehem were buyers who purchased daily commodities. Even though the friars received food, clothes, and objects among the alms that arrived from Christendom, they would still buy local products such as eggs, hens,[20] straw,[21] wood,[22] and grapes to make wine.[23] Franciscans also turned to locals for services of different kinds. Sometimes the account book mentions salaries paid generally to the "workers" in Bethlehem.[24] In other cases documents are more detailed. In 1672, for example, the friars paid some villagers to build a fence around a newly purchased plot of land in Bayt Sāḥūr.[25] Account books also list the wage paid to locals to graze the oxen[26] or to shoe the friars' mules[27] along with the expenses related to a grazing easement.[28]

Local Christians were also employed as dragomans by the convent, acting as interpreters and porters; their salaries are dutifully recorded in the account books of Jerusalem.[29] At St. Catherine there were usually two porters, one at the main gate and the other employed for different services. Dragomans also acted as intermediaries between the friars and the local administration, as has been pointed out by Jacob Norris.[30] Accordingly, the sums of money occasionally paid to them in relation with burials may have been taxes due to the Ottoman authorities.[31] The economic relations between the friars and dragomans were not limited to the latter's employment in the convent. One of the dragomans "Elias il dottore," for example, is mentioned among those who sold grapes to the friars.[32] The same name appears years later, in 1647, when the list of expenses records the money given to him to repay a debt incurred by the friars.[33] Moreover, despite explicit prohibitions, evidence suggests that the friars in Jerusalem and in Rama regularly sold textiles to the dragomans;[34] this may have occurred in Bethlehem as well. Finally, ties with the dragomans overlapped with the growing network linked to the production of devotional objects in the village, as the dragomans became more and more specialized in handicraft.[35]

The Franciscans' involvement in the production and trade of craftwork in Bethlehem is well known and testified by numerous sources. Actually, the production of "souvenirs for pilgrims" in the village is amply attested since as early as the Late Antiquity, well before the arrival of the friars. However, from the end of the sixteenth century the friars contributed to the refinement of local skills, especially with regard to the use of mother-of-pearl and the creation of models of the Holy Sites (see Figure 8.1). They established schools

Figure 8.1 Model of the Church of the Holy Sepulchre, seventeenth century, olive wood embedded with ivory, mother-of-pearl and ebony

Source: Courtesy of MuCEM, Paris-Marseille, Inv.1010.7.1, photograph: Christophe Fouin where local artisans would be trained, and they contributed to the spread of workshops and ateliers. As time passed, the friars also became important buyers of these products, which they donated to their benefactors.[36]

2 Ownership and land use

Another important aspect of the friars' involvement in local life is the acquisition and usage of land, with the connected productive activities. In Palestine the acquisition of land has been considered a characteristic policy of Christian churches, with important repercussions for the landscape. In this respect, the Custody of the Holy Land has mainly been recorded as the purchaser of land with religious and historical significance.[37] However, over the centuries the friars also acquired buildings, arable land, vineyards, and orchards. As a mendicant order the Franciscans could not in theory own and manage properties, administer the alms received, or engage in economic transactions.[38] Therefore the Pope Clement VI when officially recognizing the Custody (with the *Nuper Charissimae*, 1342) decided that the friars would be joined in Jerusalem by a lay person who would have the same function as performed by the *sindaci apostolici* in the other Franciscan provinces. In Palestine, however, this arrangement proved to be difficult due to the paucity of men who wanted to spend a long time in the area. Because of this, the friars were awarded some dispensations. Before officially recognizing the Custody, Pope Clement VI had already allowed them to own and administer properties (1307). This arrangement was confirmed in 1458 by Pope Callisto III,[39] who – with the *devotionis vestrae ardor* – allowed the Franciscans to directly manage the alms received and properties acquired. These faculties were bestowed to the Guardian, who could choose a member of his convent instead. This arrangement led to the development of the office of the *procuratore generale*, who was in fact elected by the Custos. In Palestine some of the friars' properties were acquired through donations. In Bethlehem, for example, they received a donation of a vineyard located near the Cisterns of David. Furthermore, purchases of land and buildings even before the seventeenth century are also well documented. Most of the Franciscans' possessions were close to the convent, such as an orchard and a small garden with bitter orange trees.[40] Furthermore, the friars also owned fields in other parts of the area, such as a large orchard cultivated with figs and olives on the road to Bayt Sāḥūr,[41] and even in the village itself, where they owned an olive grove.[42]

Regarding the friars' integration in Ottoman Palestine, these investments are interesting on several levels. The purchase of orchards and vineyards testifies to the participation of the friars in the larger economic processes that affected the land tenure system in the sixteenth and seventeenth centuries. In theory, as most of the land had been owned by the sultan since the Ottoman conquest, peasants could only enjoy the usufruct of the plot they cultivated. Although they did not own the land, according to the Islamic law they had the property of the orchards and plants they grew and could therefore sell them. Such sales – which became more common in the seventeenth century, as a result of the peasants' indebtedness – would lead de facto to a change of ownership, or more precisely, to the transformation of what was once sultanic land into private property (*mülk*).[43]

The friars' investments are equally significant when considered in the light of their involvement in village life. Land was very important both for the sociopolitical life of the community and as a means of subsistence. Despite the presence of craftsmen, villagers were mostly devoted to the cultivation of wheat and barley, as well as grapes and olives as fruit crops. Agricultural production was primarily intended for the internal consumption of the village and ensured its subsistence. Accordingly, most of the conflicts within the village community arose over ownership or access to land.

The acquisition of land spurred the Franciscans' involvement in the rural economy in various ways. First, the friars rented out arable land to the inhabitants of the area. Such was the case with the already mentioned vineyard near the Cisterns of David.[44] Second, land was managed by employing locals as wage laborers. Account books, for example, mention the villagers helping the friars with the harvesting of grapes and the production of wine,[45] or the pruning (*potura*).[46] Finally, since as early as the fifteenth century, the friars' acquisition of land caused conflicts with the locals, in particular over the ownership of some fields and their usage.[47] In general, considering conflicts may contribute to an understanding of the relations between missionaries and locals, in that conflicts represent a distinct, albeit problematic form of interaction. The way conflicts were solved is therefore meaningful as well. The friars' choice to appeal (or not to appeal) to the Ottoman authorities, for example, testifies to their knowledge of the local system of conflict resolution.[48]

The existence of tensions between the friars and the inhabitants of Bethlehem in the seventeenth and eighteenth centuries has been described in relation to the friars' missionary activity[49] or to their production of devotional objects.[50] Actually, conflicts started well before this, and were related to the use of natural resources and to the very presence of the friars. In the sixteenth century, for example, the existence of tensions with the local population emerges from a set of firmans that prevented the villagers of Bethlehem from bothering the friars.[51]

Regarding the use of local natural resources, besides the previously mentioned litigations over land ownership, conflicts also arose over the use of the convent's water tank. In the Palestinian countryside ovens, mills, and wells were normally used by all the inhabitants of a given area. Consequently, they also became places where people met to sell and buy products. Franciscan convents in Palestine, like their European counterparts, had their own facilities: ovens, water tanks, wine presses, and, in Jerusalem, a mill. But whereas medieval monasteries allowed (and often forced)[52] the local population to use their wells and ovens, in Bethlehem the Franciscans – at least before Catholicism spread in the village – showed a different attitude. This is suggested by a set of firmans reaffirming the friars' right to close the pipes of the water tank when they pleased. The documents also stated that the friars were not obliged to let the inhabitants of the village use the water tank and that the villagers had no rights upon it.[53]

The sources analyzed up to now testify to the extension and complexity of the friars' entanglement with the population of Bethlehem, as owners, buyers of goods and services, employers, users of local resources, and litigants. The role the Franciscans came to occupy in the production and sale of religious craftworks, alongside their engagement in agriculture and farming, also testifies to their adaptation to the village's economy, traditionally centered on agriculture and handicraft. Coherently, they would also take advantage of the growth of French commerce in the eastern Mediterranean, which would facilitate their trade in devotional objects with European buyers.[54] The data also highlight the fundamentally economic nature of the friars' entanglement in the local society. How did this picture change after the beginnings of the missionary activity?

3 Interactions and missions

When the Franciscans of Bethlehem embarked on missionary activity in the 1620s, they used their already established networks to spread the new faith. These patterns of interaction with the local society, as developed over the previous centuries, influenced their model of mission, which remained strictly centered on economic exchanges and linked to the presence of the convent and its productive activities. In this respect, the spread of Catholicism in the area aligns with some of the research findings on the diffusion of religion in rural settings. Taking into consideration different historical contexts, these findings have fostered a model of missionary activity strictly entangled with the economic and daily interactions that resulted from the very establishment of a monastery. Works on the subject have shown how monks facilitated the spread of the new faith by interacting with the surrounding area through the exchange of goods and services and through charitable and pastoral work among the local population.[55] This is the case, for example, with the role played by Benedictine monasteries in the spread of Christianity in rural Europe, during the sixth and the seventh centuries.[56] More recently, scholars have highlighted the role of rural monasteries in the "colonization" of Southern Mount Lebanon by the Maronites in the seventeenth and eighteenth centuries and earlier in the Christianization of the Palestinian countryside during the Byzantine period.[57] Finally, with regard to the Ottoman Empire, according to Ömer Lütfı Barkan in the newly conquered Balkans, dervish monasteries greatly facilitated conversion to Islam, starting with their servants.[58]

Likewise, in Bethlehem Catholicism spread initially among the dragomans and those who worked for the friars and their families. The recurring presence of their names as witnesses and godparents in seventeenth-century parish books suggests the existence of an initial nucleus of Catholics whose members had tight ties to one another and with the convent.[59] From this first nucleus the new faith spread through familial bonds and social relationships until a snowball effect was achieved. As a result, in Bethlehem the number of converts grew as the century advanced, reaching the neighboring Bayt Jālā and Bayt Sāḥūr.[60] In this respect, the importance of the friars' participation in the local economy is confirmed by the growth of the network linked to the production of craftworks in Bethlehem. In fact, conversion to Catholicism, the growing production of devotional objects, and the development of a Catholic community are all different aspects of the same process. This continued throughout the course of the century, to the point that the very definition of the word "dragoman" would come to include not only interpreters of the convent (as in the Ottoman tradition) but also craftsmen, all of them Catholic.[61]

The beginning of the mission also introduced changes in the existing patterns of interaction: First, as a consequence of the previously mentioned development of a local Latin-rite community the friars began to engage in pastoral activity. Even though an Arabic parish priest was normally charged with the care of souls, sacramental books suggest that, especially in the first decades after the spread of Catholicism began, it was often the Guardian of Bethlehem who administered the sacraments to locals.[62] In addition, with the beginning of missionary activity the friars bestowed their charity upon local Catholics and new converts, clearly an incentive for conversion and a means to build a local Catholic identity.[63] In doing so, they took advantage of the large sums of money conveyed to Jerusalem as alms for the Holy Sites, despite the opposition of *Propaganda Fide*.[64]

In fact, the very use of charity, alongside the entanglement between the production of craftworks and the development of the Catholic community, suggests that the fundamentally economic nature of the interactions between the friars and the locals was not altered by the beginning of missionary activity. On the contrary, the economic power acquired by the friars – especially with respect to the production of devotional objects – in an economic environment that offered limited opportunities might even explain the higher rate of conversions in Bethlehem as compared with Jerusalem.[65] This hypothesis is also strengthened by the prominent position acquired by some of the dragomans' families in the social and economic life of the village. In fact, besides employment, the friars also gave these families the opportunity to train their children, to acquire linguistic and artisanal skills that would boost their prospects as traders, and therefore to strengthen their economic position.[66]

Is the role played by pre-existing relationships in the spread of Catholicism an exclusive characteristic of Bethlehem, or is it attested in Jerusalem as well? And more generally is it possible to identify differences in the way the friars participated in local networks in Jerusalem and in Bethlehem?

The nature of the Franciscans' settlement in both Jerusalem and Bethlehem led to close and complex relationships with the dragomans of the convents, the employment of locals for various services, and the purchases of daily commodities. As a result, in both places, a high percentage of reconciliations occurred among those who had close ties with the convent and their acquaintances. Nonetheless, due to the presence of a larger variety of people and social interactions, in Jerusalem the acceptance of Catholicism was favored by a wider range of circumstances, such as recent migrations to the city.[67] More generally, in the Holy City the friars took advantage of the greater variety of economic and social networks. For example, their role as financial actors was more developed than in Bethlehem: They acted as moneylenders, mostly to the other churches, and also became debtors of Jews and Muslims, sometimes paying high interest rates.[68]

These data suggest that the different characteristics of villages and cities shaped the friars' participation in local life. Such a hypothesis is further strengthened by looking at the friars' interactions with the Ottoman authorities in Jerusalem. Generally speaking, although cities and villages could share similarities as to the number of inhabitants, occupational structure, and even the presence of markets, scholars agree that a distinctive characteristic of cities was the presence of certain administrative institutions.[69] This is particularly true when we consider a city such as Jerusalem, which was a district capital. Here the presence of Ottoman officials and the position that the city occupied in the empire's administration system determined the groups with whom the Franciscans interacted.

4 Friars and local authorities

According to the Ottoman administrative division, the Jerusalem district was part of the province of Damascus. It was controlled by a *sanjaq-bey*, who was the chief military and civil authority. In addition, different officials guaranteed the functioning of the administration and a permanent military presence at the district level.

Within the districts, villages were fiscal and administrative units whose borders were recorded in official documents.[70] Villagers interacted with Ottoman officials mostly for the purpose of tax collection. Occasionally they also turned to the Ottoman court, mainly for matters of taxation, to record loans and sales, and sometimes to resolve litigations. Accordingly, in Bethlehem, Franciscan interactions with the local authorities were mostly centered on the payment of taxes. In this regard, the poll tax – imposed on all non-Muslim male subjects of the sultan – did not apply to the Franciscans, as they were "foreigners."[71] Nonetheless, account books mention the taxes paid by the friars to the *subaşi* of Bethlehem (an Ottoman official assigned one or more villages where he collected taxes and performed police functions) on the occasions of Ramadan, Christmas, and the grape harvest.[72] The last of these is not surprising; since in Ottoman Palestine taxes were levied in kind, the harvest was usually supervised by officials and tax recipients, in order to prevent fraud. In some of the friars' documents the tax collector is called *cafariero* or *cafarieri* (plural). The term (derived from *cafarro*, or poll tax) may have designated the *subaşi*, but in some cases it seems rather to indicate the heads of the villages (*shuyūkh al-qarya*), who were designated members of the village community and acted as intermediaries between the community and the Ottoman authorities in matters of taxation.

Leaving aside the tax payments, the Franciscans of Jerusalem were those who dealt the most with Ottoman authorities, even for matters regarding other convents, including the one in Bethlehem. This is consistent with the position of the St. Savior convent as the administrative center of the Custody and with the presence in Jerusalem of numerous high-ranking officials and Ottoman institutions. Besides the governor, the city hosted a unit of janissaries (infantry troops), the previously mentioned *subaşi*, and other officials bearing more specialized functions, such as the *muḥtasib*, a market inspector. Jerusalem also had a district court with its personnel. The Franciscans frequently resorted to the Ottoman judge for matters related to the convents of both Jerusalem and Bethlehem. Represented by a dragoman,[73] the friars in the court recorded purchases of land and settled litigations with locals,[74] for instance, the previously mentioned court ruling regarding the use of the water tank in Bethlehem.[75] When a Muslim wanted to move to a property next to the convent of St. Savior, as another example, the friars, unwilling to have a Muslim neighbour, brought the case before the court and the judge ruled in their favor.[76] In addition, the judge's rulings were requested by the friars in order to avoid future contestations on their property rights and to avoid fraud and bribes. This is the case, for example, with the permission to make wine and oil or with the ruling stating the friars could not be charged higher than the market price for wheat.[77] In the same way, to avoid future problems, the friars in Jerusalem also requested the presence of officials during the purchase of grapes.[78]

Further details on the friars' interactions with the local authorities are furnished by some entries of the account books, suggesting that they sold textiles to Ottoman officials.[79] The same source also reveals that all the Franciscan convents and hostels, including Bethlehem, sent garments to district officials on specific occasions, such as the arrival of a new governor. This was part of a wider policy pursued by the friars and aimed at establishing clientelist relationships with local Ottoman authorities. Such a policy is amply attested by sources and was much more developed in the city because of the presence of high-ranking officials. Father Pietro Verniero di Montepeloso mentions, among various other pieces of advice to a newly arrived guardian, a list of gifts that the friars customarily gave to Ottoman authorities on Muslim festivities and on other occasions. For example, friars would give a garment to the newly appointed qadi upon his arrival, and, when he left the city, one was given to the remaining vice-qadi. Similarly, garments were given to a new *subaşi* and, naturally, to the *sanjaq-bey*.[80] The presence of such a list of "gifts" seems aimed at establishing and reinforcing customary norms while preventing fraud and conflicts with the Ottoman authorities. Such a practice is also corroborated by the lists of incomes and expenses presented by the Franciscans to *Propaganda Fide* in the 1650s. It is not easy to say to what extent the friars' "gifts" were voluntarily given. Among the yearly expenses of the St. Saviour convent, the friars mention commodities that were given to the "Turks" as taxes or "per usanza, per cortesia, o per forza." Among them, records mention sugar, candles, wax, and various kinds of textiles such as silk, all of them from Europe. Similar evidence is yielded from the records of the Commissariats of the Custody of the Holy Land, established in all the Franciscan provinces. Commissariats were institutions charged with the collection of money and goods for the maintenance of the Custody, sometimes upon the request of the Guardian himself. Among the other necessities of the convent, the lists of requests mention objects to be given as "a gift to the Pasha" and to other local authorities: textiles, garments, mirrors, and snuff boxes.[81]

In addition to the gifts, the *sanjaq-bey* and its entourage were also occasionally invited for dinner at the St. Saviour convent. One of the previously mentioned pieces of advice warns newly elected guardians to respect the Muslim method of slaughtering when inviting Ottoman authorities for dinner.[82] Furthermore, among the objects requested for the Commissariats, the friars also list plates "for when the Pasha has dinner in the convent."[83]

The results of the friars' efforts varied over time and were influenced by the personality of the officials. This information, however, further testifies to the friars' adaptation to the local context. Furthermore, some clues suggest that over the centuries they succeeded in establishing fruitful relationships with the local authorities, to the point that newly elected guardians were warned not to carry over to Istanbul the frequent conflicts with the Greek Orthodox Christians because the latter had a better power base in the capital. In Jerusalem, by contrast, the friars were more likely to be successful thanks to their bribes and gifts.[84]

5 Concluding remarks: Going local?

The reconstruction of the friars' entanglements with local Bethlehem society shows differences and similarities with other Catholic missions in Asia. Although, in contrast to other missionaries, Franciscans could count on the arrival of alms from the other provinces, they were also active local economic actors. As Jesuits in Asia, they adapted to the economic context, participating in the main traditional sectors of the local economy: agriculture and the production of devotional objects. In the Franciscans' documents, the friars' entanglements in local life is conveyed by numerous routine interactions in which the friars are buyers, employers, and even litigants. All these findings suggest the fundamentally economic nature of the friars' integration in Bethlehem. This would not be altered by the friars' engagements in the reconciliation of local Christians; rather, it helped to shape the missionary activity and the future relations with new converts.

The presence of the friars in both Jerusalem and Bethlehem allows us to consider how the two different settings influenced their participation in social and economic networks. In Jerusalem the friars engaged in more varied economic activities and interacted with different social groups. The administrative structure of Ottoman Palestine – and the political centrality of Jerusalem – strongly influenced the role the friars played in the already existing power relationships and in shaping new ones. Indeed, the presence in Jerusalem of the district's administrative and judicial authorities encouraged the friars to develop clientelist relationships within already existing power hierarchies. In Bethlehem, by contrast, the Franciscans' clientelist activities contributed to the very shaping of new social hierarchies, boosting the economic and social role of some families affiliated with the convent. This was made possible by the economic position acquired by the friars in a poorer economic context.

Overall, the case of the Franciscans in Palestine sheds new light on the meaning of the term "localized actors" for missionaries. My analysis shows that the friars' frequent interactions with locals and participation in economic networks did not necessarily mean their full integration in local societies. For example, the friars' use of the Arabic language remained extremely limited. Moreover, the request of decrees preventing locals from using the water tanks and the importance given to the demarcation of clear borders for their properties and to the construction of walls to protect their buildings all suggest the friars' desire to distance themselves from the context. This impression is further strengthened by the lists of objects that arrived from Europe. In contrast to missionaries of other orders, the Franciscans never adopted local habits with regard to clothing and food. Their garments and the food they consumed mostly arrived from Europe or were produced by the friars themselves.

Not only did the friars never go local; they also fostered European influence among the local Christians in various ways. They not only pushed for the converts' adoption of the Latin rite but also contributed to the spread of Italian-style and, more generally, European-style craftwork through their schools. In the centuries to follow, this process would be further consolidated by the growing of local powers and the increasing French dominance of Mediterranean trade, leading the Catholic community to acquire not only economic power but also unprecedented social prestige.

Notes

* This research has been funded by the European Union's Horizon 2020 Research and Innovation Programme, MSCA, Project: MIGMED 65711.

1 Heyberger, *Les chrétiens du Proche-Orient*, 350–377. On Catholic missions in the Middle East see Windler, *Missionare in Persien*; Frazee, *Catholics and Sultans;* Masters, *Christians and Jews*; Valensi, "Inter-Communal Relations and

Changes"; Heyberger, "Frontières confessionnelles"; Tramontana, *Passages of Faith*.

2 Heyberger, *Les chrétiens du Proche-Orient*, 370–377.

3 Roger, *La Terre Sainte* and Lemmens, *Acta S. Congregationis*, vol. 1, 374–377, both cited by Heyberger, *Les chrétiens du Proche-Orient*, 286. Specifically concerning the area of Jerusalem, however, the number of friars allowed to stay was limited by the decrees issued by the Ottoman authorities. In general, it ranged between 36 and 60, and it was an object of contention between the Orthodox Greeks and the Catholics, each party exerting pressure on the Ottoman authorities. See for example Jerusalem Court Record vol. 139, 122; vol. 146, 296–297, cited by Peri, *Christianity under Islam*, 36.

4 In 1680, out of 125 friars, 44 were lay, cf. Lemmens, *Acta S. Congregationis*, vol. 1, 374–377.

5 Eastern Catholic Churches are formed by Eastern Christians who have left their mother church to join the Catholic communion. They are in full communion with Rome but retain their own liturgy and organization.

6 Heyberger, *Les chrétiens du Proche-Orient*, 275.

7 Norris, "Dragomans, Tattooists, Artisans," 86–104.

8 The first available archival documents pertaining specifically to the Bethlehemite convent date back to the 1740s (ASCTS, CC, PG, Carteggio Conventi, Bethelehem 1). Therefore this work is mostly based on seventeenth-century account books of the St. Savior convent, which provide information on Bethlehem as well (ASCTS, CC, PG, Libri Mastri, vols. SN [1619–1620]; Entrate e uscite Monte Sion; SN [1620–1625]; Entrate e uscite del Monte Sion; 1, Conti del S. Salvatore [1642–1648]; 2 [1665–73]). Further information has been gathered from lists of expenses regularly sent by the Custos to *Propaganda Fide* (APF, SC, Terra Santa. Miscellanea, vol. 1; APF, SOCG, vol. 104); from chronicles and other narrative sources: Horn, *Ichonographiae*; Pietro Verniero di Montepiloso, *Croniche*; Francesco da Serino, *Croniche*.

9 Traditionally, in definitions of "rural" the most important dimensions are: not urban, low population density, extensive land use, primary economic activity and employment, community cohesion, and governance. However, in the last decades the classic dichotomy between "rural" and "urban" has been questioned by a growing number of works, such as Champion and Hugo, *New Forms of Urbanization*.

10 Ze'evi, *An Ottoman Century*, 100–104.

11 Peri, "The Christian Population of Jerusalem."

12 Singer, *Palestinian Peasants*, 80.

13 Swierenga, "The New Rural History."

14 See for example Pietro Verniero di Montepiloso, *Croniche*, vol. 3, 304.

15 APF, SOCG, vol. 104, fol. 118v.

16 Kolovos, "Monasteries," 165–171; Vatin and Zachariadou, "Le monastère de Saint-Jean," 193.

17 Religious minorities living under Muslim rule enjoyed the status of *ahl al-dhimma*, protected people. They were granted protection, as long as they paid the poll tax and recognized the superiority of Islam. See Friedmann, "Dhimma."

18 Khalilieh, "Amān."

19 On the economy of the Discalced Carmelites in Persia see Windler, *Missionare in Persien*, 539–573.

20 ASCTS, CC, PG, Libri mastri, 1 (1642–1648), 1644 (pages unnumbered).

21 ASCTS, CC, PG, Libri mastri, 1 (1642–1648), 1647 (pages unnumbered); see also ASCTS, CC, PG, Libri mastri, SN (1620–1625), fol. 44v–46r.

22 ASCTS, CC, PG, Libri mastri, 2 (1665–1673), 1665 (21 June, 1 July), (pages unnumbered).

23 For example, ASCTS, CC, PG, Libri mastri, SN (1619–1620), fol. 58v. On the production of wine, see Horn, *Ichonographiae*, 204.
24 ASCTS, CC, PG, Libri mastri, 2 (1665–1673), 1665 (pages unnumbered); SN (1619–1620), fol. 59v.
25 October 1672 (ASCTS, CC, PG, Libri mastri, 2 [1665–1673] [pages unnumbered]).
26 ASCTS, CC, PG, Libri mastri, SN (1619–1620), fol. 80v, SN (1620–1625), fol. 49v.
27 ASCTS, CC, PG, Libri mastri, 1 (1642–1648) (pages unnumbered).
28 ASCTS, CC, PG, Libri mastri, SN (1619–1620), fol. 80v, 87v.
29 ASCTS, CC, PG, Libri mastri, SN (1619–1620), fol. 80v, SN (1620–1625), fol. 49v.
30 Norris, "Dragomans, Tatooists, Artisans."
31 ASCTS, CC, PG, Libri mastri, SN (1620–1625), fol. 48r.
32 ASCTS, CC, PG, Libri mastri, SN (1619–1620), fol. 58v.
33 ASCTS, CC, PG, Libri mastri, 1 (1642–1648), 1647 (pages unnumbered).
34 ASCTS, CC, PG, Libri mastri, SN (1620–1625), fol. 9r, 11v.
35 See Francesco da Serino, *Croniche*, vol. 11, 200, mentioned by Bagatti, "L'industria della madreperla," 135–140, here: 136.
36 Bagatti, "L'industria della madreperla," 135–140; Norris, "Exporting the Holy Land"; Girard and Tramontana, "La fabrication des objets de dévotion en Palestine."
37 Frantzman and Kark, "The Catholic Church in Palestine/Israel."
38 On the topic see Todeschini, *Il prezzo della salvezza*.
39 This arrangement was also confirmed in 1632 by Urbano VIII (*Ut dilecti filii*).
40 Pietro Verniero di Montepiloso, *Croniche*, vol. 4, 86–87. See also Castellani, *Catalogo dei Firmani*, concerning the donation of a field in Ayn Karim.
41 The Franciscan property rights over these places are attested by firmans (decrees issued by the sultan). Castellani, *Catalogo dei Firmani*, nos. 100, 136, 181, 205, 381, 499. See also Pietro Verniero di Montepiloso, *Croniche*, vol. 4, 86–87.
42 See Pietro Verniero di Montepiloso, *Croniche*, vol. 4, 118. It mentions the purchase of an orchard near Bethlehem with olives and figs in 1593, and the purchase of a land cultivated with figs in Bethlehem in 1597 and 1612.
43 Mundy and Smith, *Governing Property*; Joseph, *Islamic Law on Peasant Usufruct*. On Palestine, see Ze'evi, *An Ottoman Century*, 113–139.
44 Pietro Verniero di Montepiloso, *Croniche*, vol. 4, 87–88.
45 Horn, *Ichonographiae*, 204.
46 ASCTS, CC, PG, Libri mastri, 2 (1665–1673), October 1672 (pages unnumbered). See also ASCTS, CC, PG, Libri mastri, 1 (1642–1648), July 1648 (pages unnumbered).
47 See, for example, Pietro Verniero di Montepiloso, *Croniche*, vol. 4, 87, 118; see also Castellani, *Catalogo dei Firmani*, nos. 58, 289.
48 Tramontana, "La corte islamica," 791–806.
49 Tramontana, *Passages of Faith*, 96–100.
50 Norris, "Dragomans, Tatooists, Artisans."
51 Castellani, *Catalogo dei Firmani*, no. 88 (1532); no. 213 (1595).
52 Ditchburn and Mackay, *Atlas of Medieval Europe*, 138.
53 Castellani, *Catalogo dei Firmani*, nos. 177–178 (1577). See also Pietro Verniero di Montepiloso, *Croniche*, vol. 3, 304, 1636.
54 On this trade, see Norris, "Exporting the Holy Land."
55 Park, *Sacred Worlds*, 139–141, 143.
56 Beatrice, "La christianisation des campagnes," 26.
57 Mohasseb Saliba, *Les monastères doubles du Liban*; Bar, "Rural Monasticism"; Perrone, "Monasticism as a Factor of Religious Interaction," 67–98.
58 Barkan, "Les fondations pieuses."
59 ASCTS, Fondo Parrocchie, Betlemme, *Register Coniugatorum et defunctorum ab anno 1669*, passim. See Tramontana, *Passages of Faith*, 93–95.
60 Tramontana, *Passages of Faith*, 86–110.

61 Norris, "Dragomans, Tatooists, Artisans."
62 Kümin and Tramontana, "Catholicism Decentralized."
63 Tramontana, *Passages of Faith*, 101–103.
64 Pietro Verniero di Montepiloso, *Croniche*, vol. 3, 71–73; APF, SOCG, vol. 135, fol. 237.
65 APF, SOCG, vol. 135, fol. 237.
66 See Norris, "Dragomans, Tatooists, Artisans."
67 Tramontana, *Passages of Faith*, 121–125.
68 Conti di Terra Santa. Entrate e uscite (1652–1656) (APF, SC, Terra Santa. Miscellanea, vol. 1 [pages unnumbered]). Although this is not mentioned by the sources, the Bethlehem friars may also have borrowed and lent money. On the subject, see Arce, *Documentos y textos*, 257; Arce, *Miscelánea de Tierra Santa*, vol. 2, 273–310.
69 For example Baer, "Village and City," 521–546; Lapidus, *Muslim Cities*, 49–79; Kark and Oren-Nordheim, *Jerusalem and its Environs*, 23.
70 Singer, "Transcrire les frontières de village," 133–143; Inalcik, *The Middle East and the Balkans*, 152.
71 In general, monks, priests, and religious men were exempted from the payment of the poll tax until 1691.
72 ASCTS, CC, PG, Libri mastri, SN (1620–1625), fol. 97v; Libri mastri, 1 (1642–1648), 1642 (pages unnumbered).
73 Castellani, *Catalogo dei Firmani*, no. 214 (1596). The decree rules that when representing the friars before the court, the interpreters must not be subjected to any threat or menace.
74 Tramontana, "La corte islamica," 802.
75 ASCTS, CC, PG, Libri mastri, 2 (1665–1673), October 1672 (pages unnumbered).
76 Pietro Verniero di Montepiloso, *Croniche*, vol. 1, 120.
77 Pietro Verniero di Montepiloso, *Croniche*, vol. 4, 136, 145.
78 Pietro Verniero di Montepiloso, *Croniche*, vol. 4, 33.
79 ASCTS, CC, PG, Libri mastri, SN (1620–1625), fol. 9r.
80 Pietro Verniero di Montepiloso, *Croniche*, vol. 4, 31–32.
81 Conti di Terra Santa. Entrate e uscite (1652–1656) (APF, SC, Terra Santa. Miscellanea, vol. 1 [pages unnumbered]).
82 Pietro Verniero di Montepiloso, *Croniche*, vol. 4, 34.
83 Conti di Terra Santa. Entrate e uscite (1652–1656) (APF, SC, Terra Santa. Miscellanea, vol. 1 [pages unnumbered]).
84 Pietro Verniero di Montepiloso, *Croniche*, vol. 4, 33–34.

9 Rural Tibet in the early modern missions

Trent Pomplun

The Jesuit missionary Ippolito Desideri (1684–1733) is now commonly celebrated for his appreciation of Tibetan philosophy, religion, and art.[1] His first impressions of Tibetans were not so favorable. When he met Tibetans in 1715, he reported to the general of the Society of Jesus that, although Tibetans were meek, docile, and averse to doing harm to others, they were "still rough and uncivilized, having neither science, nor art, nor communication with other nations apart from some porters from Kashmir, who come to take wool."[2] This passage, which stands in stark contrast to Desideri's other depictions of Tibetans, is one of the very few examples in which he acknowledges rural Tibetans. Compare the following passage from the *Historical Notices of the Kingdoms of Tibet*:

> Tibetans are a people of lively spirit and subtle intelligence, with a cheerful and active genius, and so are neither idle nor lazy, but for the most part almost always occupied. Almost everyone commonly knows most of the arts necessary for humane living, like spinning, weaving, sawing, rope-making, hide-tanning, shoe-repair, woodworking, housebuilding, papermaking, the making of gunpowder, cooking, farming, animal husbandry, butter-making – in sum, they know how to do everything or almost everything that might be needed for the maintenance or running of a household.[3]

Most scholars – myself included – explain the Jesuit's apparent change of heart as a result of his increased familiarity with Tibetan culture.[4] Others have pointed to such passages as evidence of a long Western fascination with Tibet.[5] Michael Sweet and Leonard Zwilling argue that these descriptions represent a deliberate attempt to present Tibet as a mission in which the church might worthily invest monies and manpower.[6] In what follows, I shall build upon Sweet and Zwilling's insights by highlighting the role that rural Tibetans played in the larger theological and anthropological categories that governed mission strategy. Missionaries' descriptions of Tibet and Tibetans were not contradictory in the least; upon closer examination, they can be seen as self-conscious attempts to situate Tibetans within the larger theological categories that governed mission strategy. As I hope to show, Tibetan nomads and herders loomed large in missionaries' imaginations – even as they were marginalized in their accounts – because the "uncivilized" peoples of any mission – traditional peoples with no science, culture, or art – posed specific theoretical and practical problems for mission strategy. In fact, missionaries suppressed much of what they knew about rural Tibet and Tibetans in order to present a coherent missionary strategy founded on the understanding of Tibet as a civilized, courtly, and economically modern nation. Their descriptions of the rural peoples of the Tibetan plateau and their social spaces were less "anthropological" than we have previously supposed; indeed, they were deliberate attempts to determine, even showcase, the utility of Tibet and Tibetans in the larger geo-political struggles of the early modern era.

1 European missionaries and the exploration of Tibet

Jesuits founded the first mission in Tibet at Tsaparang in 1624. They entered Bhutan in 1627 and traveled through Sikkim to Shigatse the following year. Capuchins established a mission to Lhasa in 1707, where Desideri arrived in 1716. Concerned chiefly with scholastic controversy and catechesis, most of the missionaries involved in these missions eschewed the accommodation of Christianity to local customs and largely sought the conversion of monarchs, chieftains, and clerical elites who could impose Christianity upon their subjects. The social spaces privileged for such interactions – the courts, universities, and monasteries – were largely urban and male. Only in rare instances did the missions expand to other social spaces. The Franciscan Domenico da Fano pursued a medical ministry that took him into the Lhasa marketplace, and the conversations of António de Andrade with the king and queen of Guge allow us a glimpse of a domestic Tibetan mission. Neither of these ministries, however, involved rural Tibetans. Da Fano's was largely an urban affair, and Andrade's was confined to the royal court.[7] If one seeks to discern patterns of localization in Tibetan Catholic churches, one finds far greater success in the nineteenth- and twentieth-century missions of the Society's great rival, the Société des Missions Étrangères, whose missionaries founded churches among Tibetan, Naxi, Nu, and Lisu minorities in Kham, Sichuan, and Yunnan that still exist today.

These missionaries traveled widely in the Tibetan countryside, and they came to possess a very good working geography. Andrade, who had traveled from Garhwal through Badrinath to Tsaparang, reported that Tibet was bordered on the north by Mongolia and on the east by China. He reported that Tibet included the kingdoms of Guge, Ladakh, Maryul, Rudok, Ü-Tsang, and "two other kingdoms in the east."[8] Desideri, who took a different route through Lahore and Srinigar to Leh, the capital of Ladakh, also remarked on the importance of Mongolia to the north, but distinguished "Upper Independent Tartary" and "Lower Tartary," that is, the Dzungar Khanate from the various Mongol tribes allied with Tibetans and/or Manchu China. After fleeing Lhasa in 1717 because of the Dzungar invasion, Desideri provided a detailed account of the monasteries of Dakpo and indications of the surrounding regions of Yarlung, É, Kham, and Kongpo to the east, Sikkim to the southeast, and Mönyul and Lho to the south.[9] The Franciscan Felice da Montecchio numbered more than 20 provinces in Tibet, naming Ladakh, Ngari, Ü, Tsang, Kyirong, Nyalam, Takpo, Kongpo, Pari, and Dartsedo.[10] The most complete account of Tibetan geography is found in Orazio della Penna's *Breve notizia del regno del Thibet*, which outlines the various states, provinces, cities, and geographical features between Kashgar and the Irtysh River, including Amdo.[11] Perhaps the most striking feature of Orazio's account, having been written after the establishment of the Manchu Protectorate in 1720, is its detailed enumeration of soldiers stationed in each state and region of Tibet.

Although the descriptions of Tibet and Tibetans in the accounts of early modern missionaries vary in tone and judgment, the subjects they took up were surprisingly uniform. Missionaries described the land and detail its commodities, particularly its produce, livestock, plants, minerals, and metals. They remarked upon the nature and character of Tibetans, their arts, crafts, sciences, government, occupations, and customs. In almost all cases, they noted the Tibetans' capacities for piety, observance, and religion.[12] When missionaries provided this information, they naturally used categories that had been long established in the colonial enterprise. In fact, their descriptions of Tibetans and their mission strategies were governed by same theological, philosophical, and anthropological categories that had been used by Las Casas and Sepúlveda in the famous debate at Valladolid in 1550–1551. The debates that informed their descriptions – whether non-Christians could be virtuous, whether they might be invincibly ignorant of the Gospel, whether they might be subject to enslavement by nature, and so forth – stretched across several genres of early modern literature.[13] All of the debates were tied irrevocably to early modern theories about the nature of individual peoples, their degree of civilization, and their capacity for warfare. After all, the colonization of rough and uncultured peoples required greater resources than the ideological conversion of a ruling elite. If European powers were concerned about the military expenditures necessary to conquer rustics, they were doubly worried about squandering them in rugged, unfamiliar territory that could support neither troops nor their mounts, especially against adversaries accustomed to such conditions. Missionaries thus noted the Tibetans' propensity to religious activity, their docility in the face of legitimate secular and ecclesiastical authorities, their willingness to punish criminals, and their readiness for war, even if these missionaries did not fully understand the intricacies of Central Asian politics themselves.

Above all, missionaries were struck by Tibet's unremitting bleakness. Astounded at its vast uninhabited – and often uninhabitable – spaces, they seemed surprised to find anyone at all, much less anyone with sciences, culture, or art. Andrade, for example, had been assured that Tibet was verdant and fertile. His shock is evident:

> Many people with experience in this country have assured us of these facts. However, the royal city where we are, which is also the most important in the region, has the most barren land that I have ever seen. It yields only some wheat in the portion that can be irrigated by the river. There are many herds of sheep, goats, and horses, but nothing else, so that not even a single tree is found for many leagues around, nor any grass in the fields, except where they can be watered by a spring or river. . . . In this region, there is no sugar or jaggery, nor fruit of any kind, no vegetables or legumes, no chickens or anything else. . . . The Kashmiri Muslims are wont to say that hell lies underneath this land, because of the great barrenness.[14]

Andrade's impression of Tibetans was more favorable:

> The people, for the most part, are very friendly, courageous, and given to warfare, in which they train continually. They are above all quite pious and well-disposed to matters of our Lord. . . . They seem a very gentle people, and even among the laypeople it is rare that one hears a harsh word.[15]

Other missionaries addressed the same subjects. Giovanni da Fano, writing from Chandernagore in 1712, mentions the barley, wheat, tea, butter, and meat found in Tibet.[16] Domenico da Fano's *Breve relazione* (1713) comments on the lack of shelter to be found on the Tibetan plateau:

> These mountains are for the greater part arid and incapable of being inhabited not only by men but also by the animals that normally dwell in forests and, being forced to pass through these mountains, one must bring food for three, four, or even six days, as well as a means to cover oneself, especially at night, for one finds neither houses nor huts along the way.[17]

His judgment of Tibetans was rather mixed:

> Tibetans are docile and easily familiar with others, especially if they hope to profit from them, being rather greedy, curious, and ungrateful unless they find themselves in need. Being craven and cowardly, they are not fierce, nor quick to object or tussle, much less to come to blows or take up arms. They are of normal stature and sufficiently robust health, lively, but not to excess. They are not especially personable or gentle in humor or appearance, but they are white. They do not apply themselves to the sciences.[18]

Desideri also emphasized the sterility of the land and its meager produce. He reports that no pack animals could make the 40-day journey from Srinigar to Leh. The land was so barren that they had to take all of their provisions, as absolutely nothing could be found, hunted, or bought on the journey:

> This country is wholly mountainous, fairly barren, and hardly inhabited. It produces barley in abundance, wheat in a small amount. There is no fruit except apricot. It does not have much commerce with other nations, except traffic in very delicate wool, gold dust (although not in great quantity), and a small amount of musk. During the last century, both the King of Independent Tartary and the famous Mughal emperor Aurangzeb attempted to conquer this kingdom. They succeeded in plundering and destroying it, but neither was able to subjugate it, since the roads are everywhere rocky and steep and entirely impracticable for foreign armies. This Tibet is wholly mountainous, arid, infertile, and horrid.[19]

Desideri and Freyre's journey from Leh to Lhasa was even more trying. The missionaries first traveled from Leh to Tashigang, where they hoped to join a trade caravan in order to take advantage of the protection it afforded but learned that the "sizeable" army of Tibetans and Mongols stationed nearby at Gartok was soon to be replaced with reinforcements. As a result, they decided to travel to Central Tibet with the military regiment instead. Desideri saw few signs of civilization during the remainder of his journey to Central Tibet. He noted a temple-cave at the foot of Mount Kailash where the semi-mythical saint Padmasambhava was thought to have meditated, pilgrims circumambulating the holy mountain, and a "crude and unadorned" monastery with a lama and a few monks.[20] He reported that the horses, mules, and yaks tended by the herdsmen who roamed Droshö belonged to the king of Tibet and the Dalai Lama, and he noted the presence of pilgrims at the lake near Rudok. The party encountered more herders in December, and Desideri remarked upon the great revenue gained by the king and the Dalai Lama from the region's gold and butter. "For three months," however, "from the time we set out from Tashigang, until we arrived at Saga, we did not meet with a single village or hamlet."[21]

As it so happens, Desideri's notes on the herders in Droshö are some of his only descriptions of rural Tibetans apart from the first impressions in his letter from Ladakh – a rather surprising lack in an account of a people so proud of its nomadic heritage.[22] Desideri arrived in Lhasa on 18 March 1716. Unlike Ngari, Central Tibet was dotted with castles, cities, and vast monastic complexes. These, of course, were the privileged social spaces in which Desideri learned Tibetan, read the Buddhist canon, and composed his Tibetan writings. Like Andrade, Desideri commented on the Tibetans' docility and gentleness, even as he remarked upon their capacity for war:

> Tibet being a peaceful kingdom, it is not their custom to maintain standing militias apart from a sufficient number of soldiers to guard and accompany the king. Another regiment of soldiers is always kept at Gartok and at Ngari Jungar from fear of an invasion of the Tartars of Dzungar-yul, that is, of Independent Tartary. . . . The people are not warlike but they rise to the occasion in times of need, because they are strong by nature and courageous, accustomed to hardships and trials, and because they are naturally docile and respectful and maintain order easily. Their arms are muskets, swords, lances, and bows. They also have some iron cannons that they transport on large wheeled carriages, large double muskets, and large culverins. But when they lack arms, it is most easy for them to defend themselves with just stones, taking their stand on top of the rugged mountains where they usually build their fortresses, which are made impregnable by their location.[23]

Orazio della Penna's *Breve relazione* describes the produce and livestock of Tibet in great detail, but it arguably provides the least favorable account of Tibetans among those of the missionaries. He judges them "inclined to revenge" (*inclinati alla vendetta*) and dedicated to lust and drunkenness, although he grants them some allowance as polyandry was acceptable under Tibetan law. He says,

> The Tibetans' bad inclinations and objectional customs notwithstanding, they still have some good qualities. They are rather good natured (although this is not equally so of the people of the state of Amdo, who are quite prickly) and show themselves to be docile and humane, submitting to reason, especially to things of the law, people in the world more than the religious, who become rather obstinate in defense of their sect.[24]

Before proceeding, let us note the remarkable consistency of these descriptions. Tibet is judged on its commodities, produce, livestock, and general fertility. Tibetans are evaluated in terms of their gentleness, docility, courageousness, lawfulness, religiosity, commerce, trade, military technology, and capacity for war. These characteristics stand in stark contrast to those found in the descriptions of the other peoples of the Tibetan plateau, whose lack of civilization is routinely noted. Among all the people described in Desideri's account, the Lhopa to the south were the least civilized:

> The Lhopa are a fierce woodland people. They live for the most part in forests and in huts and are always occupied in hunting all sorts of animals, which they eat raw or poorly roasted. At times they even feed on human flesh, killing men without the slightest difficulty if they find them ruddy and young.[25]

Desideri had no experience of southern tribes and was almost certainly aping Central Tibetan prejudices; for our purposes, we need only note the Lhopas' perceived savagery.[26] But he also judged Mongols to be uncivilized:

> Leaving the Lhasa countryside from the east, from the eastern part of Lhasa countryside by the road, adjoining the Ganden mountain and turning left toward the north, one finds a province whose customs are uncivilized, called Hor, and whose inhabitants are rustics and herders for the most part.[27]

Desideri reserved a special animus toward the Dzungars, whom he characterized – in contrast to both Tibetans and Mongols – as haughty, unfriendly, and disrespectful. It suffices for now to note that Desideri distinguished the rural peoples of the Tibetan plateau from their neighbors in its cultured and civilized regions. We shall take up the problem of rural Tibetans again in the third and final part of this chapter; before doing so, we need to address the political importance of the regions they inhabited.

2 The importance of Western Tibet

As the missionaries' accounts indicate, the civilized social spaces in which they interacted with rulers and ecclesiastic dignitaries were often separated by vast distances. Their accounts give us some hints of the strategic importance of these areas, but we should fill in a little of what is missing. First – as John Bray reminds us – missionaries did not "discover" Tibet in the way that later explorers "discovered" the poles; they sought passage with trade companies that had managed the logistics of Himalayan travel and followed trade routes that had existed for centuries.[28] In fact, almost every missionary who entered Tibet did so with the help of merchants who worked with well-established companies.[29] The Jesuit brother Bento de Goís, who passed through Agra, Lahore, Peshawar, Kabul, Yarkand, and the Tarim Basin before dying in Suzhou in 1607, traveled with a Greek merchant. Andrade traveled with a trade caravan from India and used a Kashmiri Muslim merchant as a translator. The first Franciscans to travel to Lhasa made use of an Armenian trade network that stretched from Western Europe to the Philippines.[30] Trading companies and caravans also served as banks and post offices. Desideri, whose well-known sympathies for Tibetan Buddhism did not extend to Islam, nevertheless instructed future missionaries to remain on good terms with Kashmiri merchants, who carried mail and managed the bills of exchange necessary for receiving money or other goods for the mission.

The political and economic health of the courts and monasteries in which Andrade and Desideri carried out their missions depended on the control of trade routes. Desideri passed through Ladakh just as the Dalai Lama's Ganden Phodrang government was losing its grip on the regions it had conquered in the late seventeenth century. The Ganden Phodrang had been engaged in a protracted war with Ladakh between 1679 and 1684.[31] The Central Tibetan invasion of Ladakh was led by the Mongol Prince Galdan Tsewang, the grandson of Gushri Khan, the Khoshuud Mongol chieftain who helped the Fifth Dalai Lama Ngawang Lopzang Gyatso and his regent Sönam Chompé conquer Central Tibet in the military campaigns of 1632–1642. For that reason, the conflict is known in Ladakhi sources as the "Mongol War," rather than the "Tibet-Ladakh-Mughal War," as it is to modern historians.[32]

Historians have largely treated the invasion of Ladakh by the Ganden Phodrang government as an inter-religious conflict between the Dalai Lama's monastic order, the Gelukpa, and their traditional political and spiritual rivals, the Drukpa Kagyü. In point of fact, both Andrade and Desideri's accounts give added weight to more recent arguments that emphasize the conflict's economic causes. Historically, Ladakh was the dominant power in the Ngari Korsum, literally, the "Threefold Dominion of Ngari," a traditional geographical designation that included – in addition to the kingdoms of Ladakh, Guge, and Puhrang – the areas of Rudok, Zangskar, Lahul, Spiti, Kinnaur, Jumla, Dolpo, and Mustang. In the decade before Andrade entered Tibet, the Ladakhi prince Sengge Namgyal captured Rudok and Puhrang, two mining towns whose gold allowed him to fund several new architectural projects, including a new palace and several Drukpa monasteries. After being elevated to the throne, he annexed Guge, Zangskar, Mustang, and Droshö. The Drukpa also managed two important temples in the region, Khochar and Pretapuri, several shrines and smaller hermitages, and the all-important pilgrimage route to the holy Mount Kailash mentioned by Desideri – all important sources of income.

This is not to say that the conflict in Ladakh did not have a religious dimension. In 1653, the Fifth Dalai Lama, with the imprimatur of the Shunzhi Emperor, declared all non-Geluk forms of Tibetan Buddhism "impure," and his armies began to spread the Geluk gospel by confiscating properties belonging to other religious orders. In the decades leading up to the events of 1679–1684, the Ganden Phodrang increasingly came to see its own existence as dependent on the suppression of the Drukpa communities that thrived on its southern and western frontiers. In 1654, authorities in Lhasa served notice to the new Ladakhi King Deldan Namgyal that the safety of the Drukpa in Ladakh would be directly proportionate to his financial support of the Geluk monasteries in his realm. The political situation was further compromised by the Ganden Phodrang government's failure to conquer Bhutan, which had repelled attacks from the Dalai Lama's government in 1644, 1648, 1656, and 1675.[33] The Dalai Lama's government attributed these humiliations to the occult power of Drukpa sorcerers whose magic had caused the death of Gushri Khan in 1655 and the death of the Dalai Lama's regent Sönam Chompé in 1658.[34] During the 1650s, Drukpas were forced to wear large woolen braids around their necks to identify themselves in public. By the 1660s, none could travel safely in Central Tibet.

Control of Western Tibet allowed the Ganden Phodrang government to maximize profits from its gold fields and monopolize the wool trade from Kashmir. It also allowed the Dalai Lama's government to replace the shrines and devotions of other religious orders with its own, thus taking advantage of a ready-made market of pilgrims and gathering income from tithes and religious donations. In fact, an army from the Geluk-controlled region of Guge had already tried to take control of the Mount Kailash pilgrimage site by force in 1628, killing several Drukpa hermits in the process. It is probably no coincidence that the various Tibetan rulers who invited or allowed missionaries into their realms during the seventeenth century often had uneasy relationships with the Geluk order or the Ganden Phodrang government. Tashi Drakpa, the "king" of Guge who welcomed Andrade in Tsaparang, was opposed by Geluk monks, not least among them his own brother, who sought the aid of Ladakh in order to depose the king. The Zhapdrung Ngawang Namgyel, who invited Estêvão Cacella and João Cabral to Bhutan in 1627, actively resisted Geluk expansion. The following year, Karma Tenkyong Wangpo received the same Jesuits at Shigatse in Central Tibet. Each of these figures ruled areas where the Kagyü order had great influence, and each found himself under increasing pressure from the Geluk order. It is difficult not to think that these rulers sought alliances that might assist them in resisting Geluk hegemony. Nor is it unlikely that they had heard that the Jesuits possessed astronomical and technological knowledge that could assist them in war. In fact, the missions of Ippolito Desideri and the Capuchins in Lhasa coincided almost exactly with the absence of Geluk control in the capital. We may presume that Lhapzang Khan was willing to consider anything, as the Geluks who resented his rule sought the aid of the Dzungars, who would eventually invade Tibet, sack Lhasa, and murder the Khan.

Although he probably did not realize it, Desideri's own perspective on these events is entirely pro-Geluk. In Desideri's account, the Ladakhis' chief geo-political foes are the Mughal Empire and the Dzungars. Senge Namgyal had not defended his kingdom from the Dzungars, however, but from the Khoshuud Mongol tribes closely related to the Dalai Lama's government. Desideri also seems to have been unaware that the Ganden Phodrang government later used Dzungar armies to attack Ladakh or that the Mughal Empire aided the Ladakhis against the Ganden Phodrang's armies. He writes, in other words, assuming Ladakh to be a tributary of the Ganden Phodrang government, which at that point it was. Ladakh had been forced to cede Guge, Puhrang, and Rudok to the Ganden Phodrang government in the peace treaty of 1684 – thus allowing the Dalai Lama to take control of the revenue generated by the gold fields in those regions – but was allowed to retain control over its shrines and pilgrimage sites. This was a bitter pill, as the Tibetan-Mongol armies had ransacked Drukpa monasteries and destroyed several of their shrines during the war. The monastery at Tashigang, for example, was forcibly converted into a Geluk institution. As

Desideri's own account notes, the Ganden Phodrang government also pursued an aggressive campaign to re-educate Ladakhi leaders in Central Tibet. Galdan Tsewang, the commander of the Tibetan armies, took Deldan Namgyal's second son and his attendants to Lhasa, where they took monastic vows in the Geluk order and later made representatives of the Ganden Phodrang government in Ladakh. As Desideri also indicates, military garrisons were stationed at the border, most notably at Tashigang, where he joined the mixed Tibetan-Mongol military caravan en route to Lhasa.

3 Conclusion

If the Ganden Phodrang government – to say nothing of the Dzungars, Ladakhis, and Mughal Empire – recognized the economic and strategic importance of the Western Tibetan plateau, it only stands to reason that Western powers would also. Europeans had long sought an overland route to Asia that would allow them to bypass Muslim control of the old trade routes. In this respect, detailed descriptions of the Himalayas were just as important in the seventeenth and eighteenth centuries as they would be in the nineteenth and twentieth. If European powers were to enter the region, they needed to know the very things about the land and its inhabitants that we find in the missionaries' accounts.

Recall again the descriptions of Andrade, Domenico da Fano, Desideri, and Orazio della Penna. Despite their quasi-anthropological tone, they are almost uniformly concerned with Tibetans' degree of civilization, their docility, and their capacity for warfare. If Desideri first judged Tibetans to be rough and uncivilized, he seems to have deliberately avoided doing so in the *Historical Notices*. He presents Tibet as a civilized – or, as rural Americans might say, "citified" – nation. He minimizes its rusticity at every turn. He neglects to mention, for example, that many of its "villages" or "hamlets" were not permanent settlements at all. Tashigang, greatly reduced by the conflicts of 1679–1684, consisted largely of a rotating military garrison. Gartok was actually two different encampment sites located 40 miles apart along the Indus River. Garyarsa, literally the "place of the summer camp," consisted of only a few permanent buildings at the foot of the Kailash Range – "three houses and twelve miserable hovels," according to the British explorer Cecil Rawling – but became a small, fully mobile town for three months of the year when the trade caravans passed through the area. Desideri, however, stayed at Gargunsa, the "place of the winter camp," which housed only a few dozen people. When given the chance, Desideri also displaces the lack of civilization to the regions surrounding Tibet – as we see in his descriptions of Dzungars, Mongols, and the Lhopa. Even when he acknowledges rural Tibetan herders, he must qualify this characterization to avoid giving the impression that they might not be able and willing subjects. He assures his readers, for example, that the livestock of the herders in Droshö belonged to the king and Dalai Lama, that is, that the herders acknowledged the proper jurisdiction of the Khoshuud chieftain Lhapzang Khan and the Ganden Phodrang government. On the only occasion in the *Historical Notices* where Desideri mentions that Central Tibetans were "rough and without any culture or religion" he refers – following Tibetans' own myths about their origins – only to Tibetans who lived before the arrival of Buddhism during the eighth century.[35]

The civilizing aspect of religion – and the Tibetans' great capacity for it – is a standard trope in these missionaries' descriptions. Missionaries routinely presented Tibetans as open, friendly, gentle, and docile. Above all, they presented Tibetans as possessing a propensity to piety, at least to the degree that it was possible for them as Buddhists. As Desideri noted, Tibetans were well versed in the principles of their beliefs and showed a tremendous reverence for religious authorities and objects; they had no problem memorizing long prayers, reciting them throughout the day, making long pilgrimages and frequent visits to temples, or giving alms to fellow human beings and their animals. "Their greatest virtue is their inclination to mercy," he says, and "their greatest enjoyment is reading religious and moral books."[36] As one sees from the course on controversial theology Desideri took under Domenico Briccialdi at the Collegio Romano, docility was the single most important trait for one to be genuinely religious.[37] The Tibetans' acquired virtues of fortitude and temperance, their love of justice, and above all their capacity for piety, observance, and religion, made them natural subjects of a Catholic monarch.

Whatever the intentions of the missionaries themselves, political powers in Europe were greatly interested in a warlike people that were docile and teachable but much less in one that was erratic or prone to rebellion according to then-current theories of civilization. Missionaries appear to have suppressed much of what they knew about rural Tibet and Tibetans in order to present a coherent missionary strategy founded on an understanding of Tibet as a civilized, courtly, and economically modern nation. In this respect at least, early modern fantasies about Tibet had less to do with an enchanted, nonviolent Shangri-la and more to do with Tibet as an able – and armed – geo-political ally.

Notes

1 Desideri's letters, accounts, and legal defenses can be found in the final three volumes of Petech, *I missionari italiani* [= MITN]. I shall follow scholarly conventions by citing Desideri's accounts and letters with the abbreviations established by Petech. All translations are my own unless otherwise noted. I sometimes opt for a slightly more literal and less fluid translation than Sweet and Zwilling's wonderful *Mission to Tibet*, usually to emphasize words with specific technical meanings in scholastic or philosophical literature.

2 DL 6 (MITN 5, 27–28). One finds an almost identical description in the letter Desideri wrote Ildebrando Grassi from Lhasa on 10 April 1716, which characterizes Tibetans as "doux & docile, mais inculte & grossier" (DL 7 [MITN 5, 37]). This letter was published without Desideri's knowledge in *Lettres édifiantes et curieuses* 15 (1722): 183–209.

3 DR 2.15 (MITN 6, 95–96).
4 Bargiacchi, "Ippolito Desideri's First Remarks."
5 Lopez, *Prisoners of Shangri-La*; Brauen, *Dreamworld Tibet*, 3–4, 116–18.
6 The great majority of the passages I discuss in this chapter are taken from books I and II of Desideri's *Notizie istoriche*. These passages are thus among the last states in what Sweet and Zwilling characterize as the "downward trajectory" in Desideri's revisions, with B_1 reflecting the Jesuit's hope of vindication in his legal battle, B_2 reflecting a more cautious – and calculating – attempt to present the Society's mission in the best light, and A evincing uncertainty and bitterness about his case, the mission, and the Society of Jesus itself. See Sweet and Zwilling, *Mission to Tibet*, 62–101.
7 Michael Sweet and Leonard Zwilling give us insight into Desideri's domestic affairs, but these did not involve any ministry beyond the bonuses he paid his help on holy days. Sweet, "Gleanings from the Account Book 1"; Zwilling, "Gleanings from the Account Book 2."
8 Sweet and Zwilling, *"More Than the Promised Land,"* 106–107. It is not clear exactly what Andrade meant by these two kingdoms. One is almost certainly Kham, but the other might be Kongpo, Amdo, Sikkim, or a more specific region like Dakpo, Yarlung, or É.
9 DR 2.7 (MITN 6, 31–32); DR 2.8 (MITN 6, 35–37); DR 2.9 (MITN 6, 38).
10 CR 2 (MITN 3, 39–40).
11 CR 3 (MITN 3, 47–55).
12 Most early modern theologians – even those who were not Thomist – shared the conception of these virtues found in Thomas Aquinas, *Summa theologiae*, IIa, IIae, q. 81. For an overview, see Strumia, *Che cos'è una religione*.
13 The literature on these topics is vast. Its touchstones are scholastic: Vitoria, *Relectio de Indis*, pars 1, 2, nn. 1–19; Vega, *De iustificatione doctrina universa*; VI, c. 16–20; Soto, *De natura et gratia* II, c. 11–12; Suárez, *De Fide*, disp. 12 and *De gratia* IV, cap. 25; Martínez de Ripalda, *De ente supernaturali* book I, tom. 1, disp. 20; and Lugo, *De Fide*, disp. 12. Important secondary works include Urdañoz, "La necesidad de la fe explícita"; Cardia, *La posizione del de Lugo*; Lombardi, *La salvezza di chi non ha fede*; Cogoni, *La dottrina di Francesco Suarez*; Jericó Bermejo, "Domingo Báñez"; Méndez Fernández, *El problema de la salvación de "los infieles"*; and Morali, "Gratia et infidelitas."
14 Sweet and Zwilling, *"More Than the Promised Land,"* 91–92.
15 Sweet and Zwilling, *"More Than the Promised Land,"* 92–93.
16 CL 19 (MITN 1, 50).
17 CR 1 (MITN 3, 4).
18 CR 1 (MITN 3, 8).
19 DR 1.8 (MITN 5, 165). Desideri also noted that Ladakh was dependent on Khotan and Yarkand for cloth and horses and dependent on Central Tibet for tea, tobacco, silk, and other Chinese goods. Desideri repeated much of this in a separate chapter on Tibet's climate and fertility. See DR 2.2 (MITN 6, 5–9), where he notes that rice, pears, apples, and some grapes can be found in Southern Tibet, but otherwise laments the Tibetans' preference for turnips, radishes, garlic, and onions over other vegetables. He also notes the salt mines of Southern Tibet and its many "extraordinary" herbs. He devotes a separate chapter to livestock. See DR 2.3 (MITN 6, 10–15).
20 DR 1.9 (MITN 5, 179).
21 DR 1.10 (MITN 5, 176).
22 On Tibetan nomads and their role in the Tibetans' own imagination, see Kapstein, *The Tibetans*, 11–18.
23 DR 2.13 (MITN 6, 79–80). Desideri altered this passage significantly as he edited his account. For example, in Ms. F and Ms. B_1, he noted that Tibet was subject

neither to revolutions or wars from surrounding nations on account of the many fortresses that could be found in "every" province. He also noted that Tibetans continued to practice archery and other exercises to be sufficiently ready for war should the occasion arise.

24 CR 3 (MITN 3, 59). Tibetans, however, are said to fear justice. In fact, Orazio della Penna devotes an entire chapter of his account to the administration of justice in Tibet: CR 3 (MITN 3, 65–70).

25 DR 2.8 (MITN 6, 36).

26 On Tibetan perceptions of the Lhopa, see Huber, "Pushing South."

27 DR 2.7 (MITN 6, 30).

28 Bray, "Christian Missionary Enterprise and Tibetan Trade."

29 We owe the first modern description of Tibetan-speaking regions not to a missionary, but to the merchant Diogo de Almeida, who stayed in Ladakh for two years around 1601–1602 before describing it to authorities in Goa. Well over a century before Desideri traveled through the same region, Almeida described the Zoji pass, the fortress at Basgo, and the gold found in Western Tibet. Hedin, "Early European Knowledge."

30 On Armenians in Tibet, see Richardson, "Armenians and Indians in Tibet"; Aslanian, *From the Indian Ocean*. The Capuchins and Armenian traders had a working relationship dating back to 1628, when the Franciscans founded a mission in Isfahan, where the Armenians had an office. Franciscans handled mail for the merchants at their mission stations in Basra and Aleppo.

31 Ahmad, "New Light on the Tibet-Ladakh-Mughal War"; Petech, *The Kingdom of Ladakh*, 70–77; Petech, "The Tibetan-Ladakhi-Moghul War (1679–1683)."

32 Modern historians have depended almost entirely on Central Tibetan sources for their description of this conflict. Compare, however, Vitali, *The Dge lugs pa in Gu ge and the Western Himalaya*; Jinpa, "Why Did Tibet and Ladakh Clash in the 17th Century?"

33 Ardussi, "The Rapprochement between Bhutan and Tibet"; Schweiger, "The Long Arm of the Fifth Dalai Lama"; Ardussi, "Sikkim and Bhutan."

34 As Bryan Cuevas has recently demonstrated, the Geluk order had its own sorcerers trained in the esoteric techniques of war magic, not least among them the fearsome rite of the "Great Iron Castle." See Cuevas, "Sorcerer of the Iron Castle," 11–13.

35 DR 2.1 (MITN 6, 4).

36 DR 2.16 (MITN 6, 101).

37 The first question of Briccialdi's lectures on controversial theology *de vera religione*, which Desideri attended in 1710–1711, concerns the docility required for true religion – the very quality Desideri repeatedly noted in Tibetans. See Archivio Storico della Pontificia Università Gregoriana, Curia, F.C. 307A, cc. 2r–143r, here 3v–13v.

Part IV

Missionaries and households

10 Holy households

Jesuits, women, and domestic Catholicism in China

Nadine Amsler

The Jesuits' mission to early modern China is one of the best-known examples of what is referred to in missionary sources as well as in historiography as "accommodation."[1] Its well-known promoter was Matteo Ricci who, in 1595, started to wear the dress of China's Confucian elite, the literati, and to present himself to the Chinese as a "Western scholar" (*xiru* 西儒).[2] In the case of the Jesuits' China mission as elsewhere, accommodation should not be mistaken for a modern "willingness to enter into a dialogue with other cultures" but must be understood as a concession that the missionaries made in order to reach their higher goal of winning souls.[3] But even so, this genuinely early modern approach to evangelization is worth examination because it deeply affected the Jesuits' mission with regard to their social networks in China, their understanding of Chinese culture, and the ways in which they presented the Christian faith to the Chinese.[4] Furthermore, it also affected the gendered spatial organization of Chinese Catholicism, an aspect that will be analyzed in this contribution.[5]

In contrast to analyses of localization, which usually give prominence to the spatial aspects of these processes, studies of the Jesuits' accommodation in China have so far not devoted much consideration to its spatial implications.[6] Because accommodation was understood as an effort to assimilate into a transregional and thus geographically scattered social elite rather than a specific local setting, it did not seem to offer much to researchers interested in concrete social spaces.[7] This chapter argues that a focus on gender arrangements brings social space back into the picture, showing that gendered spaces are crucial for understanding the Catholic communities administered by the Jesuits in seventeenth-century China.

In China's Confucian tradition, gender arrangements were thought of in spatial terms. The ancient Confucian ideal, according to which "men and women should be separated" (*nan nü you bie* 男女有別) was closely connected with a spatial binary, the inner (*nei* 內) versus the outer (*wai* 外).[8] The eleventh-century philosopher Sima Guang 司馬光 thus stated that women should stay in the inner sphere, whereas the outer sphere was reserved for men: "In housing, there should be a strict demarcation between the inner and outer parts with a door separating them. . . . The men are in charge of all affairs on the outside; the women manage the inside affairs."[9] Sima Guang's ideal view of gender separation was also important for Chinese ideas of gender propriety in early modern China.[10] Different than European homes, whose interior was often intricately connected with the street life, Chinese homes typically consisted of closed architectural structures built around one or several courtyards so that the inner realm was clearly separated from the outer one.[11] According to Confucian ideals, the domestic altar was the proper place for women's worship. In contrast, Buddhist temples were the despised "other," and Confucian moralists looked with scorn on women's visits to such temples.[12]

In seventeenth-century European Catholicism, space played a much different role than in contemporary Chinese Confucian tradition. Although Catholic devotees were acquainted with gender separated spaces in churches, it was normal for them that churches were the primary spaces for religious worship for women and men alike.[13] That early modern Catholicism was a genuinely public religion with the church as its primary focal point can also be seen from the fact that the post-Tridentine Church increasingly perceived of masses read in private homes as a problem.[14]

Due to these differences, a reconciliation of Catholic worship and Confucian gender arrangements was not easily achieved and required that the organization of Chinese Catholic communities undergo a process of localization. This process of localization and its consequences for the spatial arrangements of Catholic women's worship are the focus of this chapter. However, before turning to this I will first discuss the mutual perceptions of European and Chinese gender arrangements in order to shed some more light on the meaning of cultural difference in the case of Sino-Western comparisons of gender norms and practices.

1 Comparisons between Chinese and European gender arrangements by Jesuits and other early modern observers

The general outline of differences between European Catholic and Chinese Confucian gender arrangements given in the introduction obscures a methodological problem of studying the role of gender arrangements within the history of Sino-Western cultural contact: the difficulty of making comparisons between Chinese and European gender practices. Due to gender practices' great diversity both in early modern China and in contemporary Europe, the attempt to compare them necessarily carries the risk of undue homogenization and generalization.[15] In order to complicate the picture given earlier, this section therefore aims at shedding light on how seventeenth-century people drew comparisons between Chinese and European gender arrangements. This will not only help us understand how *they* made sense of the differences and similarities of gender arrangements in Chinese and European localities, and which conclusions *they* drew from their exercise of cross-cultural comparison. It will also help us better grasp the Jesuits' perspective on Chinese women and gender relations as a starting point for the process of localization described later in this chapter.

Luckily, there is an eighteenth-century source that documents a Chinese traveler's view on contemporary French gender arrangements.[16] This is the *Récit fidèle*, a manuscript written by the French Jesuit François Foucquet to justify himself after his failure to collaborate with his Chinese aid, Jean Hu. The *Récit fidèle* is an impressive testimony on how eighteenth-century France's mixed-sex sociability could be a disturbing experience for a Chinese observer. Jean Hu, who is described as a man of humble social background in his forties, lived in France from 1722 to 1725, where he should have been helping Foucquet with the translation of Chinese texts. However, Hu found it extremely difficult to adapt to the new circumstances in France and was especially irritated by the omnipresence of women in Paris's public life. Soon he started to refuse go to church because he thought that there were too many women attending mass. The situation escalated when, one day, Hu went to St. Paul's Church with a banner on which he had written the Chinese sentence *nan nü fen bie* 男女分別 ("men's and women's roles should be separated"). In front of the church Hu started to wave his banner, hit a drum, and orate in Chinese to the curious crowd that soon started to flock around him.[17] Hu clearly thought the gender arrangements of France differed considerably from those back home. For him, the Confucian ideal of the separation of the sexes was seriously neglected in the social life of the French capital.

Not all Chinese visitors of early modern France perceived of the French gender arrangements as a problem. Arcade Huang (Huang Jialüe 黄嘉略), for instance, seemed to adapt very well to the new social environment. Huang traveled to Europe with a missionary of the Missions Étrangères de Paris and worked as a translator in the royal library during the first two decennia of the eighteenth century. When living in Paris, Huang abandoned his plans to become a Catholic priest, married a Parisian woman, and had a child with her. But even Huang seemed to feel obliged to conform to the norm of the separation of the sexes to a greater extent than most ordinary Parisians. From the entries in his personal journal, written in French and Chinese, we know that he never went to mass at the same times and places as his wife. He thus adopted the practice of gender separation that was common in Christian communities of rural China.[18]

The Chinese Christian travelers' views on European gender arrangements are an important complement to our picture of early modern Sino-Western comparisons of gender arrangements. For the overwhelming majority of early modern comparisons were made by Jesuit missionaries, who were the best-established missionary order in early modern China and who published a large number of accounts on the Middle Kingdom written for a European audience.[19] Most Jesuit accounts of China describe Chinese women in a curiously uniform way, stressing their reclusiveness and modesty. The Flemish Jesuit Philippe Couplet's description serves as an example.

In his *Histoire d'une Dame Chrétienne de la Chine*, published in Paris in 1688, he wrote that

> Chinese girls and women have so little contact with the world that you see them very rarely. They live shut away in apartments which are so retired that there is no greater solitude than the one in which they pass the most part of their life.[20]

With this statement, Couplet perpetuated a view held by the overwhelming majority of Jesuit missionary authors of published accounts.[21] These authors also unanimously praised Chinese women's modesty, especially their modesty of dress, which was, according to the Spanish Jesuit Alvaro Semedo, "closed up to the neck."[22] What Couplet and Semedo (and many other Jesuit authors) had in common was that they did not make distinctions between different geographical regions, social classes, or ethnic groups but focused exclusively on women of the literati class, the class into which they aimed to assimilate.[23] Only occasionally did an author mention that "in such a large country like China, it is impossible that all women live such a retired life," and that in some regions the "burgher women move as freely as (our women) do."[24]

Other European sources on seventeenth-century China were more explicit about regional, social, and ethnic differences. Thus Johan Nieuhof, who traveled through China with a Dutch embassy in 1655–57, repeatedly mentioned the visibility and boldness of Manchu women. Recounting an encounter with a Manchu dignitary and his wife, he expressed astonishment about the fact that the wife "was very assertive, spoke up boldly, and talked more than [her husband]. She asked the embassy's members about everything and even took their rifle into her hands, like a cavalier."[25] That such remarks are missing in the Jesuits' accounts about women in China should make us wary about the Jesuits' constructions of differences between European Catholic and Chinese gender arrangements. Even though the views of Chinese Christians on Europe (as well as the Jesuits' experiences in China, which will be discussed later in this chapter) suggest that differences between the visibility of women in early modern China and Europe existed, it is important to ask why the Jesuits' representations of Chinese women stress their reclusiveness and modesty.

One possible explanation for the Jesuits' great emphasis on Chinese women's modesty is that it was connected with their accommodation, and with the ways in which the missionaries tried to justify their accommodating practices in Europe.[26] As I have argued elsewhere, the Jesuits' accommodation to the literati elite also implied that they tried to adapt themselves to the norms of literati masculinity, an important part of which was paying attention to the rules of gender separation.[27] This, however, was not easily reconciled with another crucial part of their mission: their evangelizing and pastoral work which addressed all Chinese people regardless of their social standing and sex. This tension had to be managed by the Jesuits, and they indeed found creative solutions in order to reconcile the priestly and literati masculine ideals. In particular, they introduced alterations into the Catholic sacraments of baptism, confession, extreme unction, and the Eucharist, in order to make them agreeable to Chinese gender propriety. For these alterations, however, the Jesuits needed approval by the Roman authorities. This was especially important in the case of baptism, where the Jesuits abstained from performing certain ceremonies that involved touching the catechumen. In order to substantiate their claim to the Roman Curia that the alterations were necessary, the Jesuits had to present a congruent picture of Chinese women, one that focused on the ideals of gender separation and female modesty.[28]

The Jesuits' effort to represent Chinese women as modest and reclusive seems to have been successful with the Roman Curia. This can be seen from the way in which the Congregation for the Propagation of the Faith (*Congregatio de Propaganda Fide*) discussed a help-seeking letter sent to Rome in 1650 by the empress dowager of the Yongli emperor, the ruler of a doomed southern satellite court of the fallen Ming dynasty of which several members had converted to Catholicism.[29] This letter, which was a beautiful scroll with Chinese calligraphy, painted dragons, and opulent seals, stirred some excitement in the Curia. However, several of its members doubted its authenticity, referring to the common knowledge about women in China: Did Chinese women not live such secluded lives that missionaries were not able to see them? How, then, could they be sure that the letter was really written by the empress? And did the retired lifestyle of Chinese women not preclude their implication into government matters? How then could it be that a Chinese empress had tried to initiate diplomatic relations with the Holy See?[30] Nothing came of the discussions in Rome, as the Southern Ming court fell in 1661 without the papal response letter having reached it.[31] But the documentation of the episode in the Roman archives is a telling example of how a discrepancy could occur between Chinese women's actual agency and its Jesuit representations for the European audience, as well as how such a discrepancy could cause puzzlement for European observers who had to rely on the Jesuits as brokers of local knowledge about China.

2 Accommodation, gender separation, and women's evangelization in China

Although the Jesuits tended to idealize their representations of Chinese gender separation, this did not mean that they concealed from their European audience the fact that their accommodation to the literati elite made it necessary for them to adjust their social behavior and network. Rather the opposite was the case. The Flemish missionary Nicolas Trigault, for instance, wrote in a printed account of 1610 that "it is important to know that, because we wear the dress of the literati, we are, according to Chinese customs, excluded from speaking with women." He explained that conversation with women was only possible on rare occasions on which the husband or father was present, and the woman was shielded from the missionary's view by a screen or a door. Trigault then justified the Jesuits' decision to adopt the literati's silk dress and abstain from contact with women:

> When we dressed like their priests (i.e., in the Buddhist monks' garb,[32] N.A.), we were not so strictly prohibited from associating with them, but we were excluded from interacting and conversing with the important and noble men.

The latter, Trigault insisted, was more important for the mission, even more so because once they won the literati's trust it would also become easier to speak with the women.[33]

Trigault's apology for the Jesuits' accommodation to the literati elite conveys the impression that their evangelization project in China excluded women altogether. This was, of course, not the case. Instead, it resulted in the establishment of patterns of indirect communication with women that relied on media (relics, sacramentals, printed texts, and devotional images)[34] and intermediaries (women's male relatives, children, or servants).[35]

There are two groups of intermediaries that were especially important for the Jesuits' communication with women. On the side of Chinese Christians, the male relatives were the most important group of go-betweens. The Jesuits made a male family head's consent a *sine qua non* for a woman's evangelization, thus showing respect to the traditional Confucian order of the family and making sure that no suspicions of indecency arose. This strategy precluded women's self-determined decisions – a drawback that the missionaries were willing to accept in order to save their reputation as "Western literati." Within the Company of Jesus, the Chinese lay brothers formed another group of go-betweens which, again, according to Nicolas Trigault, had easier access to women than ordained priests. As Trigault explained, this was again connected with their way of dressing: "Since our brothers do not use a dress that is so much honored [as ours is], speaking with women is not difficult for them." But even they, Trigault explained, had to be cautious in order not to damage the mission's reputation:

> On orders of the fathers, [the brothers] use this freedom with so great a moderation that they never speak to them one by one, but make sure the husband, father, or another adult relative is always present. And if this is not possible, our brother takes with him two or three esteemed neophytes who are present during their conversation.

According to Trigault, this way of dealing with women was much applauded by the Chinese and gave Christianity a "holy reputation."[36]

Although sources show that the Jesuits attached great importance to keeping their distance from Chinese women, it is not entirely clear how consistently they could have implemented this strategy. A number of anti-Christian pamphlets written in the 1610s and early 1620s show that not all Chinese were convinced of the Jesuits' consideration for gender propriety. In one of these pamphlets, the lay Buddhist Xu Dashou's 許大受 *Assisting the Holy Dynasty in Refuting [Heresy]* (Shengchao zuopi 聖朝佐闢, 1623), the Jesuits were accused of letting wives and daughters of their followers "mingle with the crowd in order to receive the secret teaching of the barbarians." For the author of the pamphlets, this was a clear sign of social disorder, as he explained, quoting from a well-known text passage in the *Book of Rites*: "'If men and women are not separated, disorder will arise and grow,' and would I not know on what their disorder is based?"[37] Xu's suspicions against the Jesuits show that not all Chinese observers accepted them as members of the Confucian literati elite. Indeed, the Jesuits were constantly in danger of being perceived as the leaders of a "heterodox" (*xie* 邪) religious movement, one of the popular religious movements that were said to transgress Confucian gender norms and were suspected to cause social and political unrest.[38] Association with heterodoxy sometimes had severe consequences for the Jesuit mission. Chinese officials who perceived of the "Teaching of the Lord of Heaven" (Tianzhu jiao 天主教), which is what Catholicism was called in Chinese, as a heterodox sect shut down churches, demolished the buildings, or transformed them into "temples of the idols," as the missionaries complained in their letters.[39] In view of this permanent threat of being identified with a socially marginal and politically persecuted set of movements it is not surprising that the Jesuits were eager to conform to the Confucian norm of gender separation and to prevent association with heterodoxy by avoiding close contact with women.[40]

Conforming to Confucian norms not only implied restricted and controlled communication between missionaries and women. It also implied the establishment of female worship spaces where women could practice their devotions in a homosocial environment. That this was necessary had already been proposed by Ricci's elder companion, Michele Ruggieri, around 1591: "The women," he wrote,

> should under no circumstances visit the churches. If a Christian husband or father takes the missionary to his house and he baptizes [a woman] after having instructed her, she [should] continue her prayers at home and not attend mass. For it is not usual for women [in China] to leave their houses.[41]

However, for these "prayers at home," a new form of worship space was necessary, and thus the Jesuits started in the early 1600s to encourage their male converts to establish oratories for the women of their families. This, in fact, initiated a process that led to a new spatial arrangement of Chinese Catholicism that also affected its social organization and devotional culture.

3 House oratories and the transformation of Catholicism into a domestic religion

House oratories destined for women's worship started to be established in the 1600s and remained an important feature of Chinese Catholicism throughout the seventeenth century. This is confirmed by a list of China's buildings for Christian worship compiled by Philippe Couplet somewhere around 1680. According to this list, cities that were renowned for their Christian communities usually boasted not only a residence and one or two churches but also a substantial number of oratories. Xi'an in Shaanxi province, for example, was recorded as having 22 oratories, and Tainan in Shandong province was listed as having 11. Shanghai, which was an especially prominent center of Catholicism in seventeenth-century China, was even said to have had 39 oratories.[42] Unfortunately, Couplet was not explicit about the exact meaning of "oratory" in his list. However, from the way he uses the term we can deduce that it denoted a room where a group of Christians worshipped together.[43] It therefore seems reasonable to assume that the oratories reported by Couplet were permanent structures within Christian private homes that provided women with separate spaces for worship.

These were, however, not the only kind of oratories that could be found in the China mission. The Jesuits' Annual Letters – accounts written by the mission's superior to report on its secular and spiritual state on an annual basis – show that, in addition to these comparably spacious, permanent, and separate oratories, less opulent oratories also existed. Even if these were not counted in Couplet's list, they were nevertheless important for women's Christian worship in China. In order to represent the importance of house oratories for Chinese Catholicism as completely as possible, the three different functions that oratories could fulfill within Christian households should each be considered: they were used for individual worship, for joint worship of the family, and for the worship of women's congregations.

Oratories used for the first function, that of a Christian woman's individual worship, seem to have been numerous in seventeenth-century China. Thus the edifying stories in the Annual Letters of 1634 and 1639, which mention how a Christian woman in Hangzhou resisted temptations when "she had retired to her oratory and was praying"[44] or how a girl was cured from an illness when "praying in her oratory" (*no seu oratorio*), are no isolated cases.[45] The particular oratories mentioned here were most probably only niches in a multi-functional room that was also used for non-religious purposes. It is probable that these niches, which were usually embellished with statuettes, images, or strips of paper with characters written on them, were set up in the same places where non-Christian women had their worship places with statuettes of Guanyin and other deities that especially appealed to women. These non-Christian oratories which, according to the Annual Letter of 1625, consisted of statues of idols and devotional objects, had to be handed over to the missionaries after conversion.[46] The personal oratories used for women's individual worship were especially important for Christian women who lived in homes of non-Christians – an arrangement that was frequent in Chinese Catholicism because the Jesuits were granted dispensations for the otherwise prohibited "disparity of cult." Sources show that many women who married into a non-Christian family were allowed to have Christian "oratories" on their own and to so continue their Christian religious practice after marriage.[47]

Second, oratories were also used for joint family worship. Thus Matteo Ricci recounted how the Beijing literatus Li Yingshi 李應試 established a house oratory in the early 1610s, where the fathers often went in order to say mass for those of his house. The family-centered function of this oratory was further stressed by the fact that Li had his son learn to serve as an acolyte during the mass, thus involving a family member in the performance of the ritual.[48] In the case of Li Yingshi, a rich member of the Confucian literati elite, the oratory was apparently a separate room especially established for this purpose. In other cases, and especially in the homes of poor Christians, the oratory was erected in a niche and sometimes combined with the altar for ancestor worship.[49] This combination is an indicator of the close association of the oratories with women, for it was the women who were in charge of tending to the domestic ancestor altar in Chinese homes.[50]

The third and most important function of house oratories – and mainly of those oratories that were established as permanent structures in elite family homes and thus counted in Couplet's previously mentioned list – was the hosting of women's congregations (*hui* 會). These congregational meetings in house oratories were usually organized by the senior lady of the family who possessed the oratory and were open to Christian women from the neighborhood.[51] As the Annual Letter of 1629 shows, they were substitutes for male Christians' churchgoing:

> The women were excluded from the solace and benefit [of churchgoing] because they were not allowed to go to the private chapel of our residence. Therefore, four Christian homes in different places that were at some distance of the city are chosen. There the women can conveniently attend the Eucharist and wash away the stains of their consciences every month.[52]

Oratories were, at least during the first decades of the seventeenth century, also the places where women met with the missionaries and received the sacraments. This only started to change in the 1630s when, in a moment of weakened government power and increasing numbers of converts, the Jesuits started to establish women's churches – called "Holy Mother's Churches" (Shengmu tang 聖母堂) – for these occasions.[53] From the 1630s onwards, the women's churches were supposed to be the places where women's congregations gathered in order to receive the sacraments, whereas the house oratories remained in place for worship that women conducted without priestly assistance. The establishment of women's churches was, however, not pervasive. Thus a set of resolutions agreed on by the missionaries in 1669 states that the celebration of mass in private houses was still permitted if this was the house of a congregation (*sodalitatis domus*). This shows that oratories remained in use for saying mass even after the establishment of women's churches.[54]

The many accounts of Christian women's domestic worship and the great number of oratories mentioned in Couplet's list suggest that the Jesuits' decision to establish separate worship spaces for women and to locate them within the domestic realm received a favorable response from Chinese Christian communities. There were probably two reasons for this. First, it was normal in early modern China to perceive of the household as a site of religious worship. As C. K. Yang has stated, "the influence of religion on traditional Chinese family life was everywhere visible." Not only were visitors of Chinese residential houses received at a door on which paper door gods were painted or written in characters, but upon entering a house, they also saw

> an altar to T'u-ti, the earth god, who protected the family against destructive influences. . . . T'ien-kuan, the heavenly Official, was in the courtyard, and the wealth gods, who brought well-being and prosperity to the family, were in the hall or the main room of the house.[55]

The residential house in early modern China was thus a sacred landscape in itself, inhabited, observed, and protected by a great number of deities from the Chinese popular pantheon.

The second reason for the favorable reception of female domestic worship was the traditionally close connection between domestic religiosity and women. In early modern China, women were responsible for tending to the domestic religious universe.[56] It was women who had the "traditional ritual authority" in the domestic sphere, tending to the ancestral shrine and organizing seasonal ceremonies for sacrifice or purification.[57] In light of this, it is not surprising that Chinese families who had converted to Catholicism found it normal to perceive of their homes as an appropriate place for worship and one for which women were responsible.

The prominence of house oratories in Chinese Catholicism resulted in a binary spatial pattern according to which the churches and residences were a predominantly male sphere of influence and the household a predominantly female one.[58] Priestly influence on the domestic sphere was generally weak, which meant that missionaries and Christian women did not have many opportunities for contact.[59] It did not mean, however, that women were less important for Chinese Christian devotional lives. Although the infrequent contact with missionaries prevented women from receiving the sacraments frequently, it also gave women considerable freedom in organizing Christian households' domestic religious life – an aspect of religiosity that was of great importance in early modern China.

While all women usually participated in domestic worship activities, it was usually the senior lady of the household – the matriarch – who was the family's religious leader. This is illustrated by the domestic devotional lives of the literati families in the Jiangnan area. Due to their special social prestige, these families are especially well documented in the Jesuits' writings. We know, for example, that Mary Sun – the 80-year-old mother of the Christian literatus Sun Yuanhua 孙元化 and matriarch of the family – made sure that the many Christian women of her household all gathered early in the morning for communal prayer in their home in Jiading during the 1630s.[60] In Shanghai, the famous Christian literatus Xu Guangqi's 徐光启 family was led in their domestic worship activities by Flavia Xu, the wife of Xu Guangqi's first-born grandson, during the 1640s and 1650s.[61] And Candida Xu, Xu Guangqi's granddaughter, who had married a Songjiang literatus in the 1620s and was widowed in the early 1650s, was the spiritual leader of an especially fervent Christian household that also became an important financial source for the Jesuits' China mission in the 1650s to 1670s.[62]

4 Conclusion

As this chapter has shown, the analysis of the Jesuits' mission to China from the perspective of gender brings the Chinese Christian household into sharp focus, showing that this eminently female space of worship was a crucial element of Chinese Christian religious culture that complemented the better known male spaces for Christian devotion, the Christian churches. The gendered spatial aspects of the China missions' "pattern of localization" structured not only Chinese Christian women's religious options and devotional practices but also the Jesuits' missionary work, defining the modes of interaction between missionaries and their flock.

The transformation of Catholicism's spatial arrangements in China according to the inner-outer binary affected many different aspects of Chinese Christian devotional lives, including visual representations. One of them, the "Visitation" reproduced in João da Rocha's *Rules for Reciting the Rosary* (Song nianzhu guicheng 誦念珠規程, 1619), illustrates this transformation in a nutshell (see Figure 10.1).[63] This woodcut print was modeled on a copperplate print published in Jerónimo Nadal's *Images of the Evangelical History* (Evangelicae Historiae Imagines, 1593; see Figure 10.2). Both show Mary and her cousin Elisabeth approaching each other with open arms. The women's postures and dresses as well as several other details of the pictures are conspicuously similar, indicating that the former was modeled upon the latter. However, there are also some significant differences between the two images. Nadal had placed the two women in the forefront. They

Figure 10.1 "Visitation" in João da Rocha's *Rules for Reciting the Rosary* (Song nianzhu guicheng 誦念珠規程, 1619)

Source: Courtesy of the Bibliothèque nationale de France, Paris, Chinois 6861

Figure 10.2 "Visitation" in Jerónimo Nadal's *Images of the Evangelical History* (Evangelicae Historiae Imagines, 1593)

Source: Courtesy of Kantonsbibliothek Solothurn

encountered each other in the midst of a large hall with open doors and windows in which the two husbands also met. The Chinese artist, however, changed the architectural setting. He placed the women in a courtyard that was shielded from the outside world by a wall. The female space in which they met was, furthermore, separated from the men's space by a small staircase. While Nadal's copperplate engraving thus conveys the impression of the women being part of a non-gendered space, gendered space is an important structuring element in the Chinese woodcut print.

The Chinese artist changed the spatial setting of the two saintly women's encounters in such a way that he did not change the core religious message of the image. However, he did change the conception of women's place within socioreligious space. He did this in order to adjust the image not only to the gender norms generally accepted in China but also to those accepted by the Chinese Christian community. For Chinese Christians, men and women alike, the Chinese version of the Visitation was probably more legible and more accessible than the European one. It conveyed an impression of orderliness and of domesticity that Nadal's engraving was lacking. While Nadal's engraving focused on the Holy Family, the late Ming artist's woodcut print depicted what we might call the "holy household."[64]

The illustrations in the *Rules for Reciting the Rosary* were structured according to Chinese ideals of gendered spaces. The book itself, however, was most probably a medium that transgressed the boundaries between the "inner" and "outer" spaces. Thanks to its illustrations, it was accessible for women who had only limited reading skills. The *Rules for Reciting the Rosary* thus remind us both of the separation and connectedness of men's and women's devotional spaces in early modern China.

Notes

1 The term "accommodation" was first used by church historians such as Johannes Bettray (see Bettray, *Die Akkommodationsmethode*). Its meaning in the context of the China mission was further elaborated by Daniel Mungello, who put forward the idea of the Confucian-Christian synthesis; see Mungello, *Curious Land*, 15. Although "accommodation" is usually associated with the Jesuits, the contributions by Christian Windler and Cesare Santus to this volume show that accommodation was by no means unique to the Company of Jesus, but – depending on the social and political contexts of the missions – was also used by other missionary orders.

2 For Ricci's account of this change of dress, see D'Elia, *Fonti Ricciane*, vol. 1, 336–338.

3 This monitum had been brought forward by Brockey, *The Visitor*, 284. However, many innovative studies have recently shown that working within the framework of "cultural contact" does not preclude an awareness of the missionaries' early modern Catholic background. See, for instance, Standaert, *The Interweaving of Rituals*, or Meynard, *Confucius Sinarum Philosophus*. Furthermore, authors such as Erik Zürcher have stated much earlier that Christianity's adaptation to the Confucian worldview was not only a deliberately chosen strategy but also the response to a "cultural imperative" from which it was difficult for

any minority religion in China to escape. See Zürcher, "Confucian and Christian Religiosity," 614.

4 On the literati converts and sympathizers, see Standaert, *Handbook of Christianity in China*, 404–422 and 475–591 respectively. On their representation of China and Confucian learning as enlightened by the *lumen naturale*, see Meynard, *Confucius Sinarum Philosophus*. For exemplary studies on the Chinese Christian writings that presented Christianity to the Chinese, see Li and Meynard, *Jesuit Chreia* and Li, *Yishu*.

5 For a broader inquiry into the gender history of the Jesuits' China mission, see Amsler, *Jesuits and Matriarchs*. For an overview on the gender history of Chinese Christianity, see Lutz, *Pioneer Chinese Christian Women*.

6 Eugenio Menegon, in his study of the Christian communities of Fujian administered by Dominican friars, analyzes the history of these communities as a process of "localization of Christianity": see Menegon, *Ancestors, Virgins, and Friars*. For Menegon, studies on Jesuit accommodation have failed to focus on localization because they follow "a long-standing tradition" that focuses on "the scientific and artistic accomplishments of the Jesuits," see Menegon, "Popular or Local?" 250.

7 On the transregional nature of the literati elite, see Heijdra, "The Socio-Economic Development of Rural China," 555–556. With respect to the spatial consequences of accommodation, research has shown that it went together with the Jesuits' preference for cities: see the contribution of Ronnie Po-chia Hsia in this volume and Standaert, *Handbook of Christianity in China*, 538–540. Furthermore, the missionaries' presence at the social space of the court is currently being researched. For this, see the contribution by Eugenio Menegon in this volume.

8 See Rosenlee, *Confucianism and Women*, 69–75.

9 Sima Guang, *Sima shishu*, translated by Ebrey, *The Inner Quarters*, 23–24.

10 This article uses "early modern" to denote the period from the late Ming to the High Qing (sixteenth to eighteenth centuries). For an overview of the ongoing debate on the periodization of Chinese history, see Dabringhaus, *Die Geschichte Chinas*, 115–118.

11 On the *nei-wai* binary in Chinese architecture see Bray, *Technologies and Gender*, 68–69. On the connectedness of European houses with the street, see Eibach, "Das offene Haus."

12 See Zhou, "The Hearth and the Temple."

13 Hersche, *Musse und Verschwendung*, vol. 2, 707–710.

14 Hersche, *Musse und Verschwendung*, vol. 1, 432–435; Windler, *Missionare in Persien*, 465–469.

15 On the pitfalls of constructing "cultures" as stable, monolithic, and homogeneous entities, see Hauck, *Kultur*, 14–141 and 180–182, and Höfert, "Gender in Trans-It." For an early critique of Western generalizations on non-Western women, see Mohanty, "Under Western Eyes."

16 Chinese voices that compare European and Chinese gender arrangements become more audible in the nineteenth century. See, for instance, Teng, "The West as a Kingdom of Women."

17 See Spence, *The Question of Hu*, 62, 82–84.

18 See Spence, "The Paris Years of Arcadio Huang," 5. On how Christian men and women in rural areas of China used to hear mass at different times and places, see François Pallu, *Praxes quaedam discusse in pleno Coetu 23. Patrum Missionariorum Chinae, quorum nomina in fide describuntur, statue et directe ad observandam inter eos uniformitatem. Mense Octobri anni 1669* (APF, Fondo di Vienna, vol. 21, fol. 136v–137r).

19 For a general overview of the Jesuit mission to China, see Brockey, *Journey to the East*. For the missionaries' publications on China, see Mungello, *Curious Lands*.

20 Couplet, *Histoire d'une Dame chrétienne*, 7.
21 See, among others, Pantoja, *Relatione dell'entrata*, 78 and Semedo, *Histoire universelle*, 47.
22 Semedo, *Histoire universelle*, 46.
23 On one interesting exception to this rule, the Jesuit Adriano de las Cortes, whose account on South China remained unpublished, see Amsler, *Jesuits and Matriarchs*, 45–46.
24 Semedo, *Histoire universelle*, 48.
25 Nieuhof, *Die Gesandschaft*, 117.
26 The Jesuits generally tended to idealize China as a Confucianized civilization in their writings for a European audience. See Meynard, *Confucius Sinarum Philosophus*, and Girard, "Les descriptions qui fâchent."
27 For this and the following, see Amsler, *Jesuits and Matriarchs*, 24–31 and 59–66.
28 It is therefore not surprising that, in the records of the Roman Curia on these dispensations, we find a vivid description of Chinese women's seclusion written by the Jesuit procurator Martino Martini: see Vareschi, "Martino Martini," 242.
29 On the Christian intermezzo at the court of the Southern Ming, see Struve, *Voices from the Ming-Qing Cataclysm*, 235–238 (including an English translation of the empress's Chinese letter) and Standaert, *Handbook of Christianity in China*, 438–441.
30 See APF, SOCG, vol. 93, fol. 44r and 138r.
31 On the fall of the Southern Ming see Struve, "The Southern Ming."
32 The Jesuits in China wore the Buddhist monks' garb during the first 15 years of their mission. See Peterson, "What to Wear?," 412–413.
33 Trigault, "Lettera annua della Cina del 1610," 49–50.
34 See Standaert, *Handbook of Christianity*, 600–620 (on printed religious texts) and 809–822 (on images).
35 See Amsler, *Jesuits and Matriarchs*, 50–52.
36 Trigault, "Lettera annua della Cina del 1610," 50.
37 Translation slightly adapted from Dudink, "The Sheng-ch'ao tso-p'i (1623)," 114–115.
38 On heterodox movements in late imperial China, see Ter Haar, *The White Lotus Teachings*. On the danger for Christianity of being confused with these movements, see Cohen, *China and Christianity*, 16–17.
39 For an account of a church being demolished, see Couplet, *Breve Relatione* (ARSI, JS 125, fol. 164r–199v, here 189r). For an account of a church transformed into a "temple of idols", see Pfister, *Notices biographiques*, 324.
40 On the prohibition of nightly gatherings, see François Pallu, *Praxes quaedam discusse in pleno Coetu 23. Patrum Missionariorum Chinae, quorum nomina in fide describuntur, statue et directe ad observandam inter eos uniformitatem. Mense Octobri anni 1669* (APF, Fondo di Vienna, vol. 21, fol. 137r).
41 Michele Ruggieri, *Relatione del Successo della missione della Cina del mese di Novembre 1577 alli 1591* (ARSI, JS 101, fol. 8r–111r, here 109r).
42 Philippe Couplet, *In Provincia Sinensi Templa, Collegia inchoata, Residentiae, et Missiones primo saeculo erecta à Patribus Societatis Jesu*, in: Litterae Annuae Vice-Provinciae Sinicae ab 1677 ad 1680, s.l., s.d. (ARSI, JS 116, 214–275, here 272r–275v).
43 See Philippe Couplet, *In Provincia Sinensi Templa, Collegia inchoata, Residentiae, et Missiones primo saeculo erecta à Patribus Societatis Jesu*, in: Litterae Annuae Vice-Provinciae Sinicae ab 1677 ad 1680, s.l., s.d. (ARSI, JS 116, 214–275, here 272r).
44 João Froes, Carta Annua da Missao da China do Anno de 1634, Hangzhou, 8 September 1634 (ARSI, JS 115 II, fol. 266r–317r, here 286r).

45 See João Moneiro, Annuae Sin[ae] 1639, 8 October 1640 (ARSI, JS 121, fol. 221r–313r, here 284r).
46 See Manuel Diaz, Annua 1625, Jiading, 1 March 1626 (ARSI, JS 115 I, fol. 30r–67r, here 63r).
47 See João Froes, Annua da V[ice]Provincia da China do anno de 1633 (BA, JA 49-V-11, fol. 1r–99v, here 37r). On the papal dispensations *in disparitu cultus* for the China mission and its consequences, see Collani, "Mission and Matrimony."
48 D'Elia, *Fonti Ricciane*, vol. 1, 263.
49 See Standaert, *Handbook of Christianity in China*, 635.
50 See Freedman, "Ritual Aspects of Chinese Kinship and Marriage," 283.
51 For a detailed discussion of Chinese Christian women's congregations, see Amsler, *Jesuits and Matriarchs*, 99–112.
52 Bernardus Regius, Annuae ex V[ice]Provincia Sinarum an[no] 1629, s.l., s.d. (BA, JA 49-V-8, 608v–627v, here 610r).
53 On this transition, see Amsler, *Jesuits and Matriarchs*, 56–59.
54 See François Pallu, *Praxes quaedam discusse in pleno Coetu 23. Patrum Missionariorum Chinae, quorum nomina in fide describuntur, statue et directe ad observandam inter eos uniformitatem. Mense Octobri anni 1669* (APF, Fondo di Vienna, vol. 21, fol. 138v).
55 Yang, *Religion in Chinese Society*, 28.
56 See Mann, *Precious Records*, 178–200; McLaren, "Women's Work."
57 See McLaren, "Women's Work," 171–172.
58 For a description of churches as the Chinese Christian worship spaces *par excellence*, see Brockey, *Journey to the East*, 367.
59 It is, however, important to remember that priestly presence and control was generally speaking rather weak compared with the situation in Europe. This was due to the Jesuits' dearth of manpower, but it simultaneously also corresponded to the traditional pattern of Chinese religiosity, which was strongly centered on lay activities, with religious specialists playing only a marginal role. See Standaert, *The Interweaving of Rituals*, 223–227.
60 See João Froes, Annua 1631, s.l., s.d. (BA, JA 49-V-10, 1r–32v, here 23v).
61 See Francesco Brancati, Annua do anno 1643 de Cum Chim da Residencia da Xam Hay, Shanghai, March 1644 (BNP, Cód. 722, 237r–252v, here 237v).
62 See Amsler, *Jesuits and Matriarchs*, 117–127 on the devotional life of the Xu household and 143–151 passim for Candida's financial contributions to the mission. Candida and other widowed matriarchs of Christian families could tap into the special social capital of "chaste widowhood," a Confucian ideal that provided women with special social prestige and freedom. See Theiss, *Disgraceful Matters*, for a thorough discussion of the ideal and the practices connected with it.
63 For a contextualization of the *Song nianzhu guicheng*, see Criveller, *Preaching Christ in Late Ming China*. For a comparative discussion of the Visitation scenes in *Song nianzhu guicheng* and *Evangelicae Historicae Imagines*, see Lin, "Seeing the Place," 203–204, and Catellani, "L'iconographie jésuite de la Chine," 120–121.
64 This term is borrowed from Lyndal Roper who, in her book *The Holy Household*, described how the household became an important focus in Protestant Germany's religiosity.

11 Women, households, and the transformation of Christianity into the Kirishitan religion

Haruko Nawata Ward

During the so-called Christian Century in Japan (1549–1650), encounters among the Jesuit missionaries and women opened up various "third spaces" for creating a new *Kirishitan* religious identity.[1] Theoreticians have conceived of the "Third Space" as both a physical space and time in which intercultural communications and negotiations take place.[2] The concept is similar to how Japanese scholars use the term *ma* (間), which denotes the "in-between" space/time, where the ordinary sense of space/time is suspended and humans communicate across fluid borders.[3] It is also a location in which new ideas and symbolic images may emerge. This chapter examines how women and the Jesuits crafted and used Kirishitan literature (*Kirishitanban*) in households (*ie* 家), which became a specific kind of "third space" where the text-creators crisscrossed between the foreign and local, public and private, communal and domestic, clergy and lay, and male and female spheres. It focuses on a range of Kirishitan texts and examines how they reveal traces of the collaboration between foreign and Japanese-born Jesuits and women. My hypothesis is that all these agents worked together to translate devotional literature into Japanese, and that Kirishitan literature can also be seen as a third space text, which was no longer a missionary product nor a simple indigenization; rather, it is one that reflects the transformation of a Jesuit-conveyed Christianity into a new Kirishitan religion.[4]

1 Evangelization in a period of political changes: The Jesuit mission to sixteenth-century Japan

The "Christian Century" was a period when rapid political and social changes took place in Japan. Arriving in 1549 during the period of the Warring States, in which the warrior lords were fighting each other and the imperial rule was declining, the Jesuit missionaries needed to rely on the Kirishitans for their work of evangelization.[5] They quickly learned to adapt to the Japanese, not only in cultural decorum but in their religious understanding about Christianity, by incorporating prominent Buddhist ideas.[6] Soon the mission admitted Japanese men into their Society by creating a special class of *dōjucu* and *cambō*, some of whom later advanced in rank to become brothers and priests. The Jesuits also worked closely with Kirishitan women although, per their constitutions, they did not establish a female branch of the Society of Jesus.[7] These Jesuits and Kirishitan associates discovered the usefulness of books for reaching a wider population, which will be discussed in this article.[8]

In spite of their willingness to adapt to Japanese customs, however, the Jesuits' mission remained on an uneasy footing because of the difficult political context in which it was situated. The first two unifiers, Oda Nobunaga (1534–1582) and Toyotomi Hideyoshi (1537–1598), permitted mission work because of their interest in foreign trade: first with Portugal, with *padroado real* supporting the work of the Jesuits, and later with Spain, with *patronato real* supporting the work of the mendicant orders from Manila. Both unifiers kept a close watch over the activities of the foreign missionaries, suspecting that they were enticing the Japanese adherents into a religion which encouraged non-conformity to their policies. Hideyoshi's *Edict of Expulsion of the Padres* in 1587 banned Christianity, but implementation was inconsistent and allowed the Jesuits to continue to work quietly with help from Kirishitan protectors. Ten years later in 1597, Hideyoshi executed 23 mendicants and three Jesuits in Nagasaki.[9]

The prospects for the missions definitely became bleak when shogun Hidetada (1579–1632; r. 1605–1623), who was the successor of the last unifier and founder of the Tokugawa government, shogun Tokugawa Ieyasu (1543–1616), came to power and adopted xenophobic anti-Christian policies. In 1612, he reissued the ban of Christianity and began arresting clergy and Kirishitans. In the Great Expulsion of 1614, he deported foreign missionaries and major Kirishitan leaders. About 30 Jesuits went underground and a few reentered secretly after being deported. The third shogun Iemitsu (1604–1651; r. 1623–1651) severed all Iberian commercial and diplomatic ties and forbade all travel to and from Japan. Harsh persecution wiped away all Kirishitan sites, books, objects, and persons, at least from the surface of Japan, by 1650.

2 Changes in Japanese households and women's space

From the beginning, households provided fertile ground for the Jesuit mission to plant the seeds of faith, which grew with a distinct Kirishitan identity. Thus, it is important to briefly examine the characteristics of households in pre-modern Japan and how they changed in the early seventeenth century. The term household (*ie*) connotes both an architectural dwelling space and the human relationships within it. The late medieval *ie* was a loosely organized "stem-family household," ruled by patriarchal or lineage heads.[10] Yet before the twelfth century, the Japanese did not have a fixed tradition of patrilineal descent nor virilocal residence.[11] The Tokugawa government adopted Confucian principles in 1607 to restructure religious, educational, and social realms.[12] This state-led imposition of Confucianism and patriarchy impacted the status of women in their *ie*, among them, the Kirishitan women, who lived through this transitional period.[13]

Earlier, medieval *ie* families were modeled after the emperor's *ie* ("court") and included biological, spousal, and adopted relatives as well as retainers and servants, all living together in compounds or neighborhoods. The *ie* was also the spiritual dwelling of the ancestors. Within the physical property, there were many space divisions according to gender and class. Women in the warrior class were most valued as the mothers of first sons, who would inherit the *ie* property. Because the *ie* was also an economic managerial system, women of all classes managed their *ie*'s internal affairs. They also worked outside the *ie*. Wives from all classes increased the *ie* economy by purchasing and selling commodities including books.[14] Upper-class women served at the imperial court and held various positions at lord's households.[15] Women in lower classes also hired themselves out. Those who could not contribute to the *ie* units were "often absorbed into Buddhist institutions as monks and nuns."[16] However, between the fourteenth and seventeenth centuries, Shinto-Buddhist nuns such as the *Cumanobicuni* (Kumano bikuni) continued to influence the public sphere by creating local infrastructure and preaching in town squares.[17] Despite such evidence of the continuity of women's autonomy throughout the medieval period, Wakita concludes that "in the sixteenth century, women's work and general activity was enclosed within the rule of the *ie*, where it was allocated a 'men's helpmate' value."[18]

As late as 1585, the Jesuit Father Luís Fróis (1533–1597) observed that Japanese women in the pre-Tokugawa period were not as strictly enclosed as their contemporary Iberian or Chinese counterparts. Young single and married women went out freely without male permission or escorts.[19] However, this started to change with the Tokugawa-Confucian regime, which stringently hierarchized the social classes as follows: the imperial aristocracy (though with little power), domain *daimyō*, warriors, landed farmers, artisans, merchants, peasants, and entertainer-prostitutes. The individual *ie* became a government-controlled unit within the pyramid of the national patriarchal household, of which the dynastic shogunal *ie* (将軍家) was located at the top. In this context a woman's vocation became tied only to her residential *ie*. This severely limited women's movement and potential to network across class. It curtailed women's rights to engage in business ventures and property ownership.[20] It also decreased women's chances of engaging in higher learning, public discourse, and religious leadership. As the Tokugawa regime reorganized the diverse Japanese religions, it remade some sectors of Buddhism into another state religion.[21] It required each *ie* to register at a precinct temple and hired Buddhist monks as anti-Kirishitan propagandists and educators of the decidedly misogynist Confucian-Shinto-Buddhist doctrines of the Five Obstructions and Three Obediences for the subjugation of women.[22]

As these political and socioreligious changes took place, the Jesuits as a male missionary religious order tried to interpolate themselves into Japanese society. Kirishitan women from different classes often provided the opening for their entry into their *ie*, where women exchanged religious ideas with European and Japanese Jesuits. The following three examples show how these households became spaces of Kirishitan text production as the result of their close collaboration.

3 A Kirishitan woman and the story of a virgin martyr saint

Hibiya Monica (c.1549–c.1577) lived in the earlier period of the Christian Century. She met with the Jesuits during the 1560s, when the mission was a small operation of four priests and five brothers struggling to gain a foothold in the greater Kyoto area. The missionaries found a safe haven in the *ie* of a merchant, Hibiya Ryōkei Diogo (n.d.), in Sakai, Monica's father. In 1561 Ryōkei invited Father Gaspar Vilela (1525–1572) to his home, where Vilela baptized Ryōkei's son, Ryōka Vicente, and most likely Monica. Ryōkei Diogo received baptism in 1564 and remained a generous benefactor of the missions and a pillar of the Kirishitan community in Sakai. His home later became the house church after the government destroyed the church building in 1587.

In 1564, Father Luís Fróis, who had just arrived in Kyushu in 1563, and Brother Luís de Almeida (1522–1583), a *converso* who had come to Japan as a trader/surgeon and joined the Society of Jesus in 1556, stayed at the Hibiyas' on their way to Kyoto.[23] Fróis describes the warm welcome the Jesuits received from the Hibiyas and how the family, including the children, appeared as if they were nobility. He also remarks that Ryōkei Diogo owned several buildings for different purposes on his property: "[He] let [us] stay in a very beautiful new house a little distance from the main house within his compound. People in Sakai are wealthy and keep multiple guest houses."[24] From this, one understands that the *ie* of the merchant class in Sakai referred to rather large complexes.[25]

Early in 1565 Fróis left for Kyoto but Almeida fell ill and remained at the Hibiyas' for another 25 days and was looked after by the Hibiya family with so much care "as if I was their own dear sibling," Almeida wrote.[26] When Almeida recovered, Ryōkei Diogo, who was one of the disciples of the famous tea master Sen no Rikyū (1522–1591) invited him to his tea house within his *ie* compound – a memorable experience for Almeida.[27]

During his stay, Almeida struck up a friendship with Monica, then about 16 years old.[28] Almeida says that he visited Monica in her own "room among many rooms which her father owns separating her from all the traffic."[29] Monica often talked to him about her aspirations of taking a vow of perpetual virginity. Almeida discouraged her because there were no Kirishitan monastic houses for women. But he also observed that she had books in her room and that she was able to read and write. Although he did not specify the book titles, they most likely included manuscript translations of stories of the early church female saints, from whom Monica must have learned the lifestyle of Christian perpetual virginity. Almeida compared Monica's devotion to that of St. Agnes and St. Catherine of Alexandria.

In fact, it was at the Hibiyas' *ie* in Sakai that translations of stories of the saints and other Kirishitan literature began. Fróis provides more information on this. He and Vilela lived with the Hibiya family when the thirteenth Ashikaga shogun Yoshiteru (r. 1546–1565), who had granted permission for Jesuit evangelization in the capital Kyoto, was assassinated and the interim imperial government under the leadership of Miyoshi Yoshitsugu (1549–1573) ordered the expulsion of the Jesuits from Kyoto, with the recommendations of powerful Buddhist temples. Fróis and his assistants again took refuge at the Hibiyas', while Vilela hid in Kawanokuchi and only later moved to Sakai. It was probably at the Hibiyas' where Vilela translated *Flos Sanctorum* and other devotional works into Japanese in 1566.[30]

Soon Fróis and the Japanese dōjucu Damião (1539–1587) moved out of the Hibiyas' because, as wanted criminals, they would have posed a danger to the Hibiyas. Ryōkei Diogo rented a small shack for them, only five houses down the street and continued to provide for them. This Jesuit *casa* ("house") was in poor condition,[31] but the Jesuits converted it into a chapel. Still learning Japanese, Fróis depended on Damião to interpret.[32] With Damião's help, he managed to say mass, "hear" written confessions, and persuade and baptize 300 people. In 1567, Damião left for Kyushu to be granted formal membership as a Jesuit brother with Fróis's high recommendation. Left alone, Fróis spent the majority of his time studying Japanese. He translated some Japanese books into Portuguese, and Gospel readings into Japanese. He also wrote a commentary on the Ten Commandments, wrote catechetical sermons in Japanese, and translated several stories of the saints into Japanese. For his translation and writing, it is likely that Fróis benefited from his continued intimate interactions with the Hibiyas and their visitors.

The early versions of stories of the saints were first rendered in oral recitations and songs. Japanese Jesuit brothers, who formerly were *biwa hōshi*, that is, visually impaired Buddhist preacher – ballad singers accompanied by the *biwa* instrument, continued to use their talents in creating Kirishitan ballads.[33] These Kirishitan *biwa hōshi* were invited into homes, where their performances called for audience participation.[34] Participants' feedback helped *biwa hōshi* improve their ballads. Although we do not have direct evidence, such a former Buddhist *biwa hōshi*, now Jesuit brother Lourenço (1526–1592) who was a close associate of Vilela, Almeida, and Fróis, might have visited the Hibiyas to try out the Sakai versions of stories of the saints.[35]

This making of texts using a writer – singer – audience-response method followed the Japanese literary tradition, in which reading texts "involved a pronounced level of orality, typically in sociable settings." While these texts preserved this communal orality, they also involved other sensory appeal "with the strongly visual component imposed by the writing system."[36] In the preparation of these and other Kirishitanban manuscripts for publication, the translator-teams made various adaptations in the writing system. In their choice among the traditional Japanese writing systems, the teams decisively chose *kanamajiri*, which combines the logographic *kanji* of Chinese origin and the phonetic *kana* in syllabic units. They chose it because it was the most accessible to women and non-elite readers. In addition, the Jesuits invented *Romaji* (a system of transliteration into the Latin alphabet) for the phonetic reading of Japanese for the non-native missionaries, but Kirishitans also learned this quickly. When no equivalent for Christian concepts existed in Japanese, the translators often used Romaji for the transliteration of Portuguese, Latin, and Spanish into the kanamajiri texts.[37] They also coined neologisms. But they regularly adopted Shinto-Buddhist concepts and terminologies that were commonly understood.

Because Japanese is a distinctly gendered and class-differentiated language, it is possible that Monica informed the Jesuits of typical expressions used by young women like herself, further refining their speeches, and the expressions and voices of young female saints, in translations and subsequent revisions. An example can be seen in the Kirishitanban story of Saint Catherine of Alexandria, in which the opening dialogue between the "Santa Virgem" [Catherine] and the "*teivō*" [Roman Emperor Maxentius] makes their hierarchical relationship obvious.[38] The emperor calls Catherine, who was the princess of his own eparch of Egypt, a "*nhonin*," thus reducing her status to that of his ordinary female subject. Later, he tries to seduce her by addressing her as "Daughter" (*musume*). Catherine, however, consistently uses polite forms and honorifics to her superiors as a young Japanese woman of Monica's time would have. The carefully nuanced expressions indicate the translators' awareness of and sensitivities toward women's experiences in their hierarchical society.

Although we cannot trace in detail Monica's role in the translation of the stories of the saints, it is clear that Ryōkei Diogo's *ie* became a third space of intellectual, cultural, and spiritual exchanges in the process. As a result of this complex translation process, Kirishitan texts, both those published by the Jesuit Japan Press and those that remained manuscripts, became a new genre of literature.[39] It is important to note, however, that collective authorship was not always made visible in the printed versions of these texts. The *Sanctos no gosagvueo no vchi nvqigaqi* (Excerpts from the *Acts of the Saints*) (Kazusa, 1591), which contains the previously discussed story of St. Catherine, only names two Japanese brothers as translators, namely Vicente Fōin (1540–1609) and Yōfō Paulo (1508–1595). However, eight stories of female saints in this volume demonstrate a high literary quality, in which Kirishitan religion speaks in a Japanese female voice, perhaps thanks to Monica.

4 A Kirishitan woman and *The Imitation of Christ*: The case of Hosokawa Tama Gracia

While Hibiya Monica was able to converse freely with the Jesuits, the situation was different for Lady Hosokawa Tama Gracia (1563–1600). Gracia became one of the Jesuits' crucial contacts with the *daimyō* households after she visited the church in Osaka incognito at Easter 1587, and subsequently received baptism from her lady-in-waiting in her quarters later that summer.[40] In 1578, Tama had been married to Lord Hosokawa Tadaoki (1563–1646), but when her father, Lord Akechi Mitsuhide (1528–1582), assassinated Oda Nobunaga in 1582, Tadaoki exiled her to Mitono. After Toyotomi Hideyoshi pardoned Tama in 1584, Tadaoki brought her back to the Hosokawa compound in Osaka and placed her under strict surveillance.

The Hosokawas were a powerful and savvy clan and remained so throughout the many political power shifts. The Jesuits hoped for their patronage and the possible conversion of Tadaoki. When Tama Gracia asked to leave her abusive husband, they counseled her to remain in confinement for the sake of the survival of the church. Thus, Tama Gracia never left the household compound after her visit to the church and died in the fiery siege by Tadaoki's enemies in 1600.[41] Although Tadaoki provided for the Jesuits in memory of Tama Gracia until 1611, the Hosokawas who were in allegiance to the Tokugawa government became some of the fiercest persecutors of Kirishitans after that date.

In her confinement, Tama Gracia relied on three sources for her knowledge of Kirishitan religion. First, she became aware of it by overhearing conversations among Tadaoki's tea circle, which included Takayama Ukon Justo (1552–1615).[42] Their exchanges made Tama Gracia desire an "extra ordinary" knowledge about this new religion.[43] The second source was her lady-in-waiting Kiyohara Ito Maria (n.d.), of an aristocratic family, who became the intermediary between Tama Gracia and the Jesuits. Since Tama Gracia did not leave her compound, Ito Maria shared knowledge of the Kirishitan religion with her, reported to her about the activities at the church, delivered Tama Gracia's letters to the Jesuits, and conveyed Jesuit messages to her. The Osaka Jesuits with whom Tama Gracia corresponded included fathers Gnecchi-Soldo Organtino (1533–1609) and Gregorio Céspedes (c.1552–1611) and brothers Takai Cosme (n.d.) and Vicente Fōin, one of the leading translators mentioned earlier.[44] When Hideyoshi issued his *Edict of Expulsion* in July 1587, the Jesuits commissioned Ito Maria to baptize Tama Gracia in her residence. After the baptism of Tama Gracia, Ito Maria dedicated her life to teaching others as a catechist and continued to baptize Tama Gracia's children and others in the Hosokawa household. Tama Gracia called Ito Maria her soul mother and trusted her as her resident pastor during her difficult years.

The most important source of Tama Gracia's spiritual knowledge came from Kirishitan books. She was extremely learned and knowledgeable about Zen Buddhism. When she visited the church for the one and only time at Easter 1587, she interrupted Brother Cosme's sermon and posed questions in the Zen disputation style. Upon leaving, she asked for a loan of "spiritual books, either written in Japanese or translated into it," so that she may "savor more of the things of God," according to Fróis. After Tama Gracia's departure, the Jesuits found out that it was Lady Hosokawa who had visited and eagerly sent her their books. These included *Contemptus Mundi* (*The Imitation of Christ*), still in manuscript form. Examining these books from cover to cover, Tama Gracia mastered *Romaji*, transliterated Portuguese, Latin, and Spanish terms and sent numerous inquiries about words and idioms via Ito Maria to the Jesuits, who sent back their explanations. Tama Gracia then gathered women to her quarters to teach Kirishitan literature. Fróis noted that she also composed catechisms and other Kirishitan books and "later she herself translated many other spiritual books in her own hand that was extraordinary in Japanese script and had a great reputation."[45] The fires of persecution destroyed all her Kirishitan works, translations, and letters while a few of her remaining "secular" letters and poems demonstrate not only her calligraphic skills but her high intellectual abilities.[46] Some may argue that Fróis used *trasladar* to mean hand-copying; however, since he used the same verb for the Jesuit translation activities, he would have recognized Tama Gracia's translation of spiritual books from European languages into Japanese.[47]

Members of Tama Gracia's study group at her residence were closely connected to the movement of women catechists, who actively promoted the Kirishitan religion in the greater Kyoto region using Kirishitan books. It is possible to imagine that each woman catechist owned a copy of these books, studied them on their own, and brought some suggestions for revisions of translated parts to the study group. Because of the long-standing Japanese practice of incorporating participatory responses from readers of manuscripts, and the Jesuit adaptation of this practice in their making of manuscripts, it is quite conceivable that multiple revisions of the manuscripts of *Contemptus Mundi* incorporated the observations, questions, interpretations, and suggestions for alternative translations by Tama Gracia and her students.[48]

Only two copies of published Japanese versions of *Contemptus Mundi* from the period exist. The 1596 Romaji version was published by the Jesuit Press, perhaps in Amakusa, and the 1610 kanamajiri version was printed by Kirishitan layman Harada Antonio in Kyoto.[49] In addition there were at least three more now nonextant revisions (1597, 1602, 1613). The "Preface to the Readers" (*docuju no fito*, literally, "those who recite it") of the 1596 version underscores the collaborative process of its translations and revisions.[50] It also suggests that the book was to be read aloud and studied in the groups of the Jesuits and laypersons.

A conspicuous feature of the *Contemptus Mundi* (1596) is the great number of Buddhist expressions that can be found in it. It is possible that these reflect ideas that Tama Gracia transmitted to the Jesuits in her correspondence about the revisions of the manuscripts.[51] Fróis noted her reputation among the Japanese such that in 1587, even as a woman, Tama Gracia was already comparable to a Zen master.[52] It is possible that this learned woman felt a special affinity for the spirituality of the *contemptus mundi* ("contempt for the world") because of its parallels to Zen Buddhism's view that people should not pin their hopes on this fleeting world.[53]

In turn, *Contemptus Mundi* probably provided Tama Gracia with opportunities to learn numerous Kirishitan terms in *Romaji* that were not translatable into Japanese. The two published versions (1596 and 1610) keep the scriptural verses in Latin in Romaji, followed by a Japanese translation. For example, Matthew 16:24 is printed in this manner in Part 2 Chapter 12, entitled "Tattoqi cruz no gocō no michi no coto" ("On the precious way of the cross").[54] It introduces readers to the meaning of the Kirishitan term *cruz* by discussing the meaning of Christ's passion and death on the cross, his commands to his disciples to "carry one's cross," and the various ways Kirishitans may face trials and temptations. Tama Gracia had discussed this chapter in her letters to Organtino in 1588.[55]

Until her death in 1600, Tama Gracia and the Jesuits continued to exchange letters and to discuss the teachings of *Contemptus Mundi* as applied to the life situations of laywomen like herself. The translators possibly utilized discoveries they made through these exchanges for their revisions toward publication. The 1610 version of *Contemptus Mundi* makes many structural changes by using far fewer loanwords (Chinese, Buddhist, or European) than the 1596 version and adds new character symbols. It removes all portions that were only applicable to the religious in the 1596 version and rewrites these with relevance for laypersons.[56] It thus became a readable guidebook for laywomen and men without the Jesuits' help in interpretation.

Because of her extreme circumstances, Tama Gracia's physical world was constrained to her quarters in the Hosokawa residence in Osaka. However, Kirishitan literature, her correspondence with the Jesuits, and interactions with the women catechists freed her mind and spirit in a third space, where she engaged in wider and loftier discourses.

5 Kirishitan women's active apostolate: The case of Naitō Julia

Women catechists connected the women in separated households with the Jesuits even while the Tokugawa increasingly restricted women's mobility and networking. Among several women associates of the mission, Naitō Julia (c.1566–1627) was the most distinguished.[57] The Jesuits noted that she was a sister of nobleman Naitō Tocuan João (c.1549–1626). After the death of her husband she was the abbess of a Jōdo nunnery in Kyoto for at least 16 years. In 1596, she heard a sermon preached by Vicente Fōin in the Jesuit Kyoto church and became a Kirishitan. She staged a religious disputation between herself and her former Buddhist male cleric colleagues and then received baptism by Father Organtino. Around 1600, she founded a society of women that followed the model of the Jesuit active apostolate and became its mother superior. She and a few other members took three vows under fathers Organtino and Pedro Morejón (1562–1639), even though the Jesuit constitutions clearly forbid establishing a female branch. The Jesuits worked closely with Julia and the *Miyaco no bicuni* ("nuns of Kyoto").[58] The bicunis' house and the Jesuit residence-church stood side by side in lower Kyoto.

Between the foundation of the Miyaco no bicuni and their arrest in 1613, Juilia and her bicunis along with some other women catechists persuaded thousands of women and men to become Kirishitans, despite warnings from the authorities and violent attacks on Julia by Buddhist clerics. When the Jesuits could no longer be out in public, Julia became the Jesuits' de facto "missionary."[59] While Julia and her bicunis preached, catechized, baptized, officiated in liturgical services, and engaged in inter-religious disputations in the open, the tide to seclude upper-class women in their *ie* was rising. As Julia used to be a well-known Buddhist teacher to ruling-class women, she continued to utilize her access to these women, who were interested in the Kirishitan religion but could not come to the church nor interact with clergy. As one Jesuit later narrated, Julia was the Jesuit key "to opening" these closed doors of households, and she baptized numerous women and their families "by her hand because we [the Jesuits] were not able to administer it."[60]

Examples of Julia and her bicunis' persuasion through personal discussions with women in *ie* must have provided the source for Fabian Fucan's *Myōtei mondō* or *Myōtei dialogue* (c.1605). The text is addressed to "ladies of quality and widows" interested in the "Kirishitan evangel"[61] and consists of fictional dialogues between two interlocutors: Myōshū, a noble widowed Jōdo nun, and Yūtei, a noble widowed Kirishitan catechist. The chapters introduce, explain, and critique the basic doctrines of the 12 schools of Buddhism, Taoism, Shinto, and Confucianism and defend the Kirishitan religion. Although Fabian (1562–1621), a Japanese brother, teacher, and apologist, claims single authorship of the work, he probably would have followed the Jesuit communal process of compilation. It is highly probable that he utilized material from the Miyaco no bicuni and especially the former Jōdo nun Julia, as Fabian was a spiritual director for the Miyako no bicuni under priestly supervision when he resided in Kyoto in the early 1600s.[62]

It is probably not a mere coincidence that one of the *Myōtei dialogue*'s protagonists, Myōshū, is a Jōdo nun, representing Naitō Julia's former religious identity. Myōshū's religious knowledge as a Jōdo nun is displayed in the chapter on Jōdoshū, which she calls "my religion" (*varafa ga xūxi*). As Myōshū describes her own life of devotion in prayer (*nembut zanmai*) to Amida Buddha, she proposes that Jōdoshū is unique among Buddhist schools in their doctrine of the promise of the glorious paradise in the West (*saifō gocuracu*) for those who call upon the name of Amida, especially at the time of death. Yūtei admits that Jōdoshū teaches an instant salvation (*socuvin vōjō*) for their followers but asserts that their sutras also require nine degrees of salvation (*cuvon vōjō*). She argues that Buddha, Amida, and paradise are nothing but *fonxō*, or one's own true nature. She further explains that navigational knowledge has proven that the world is round and the "West" is all relative, and so Jōdo ("Pureland") in the Western paradise is only an illusion.[63] Thus, she continues, Myōshū's *nembut* only leads her to the status of empty mindedness, and Jōdoshū, like all other Buddhist schools, ends in nothingness.

The *Myōtei dialogue* takes a decisive turn at the end of the dialogues on Japanese religions, when Yūtei starts to talk about the Kirishitan teachings:

> Now, I will speak to you about the teachings of my religion, Kirishitan. So far, I spoke to you in a lengthy discourse that neither Buddhism nor Shinto knows the True Lord of Heaven and Earth and thus they do not have the truth. Even though you have already been praying for safety in this world and a good place in the afterlife, you must know now that there exists this one Lord of Heaven and Earth.[64]

In the course of instruction, Myōshū gives her consent that there must be a creator and sustainer of all things in heaven and on earth. She affirms that Yūtei is her teacher and she begins posing questions about the Kirishitan religion.

Overall, these dialogues, taking place in Yūtei's bicuni house, convey Yūtei's expansive religious knowledge and self-confidence, as well as the loving relationship between her and Myōshū. They may suggest how Naitō Julia might have persuaded women like Myōshū, who sought her out, to embrace the Kirishitan religion when the Jesuits no longer had access to women's *ie*.

Around 1608, Fabian renounced his Kirishitan faith, left the Society, eloped with one of the bicunis, and, in 1620, wrote his famous anti-Kirishitan work *Ha daiusu* for the Nagasaki magistrate (*bugyō*) for use in its interrogation of Kirishitans. The shared space of the Jesuits and women catechists, both in public and clandestine places, continued to expand until, following the edict of the Shogun Hidetada, the authorities arrested the Miyaco no bicuni and closed the Jesuit mission in 1613. After public torture and imprisonment, the bicunis were marched to Nagasaki for inquisition. The authorities must have perceived that the Jesuits and the Miyaco no bicuni belonged together, as in late 1614, they deported Naitō Julia and 14 bicunis on the same ship with Father Morejón, 15 dōjucu, and 23 other Jesuits with the families of Naitō Tokuan João and Takayama Ukon Justo. Upon arrival at Manila in early 1615, the bicunis settled in a house next to the Jesuit house in the village of San Miguel and lived in total enclosure until 1656. There, instead of going out into the world to preach, these women shared another secret space with their Jesuit confessors in revealing their heavenly visions, intercessory prayers, and prophetic words, some of which the women wrote down in their diaries and were published posthumously by the Jesuits.[65]

6 Effacing women's spaces

Throughout the Christian Century, the Jesuits and women constructed multiple third spaces for their shared ministries, especially through the literature mission, within and beyond Japanese *ie*. Kirishitan women went through these new gateways to seek spiritual liberation even as Japanese society and religion decreased women's freedoms. This history of Kirishitan women broadens the definitions of "missionary" and "households." The household spaces of the merchant class Hibiya Monica and *daimyō*-class Hosokawa Tama Gracia were nurseries for Kirishitan literature. Aristocratic Kiyohara Ito Maria became a type of "domestic" missionary within the Hosokawas' household. As missionaries, like the Jesuits, Naitō Julia and her bicunis brought both books and new religious ideas to private households and the general public.

During the 1630s, hundreds of Kirishitan women and men were executed for harboring fewer than 20 fugitive Jesuits in their homes. After the martyrdom of the last recorded priest, Konishi Mancio, SJ (1600–1644), in 1644, visible signs of Kirishitan spaces disappeared at least from the surface, and all Kirishitan activities were carried out in extreme secrecy in remote communities for generations. By the 1650s, the Tokugawa government took control of the Japanese population and religions through the perpetuation of the *ie* system. Its bureau of religious inquisition (*shūmon aratame*) conducted an annual examination of religious affiliations of each household and kept census records of the descendants of former Kirishitan families.[66] Its rigid demands about social status and residency fixed in one's *ie*, as well as the indoctrination of Confucian filial piety, left little room for women to publicly exercise religious autonomy, networking, or leadership.

Despite the relentless raids throughout the 1850s, underground Kirishitan households in Urakami in Nagasaki continued to instill a strong sense of Kirishitan identity among their youth, orally teaching them foundational beliefs, prayers, and other rituals. They also continued to secretly circulate the Kirishitan texts. Among the documents that the inquisition confiscated from these households toward the end of the underground period was a collection of stories of three women saints, including that of St. Catherine of Alexandria.[67] The new Meiji imperial government, established in 1868, continued to persecute the Kirishitan communities who had resurfaced in 1865. The Kirishitan ban was only lifted in 1873 and the Constitution of 1889 finally guaranteed freedom of religion. How Kirishitan women created a new space for their leadership in their communities throughout this transition is a story for another time.

Notes

1 The term *Kirishitan* is derived from Portuguese *cristão* ("Christian"); as an adjective it means "Catholic," and as a noun it refers to a Catholic convert or converts, primarily during this period. The Japanese people simply pronounced and transcribed the Portuguese word *cristão* or *Christam* (alternative Portuguese spelling) as *Kirishitan*. The term also applies to the descendants of Kirishitan communities who went underground after 1650 and resurfaced in the mid-nineteenth century. Modern Japanese and English historiography uses *Kirishitan* for the Catholics

of the sixteenth and seventeenth centuries, differentiating them from Catholics (*katorikku*) who converted after the Meiji Restoration government lifted the ban on Christianity in 1873.

2 I am borrowing the term "third space" from postcolonial critics with caution. Since the 2004 publication of *The Location of Culture* by Homi K. Bhabha, various thinkers have redefined this concept. See Ikas and Wagner, *Communicating in the Third Space*. To apply this twentieth-century theoretical term to a pre-modern historical case, I am modifying "the" Third Space into a diversity of third spaces.

3 I am grateful to Nicolas Standaert, who pointed me toward studies on Japanese *ma* 間 (and Chinese *shi* 勢) as another methodological possibility. In his "Don't Mind the Gap," Standaert states that "many human activities come into being due to the existence and creation of space 'between' the Self and the Other. This space acts both as that which allows an encounter to take place (leading to interaction and communication) and as that which is produced by the encounter as such" (p. 98). Such observations can be applied to this research.

4 The mission's printing press produced at least 60 Kirishitanban ("Christian edition") titles between 1590 and 1614.

5 On the Jesuits and Kirishitans, see Boxer, *The Christian Century in Japan*; Higashibaba, *Christianity in Early Modern Japan*; and Ward, *Women Religious Leaders*.

6 On Jesuit accommodation, see Schütte, *Valignano's Mission Principles for Japan*; Üçerler, "The Jesuit Enterprise in Japan"; and Moran, *The Japanese and the Jesuits*.

7 The topics of the exclusive maleness as one of the distinctive marks of the Society of Jesus and of women who embraced Jesuit-style active vocation in the missions in England, New France, and other places, in relation to the post-Tridentine regulations of the enclosure of religious women, have become standard in Jesuit studies. See Simmonds, "Women Jesuits"; Ward, "Jesuits, Too."

8 On the spread of literacy from the elite classes to commoners between the late fifteenth and mid-seventeenth centuries in Japan, see Lieberman, *Strange Parallels*, 63; on writing and reading practices of Japanese women, see Endō, *A Cultural History* and Ericson, "The Origins of the Concept of 'Women's Literature'," 77–78. The Jesuits favorably compared Japanese women's higher literacy to the lower literacy of European women. See Fróis, *Kulturgegensätze Europa-Japan* (1585), 128 and Danford, Gill, and Reff, *The First European Description of Japan*, 74–75.

9 On the history of Japanese persecution against Kirishitans, see Gonoi, *Tokugawa shoki Kiirishitan shi kenkyū*.

10 Bernstein, "Introduction," 3.

11 See Sekiguchi, "The Patriarchal Family Paradigm," 27–46.

12 The consensus among religious scholars and historians is that "Confucian" discourses do not designate one universal, coherent, and hegemonic religion. Here I am using the term specifically for the Tokugawa states' selective adaptation, codification, and implementation of Chinese principles (儒教) on rulership and institutions.

13 For a nuanced understanding of the historical development of official "Confucianism," male domination of politics, families, and texts in East Asian Confucian societies, and evidence of women's embodied negotiations for their own empowerment in these societies, see Ko, Haboush, and Piggott, "Introduction." Particularly applicable to this essay is the authors' caution (p. 7) that the modern Euro-American notion of public versus private spheres did not correspond to pre-modern East Asian ideas of official and unofficial realms.

14 See Wakita, *Women in Medieval Japan*. Also see Wakita, "The Medieval Household and Gender Roles." For women in the book industry, see Smith, "The History of the Book in Edo and Paris," 339; and Kornicki, *The Book in Japan*, 12.

15 See Uno, "Women and Changes" (especially 22–30).
16 Wakita, "The Medieval Household," 82.
17 See Wakita, *Women in Medieval Japan*, 115–118; also see Ruch, "Woman to Woman," 567–575; and Ward, *Women Religious Leaders*, 145–156.
18 Wakita, *Women in Medieval Japan*, 121.
19 See Fróis, *Kulturgegensätze Europa-Japan* (1585), 126. See also Danford, Gill, and Reff, trans. and ed., *The First European Description of Japan*, 69–70.
20 Women in the early Edo period not only lost their rights to own property, but their bodies also became the property of their husbands. See Tonomura, "Sexual Violence Against Women," 144.
21 See Hur, *Death and Social Order*.
22 On these misogynist Buddhist doctrines, see Yoshida, "The Enlightenment of the Dragon King's Daughter." On Shōsan Suguki, one of the Confucio-Buddhist educators of women, see Elison, *Deus Destroyed*, 223–231. On the nature of Confucian anti-Kirishitan discourses of the early Tokugawa era, see Paramore, *Japanese Confucianism*, 34–77.
23 On Luís de Almeida and Luís Fróis, see Schütte, *Textus catalogorum*, 1124–1125; 1176–1178.
24 Fróis, *História de Japam*, vol. 2, 5. The English translations from all non-English sources in the following are mine.
25 On the merchants of Sakai, see Morris, "The City of Sakai and Urban Autonomy," 23–54.
26 Fróis, *História*, vol. 2, 35. This and other descriptions hint that the Jesuit missionaries genuinely appreciated the hospitality at the Japanese *ie* with little sense of European colonial superiority.
27 Fróis, *História*, vol. 2, 40. On the shared aesthetic space between Jesuit missionaries and the Japanese in tea ceremonies, see Hioki, "Tea Ceremony as a Space for Interreligious Dialogue."
28 On Hibiya Monica, see Ward, *Women Religious Leaders*, 37–60.
29 Fróis, *História*, vol. 2, 37–38.
30 Fróis, *História*, vol. 2, 170. See also Fróis's letters dated 20 February and 30 June 1565, on Vilela translating several books including *Flos Sanctorum* in CE 1, fol. 177r and 206v. The 1565 incident eventually led to Oda Nobunaga's overthrow of the dynastic Muromachi government (established in 1338) in 1573.
31 Fróis, *História*, vol. 2, 115. The Jesuit communities lived in professed houses where there were no colleges. See O'Malley, *The First Jesuits*, 356.
32 See Fróis, *História*, vol. 2, 175, 184. Very little information on this Damião is known.
33 On *biwa* minstrel-priests and sermon ballads, see Shirane, *Traditional Japanese Literature*, 1159–1160. On the Jesuit *biwa hōshi*, see Ruiz-de-Medina, *Iezusu kaishi to Kirishitan fukyō*, 131–168. Among these entertainer groups who inspired the Noh and Kabuki, *goze*, the female counterpart to *biwa hōshi*, were already marginalized by this period, and perhaps no *goze* participated in the Jesuit circles. See Wakita, *Women in Medieval Japan*, 94–95.
34 On the audience participation in Jesuit translations, see Obara "Kaisetsu," in *Santosu no gosagyō*; also see Ward, "Women and Kirishitanban Literature"; and Ward, "Images of the Incarnation."
35 On Lourenço, see Schütte, *Textus catalogorum*, 1211–1212.
36 Smith, "The History of the Book," 348–349. On a similar tradition in China, see Tymoczko, "Ideology and the Position of the Translator," 224.
37 On the European loanwords, see Fukushima, *Kirishitan shiryō to kokugo kenkyū*, 142.
38 *Sanctos*, 2, 61–85. For a more detailed examination of the texts of Kirishitanban stories of St. Catherine of Alexandria, see Ward, "Images of the Incarnation."

Two surviving copies of *Sanctos no gosagveo no vchi nvqigaqi* are preserved in the Biblioteca Nazionale Marciana, Venice, Italy, and the Bodleian Library, Oxford. The facsimile of the Marciana copy is published in Kōso, *Sanctos no gosagveo no vchi nvqigaqi.*

39 On the similar results in their contemporary Jesuit translations of French devotional literature into English, see Coldiron, "Translation's Challenge to Critical Categories."

40 On Hosokawa Tama Gracia, see Ward, *Women Religious Leaders*, 193–292.

41 As a high-ranking warrior class woman, Akechi-Hosokawa Tama lived in castles before exile (Akechi's Sakamoto castle, Hosokawa's Shōryūji castle, and Tanabe castle). Beginning in 1583, the unifier Hideyoshi ruled from the Osaka castle and ordered *daimyō* to construct their residential mansions in Osaka. Tadaoki obliged, and that was where Tama Gracia spent much of her adult life in confinement and where she died.

42 The Catholic Church beatified Takayama Ukon Justo in 2017.

43 Fróis, *História*, vol. 4, 487.

44 See Schütte, *Textus catalogorum*, 1261 (Gnecchi-Soldo Organtino), 1152 (Gregorio Céspedes), and 1304 (Takai Cosme).

45 Fróis, *História*, vol. 4, 492.

46 Reproductions of Tama Gracia's handwritten letters can be seen in an exhibition catalogue, *Ai to shinkō ni ikita Hosokawa Garashiya ten*, 108–115.

47 On Tama Gracia's literacy in European languages, see Ward, *Women Religious Leaders*, 203–209. See also Guerreiro, *Relação Anual*, vol. 1, 126–127. Since the first dictionary/grammar, *Dictionarium latino lustitancum ac japonicum*, was not published until 1595, Tama Gracia and the Jesuits must have used manuscript forms of Abecedarios and grammar/dictionaries.

48 See Ebisawa, *Kirishitan nanban bungaku nyūmon*, 160–161, on the prepublication history of *Contemptus Mundi* in Japan. A version of the original, which the Jesuit called *Gersom* according to the attributed author Jean Gerson, was included in the catalogue of books sent to Japan in 1554. The Jesuit annual letter of 1582 mentions a Japanese translation for the Novitiate in Usuki. Ebisawa says that in 1585, Pope Sixtus V gave the Japanese readers an indulgence of ten years for a chapter reading.

49 Three copies of the 1596 version of *Contemptus mundi jenbu* survive in Biblioteca Ambrosiana, Milan and the Bodleian Library, Oxford. A critical edition of Biblioteca Ambrosiana copy is available in Obara, ed., *Kontemutsusu munji.* A copy of the 1610 version is preserved in Tenri Central Library, Nara, and its facsimile is found as *Kontemutsusu munji* in *Kirishitanbanshū*, 369–538.

50 *Kontemutsusu munji*, 14.

51 See Obara's list of Buddhist terms in *Contemptus Mundi* and other Kirishitan literature in *Kontemutsusu munji*, 296. He observes that *Contemptus Mundi* contains far more Buddhist terms than others.

52 Fróis, *História*, vol. 4, 485. See also Ward, *Women Religious Leaders*, 268–271. There were several Jesuit dōjucus and brothers who were also knowledgeable about Zen, but none received such praise as Tama Gracia.

53 See Farge, *The Japanese Translations of the Jesuit Mission Press.*

54 "Si quis vult post me venire, abneget semetipsum, et tollat crucem suam, & sequatur me. Matt. 16. Tarenitemo are vaga atoyori qitaran to vomofuni voite ua, mi vo sutete sono mino cruz vo totte vare vo xitaye." The NRSV has: "If any want to become my followers, let them deny themselves and take up their cross and follow me. See *Kontemutsusu munji*, 80; and *Kirishitanbanshū* vol. 1, 465 (Chapter 9 in this version).

55 See Fróis, *História*, vol. 5, 35.

56 See Hiiragi, "Kaidai," 27–38.

57 On Naitō Julia, see Ward, *Women Religious Leaders*, 61–81; and Ward, "Women Apostles in Early Modern Japan, 1549–1650."
58 Also see Kataoka, *Kirishitan jidai no joshi shūdōkai.*
59 ARSI, Phil. 7I, 197v–198.
60 Colín, *Labor Evangélica*, 3:500–501.
61 Elison, *Deus Destroyed*, 438, note 71.
62 On Fabian Fucan, see Schütte, *Textus catalogorum*, 1168 and Cieslik, "Fabian Fukan den nōto"; on Fucan's Kirishitan and anti-Kirishitan writings, see Ide, *Kirishitan shisōshi kenkyū josetsu*; and Elison, *Deus Destroyed.*
63 *Myōtei mondō*, 348–351.
64 *Myōtei mondō*, 383.
65 On these diaries, see Colín, *Labor Evangélica*, 3:512. On the life of the Miyaco no bicuni in the Philippines, see Ward, *Women Religious Leaders*, 83–104.
66 For an edition of massive records from more than a dozen regions, see Yajima, *Bungo no kuni Kirishitan ruizokuchō.*
67 On these stories of the saints confiscated from Kirishitan communities in Urakami in 1789–1800, see Anesaki, *Kirishitan shūmon*, 131–239.

12 Missionaries and women

Domestic Catholicism in the Middle East

Bernard Heyberger

Even today, states with an Islamic rule and a Muslim majority do not tolerate Christian proselytizing. Catholic authorities have been aware of the impossibility of addressing Muslims in these regions since the first attempts in the Middle Ages. Therefore, as missions in the Ottoman Empire first targeted Eastern Christians, they could to some extent be compared to the home missions, which, in Catholic countries, from the beginning of the seventeenth century, tried to "convert" the Catholic faithful, who were considered to be bad and ill-educated Christians.[1] In his report for the year 1652, the Jesuit Nicolas Poirresson asserts that the tasks of the missionaries in Syria were the same as those in France: schools, predication, confraternities of laymen, catechism, confession, and conversation with Catholics and others.[2]

However, Eastern Christians were not Roman Catholics. The term "Eastern Christians" encompasses a wide range of different churches: Maronites, Melkites, Armenians, Western Syrians, Eastern Syrians, and Copts were represented in the Arabic part of the Ottoman Empire.[3] Each Christian belonged to his own church and was submitted to his own hierarchy. Even if some hierarchies like that of the Maronites were considered Catholic and in union with Rome, the freedom of the Latin missionaries in interacting with the faithful was limited and dependent upon the ordinary local authorities, bishop, or patriarch. Moreover, whereas the local Christians were subjects (*dhimmī*) of the Sultan, Western missionaries were only tolerated as strangers. Locally, their position depended on the importance and the sectarian balance of the Christian population, the presence of a French consul, and the strength of the Islamic framework (presence of Islamic courts and other Islamic institutions, with a strong class of religion-officers, ulama). Aleppo offers an opportunity for a thorough survey of the way in which Catholicism spread locally under these circumstances. Between the seventeenth century and the beginning of the nineteenth century, this city, deeply marked by Islamic institutions, included several thousand Christian inhabitants, with a strong presence of Latin missionaries under the protection of the French consuls. These features, as well as the rich documentation conserved on the issue, make it an especially interesting case for investigation.

In the specific context of Aleppo, Catholicism appears rather as crypto-Catholicism, a semi-clandestine denomination, mostly private and individualistic in its practice. This context of secrecy and privacy, as in other cases,[4] fostered a specific gendered religiosity, characterized by the active participation of women. The link between women and Latin priests through spiritual guidance strengthened and produced new kinds of behaviors and mentalities, which sometimes encountered opposition from the local clergy and the relatives of these devotees.

1 Missionary activities in a constrained context

In the Islamic context, Christians were submitted to specific constraints concerning the practice of their religion. These constraints were more stringent in ancient cities like Aleppo, Tripoli, or Damascus, where a class of religious officers attended to the implementation of *shariʿa*, than in the highlands or the countryside, where more relaxed local customs often prevailed.

The Latin missionaries were regarded as strangers by the Ottoman State. They were *mustaʾmin* ruled by the agreements between the Sultan and the French king. Their presence was generally tolerated because they were supposed to serve the European Catholic people settled in the Ottoman Empire. They served as chaplains of the consuls and vicars of the Frankish communities, but officially, they were not to interfere in local Christian affairs.[5] Therefore, missionaries were often sheltered in the neighborhoods of the French consuls and merchants, in specific commercial buildings called *khans*, where they rented a number of rooms. These estates generally belonged to Islamic foundations, called *waqf*, which were under the administration of a manager linked to the religious elite of the city.[6] And they were located in the trading heart of the town, the market or the harbor. This was the case for instance in Smyrna, Sidon, Acre, Tripoli, Aleppo, Cairo, and Constantinople.

In Damascus, where there were no foreign consuls and no foreign merchants, the missionaries had the liberty of living in the midst of the Christian neighborhood, within the old city, between Bāb Tūma and Bāb Sharqī.[7] In Aleppo, in contrast, the Catholic missionaries dwelled in *khans*, in the central bazaar, while the main Christian district was located in the northern suburb of the city. The distance was no more than a kilometer, but in order to visit the Christians and their churches, the Latin priests had to walk through the narrow streets of the medina and to cross the city's gates, where they were sometimes physically assaulted.[8] It was also very difficult for the Eastern Christians to visit them, and sometimes the gathering of young men in the missionaries' dwellings prompted clashes with the Muslim neighborhood.[9] It was even more difficult for women to attend the Western chapels in the center, and several incidents occurred with Muslim officers regarding their attendance there. In 1710, for instance, the rush of Christian women for the Feast of Saint Anthony of Padua caused an action of the qadi against the church of the Franciscans.[10] In Acre, which in the eighteenth century was a boomtown, where the Islamic framework was less strong than in Aleppo,[11] the Franciscan Minor Friars succeeded in building a church in the Christian district that was specifically intended for women, who could not attend the chapel in the central *khan*, where the missionaries were dwelling.[12]

Eastern Christians officially belonged to a congregation in which they received the sacraments and attended liturgy but also paid the poll tax and other taxes, under the jurisdiction of their patriarch or their bishop. In this context, religion is overall a communal practice, where attendance at liturgy is the main expression of faith, and the main way to be instructed in it. Individual conviction does not really matter, but social conformity is required, as a part of political order. Under these conditions, it was almost impossible for people to change affiliation and to attend the Latin worship instead of that of their own church. When from the beginning of the eighteenth century, the struggle between the Eastern Christians "united" to Rome and the "orthodox" became stronger, those who leaned to Rome could be charged in the *shari'a* court with "becoming Franks," that is, with betrayal of the Sultan. As a result, Catholics belonging to Eastern denominations could not have their own churches and worship freely, until their recognition as autonomous *millets* as late as 1848. Before this date their situation varied from place to place, and time to time. Sometimes they were free to meet and worship, sometimes they attended the Latin churches, and sometimes they practiced their devotions privately in their houses.

Under these circumstances, the pastoral tools commonly available for Catholic missionaries in the seventeenth and eighteenth centuries to address the Christian faithful were not easy to use. Predication was the first of these tools. But even for preaching in their own chapel, the Latin priests had to take into account the competition between the different religious orders present (Jesuits, Capuchins, Discalced Carmelites, Minor Friars), each of them wanting to give the homily for the consul or for the European community. When they wanted to preach in an Eastern church, they had to secure the agreement of its bishop or of its parish priest, who was often reluctant to give it, even when they belonged to a Catholic denomination, like the Maronites.[13] The second important pastoral tool typical for baroque Catholicism, public meetings and demonstrations of devotion like processions and Stations of the Cross (for which missionaries had a fondness), was almost impossible.[14] In Aleppo, in 1658, fearing persecution, the Discalced Carmelites had to give up the modest monthly procession of the Virgin of Carmel, in their small chapel of the *khan*, which was provided with indulgences for those who belonged to the friary of the Scapular.[15] The Capuchin Justinien de Neuvy describes in great detail the Christmas festival of 1668 in Aleppo, with a very well-ordered procession. But this entire beautiful ceremony happened in the very tiny chapel of the friars and involved no more than 20 people, who had to take care not to attract the attention of neighbors when entering the *khan*.[16]

The missionaries had to adapt to this specific context. As Joseph Besson asserted in his *Syrie Sainte* (1660):

> Missions in Syria are not royal missions, which put on the feet of missionaries crowned heads to be baptized and give them Princes listening to their teaching. . . . I confess that these missions have less radiance, either because new churches are not erected and they are only allowed to repair the Ancients (which are falling due to their old age), or because you have to serve God with a hidden hand and to be consumed with a concealed zeal.[17]

In Aleppo, which had nearly 30,000 Christian inhabitants at the end of the seventeenth century, the pastoral care of the Latin missionaries took place in an almost clandestine way, with most of their activity consisting of visiting the families in the courtyards and the blind alleys of the suburb of Jdayda. In 1655, Anselme de l'Annonciation, a Discalced Carmelite missionary, although in rather idealistic and apologetic terms targeting a European readership, detailed several interesting elements concerning his working method. He begins his day at three o'clock in the morning. After having said mass, he spends the morning in the suburbs, until noon. He is welcomed by the women and girls, who, he asserts, do not hide from his presence, contrary to what they do with the other men. Once he has entered a home, he pulls out a crucifix from his clothes and makes known to the inhabitants that he does not want their gold or their money. And he always refuses food and drink from his hosts.[18]

The dwellings of the Christians were generally one room, with three or four families living in the same building. Several families could live in the same blind alley, which appeared as a semi-private space.[19] Following Father Anselme's account, when the missionary enters a dwelling, people gather, so that often he becomes surrounded by 10 or 12 people. He also visits the workshops, where men and children produce textiles. Entering the building, he informs everyone that he does not want the workers to stop working. He needs only their heart and their ears. Following the method of Saint Ignatius, he asserts (a rather amazing point, coming from a Discalced Carmelite), he begins modestly, asking how their business runs, and if the children have prayed. Then he gathers the children, asking them to make the sign of the Cross and to repeat the *Pater, Ave*, and *Credo*. He advises them to be obedient to their parents and their masters; not to steal, swear, or talk with Muslims; to avoid the company of bad children; and to pray in the morning and evening. By addressing the children, the missionary is of course also targeting the adults, and he sometimes asks them questions afterward. He recites different acts of faith and contrition, with the crucifix in the hand, "the all briefly, but fervent and inflamed." When they tell him about their problems, he dispenses advice and promises relief.[20] During these visits, all the missionaries generously dispatch images and medals to their hosts and try to collect in return the amulets Christians are often using. They write short spiritual exhortations in Arabic, which they hand out.[21]

Once people have agreed to listen to the missionary and to follow his directions, he has them prepare for confession. The sacrament of penitence is indeed the main tool for the Latin priests to forge a narrow and personal relationship with the people. As in the home missions in Europe, this becomes the main indicator of their activity: in 1669, the Capuchin Jean-Baptiste de Saint-Aignan gives a number of 500 to 600 people who confessed to the Latin priests in Aleppo every month;[22] at the beginning of the eighteenth century, the Jesuits announce triumphantly in their annual reports the number of the confessions they have received each year. In 1713, for instance, they achieved a total of 3040 in Aleppo.[23]

Among Eastern Christians, private confession was not systematically practiced and was not based on the same principles and rules as in the Roman Church. In the Eastern tradition, sins were considered a disease, and the confessor a physician. Absolution was like a remedy. In the Catholic scholastic theology, in contrast, as it developed from the thirteenth century, the faithful appeared individually before court and the confessor was considered a judge. Sins had to be precisely defined and confessed because the confessor had to assess their gravity and determine the penitence based on their importance.[24] This kind of confession required daily training. Books like the famous *Penitente istruito* from the Italian Jesuit missionary Paolo Segneri[25] were translated into Arabic and dispatched among the people, in order to teach them how to prepare for the sacrament of confession. This intense and frequent training of soul searching and confession could develop beyond the sacramental confession into spiritual guidance, a practice also attested in the Eastern tradition, but in this case in a monastic context.[26]

It seems that confession, the technology of soul searching, and moral theology all encountered real success and became widespread not only in Syria but everywhere in Eastern Christianity starting in the seventeenth century.[27] Nevertheless, the Eastern clergy never matched the Latin priests in this field.

2 Women and domestic Catholicism

In this context, women became one of the main targets of the missionaries. Generally, they belonged to those categories of people considered ignorant and spiritually derelict, which became a problem for post-Tridentine Catholicism. Thus, it was a prime task for the clergy to give women access to religious services and the sacraments in order to ensure their salvation and to take control over their role as educators of their children.

As Joseph Besson wrote:

> Besides, the lack of devotion among the women, and their extreme ignorance, which is significantly higher than that of the men in all that pertains the mysteries of our religion, are the causes of the perdition of the

> young people, who do not receive any kind of education from their parents. It must be said that the condition of the children is pitiful due to their mothers . . . in that, they are similar to the Mohammedan women who are banished from the mosques, and who even the Koran does not welcome in Paradise.[28]

The local conditions generated a specific position for women. The honor code that ruled the local society as well as living among Muslims did not necessarily limit women's agency within their households, but it seriously restrained their mobility in the public sphere. In 1738, a governor of Aleppo forbade the Christians to go to the gardens and Christian women to go to the cemeteries.[29] In 1764, the Maronite bishop proclaimed that women going to the gardens without his authorization or to the countryside on Sundays or holydays without a legitimate reason, committed a sin of which the absolution was reserved to himself.[30] His successor in 1807 issued a very strict regulation concerning women, forbidding them from attending funerals even in the church, as well as every kind of outside festivity.[31]

Women often did not visit their church for several reasons. Father Besson asserts,

> The second [source of disorder] concerns the women, whose decency could not be praised enough, but this utmost restraint causes great disorder. That is, that the most qualified of them almost never hear the mass, neither on Sundays, nor on the biggest days of the year, and in this consists the greatness of the ladies, that as their beauty or their social level rises, they proportionally less show up in the churches. . . . They attend baths and weddings, but never the church.[32]

Moreover, the canonic rules forbade women from entering the church during their periods and for 40 days after the childbirth of a boy, 80 after that of a girl. If a woman was too poor to be properly dressed, or if her husband converted to Islam, she was supposed to abstain from attending the services. In churches, women had a special space in the back – and even a special entrance gate. The missionaries worked so hard to convince them to attend worship in church, that, for instance, the Maronite church of Aleppo had to be enlarged in 1686, when women began to more frequently attend the services.[33] Nevertheless, it is noteworthy that in the confraternity of the Sacred Heart founded in 1750 by the Maronite devout woman Hindiyya, to whom I dedicated a book, there were still specific rules for women, in order to allow them to practice privately within the domestic setting.[34]

On the other hand, in the context of the Ottoman social and political organization, it seems that the roles were differentiated within the families: to the men belonged the spaces of the street and the church, the obligation of taxpaying, and the official affiliation with a denomination. To the women belonged the domestic space. Women could discretely keep company with the Latin missionaries who could provide them and their family with some advantages. Actually it was possible to be a secret follower of Catholicism while being publicly affiliated with an Eastern church. Furthermore, it was also possible for only the women of a household to convert to Catholicism, as the conversion of a woman had fewer serious consequences than that of a male household head.[35]

Eastern Christian families did not necessarily fit with the common conception: extended, patriarchal, with women and young men dependent on or protected by elder men. Recent scholarship provides a more nuanced picture of family and households in the early modern Middle East, with the predominance of conjugal family over lineage and patriarchy. Overall, they show the notions of family and household as moving and dynamic realities, dependent first on the demographics.[36] Nevertheless, we might state that, like in other societies, Eastern Christian women and young people belonged to socially weak categories, which needed outside support. Among the women who became followers of the Latin priests were a number of widows or wives whose husbands had disappeared or converted to Islam, or younger girls who did not have family support and who had few hopes of getting married.[37] A corpus of recorded conversions operated by the Discalced Carmelites in Aleppo during the second half of the seventeenth century shows that more than half of the households that converted did not have a male head. These families typically consisted of a mother with her children or of brothers and sisters. From a strong link to the Latin missionaries, such families could expect material relief and a form of protection. The missionaries could provide their followers with contacts to the European consuls and residents, who on their side could supply their "protégés" with alms, jobs, or useful information concerning trade. Overall, missionaries swiftly gained a reputation for being physicians and apothecaries. It is noteworthy that fathers and husbands, if they were mentioned, were hardly ever the first to convert. The connection to the missionaries was carried out through the wife, the mother, or the children. The specific sociability between women in the domestic neighborhood often appears in the accounts of the missionaries. The links between the housemaid and the women of a household, for instance, are mentioned several times as a key to conversion.[38]

Meeting women in a domestic context, especially for confession, was not without danger for the conscience and the reputation of a missionary. Father Anselme de l'Annonciation gave advice on how to proceed for hearing women's confessions. The missionary should be very prudent with women, he asserted because they wear light clothing, especially during summertime. He should stretch a blanket between him and the penitent, hang a crucifix on it, and hold another one in his hands. He should always take care to leave doors and windows open.[39] Two centuries later, in 1838, the Apostolic delegate Jean-Baptiste d'Auvergne issued a rule for confessions at home in order to bring an end to neverending controversies and scandals. He ordered that no woman could be confessed at home after the evening's *Ave Maria*, and that the confessor will always wear a stole on his neck, the door of the room will always stay open, and the woman, kneeling quite far apart from him, will wear a veil on her head.[40]

Like in Western Catholicism, confession tended to become an intense guidance of the conscience, exclusive and frequent, especially with women. In the rules of the confraternities that were initiated by the missionaries, access was only granted after a previous general confession, which was far more than a simple confession of the sins. It was actually an unveiling of the inner self, based on which the relationship between the penitent and his spiritual father would afterwards be established.[41] When, in 1736, the Jesuit Antonio Venturi became the spiritual father of the young Maronite devotee Hindiyya, he visited her at her home once a week.[42] In the rule of the confraternity of the Rosary, intended for widows and maidens and founded by a Lazarist in 1794, it was said that the members of this pious association have to recognize the spiritual adviser as "a father, a physician, a judge" and have to open their conscience at the end of every month because "nothing helps to improve the spiritual health like soul-searching."[43] In the confraternity of the Holy Heart of Jesus, initiated in 1817, the "disclosure of conscience" took place over fixed intervals of time, with a spiritual adviser who was not necessarily the confessor. According to a report of a Melkite bishop, in 1829, the female members of this association visited their spiritual adviser several times a day and spent time with him alone. He ordered that they should only confess once a week, and the duration of the confession was not to exceed three quarters of an hour.[44]

The first rules of confraternities, at the beginning of the eighteenth century, were less precise and placed less emphasis on spiritual and psychological improvement through soul searching. Yet, from the very beginning of their activity the missionaries began to encourage girls to renounce marriage and to commit themselves to a religious life. Around 1670, the capuchins gathered Syrian, Armenian, and Melkite women involved in a project of a consecrated life. However, a secluded life like in a monastery was not possible in an Islamic city. Instead the women had to live as Franciscan Tertiaries, continued to stay in their parents' homes, and worked to make a living. However, they renounced the idea of marriage, tried to abstain from meat, recited the Holy Virgin's Office every day, went to church three or four times a week, and confessed every two weeks. Although this Third Order eventually lasted more than 30 years, until 1700, it was met from the beginning with resentment and opposition, especially on the part of the Eastern clergy. After the Third Order vanished, the Jesuits initiated another group of women, living with the rule of Saint Francis of Sales. Through controversies and conflicts, this second experience of female consecrated life led to the foundation of several female religious orders in Mount Lebanon around 1750, among them that of the Sacred Heart of Jesus led by Hindiyya.[45] However, devout women living like Tertiaries in their homes under the guidance of missionaries existed in Aleppo until the mid-nineteenth century, and there is evidence of the presence of similar groups in other cities, like Damascus and Acre.[46]

3 A new education, a new behavior

The intense relations between the Latin clergy and the women generated a new kind of habitus among the Christian women. As early as 1630, a Friar Minor envisaged beginning to teach catechism to the women in Aleppo, but apparently, requests also came from the families themselves. We find evidence of girls studying with missionaries and even teaching others to read as early as 1660.

During the eighteenth century, reading became widespread among women. In the rules of the Congregation of the Rosary mentioned earlier, article one requires its members to possess spiritual books. Article two states that the main purpose of this association is the instruction of young women, who must then report back to their individual homes on what they have learned during the meetings. In addition, the devotees of the Rosary had to meet on Sunday afternoons to repeat the catechism and teach it to girls, especially to those preparing for their first communion.[47]

Markings in some books from the eighteenth century offer evidence that they belonged to women. For example, a printed volume of Paolo Segneri's *Sinner's Guide* (*Murshid al-khāṭī' fī sirr al-tūba wa-l-i'tirāf*), edited in the Lebanese monastery of S. John of Shuwayr in 1747, became the property of the Aleppine Maryam bint Bashāra ibn Ni'mat Allāh Sā'igh in 1764. Furthermore, in 1797, a small catechism was given to the Capuchin Philibert by Theresia bint Jibrā'īl Banna so that he could learn Arabic. Finally, we also know of a handbook for a good communion (*Muḥtawiyya 'alā l-isti'dād wa-shukr wa-tilba al-qurbān*) that was owned by Madalena Sā'igh, a daughter of the deceased Yūsuf Sā'igh.[48]

The British physician resident in Aleppo, Alexander Russell, reports in about 1790 that Christian women of higher classes were known to read and write, although they scarcely considered reading to be entertainment.[49] In these circles, reading was mostly a rather mechanical, oral, and collective exercise (although the practice of silent and solitary reading was one of the goals stated by the rules).

What did these women read? They could have read all the classics of baroque spirituality, widely available in Catholic Europe and translated into Arabic from the middle of the seventeenth century. In 1831, a report to Rome listed the books in use by the spiritual advisers and their devotees. There were, unsurprisingly, five or six exemplars of *Castello dell'anima* of Theresa of Avila, two exemplars of the biography of Marguerite-Marie Alacoque by Jean-Joseph Languet de Gergy, both in an Arabic translation, and *Al-Sabīl al-Afḍal* (*The most Perfect Way*), "a collection of ascetic texts, without connection and without taste."[50] Thus this literature helped to conform to the literary pattern of spiritual women as illustrated by many Western holy women, whose writings were available in Arabic as early as the second part of the seventeenth century.

Most of these books translated into Arabic taught a way of life which broke with some of the most atavistic customs of the reader's everyday life. Handbooks were available in Arabic, which analyzed and commented on behaviors linked to specific social conditions and delivered judgments on good or sinful conduct according to each social situation: duties of the mother, characteristic sins of youth, spiritual dangers incurred by merchants. At every moment of the day, self-control must be maintained; nothing can be left to chance or escape the attention of the devout. For instance, the rules of the Rosary Sisterhood specify that, in the evening, at bedtime, women must offer their heart to Jesus, their beloved. In the morning, they must wake up half an hour before sunrise, jump out of their bed and begin to recite various prayers. They must not take more than three meals a day. They must show proof of temperance and decency (*iḥtishām*) while eating and not forget to rinse their mouth after a meal. They must keep their senses in check. They must not cast their glances around in every direction; they must not stare at bystanders or passers-by and they must not peep out of windows out of curiosity. They must not walk swiftly, must never joke together, never hold or touch one another, and never shake a man's hand, not even a priest's. It is better that they always hold something to work on or a book or a picture of Jesus Christ in their hands.[51]

Beyond these practical injunctions, the handbooks initiate the reader toward a psychological self-consciousness, providing the necessary keys for telling oneself or one's confessor about the state of one's soul. Internalization of this discourse is the best proof of its authenticity and truth. The handbooks teach that even temptation can become a sin; thus, one must gain conscious awareness of it and express it through self-confession. Paolo Segneri explains, for instance, how temptation moves from the object to the senses, then toward understanding and the will. In order for temptation to become a sin, it must reach the will. This can eventually lead to sin in two different ways: through desire (ardently desiring the realization of the temptation) or by complacency (when pleasure is derived from the realization of the temptation, without nonetheless having wished it). These patterns of education had actual consequences. Alexander Russell relates that households, especially Maronites, began to adopt European customs. Most Christians in the service of "Franks" ate their meals at tables, seated on chairs, and admitted the company of their wives, sometimes even allowing them to appear unveiled in front of European guests. Russell notes that Christian women had more distinguished, or more affected, manners than Muslim women. According to the author they were less inclined to venture bold comments or to constantly invoke the name of God.[52]

Yet these developments were also met with resentment and opposition. As early as 1711, the representatives of four Aleppine congregations challenged the intentions of missionaries who were involved in educating women. Armenian leaders sent a protest, also undersigned by Maronites, Melkites, and

Chaldeans, to the Guardian of Jerusalem, objecting to the Jesuits and the Capuchins who visited women's houses "where they go to mislead women and children, giving them medals, crosses and money, and in this way Turks increase pressure on us."[53]

In 1757, the Armenian Catholic Patriarch complains to *Propaganda Fide* against the Minor Friars and requires the removal of their Third Order in Aleppo, arguing that:

> [They] ask these women, who register with them, to wear a black tunic with a belt consisting of a big rope with a big Rosary at its end, and a proportionated cross. This, being an innovation, causes astonishment among the Orientals, and the Turks do not abstain from making fun of it and blaspheming the cross.[54]

It is not appropriate, he asserts, for women to go through stores, coffee shops, and markets that are crowded with Muslims. Moreover, this Third Order spreads mischief within the households because these women forget their domestic duties.[55]

Confraternities and confession were instruments used to attach the faithful to a spiritual adviser. The local clergy often protested against the actions of the missionaries that encouraged their flock to escape its own authority and tried to restrain confession and worship to the parish priest, exclusively within the parish church. From the end of the seventeenth century until the mid-nineteenth century, several scandals arise concerning the close relationship between missionaries and women, out of the control of the ordinary authorities. In Aleppo, a scandal of *ʿābidāt*, devotees closely linked to French missionaries, lasts more than 30 years, at the beginning of the nineteenth century. As with the scandal around Hindiyya, in 1750–1770, women were charged with seducing their spiritual adviser, reversing the roles between the weak or incompetent confessor and his penitent, as had often happened in Catholicism (remember Madame Guyon and Fénelon, Marguerite-Marie Alacoque and Father La Colombière).[56]

Spiritual guidance and confraternity rules explicitly incited women to break off with traditional female behaviors. For instance, the previously mentioned rules of the Rosary Sisterhood order the girls not to stretch their legs when they are sitting, as the Eastern women used to do. In 1803, a conflict arises when the Lazarist Dellardes intends to forbid his penitents to use kohl as eye makeup, which was a usual and time-honored practice, with the reputation of keeping the eyes healthy. The ban on sexual interference with a pregnant or a sterile woman can be ascribed to the same missionary.[57]

But there were also people and families supporting the missionaries and their devotees. A new pattern of female life, in which celibacy and chastity helped women escape their traditional domestic functions, could attract the groups of Eastern Christians who were most concerned about connections with Western priests and merchants, and about various forms of "modernity."

The new literacy and new social discipline of everyday life, taught by missionaries and Catholic literature, could lead to an improvement of economic efficiency. Furthermore, keeping a consecrated girl at home or sending her to a monastery in Mount Lebanon not only could resolve the delicate questions of concluding matrimonial unions and distributing the estate; it also reinforced the economic and cultural links between Mount Lebanon and Aleppo or Damascus, and could provide the family with prestige. Marriages with "Franks" were rather frequent in this micro-society. Local families were part of networks deployed across the Mediterranean, as far as Istanbul, Cairo, London, Livorno, and Paris. A shared Catholic culture helped to improve the position of Eastern Christians in these networks.

This new pattern of behavior, widespread in the region thanks to Catholic missionaries' activities, may have contributed to introducing "modernity" among the Eastern Christians, and it surely helped them stand out from the Muslim majority through a specific "confessional culture."[58] The new education and behavior of women were two of the main markers of this Christian-Catholic specificity, before becoming, at the end of the nineteenth century, a general goal of all kinds of Ottoman reformists, including Muslims.

Modernization in this context means, above all, a more intense formalization of some social rules under the control of the clergy and the will to centralize each church and confessional group. Nevertheless, this last goal encountered fierce opposition, due to the local sectarian pluralism and its range of conflicts, both between Latin missionaries and local Catholic clergy as well as between Catholics and non-Catholics, fueled by a lack of recognition through the Ottoman State and the simultaneous functioning of patronage and clientelism. It was only in the mid-nineteenth century that controversies about female religious practices faded. The official recognition of the Catholic congregations by the Sultan as autonomous *millets* helped the ordinary clergy to impose its authority. From that point on, worship could be freely celebrated, and women could freely attend churches. The semi-clandestine and domestic meetings for confession and spiritual guidance became less necessary. Yet, as elsewhere, Catholicism gave more space to women participating in the services and in charitable action. In contrast to seventeenth-century Tridentine discipline, which forbade women from participating in public activity, nineteenth-century Catholicism saw the emergence of a new pattern of consecrated maidens, living in the world and acting through education and healthcare. This offered to girls an attractive alternative to the life of a housewife, as well as to the social role of a mystic or prophet. In the nineteenth century, numerous female congregations acting in schools and hospitals settled in the Eastern provinces of the Ottoman Empire.[59]

Notes

1 Châtellier, *La religion des pauvres*.
2 Sidon, 16 April 1653, edited in Rabbath, *Documents inédits*, vol. 1, 50–51.

3 To some extent, this presence of Roman Catholic missions in a pluralistic context could be compared to what has been observed in non-Catholic Europe, for instance: Forclaz, *Catholiques au défi de la Réforme*.
4 For instance: Muchnik, *De paroles et de gestes*.
5 Boogert, *The Capitulations and the Ottoman Legal System*.
6 For *waqfs* in Aleppo, see Knost, *Die Organisation des religiösen Raums in Aleppo*.
7 Heyberger, *Les chrétiens du Proche-Orient*, 346.
8 Heyberger, *Les chrétiens du Proche-Orient*, 342.
9 Heyberger, *Les chrétiens du Proche-Orient*, 344, 495.
10 Heyberger, *Les chrétiens du Proche-Orient*, 344–345; APF, SOCG. vol. 574, fol. 23r–24r, 16 December 1710.
11 Philipp, *Acre*.
12 Lemmens, *Acta S. Congregationis*, vol. 2, 187; Heyberger, *Les chrétiens du Proche-Orient*, 345.
13 Heyberger, *Les chrétiens du Proche-Orient*, 356–357.
14 In Constantinople's suburb of Pera, where a Latin presence was strong and ancient, processions could take place on the streets but within certain limits: Binz, *Latin Missionaries and Catholics in Constantinople*, 63–65.
15 *Relation succincte des choses qui se sont passées . . .*, Aleppo, 12 March 1658, edited in Rabbath, *Documents inédits*, vol. 1, 60–85.
16 APF, SC. Francia, vol. 3, fol. 58r–59v, Aleppo, 1668; Heyberger, *Les chrétiens du Proche-Orient*, 360–362.
17 Besson, *La Syrie sainte*, vol. 1, 1–2.
18 ANF, L 932, 3, 1657, p. 2, p. 7.
19 Marcus, *The Middle East on the Eve of Modernity*, 314–328. For a general view on the townscape in the Early Modern Middle East, see Raymond, *Grandes villes arabes*, 166–326.
20 ANF, L 932, 3, 1657, p. 2, p. 7.
21 Heyberger, *Les chrétiens du Proche-Orient*, 363–364.
22 APF, SOCG, vol. 423, fol. 178r–195r, point 86, 20 March 1669.
23 ARSI, Gallia 96, vol. 1, fol. 504, 20 May 1714.
24 Getcha, "Confession or Spiritual Direction in the Orthodox Church"; Heyberger, "Morale et confession chez les melkites d'Alep."
25 Segneri, *Il penitente istruito a ben confessarsi*.
26 For a good testimony about the training for soul searching and confession, concerning a young Maronite native from Aleppo, see: Dyāb, *D'Alep à Paris*, 56–62.
27 Tsakiris, *Die gedruckten griechischen Beichtbücher zur Zeit der Türkenherrschaft*. On the innovations in the Greek conception and practice of confession starting in the seventeenth Century, see Getcha, "Confession or Spiritual Direction in the Orthodox Church."
28 Besson, *La Syrie sainte*, 117–118.
29 Rabbath, *Documents inédits*, vol. 2, 55. The same ban was implemented by the governor in other circumstances. Russell, *The Natural History of Aleppo*, vol. 1, 257. On 16 April 1804, the governor also forbade all the inhabitants to allow their women to go outside to the gardens: Seetzen, *Tagebuch*, 103.
30 Idlibī, *Asāqifa al-Rūm al-Malakiyyīn bi-Ḥalab*, 188–189; Rome, Archivio Generale dei Cappuccini, AD 106, 84, 93.
31 Tawtal, *Wathā'iq tārikhiyya ʿan Ḥalab*, 1:109–111.
32 Besson, *La Syrie sainte*, 117.
33 Tawtal, *Wathā'iq tārikhiyya ʿan Ḥalab*, 41–42.
34 Heyberger, *Hindiyya*, 125; Heyberger, *Les chrétiens du Proche-Orient*, 484–485.
35 See Santus, "Conflicting Views," in this volume.
36 Mayeur-Jaouen, "Les familles au Moyen-Orient"; Meriwether, *The Kin Who Count;* Doumani, *Family Life*.

37 In a census of the Maronite population of Aleppo by households, in 1740, a significant number of widows or other single women are mentioned: Census (in Arabic) dated 1 June 1740 (Archives of the Maronite Bishopric of Aleppo).
38 Heyberger, "Les chrétiens d'Alep."
39 AGOCD, 245/c/1, p. 3–4. On women, confession, and spiritual guidance in this context, see Heyberger, *Hindiyya*.
40 APF, Acta, vol. 201, fol. 156v, 12 March 1836; fol. 133v–134r.
41 Adriano Prosperi, "Diari femminili e discernimento degli spiriti," 85.
42 Heyberger, *Hindiyya*, 38–46. Having to justify his spiritual guidance of the young woman, Antonio Venturi wrote a long and precise report on the matter: *De directione Nobilis Virginis Alepensis ejusque spiritus Ad dm. Rdo. Nro. Generali Francisco Retz* (APF, CP Maroniti, vol. 118, fol. 311r–327r).
43 *Rusūm al-Akhawiyya al-taqawiyya li-l-Akhawāt al-ʿābidāt al-ʿāʾishāt fī-l-ʿālam bi-madīna Ḥalab al-muʾassasa taḥta kataf al-wardiyya al muqaddasa*, unpaginated (Aleppo, Archives of the Melkite Archbischopric, 508).
44 APF, Acta, vol. 194, fol. 483rv, 484v.
45 Heyberger, *Hindiyya*, 13–15, 42–46.
46 Heyberger, *Hindiyya*, 13–15, 42–46, 57–61, 211–214; Heyberger, *Les chrétiens du Proche-Orient*, 489–493. Seetzen, *Tagebuch*, 105, mentions (as late as 1804) the presence in Aleppo of men and women who stay unmarried in their parents' homes, living a religious life.
47 *Rusūm al-Akhawiyya*... (Aleppo, Archives of the Melkite Archbischopric, 508).
48 Gonzague, "Les anciens missionnaires capucins de Syrie," 67; Sarba (Lebanon), Monastery of Dayr al-Shīr, manuscript n. 232.
49 Russell, *The Natural History of Aleppo*, vol. 2, 45.
50 APF, Acta, vol. 194, fol. 452r and 504v.
51 *Rusūm al-Akhawiyya*... (Aleppo, Archives of the Melkite Archbischopric, 508).
52 Russell, *The Natural History of Aleppo*, vol. 2, 43, 45.
53 APF, SOCG, vol. 578, fol. 233r; Heyberger, *Les chrétiens du Proche-Orient*, 369.
54 APF, Acta, vol. 127, 8 March 1757.
55 APF, Acta, vol. 127, 8 March 1757. The same accusation against a confraternity of the Holy Virgin's Belt, founded by Maronites but attracting Melkite women: APF, Acta, vol. 136, fol. 29r–33r, 3 March 1766. As late as 1804, the German traveler Seetzen mentions unmarried women wearing a special black dress. Seetzen, *Tagebuch*, 105.
56 Heyberger, *Hindiyya*, 37–46, 212–214; Heyberger, "Individualism and Political Modernity."
57 APF, SC Melchiti, vol. 11, fol. 337r–340r (Italian translation), fol. 335r/v (Arabic), 20 July 1801.
58 Among the vast literature on the issue, see Reinhard, "Gegenreformation als Modernisierung?"
59 Verdeil, *La mission jésuite*, 375–392.

Afterwords

History as the art of the "other" and the art of "in-betweenness"

Nicolas Standaert

History can be considered the art of the "other" because historians investigate actions of people who lived in other times or places. In particular, in the study of contact between cultures, this "other" occupies a central position, since historical events being studied concern encounters with another culture. This is also the case with the mission history of the early modern period, such as that represented in this volume. In one way or another, all the chapters relate to one question: what happened in the encounter between the missionaries from Europe and the multiple "others"?

The starting point of such historical investigation is the "encounter" with the "other" that occurs in a "place," which through the encounter becomes a "space." Any such encounter "between" people can lead to a "story," in which the story of the encounter is told. This story can be expressed in multiple ways: usually using texts or images, and even artifacts but also using buildings, and less tangible expressions such as communities, social networks, and rituals. These are the sources to which historians have access. One possibility for historians interested in the "other" is to try, via the story expressed in these sources, to catch a glimpse of the original encounter between these groups of people, in other words of their "in-betweenness." By thus taking the encounter as the center, there is a shift from the focus on the "other" to the event "between" those who are "other" to each other. In this sense, history is also the art of "in-betweenness."

Without covering all aspects, this afterword attempts to reread the contributions from this perspective. The chapters illustrate the key issues that I will treat in the following order: an encounter with a diverse other, which transforms a place into a space, and is then told in a story, revealing in-betweenness and in-between persons. In this volume, their interaction concerns patterns of localization that involve tensions related to accommodation and conflict.

Encounter with a diverse other

The starting point is the encounter with the "other." Given the theme of the volume – Catholic missions – most of the chapters of this book take the European missionaries as the primary point of reference. It is primarily but not exclusively their encounter with the "other" that is narrated. This "other" is, foremost, the cultural other, since the missionaries traveled to non-European areas. There they met with people who ordered their lives according to rituals belonging to different traditions: they not only met with Muslims, who were known to Europeans before the sixteenth century but also with those who followed largely unknown traditions, such as Confucian, Shinto, or Buddhist traditions. The types of encounters with the "other" were multiple. For instance, in India, on the one hand there were the courtly discussions at the Mughal court "between a Muslim king, Akbar, and a vassal-cum-ambassador-cum-spiritual-teacher, Acquaviva," and on the other hand there was the violent encounter between the villagers of Cuncolim in the province of Salsete and Acquaviva, which led to the latter's death (Županov). In Persia, the forms of integration of Augustinians into local society "ranged from practices of social interaction with Muslims and 'heretics'. . . to economic integration into, and dependence on, local society" (Windler). In the Japanese port town of Nagasaki there was a self-administered Christian community as well as Jesuits, their disciples and Christian local elites (Tronu). In China there were women's congregations (*hui*) with "congregational meetings in house oratories . . . [that] were open to Christian women from the neighborhood" (Amsler). The advantage of bringing these papers from different areas together is that they underscore the diversity of the "other," which is not only present between cultures but also within cultures. This wide diversity takes the reader beyond the binary oppositions of self/other (Other), religious/non-religious, foreigner/native, and man/woman, and it moves the focus of several authors to the "between," to the search for the "inter-action" "between" the opposites (Ward).

Yet this attention to "between" brings about a second shift in focus. The self/other approach may tend to view only the missionary as an agent who brings about the encounter with the "other"; in this view, the missionary is the subject and the other the object. Basing themselves on missionary sources, many chapters inevitably tell the story of these encounters from the perspective of the missionary and not so much from the perspective of the "other." Yet the previous examples, and others mentioned in this volume, indicate that missionaries were not the only agents, and at times not even the primary agents. The case of Japan, where women became primary missionaries, best exemplifies this shift in agency: the "history of Kirishitan women broadens the definitions of 'missionary' and 'households.'" The household spaces were nurseries for Kirishitan literature; aristocratic women became a type of "domestic" missionary within the Hosokawas' household. As missionaries, like the Jesuits, these women brought both books and new religious ideas to private households and the general public (Ward). A similar phenomenon happened in the Ottoman Empire, where the connection between the missionaries and the families was guaranteed by the women (Heyberger). These cases exemplify the possibility of writing history not only from the perspective of the receiver but of also conceiving this receiver as an agent who participates as a subject in the encounter and who thus co-creates an in-between space.

Transforming a place into a space

Encounters occur in a "place" and transform the place to a "space." One way to investigate the "localization" is to examine how specific encounters in places transformed these places into spaces.

I refer to the difference between "place" (*lieu*) and "space" (*espace*) as proposed by Michel de Certeau:

> A place is an instantaneous configuration of positions. It implies an indication of stability. By contrast, a space exists when one takes into consideration vectors of direction, velocities, and time variables. Thus space is composed of intersections of mobile elements. . . . In short, space is a practised place.[1]

Central to the concept of space is the human interaction that takes place in it. This volume brings "social space" into the picture by organizing the chapters into four spatial dimensions: princely courts, cities, countryside, and households. Some theoreticians, such as Homi K. Bhaba, Karin Ikas, and Gerhard Wagner, have even conceived this space as the "Third Space" (or better yet as a diversity of third spaces) as both a physical space and time in which intercultural communications and negotiations take place (Ward). These places were transformed into spaces: "Ryōkei Diogo's *ie* became a third space of intellectual, cultural, and spiritual exchanges" (Ward).

All these social spaces are located in specific places with a certain dimension of stability: the Safavid court in Isfahan (Windler), the Qing court in Beijing (Menegon), and the Mughal court in Fatehpur Sikri (Županov); cities such as Zhaoqing, Nanchang, Shanghai, . . . (Hsia), Nagasaki (Tronu) or Constantinople, Smyrna, Aleppo, Damascus, Sidon, Jerusalem, and Cairo (Santus, Heyberger); villages such as Cuncolim in the Salsete region of Goa (Županov), the countryside of Kyūshū in Japan (Vu Thanh), or rural villages in Galilee (Tramontana) and Tibet (Pomplu); and finally households in China (Amsler), Japan (Ward), and the Near East (Heyberger).

Though places tend to be rather stable, they can also move in at least three senses. As the case of Tibet shows, there is external movement due to nomadic existence. Many of the "villages" or "hamlets" were not permanent settlements at all. For instance, Tashigang consisted largely of a rotating military garrison while Gartok was actually two different encampment sites located 40 miles apart along the Indus River (Pomplun).

There is movement not only of places but also within places. This can occur through interactions in the space of an encounter. This is exemplified by several examples of the household space, which was clearly divided, often based on gender. For instance, in China's Confucian tradition, gender arrangements were thought of in spatial terms, especially the spatial binary, the inner (*nei*) versus the outer (*wai*) (Amsler). Similar spatial divisions existed in the context of the Ottoman social and political organization, where men and women had differentiated roles and disposed of different spaces, with gendered spaces existing not only in the household but also churches (Heyberger). That the relationship between the inner and outer could shift is illustrated by changes that households underwent in pre-modern Japan in the early seventeenth century. They changed from relatively open spaces (not as strictly enclosed as their contemporary Iberian or Chinese counterparts) to more closed and even government controlled environments, especially for women (Ward). In China, households were already much more closed environments with the inner space reserved for women. This space underwent change through the encounter with Catholicism, which was itself transformed by the encounter as well. The process of localization, which consisted of the promotion of "prayers at home" (instead of at church) had consequences for the spatial arrangements of Catholic women's worship. A new form of worship space was necessary, and thus the Jesuits encouraged male converts to establish oratories for the women in their households. These household oratories transformed Catholicism into a domestic religion (Amsler).

Besides the movement of places and within places there was also movement between places. Moving from one place to another can be called an essential characteristic of missions, of which the first mission history (the *Acts of the Apostles*) is the prime example. It contains many summaries that simply enumerate the cities through which Paul and his companions traveled (e.g., *Acts* 17.1: "Paul and Silas traveled on through Amphipolis and Apollonia and came to Thessalonica, where there was a synagogue."). One finds similar descriptions in the chapters of this book (e.g., Tramontana). Some chapters also examine the movements of missionaries in different directions: in the case of China, the movements can be described as ascending, horizontal, and descending across the system of urban hierarchy and macroregions (Hsia). Movements often include an element of choice regarding where to go, as clearly illustrated by urban-rural movements, not only in China (Hsia), Japan (Vu Thanh), or Tibet (Pomplun) but also in semi-rural Palestine (Tramontana). Movements between places created the networks that made missions possible. These could be social networks determined by patronage (Hsia), or economic and productive networks (Tramontana). All these patterns of interaction determined the missionary activity.

Telling the story

Encounters that take place in a space can lead to a story. The ways in which this story is expressed and preserved for historians can be very diverse. Most contributions investigate the encounters based on letters sent by the missionaries. These letters not only report about events and encounters, but, as in the case of the meetings of Acquaviva with Akbar, sometimes record in detail the ups and downs of a relationship (Županov).

But a wide variety of other written sources is also used: an obituary notice at the end of his *History of Shah 'Abbās* by a secretary at the court of the shah (Windler); Antoni de Monserrat's manuscript biography of Rodolfo Acquaviva (Županov); Valignano's instructions, statements, and accounts submitted to the Roman Curia (Vu Thanh); and the *Récit fidèle*, a manuscript written by the French Jesuit François Foucquet to justify himself after his failure to collaborate with his Chinese aid, Jean Hu (Amsler) are just a few examples.

Worth noticing is that some of the sources are themselves constructed in the form of an encounter or dialogue. Thus they reproduce the basic pattern of the missionary encounter. Fabian Fucan's *Myōtei mondō* or *Myōtei dialogue* (c.1605), for instance, is addressed to "ladies of quality and widows" interested in the "Kirishitan evangel" and consists of fictional dialogues between two interlocutors: a noble widowed Jōdo nun and a noble widowed Kirishitan catechist. Another example in Japan is the Kirishitanban story of Saint Catherine of Alexandria, which starts with a dialogue between Catherine and the Roman Emperor, which could have served as inspiration for young Japanese women to confirm them in their Kirishitan faith (Ward). Such encounter stories of the past are linked to encounter stories of the present, a storytelling method that is also characteristic of retellings of the encounters of Jesus in the gospels.

Although these sources tell the story of the encounter from a certain perspective, mostly missionary, since the local sources are relatively limited, it is nevertheless still possible to narrate the story of the "other" through these sources, as is the case with the chapters on women in this volume (Amsler, Ward, Heyberger). By giving prominence to the spatial aspects of the process of localization, they retell the story from the point of view of the gendered spatial organization of Chinese, Japanese, and Near Eastern Catholicism. Telling the encounter from the perspective of the "other" also means paying attention to the "other," especially the "other" within the missionaries and converts, their internal motivations and desires, their spirituality, hopes, and dreams. This internal drive was often an important motive for the missionaries and the converts to become what they became.

Not only modern historians but also contemporary authors tell and retell the story of an encounter. In this retelling, the transformation which occurs can be made explicit. Some stories were "narrativized" anew. For instance, Acquaviva's missionary loss or "error" was narrativized into hailing the advantages of such "pious deaths" (Županov). To a certain extent, although with different objectives, each contribution to this volume conducts such narrativization.

Yet the stories of encounters also take forms other than texts: visual expressions are clearly present in the images of clothes (Menegon). Through these images one can not only grasp the encounter between the missionary and the local culture but also between the missionary and the artist who made the drawing. Another source that tells stories of encounters is architecture. Archeological findings of buildings relate the stories not only of encounters of individuals but also of communities. These communities built places of gathering and had to make choices between local and new traditions: the early churches in Japan were built in the Japanese style, in wood with tatami floors, and Christian elements were mainly to be found inside the churches, in their decoration and furniture (paintings, altars, textiles, liturgical objects, etc.). There were also some hybrid elements such as the cross-pattern roof tiles used by all the churches in Nagasaki (Tronu) or the Jesuit residences which resembled Buddhist temples (Vu Thanh). These buildings are themselves stories of intercultural encounters.

In-betweenness and in-between persons

One can notice the presence of the "between" in this volume. It is striking that the term "between" appears five times in the main or subtitles of the contributions (Windler, Županov, Santus, Amsler, Vu Thanh); in two other contributions it is taken as topic of the research question (Hsia, Tramontana). The titles and questions underscore that there is a wide variety of sometimes even contradictory meanings related to the English word "between" (or "betwixt," etymologically derived from earlier forms meaning "by – two each"; the same concept is rendered by the term *inter* in Latin or *entre* in French). "Between" can express: (1) the position or interval that separates two things, such as in "standing between A and B" ["the various states, provinces, cities, and geographical features between Kashgar and the Irtysh River, including Amdo" (Pomplun)], or two moments in time, such as "between one and two in the morning" ["the period between 1580 and 1800" (Hsia)]; (2) the intervening space either as separating, such as "the vast distance between heaven and earth" ["Jesuits' adoption of long beards was an attempt to put a greater distance between themselves and women" (Menegon)], or as connecting, such as "to stretch a rope between the two rafters" [the "trade between Japan and Mexico" (Tronu); "What was the relationship between missionaries' entanglement with local society and their evangelizing activities?" (Tramontana)]; (3) confinement to two or more parties acting conjointly, such as "between ourselves" ["the practice of sacramental intercommunion between Catholic converts and non-Catholics" (Santus)]; (4) after verbs and nouns of action a (subjective) separation, division, distinction, or discernment, such as "the choice between A and B" ["traditional contraposition between rigorism and accommodation" (Santus); and "differences between European Catholic and Chinese Confucian gender arrangement" (Amsler)].[2] These different meanings also appear in the words that are built on "inter": interval, interstice, interact(ion), intervene, intermediary, interlocutor, interpolate, interpreter, etc.

The concept of "in-between" is at the center of the "encounter" that takes "place" in "spaces." "In-betweenness" or "the between" draws the attention to one particular aspect of space: instead of focusing on oppositions, on either/or, on "self" or "other," the focus moves to the "between," to the search for the "inter-action" "between" the opposites, and to various forms of encounter and conversation ("*entre-tien*" in French). Attention to in-betweenness means attention to intervals, gaps, cracks, in-between moments, or zones in culture and human life. This notion of in-betweenness shows that many human activities come into being due to the existence and creation of space "between" the "self" and the "other," or between the transmitter and the receiver, between the missionary and the convert, etc. This space acts both as that which allows an encounter to take place (leading to interaction and communication) and as that which is produced by the encounter. The interaction is considered a permanent tension: between the possibility of understanding (and being understood) and the impossibility of such an understanding, between the local and the global. The interaction therefore causes the partners to readjust, rethink, and reformulate ideas of themselves and of others. Thus in-betweenness is the space in which an encounter can take place.[3]

By focusing on the in-between one discovers the identity of the agents as "in-between persons" or "between-beings, intermediates."[4] The missionaries left their countries and culture(s) of origin and tried to accommodate and localize to different degrees so that they no longer belonged entirely to their own culture(s) and yet did not belong to the other multi-faceted culture, while at the same time belonging to both the culture of origin and the new culture. This led to their intermediary identities because they functioned "in-between" two (or more) categories or multi-layered cultures, belonging at the same time to both of them and to neither of them. This in-between identity was not merely a matter of choice: it came into being through interaction, as the Europeans were "shaped by the other." That is why such "in-between" identities were not only characteristic of the missionaries but also of the converts. Converts also "left" their cultures of origin, practiced new rituals, and adopted the ways of life and the rhythms of new cultures. They started to organize their lives according to new rituals without entirely leaving behind the local rituals.

The story of these in-between people, both missionaries and converts, is told throughout the book. A typical in-between identity is that of a translator, or better *inter*preter, such as the interpreters of European languages at the Safavid court (Windler). This in-between position of translator was occupied by missionaries or by local people. Their intermediate position, though, could also change like in the case of the Jesuits in Japan, whose complex work of mediation was closely controlled by local authorities (Tronu). In the Ottoman empire, "local Christians were also employed as dragomans by the convent, acting as interpreters and porters"; these dragomans "also acted as intermediaries between the friars and the local administration" (Tramontana). There were also tax collectors (*cafarieri*), "who were designated members of the village community [and] who acted as intermediaries between the community and the Ottoman authorities in matters of taxation" (Tramontana). These examples also underscore the multifaceted aspect of the cultures involved, a choice that appears saliently throughout the volume. A clear illustration of the importance of intermediaries can be found in the ways in which the encounters between the Jesuits and women could be mediated in China. There were "two groups of intermediaries that were especially important for the Jesuits' communication with women," namely Chinese Christian men and Chinese lay brothers who became "go-betweens" with easier access to women (Amsler). These examples indicate that the identities of the in-between people were subject to continuous change; this change was subject to the interactions with the "other."

Patterns of localization

The encounter that takes place in the in-between involves an interaction between agents. The leading question regarding interaction in this volume is the process of localization, a well-chosen term since it takes the process of becoming local, i.e., becoming inserted in a "place" (locus = place), as a central point of investigation. The question is how the missionaries "interpolate" in a society, and how through interaction in a specific place this affected their identity and the identity of the converts and the Christian community. In Japan, for example, the households became spaces of Kirishitan text production because women had opened them to Japanese and European Jesuits (Ward).

One pattern of achieving this localization is so-called "accommodation," which is a practice by which missionaries adapt to the local culture in various ways in order to spread the gospel better through encounters. The degree of accommodation, however, is often seen as a choice taken by the missionary agent, while in fact these missionaries were often "shaped by" the receiving culture, as the case of the Japanese women shows. Moreover, variations and opinions about accommodation led to tensions and conflicts that are also a form of cultural interaction.

Clothing, a topic that appears in several of the contributions, is an attractive paradigmatic example of studying the role of "accommodation" in the process of localization. This topic also exemplifies the tension that exists in other forms of accommodation: when missionaries moved to another culture, the question was whether they should keep the habit that marked their religious status in their culture of origin (distinguishing priests and nuns from laity), or "accommodate" the habit to the new place, and if so, to which (local) habit? In general, "clothes were a tangible way to construct a hierarchy, to mark distinctions, and to affirm social status, in early modern Europe and late imperial China alike" (Menegon). Clothing can create distance but also rapprochement: in the early China mission, Chinese lay brothers had easier access to women than ordained priests because of their simpler way of dressing (Amsler). Moreover, the use of clothing is linked to one's identity: for instance, wearing a particular habit or an identifiable mark on one's external attire makes one more recognizable as a member of a specific family or congregation. Thus conflicts regarding styles of dressing "demonstrates clothing's importance in society" (Menegon).

The China case regarding this issue is well developed in this volume. In China, some missionaries, such as Johann Adam Schall von Bell, chose to accommodate and were denounced for their great expenses for an excessive number of personal fine silk clothes and hats, as well as for official robes decorated with dragons. Others, such as Matteo Ripa, bewildered by the complexity of Chinese clothing, resisted doing so because this accommodation in terms of clothing seemed to him to completely undermine the very essence of the priestly and missionary vocation, and the vow of poverty (Menegon). In Persia, there were similar tensions regarding the adoption of local "signs of social distinction" (Windler).

Yet accommodation was not only a matter of personal choice on the part of the missionary; it was also shaped by the cultural environment and in certain cases determined by what Erik Zürcher has called the "cultural imperative."[5] This is the obligation to conform to what was considered correct, orthodox, and good behavior in the religious, ritual, social, and political sense by the culture that the missionaries entered. In this sense the decision for a certain attire was only taken after having been counseled by diverse local interlocutors (Menegon). And in the Chinese rendering of the choices, missionaries such as Ricci hardly seem to have been the ones in charge (Menegon). This was not only the case in China, but in other places in Asia such as Persia, where "clerics and laymen subordinated themselves to local ceremonial practices" (Windler). Missionaries thus "became part of non-European centers of power . . . at the service of rulers in whose view Rome was not the center of the world but, at best, that of a distant European periphery" (Windler). The submission to rituals is closely linked with clothing, as the rituals often require corresponding ways of dressing. It is this cultural imperative that shaped the missionaries' actions and behaviors, making them become who they became. There is a clear contrast with other mission areas, especially Latin America, where the colonial power went together with the imposition of a new language. In China the language of communication was Chinese: hardly any Chinese person learned a European language in the seventeenth or eighteenth centuries, while the missionaries were subjected to the imperative of the Chinese language.

This dependence on the local environment was not only a matter of ritual and language but also of economic and financial interaction. For instance, the patterns of interaction of the Franciscans of Bethlehem with the local society influenced their model of mission, which remained strictly centered on economic exchanges and linked to the presence of the convent and its productive activities (Tramontana). The Jesuit success at integrating the Japanese countryside "can be attributed to the Society's efforts at blending in the local social structures but also to the material support it found among the population." Jesuits relied on the *daimyō*'s financial support and were helped by the material services of the peasantry (Vu Thanh).

The styles of accommodation differ from one culture to another, and at times missionaries are well aware of this variety. In response to the criticism that missionaries go around dressed in silk in China, one missionary answered, while referring to Madurai (in India), Canada, and China: "What is good and sufficient in one country to have the Gospel accepted, in some cases does not work at all or is insufficient in another country" (Menegon). The degrees of accommodation are also very diverse and can be visualized as a gradient scale. On one end is total accommodation and on the other end no accommodation at all (rejection of any accommodation). In certain cases accommodation led to a radical and total change, though this was rather exceptional. In Persia, for instance, the process culminated in the conversion of the prior of the Augustinians, António de Jesus, to Islam in 1697 (Windler). In other cases it was not accommodation but the maintenance of the culture of origin that was stressed, such as the promotion of some forms of Latinization in the Middle East (Santus). Yet, in most cases the localization was situated somewhere between accommodation and no accommodation, as the chapters in this volume extensively show. Accommodation and non-accommodation were therefore not necessarily opposites. Precisely, the Jesuit self-conscious and systematic effort to accommodate and their deep entanglement with the local community made it possible for bishop Luis Cerqueira to train diocesan native priests and implement the post-Tridentine parish system and the Roman Calendar (Tronu).

The encounters in the processes of localization and accommodation were not always harmonious. The space in between was often one of conflict. For instance, there was the struggle between the Eastern Christians "united" with Rome and the "orthodox" in the Ottoman Empire (Heyberger). In this regard the case of Damascus is particularly interesting because it introduces a "complex system of rivalry" and simultaneously also "conflicts of jurisdiction" between diverse religious orders and Eastern Catholic clergy (Santus). Another example, in China, was the rivalry between Franciscans, Dominicans, and Jesuits (Menegon). In Japan, tensions between missionaries and diocesan priests even led to "the so-called Schism of Nagasaki after the bishop died in early 1614" (Tronu). In the Middle East, "the existence of tensions between the friars and the inhabitants of Bethlehem in the seventeenth and eighteenth centuries has been described in relation to the friars' missionary activity or to their production of devotional objects" (Tramontana). There were also violent conflicts, such as the killing of Acquaviva and four other Jesuits in a village disturbance in the province of Salsete (Županov).

As some of the articles in this volume point out, these conflicts are complex issues. The competition between the missionaries cannot be easily explained by traditional or stereotypical contrapositions (such as "Jesuit accommodation" versus "Franciscan rigorism"), which have been increasingly questioned by scholars (Santus). Most importantly, they are worth studying because they are also a form of interaction: as such, their study may contribute to an understanding of the relations between missionaries and locals, in that conflicts represent a distinct, albeit problematic form of interaction. The way in which conflicts were resolved is also meaningful because it can testify to the missionaries' knowledge of the local system of conflict resolution (Tramontana). This shows that conflicts can be resolved through localization.

Conclusion

I have tried to show that by shifting the historian's attention from the "other" to "betweenness," the focus moves to the in-between "space," in which the agent of mission history is not only the missionary but also the "other," especially the convert. This "other" shapes the interaction between them, makes new things possible, and rewrites the story. Moreover, in the eyes of missionaries and converts, their interior encounter with an "Other" was also shaping them.

This idea of "being shaped by" leads to the question: Where is the center of (research on) the mission? European missionaries were at times seriously decentered, as exemplified by their subordination to local ceremonial practices at Asian princely courts or the emergence of women missionaries in Japanese or Chinese households. This decentralization seems to call into question the papacy's claims to universal validity and the universal aspirations of the religious orders active in the missions. Yet I hope to have shown that the center is the encounter, the interaction between the missionary and the other/Other. Perhaps this interaction expressed in various forms of localization made universalization possible.

By being engaged in "thinking the between," one can try to rethink the stories that emerged from the encounters between the different agents. These stories need to be re-examined and adjusted continually and repeatedly. It is often in the *inter*stices – the spaces *between* cultures – that concepts are reformulated and recreated, and that mission is localized.

Notes

1 Certeau, *The Practice of Everyday Life*, 117.
2 *The Oxford English Dictionary*, 154–156.
3 Standaert, "Don't Mind the Gap"; for Michel de Certeau on in-between, see Standaert, "Attention à l'écart."
4 Leung, *Bianyuan yu zhijian*; Desmond, *Being Between*, 12.
5 Zürcher, "Jesuit Accommodation and the Chinese Cultural Imperative," 40ff.

Localizing Catholic missions in Asia

Framework conditions, scope for action, and social spaces

Birgit Emich

An overview of the 12 contributions in this volume reveals the richness of its findings. Even though the book deals with very different regions from the Middle East to Japan and with such diverse aspects as the clothing of missionaries, the variety of their roles at court, and the seclusion of Asian households, the contributions largely adhere to the central questions outlined by the editors. From a concluding look at the contributions as a whole, a snapshot picture should emerge of the localizing of the Catholic mission in Asia during the early modern period. We should now be able to consider the problem introduced by the editors of how the missionaries integrated themselves into the networks of interaction that they found in the various, localized communication spaces.

To sketch this picture, one could follow the structure of the volume and ask how and to what extent the missionaries adapted to the local societies at court, in the city, in the country, and in the household. I will return to this question, but I would like to start with a look at some questions and themes that run counter to the structure of the volume. The diversity of the contributions provides insights into both the general framework conditions of the mission in Asia, and the factors that determined the roles and the scope of action of the actors. Most likely it was these same framework conditions and factors that shaped the processes of rapprochement with local societies. I would therefore like to gradually approach the core question of the volume about the integration of the missionaries into interaction networks on the ground starting with some very general observations.

The following questions will be dealt with: (1) Which framework conditions and prerequisites made the mission in Asia possible in the first place? (2) Which factors shaped the respective situations on the ground? (3) How did the situation differ in various communication spaces, ranging from the court to the household? In doing so, what all this means for patterns of localization should become apparent.

All of this will be discussed in light of the present contributions. There is, of course, no intention of a broader literature review on the subject of mission. Some of the distinctions made here, between framework conditions and factors developing an active influence, will necessarily be debatable. But what will emerge is a picture of the overall complexity of the environments within which the localizing of the Catholic mission in Asia took place.

Framework conditions of the Catholic mission in Asia

When one inquires after the conditions and prerequisites for the mission, a number of overarching themes come to the fore. Structural issues of a political, social, and economic nature need to be considered here. However, the actor-centered approach of this volume makes it seem more appropriate to begin elsewhere. The prerequisite for any mission is the will to evangelize, and this is demonstrated clearly by the initial restraint of the Protestant churches in this field. It is also known that this will was not consistently in place on the Catholic side. This is underscored by the Franciscans in the Holy Land, who decided only in the 1620s to engage in missionary activities (Tramontana).

Just as important as the will to conduct missionary activities, however, would have been the willingness on the ground to tolerate or even promote such efforts. The danger of suffering martyrdom permanently accompanied the missionaries in Asia. Some of them were even motivated for this task in the first place by the prospect of such an end and the salvation of the soul that was promised by it (Županov). For the mission to be successful, a minimum of tolerance, protection, and support from the local population was required. In fact, the contributions to this volume show time and again that patronage played a decisive role in the survival and progress of the mission in Asia. This applies above all to patronage in the narrower sense, i.e., to relationships with a patron who was permanently more powerful than oneself. Landowners like the *daimyō* in Japan could be such patrons but also high officials like the provincial governors in the Ottoman Empire or the mandarins in China. This short list alone shows that patronage of the mission could be linked to the conversion of the patrons themselves. And indeed, this was the rule in Japan and also occurred with some Chinese mandarins, although others protected the mission without becoming Christians themselves. The promotion of patrons, who gave the missionaries access to places and people and paved their way from the province to Beijing, proved to be so influential that neither the movement patterns of the missionaries nor the geographical expansion of the mission in China could be explained without the patronage factor (Hsia). In Japan, too, the special role of Nagasaki as a Christian city was due to the donation of a local magnate (Tronu). The Ottoman Empire offers another variation: the Sultan and his local representatives were not themselves the goal of the mission. Nevertheless, they were courted through the use of patronage, for example, by the Franciscans in the Holy Land, who obtained the protection of the Ottoman territorial rulers with gifts and invitations to dinner (Tramontana). The support of local rulers was essential for the success of the mission.

The possibilities of territorial rulers were, above all, limited by the attitudes of their own superiors. Instances of the mission being outlawed, as in Japan in 1587 or 1614, and in China in 1705, were usually spearheaded by rulers. Consequently, their attitudes toward the mission played a decisive role. The missionaries were of course well aware of this and they concentrated their efforts on the top tiers of society. It was never possible to persuade the rulers to convert, even if hopes were at times high. Yet the missionaries were often successful in wringing the tolerance of the mission from them. Hence, the question arises of what determined the rulers' attitude toward the Christian missionaries.

First of all, we must consider the concepts of rule held by the sovereigns as well as their take on religion. In heterogeneous empires with universalist aspirations a policy of inclusiveness that demonstrated the greatness of the ruler was the obvious choice. This left room for most groups to be integrated into society, and it also meant that the presence of Christians at the ruler's court did not cause offense. This applies to the Mughal emperor Akbar the Great, whose interest in public debates but also in personal conversations and even visits to the residence of the Jesuits, aroused the – ultimately false – hope of the missionaries for his conversion to Christianity (Županov). But it also applies to the Persian Shah Abbas I, who believed that Christians possessed some knowledge of the revelation of God, although their insight remained incomplete (Windler).

The example of the Shah in particular also refers to other motifs behind the rulers' interest in the missionaries from Europe. Abbas I hoped for foreign policy mediation and for alliances with Rome and secular European courts against the Ottoman Empire (Windler). Missionaries acting in a dual capacity as preachers of the cross and as representatives of the European powers are also found in other constellations. Just as the prior of the Augustinians acted as an agent of the Portuguese crown at the Persian court (Windler), mendicant monks were sent as envoys from the Spanish Philippines to Japan (Tronu), while Jesuits were deployed as middlemen between Portuguese Macao and Japan (Vu Thanh). It is thus obvious that political interests were among the factors that made missionary travel possible in the first place.

An even greater role for access to Asia than this political co-optation of the missionaries was probably played by the prospect for the Asian and European rulers of establishing or intensifying trade relations. Thus the interest of the Japanese warlords Oda Nobunaga and Toyotomi Hideyoshi in long distance trade not only facilitated the missionaries' access to Japan in the first place, such trade relations also determined which orders were preferred. Since the Portuguese patronate supported the Jesuits, the trade with Portugal brought the Society of Jesus into play; and because the Spanish crown extended its patronage to the mendicant orders, the trade with Spain since 1580 had also promoted the presence of the Dominicans, Franciscans, and Augustinians from Manila in Japan (Ward). The Spanish mendicants used the Philippines as their starting point from which they eventually also reached China. They found their way via the Hokkien trade routes to the Chinese southeast coast across the sea (Hsia). But missionaries also benefitted from the protection and the routes of trade companies on land (Pomplun) as, for instance, in the impassable Tibet. The fundamental importance of trade relations for the success of the mission in Asia is further underscored by the fact that even the financing of the local mission sometimes depended on the participation of the orders in trade, as in the case of the Jesuits in Japan and their investments in the Portuguese silk trade (Vu Thanh).

It was only natural that trade contacts also shifted the balance of power on the ground. The Franciscans in Jerusalem were not only able to expand their business with homemade devotional objects but also to increase their social prestige and political weight in the same measure, as their French trading partners penetrated the region economically and diplomatically (Tramontana). Conversely, the exclusion of the Jesuits from trade between Japan and Macao went hand in hand with the prohibition of the mission in Japan (Vu Thanh).

These indications draw attention to the international balance of power and the competition between powers as an essential framework of the mission. Moreover, the opportunities of the individual orders did not only depend on which crown supported them most. It was always necessary to keep in mind which of these crowns was most influential on the ground. Thus, thanks to its commercial dominance in the Middle East, France became central not only for the Franciscans but also for all other orders with interests in the region. Local settlements in the Ottoman Empire without the support of the French ambassador and his consuls came to be difficult starting around the second half of the seventeenth century (Santus). However, the dominance of a specific power on the ground of the mission could also end in disaster. The martyrdom of the Jesuits in Salsete cannot be explained without taking into account the territorial rule of the Portuguese in Goa and their fiscal claims on the indigenous population (Županov).

While the military subjugation of the region by European powers and the establishment of a proper territorial dominion remained the exception in early modern Asia, the missionaries encountered another claim to dominion time and again: namely, the claim of Rome to be the ecclesiastical center and to act as the supreme normative authority in all that concerned the mission. As in other areas, Rome tried to assert this claim to centrality in the mission with the help of a new institution. The foundation of the Sacred Congregation for the Propagation of the Faith in 1622 was aimed at enhancing Rome's role in missionary activities. The fact that, starting in the second half of the seventeenth century, the access route to Asia for the missionaries increasingly included other options than the Portuguese ships traveling via Goa constituted a success of this Roman policy.

In addition to such international and church-related constellations, the internal conditions in the mission's target countries also played a role. Above all, internal power shifts and power struggles opened up mental and geographical spaces for the missionaries. The decline of the Ming dynasty in

China not only resulted in an increased freedom of movement for the Jesuits and their patrons but also in Chinese locals searching for alternatives to the ruling neo-Confucian orthodoxy. In Japan the consolidation of imperial power went hand in hand with the end of the local mission. Its eventful history in between massacres, bloom, and ban cannot be understood without considering the shifts in power among the elite (Tronu). In Tibet it is also noticeable that the regions which opened themselves up to the mission were those most threatened by the superiority of the Dalai Lama and his Gelupka order (Pomplun). Christian observers were likely also aware of these connections.

The legal situation was one of the conditions of the mission that was closely linked to the internal situation of the countries affected. Explicit bans on the missions severely restricted opportunities for the missionaries, although the Ottoman case, where missionaries were allowed to evangelize among the Eastern Christians and sometimes turned to Muslim legal authorities in order to solve their conflicts, demonstrates how differentiated legal situations could be (Tramontana).

The legal conditions have to be considered alongside sociostructural and geographic conditions, such as accessibility – for instance, in the mountains – and the connection to trade routes. These reflections underscore an obvious observation: the conditions encountered by the Catholic mission in Asia could be extremely variable. Even within a single country a broad spectrum of variants is to be expected. Thus it seems likely that without a nuanced perspective it will prove difficult to approach concrete missionary activities.

With attention being paid to the differentiating categories of time, geographic location, and social space, the image becomes a little sharper. After having considered the general conditions that determined the limits and opportunities of mission throughout Asia, the focus will now shift to the factors that directly influenced the concrete actions of the missionaries. We will explore the scope for action that was available to the missionaries. Here, too, systematization is called for. The focus will therefore lie on the factors that prescribed the actors' model roles and thus shaped their concrete behaviors.

The choice of roles and the scope for action on the ground

Some decades ago, historians were quick to answer questions about the norms governing the behavior of the missionaries. In their view, the constitutions of the orders prescribed to the missionaries a life of varying degrees of contemplation, poverty, and modesty, and thus clearly distinguished them from other clerics and their scope for action in the world. Even today, there is no doubt that the varying religious norms played a role for the actors: although the disputes in which regular clerics were engaged in many places of mission were energized by the respective "national" classifications of the communities, by conflicts of jurisdiction, and by a certain degree of competition, the respective religious profiles also contributed their part. This also applies to the varying degrees of proximity to Rome, which, for instance, caused conflicts between the Jesuits and the missionaries of the *Propaganda Fide* in China (Menegon). Finally, it is also evident that the missionaries were measured both by Rome and by their local critics against the normative guidelines prescribed by their respective orders.

The contributions in this volume, however, highlight the corrections and additions that recent research has brought to this picture. Many regular clerics found pragmatic answers for existential questions. For instance, the Franciscans in the Middle East, who, as a mendicant order, were not allowed to administer possessions, delegated this necessary task initially to a layman and later even to a religious office (Heyberger). Moreover, comparisons among the regions demonstrate that members of the same order sometimes behaved differently in different places. This flexibility was at times explicitly encouraged: even if the Jesuits adapted to the different needs of the respective localities of their mission, it was affirmed in the Society of Jesus that they would all remain brothers (Menegon). But this willingness to adapt was not due to the oft-cited elasticity of the Jesuit program. Under specific circumstances members of the Society of Jesus were sometimes set more strictly against adaptation to requirements on the ground than members of other missionary orders. This emerges clearly in the controversy about the *communicatio in sacris*. These debates mobilized many actors between Rome and the Middle East. They focused on whether *communicatio* was indeed unavoidable for Catholics and for Eastern Christians willing to convert, and on how this difficult liturgical mixture could succeed without turning those participating into a false "sect." Orders did not follow consistent lines of argumentation. Not only the affiliation with a specific order but also the local context were both decisive for missionaries' positions in these debates. Where the missionaries were politically isolated and economically weak, they showed a willingness to adapt; where they felt they were in a strong position, they might have rejected such compromises (Santus).

In practice, the orders left their members with significant scope of action. Thus the question remains which factors determined the missionaries' actions and shaped their engagement with local conditions. Let us begin with the obvious. The roles that were available to the missionaries were determined by the benefits they offered their host society. Missionaries worked as translators at courts. They were also welcomed for their capacities as learned interlocutors and participants in disputations. Nowhere was the demand for the cultural capital of the missionaries more evident than in China. In view of the interest in Western knowledge harbored by potential patrons ranging from the mandarins to the emperor himself, Matteo Ricci made European educational resources and skills, especially in the fields of mathematics and astronomy, an important part of his mission strategy in China. However, this decision meant that many of the Jesuits' roles were predetermined, for instance in terms of their clothing and their understanding of gendered roles. In order to be able to convey their offerings with credibility to the social elites at court and elsewhere, the Jesuits adopted the role model of the literati. Just like these Confucian scholars, the Jesuits now also clothed themselves in silk, and since they associated themselves performatively with a socially exclusive milieu, these practices gave them access to the courtly elites. On the other hand, adherence to this model of behavior complicated their access to other milieus. As a result of their courtly literati dress, Jesuits only had limited access to women (Amsler).

Similar commitments to specific roles, which included adhesion to rules of dress and behavior with their respective advantages and disadvantages, sometimes meant that missionaries were co-opted for political goals. Whoever came to court as an agent of a crown had to respect rules concerning courtly and diplomatic behavior in order to fulfill their representative role. These requirements remained valid even for actors who were already committed to other sets of rules, as is illustrated by the case of the prior of the Augustinians in Persia (Windler). The tensions that arose between the religious aims and duties of the missionaries and their political mission were often expressed in their clothing (Menegon). How difficult it was to make the right decisions on the courtly stage is evidenced by the great appetite missionaries displayed for guidance from the "genuine" literati and ministers.

Just as the demand for missionaries' cultural capital and their political services were sometimes decisive for the societal roles they would fulfill on the ground, the need to meet the challenge posed by Rome's dramatic underfunding of the mission developed at least equally compelling imperatives. This is particularly evident in the case of the Jesuits in Japan. Since their participation in the Portuguese silk trade was not only controversial within the order but also yielded too little, the Jesuits had to find further sources of local income. In doing so, it proved to be especially helpful for them to follow the model provided by Buddhist monks. The Jesuits dressed like the monks and made use of the same structures, as they developed streams of income in rural areas. With the help of the *daimyō*, i.e., the local magnates and landowners, who gave the missionaries access to income from land ownership and helped them secure the support of the population, the Jesuits not only took over buildings previously inhabited by Buddhist monks in the countryside but also their style and social roles (Vu Thanh).

If one compares the roles chosen by Jesuits in China and Japan, the same basic pattern emerges despite the many differences on the ground. This pattern might be described as the double preservation of the social order. The Jesuits accepted traditional local structures and social hierarchies and adapted their behavior to a role that was already in place in each locality. This role, however, was meant to situate the missionaries as high up in the societal hierarchy as possible, and thus to reflect their social status in their European homeland. This social positioning gave them the scope for action that was needed for the religious dimension of the mission.

The Franciscans in the Holy Land were less keen to adopt local roles. In terms of their clothing and their food they remained committed to European patterns. But here, too, Tramontana's explanation fits into the broader picture. The Franciscans had been in place long before they engaged in missionary activities, and since their daily exchanges had resulted in the close economic integration of their community with their Muslim environment, the conditions here were very different. For them it was not necessary to adopt local roles in order to prepare the ground for their religious activities, as the structures that were already in place were sufficient.

The fact that conversion usually did not affect the social status of the person concerned underscores the importance of social stability for the mission. Ward's contribution provides evidence of a Buddhist scholar who after her conversion to Christianity was allowed to continue to debate with other scholars and worked self-confidently on the foundation of women's groups that were analogous to the brotherhoods and orders of men. Conversely, even if a missionary converted to Islam he could maintain his status as a scholar (Windler).

The conversion of a missionary refers to the dangers to which the mission was exposed and which in turn limited the actors' room for maneuvering. On the one hand, limits were set by the dangers that could arise from a violation of cultural norms. For example, excessive deviations from local notions of gender relations carried the risk of aligning one's behavior with that of local heterodox non-Christian groups and of subsequently being perceived as a member of one of these groups (Amsler). Above all, however, accusations of sexual rapprochement with women had to be avoided, as this would have endangered the mission in its entirety. Correspondingly, the rules for confession in the Middle East stipulated that doors and windows had to remain open when a missionary held a confessional conversation with a female penitent (Heyberger). In China, too, the missionaries attached the greatest importance to steering clear of any moments that might offer the opportunity for sexual assaults, for example, by calling in witnesses or veritable chaperones (Amsler).

On the other hand, there was also the danger of becoming overly assimilated. In specific cases, intensive engagement with the cultural and religious other could lead to the aforementioned conversion of a missionary (Windler). Furthermore, structural adjustments could also cease to be advantageous and turn into a risk factor. Thus the adoption of the model of Buddhist monks by the Jesuits in Japan was initially viewed as a foundation for missionary success. However, it was exactly this success that aroused distrust among the elites and the population, which was, in turn, directed at the missionaries and which led in the long run to the ban and failure of the mission (Vu Thanh).

It remains to be explored to what extent the scope for action and its limits outlined here varied according to the communication spaces in which the actors moved. The following section will concentrate on the insights arising from this volume's focus on various social spaces.

Scope for action and social spaces

Missionaries acted in contexts, and these contexts can be categorized into specific social spaces or localities. The court is such a locality, as are the urban and rural spaces and the household. The contributions which focus on the household show the benefits of organizing analytical work in accordance with social spaces in an exemplary manner. The focus on domestic spaces, which has often been overlooked in previous research, immediately opens up new perspectives for research in the histories of the mission and the church. What emerges are insights on the role of women in the sense of classical women's history, on the significance of gender for both men and women, and on the role of media and mediators, who were not only able to overcome linguistic and cultural boundaries but also to transcend the access restrictions of a society separated by gender. Finally, "third spaces" come into view, in which something new emerged from the contact between different cultures. This perspective, however, distances itself from the focus of traditional church history, which centered on the priest, the Eucharist, and the church space as the center of Christian life. In situations where women were strictly forbidden to attend church services, gender-aware mission research must seek out spaces other than the public sphere of the church and cultivate an interest in media and mediators.

We thus follow the missionaries who were themselves confronted in their everyday lives with a much stricter gender separation than they were used to from their home countries in Europe. Above all, the sharp inside versus outside dichotomy in China spatially conceptualized the separation of genders and thus turned the household into a self-contained, enclosed space. Simultaneously, households made visible the broader categorization of societal roles. In order to not violate these cultural norms, missionaries in China did not begin to turn their efforts toward women until after the male head of household had been converted. And even then, their missionary efforts remained indirect, as they relied on male relatives, servants, or Chinese lay brothers as mediators (Amsler). Things were different in the Middle East. Here the missionaries focused their efforts decidedly on women in view of the legal conditions that required the Sultan's Orthodox subjects to remain in the church appointed to them by the Ottoman authorities and which amounted to a conversion ban for men. This was a successful strategy. In Aleppo, for instance, women and families without male heads of household formed the bulk of those who converted from the Eastern Church to Roman Catholicism (Heyberger). This shows that gender roles could both promote and hinder the mission. In Ottoman rule, the legal disadvantage of women not counting as fully fledged subjects increased their religious mobility.

In Japan, the missionaries were able to initiate contact with women even if no male member of the family had yet chosen Christianity. More than in the other case studies, the social space of the Japanese household presents itself as a "third space" in the sense of Homi K. Bhaba: it acted as a cultural contact zone, in which the actors transgressed and shifted boundaries in various ways. They talked, sang, and wrote together, thus producing texts that represented something new, something third (Ward). Through this cooperation, documents were created that took into account the linguistic differentiations of Japanese in accordance with gender and status. These texts do not only document the formation of the Kirishitan religion as an independent Christianity. They also deliver an important example of the emergence of new mission techniques and media and demonstrate that other actors had come into play in addition to the European missionaries. Even Christianity itself would come to present itself in a new light. The public religion of Europe became domestic in China, where even the practice of the sacraments was differentiated according to space and gender (Amsler).

Through a consideration of the household, the importance of the spatial order of the mission becomes apparent. It is here that the gendering of the mission becomes tangible, since it is evident that the mission was by no means limited to men. Nevertheless, it should not be forgotten that the category of gender also played a central role in other social spaces. Still, this perspective helps to clarify the analytical benefits of the "spatial view," which go beyond the delivery of insights about specific forms of the mission. At the same time, this approach reveals specific aspects that were particularly important in a given space and have therefore left traces in the sources but are often also of fundamental importance in other settings. For the household, this is the category of gender; for the court, it is the variety of roles open to missionaries depending on the demands of the political context and the cultural capital available to them. Moreover, the richness of sources concerning the courtly space make it the ideal setting for highlighting the importance of individual decisions.

The urban space firmly directs one's attention to questions of church organization and hierarchy, not only because an astonishing and singular attempt was made to introduce the Tridentine parish model to Asia in Nagasaki (Tronu). Beyond this, the diversity of urban spaces promoted a diversity of opinions among the actors on the ground, which severely complicated the claims of the Roman Curia to centrality and normative authority. At the same time, cities reveal the overlapping of social spaces. Thus the European model of rural mission was also applied in Asia. Preachers traveled to the often-scattered small communities in the countryside from the urban residences of the missionaries, and the actors of the rural mission could therefore also be found in the cities. A second model of rural mission also became increasingly popular. In view of the scarcity of local staff, the missionaries began to leave village congregations to the leadership of converted locals and to instruct them using letters and messengers from their urban residence. Converts with previous experience in leadership roles were particularly suitable for this task: former Brahmins in India and former Zen monks in Japan. Apparently, the missionaries' goal of maintaining social stability also had to be applied in the selection of local employees, and not only in India with its rigid caste system. Nevertheless, in rural areas in particular, it is evident that stability was not always a matter of course and that the agency of the population was a crucial factor for the success of the missionaries. When the indigenous inhabitants of even remote regions turned against the missionaries, it could mean the end of the mission or the end of individual missionaries (Županov).

The Salsete massacre, which claimed the lives of the group of Jesuits around Rodolfo Acquaviva, was due to Acquaviva's second mistake after his failed mission attempt at the Mughal court. This instance underscores the interconnectedness of the social spaces discussed here in the life of the actors (Županov). Acquaviva had traveled from the Mughal court to the jungle of Goa only a short time before his martyrdom. That he died there was due in no small part to his failure to familiarize himself with the problems and rules of rural areas.

There was no mention of this failure in the reports of his contemporaries. In the context of actual or aspired canonizations, certain narrative strategies are to be expected. Here they turned an impatient and poorly informed Italian nobleman into a humble martyr and thus revealed some of the potential pitfalls that missionary history has to contend with in terms of sources (Županov). The presumed expectations of the addressees shaped the reports of the missionaries in various ways. Events and decisions that would have presumably been met with incomprehension or even criticism in Rome were often concealed or translated into European thought patterns (Amsler). All the while, attempts were made to fuel the zeal for the mission of the European powers by resorting to stereotypes such as the notion of the uneducated but gentle and religiously open-minded indigenous people (Pomplun). The mental landscape of the addressees thus represents another dimension that has to be taken into account when conducting research into the history of missions. Europe was always present in the minds of the missionaries in Asia.

One thing can be learned from Acquaviva's mistakes: going local was an ongoing task, not a one-off process. Localizing the Catholic mission in Asia can therefore be understood as a process that took place through multiple interactions and that differed according to social space, geographic region, and time. This commentary has sought to highlight the diversity of the framework conditions and other factors that shaped this process. The extent to which these findings on Asia can be transferred to other regions of the world is open for discussion. But it is also worthwhile for the Asian region to continue along the path outlined here and to take up the methodological suggestions of this volume.

Some final thoughts might be of interest in this context. The analysis of "local religions" that focused on individual case studies undoubtedly liberated us from old fixations and offered valuable insights. It might now be useful to take these individual cases as starting points from which to extend perspectives focusing both inward and outward and to systematically consider the polycentric structure of pre-modern Christianities. Within these Christianities, one promising endeavor would be an inquiry about overlapping structures and organizations, such as the orders and their networks, but which is also about the coexistence of different religious, liturgical, and ecclesiastical models, as well as about the development of competing centers and authorities. Outwardly, the contacts of local Christianities to Rome and to Europe should be considered just as much as their relations with one another, even where boundaries of confession were transgressed. These perspectives present themselves when we understand Christianities as communities of interaction that give shape to their centers and margins through communication. This directs our attention to the boundaries drawn by the actors, not to those imposed later by church historiography or national historical research. In this way new connections might become visible. Parallels and affinities between dogmatically separated Christianities might emerge, as well as variants within a single confession. Christianities might reveal themselves to be fundamentally polycentric and equally dynamic, and their contribution to the interconnectedness of the world might become more apparent. This can only succeed as a joint project that unites numerous researchers who are willing to contribute their perspectives and expertise. This volume represents an important step along this path.

English translation: Regine Maritz (Paris)

Abbreviations

ACDF	Archivum Congregationis pro Doctrina Fidei, Rome
Add Mss	Addington Manuscripts
AE	Affaires Étrangères
AGOCD	Archivum Generale Ordinis Carmelitarum Discalceatorum, Rome
ANF	Archives Nationales de France, Paris
ANTT	Arquivo Nacional da Torre do Tombo, Lisbon
APCP	Archives Provinciales des Capucins de Paris
APF	Archivum Sacrae Congregationis de Propaganda Fide, Rome
ARSI	Archivum Romanum Societatis Iesu
ASCTS	Archivio Storico della Custodia di Terra Santa, Jerusalem
BA	Biblioteca da Ajuda, Lisbon
BAV	Biblioteca Apostolica Vaticana
BL	British Library, London
BNP	Biblioteca Nacional de Portugal, Lisbon
BRAH	Biblioteca de la Real Academia de la Historia, Madrid
CC	Curia Custodiale
CCT BnF	Standaert, Nicolas, Adrian Dudink, and Nathalie Monnet, eds. *Faguo guojia tushuguan Ming-Qing Tianzhujiao wenxian* 法國國家圖書館明清天主教文獻 – *Chinese Christian Texts from the National Library of France – Textes chrétiens chinois de la Bibliothèque nationale de France*. 23 vols. Taipei: Taipei Ricci Institute, 2009.
CE 1	*Cartas que os padres e irmãos da Companhia de Jesus que andão nos reynos de Japão escreverão aos da mesma Companhia da India, e Europa, desdo anno de 1549 atè o de 1580, Primeiro tomo, Nellas se conta o principio, socesso, la bontade da christandade daquelles partes, los varios costumes, las idolatrias da gentilidade, Impressas por mandado do Illustrissimo, & reverendissimo senhor dom Theotonio de Bragança Arcebispo d'Evora*. Évora: Manoel de Lyra, 1597.

CE 2	*Segunda parte das Cartas de Japão que escreverão os padres & irmãos da Companhia de Jesus*. Évora: Manoel de Lyra, 1598.
CP	Congregazioni Particolari
DAAG	Directorate of Archives and Archeology, Goa
DI	Wicki, Joseph, ed. *Documenta Indica*. 17 vols. Rome: Institutum Historicum Societatis Iesu, 1948–1988.
FR	D'Elia, Pasquale M., ed. *Fonti Ricciane: Documenti originali concernenti Matteo Ricci e la storia delle prime relazioni tra l'Europa e la Cina (1579–1615)*. 3 vols. Rome: Libreria dello Stato, 1942–49.
JS	Japonica Sinica
JA	Jesuítas na Ásia
LEC	Aimé-Martin, M. Louis, ed. *Lettres édifiantes et curieuses concernant l'Asie, l'Afrique et l'Amérique, avec quelques relations nouvelles des missions, et des notes géographiques et historiques*. Pantheon litteraire. Paris: Paul Daffis Libraire-Éditeur, vol. 3, 1843.
MITN	Petech, Luciano. *I missionari italiani nel Tibet e nel Nepal*. 7 vols. Rome: Libreria dello Stato, 1954–56.
NA	Nationaal Archief, The Hague
OS	Tacchi-Venturi, Pietro, ed. *Opere Storiche del P. Matteo Ricci, S.I. Edite a cura del Comitato per le Onoranze Nazionali. Vol. 2: Le Lettere della Cina (1580–1610) con appendice di documenti inediti*. Macerata: Giorgetti, 1913.
Ott. Lat.	Ottoboniani Latini
PG	Procura generale
SC	Scritture riferite nei Congressi
SN	sine numero/without number
SO	Sanctum Officium
SOCG	Scritture originali riferite nelle Congregazioni Generali
SOCP	Scritture originali riferite nelle Congregazioni Particolari
St. St.	Stanza storica

Bibliography

Primary sources

Abū l-Fażl ʿAllāmī. *Akbar-nāma*. Abdur Rahim (ed.). 3 vols. Translated by Henry Beveridge. New Delhi: Ess Ess Publications, 1979.

Acosta, José de. *De procuranda Indorum Salute*. Edited by Luciano Pereña Vicente, V. Abril, C. Baciero, A. García, D. Ramos, J. Barrientos, and F. Maseda. 2 vols. Madrid, CSIC, 1984, 1987.

Aduarte, Diego. *Historia de la Provincia del Sancto Rosario de la Órden de Predicadores en Philippinas, Japón, y China*. Manila: en el Colegio de Sancto Thomas, por Luis Beltrán, 1640.

Aleni, Giulio. *Vita del maestro Ricci, Xitai del Grande Occidente (Daxi Xitai Li xiansheng xingji*, 大西西泰利先生行蹟), Chinese text translated into Italian by Gianni Criveller. Brescia: Fondazione Civiltà Bresciana/Centro Giulio Aleni, 2010.

Alonso, Carlos. "El convento agustiniano de Ispahan durante el período 1621–1671. Documentación inedita." *Analecta Augustiniana* 36 (1973): 247–308.

Aquinas, Thomas. *Summa theologiae cum supplemento et commentariis Caietani*. In *Sancti Thomae de Aquino Opera omnia, iussa impensaque Leonis XIII. P.M. edita*. Vols. 4–12. Rome: Ex Typographia Polyglotta S. C. de Propaganda Fide, 1888–1906.

Arce, Agustín. *Documentos y textos para la historia de Tierra Santa y sus santuarios, 1600–1700*. Jerusalem: Franciscan Printing Press, 1970.

———. *Miscelánea de Tierra Santa*. Vol. 2: Ex archivis Custodiae Terrae Sanctae. Jerusalem: Franciscan Printing Press, 1973.

Banerjee, S. N., and John S. Hoyland, trans. *The Commentary of Father Monserrate S.J. on His Journey to the Court of Akbar*. New Delhi: Asian Educational Service, 1992.

Bastiaensen, Michel, ed. *Souvenirs de la Perse safavide et autres lieux d'Orient [1664–1678] en version persane et européenne*. Brussels: Éditions de l'Université de Bruxelles, 1985 (partial edition and French translation of *Angelus a Sancto Ioseph. Gazophylacium linguae Persarum*. . . . Amsterdam: ex officina Jansonio-Waesbergiana, 1684).

Besson, Joseph. *La Syrie sainte ou la mission de Jésus et des Pères de la Compagnie de Jésus en Syrie*. Vol. 1: *L'establissement et le progres de Mission de la Compagnie de Jésus en Syrie*. Paris: J. Hénault, 1660.

Bognars, Jacques, and Robert Sourgenolle. *Alcune lettere delle cose del Giappone dell'anno 1579 infino al 1581*. Milan: Pacificio Pontio, 1584.

Carvalho, Valentim. *Apologia*. Edited by José Eduardo Franco. Lisbon: Centro científico e cultural de Macau, 2007.

Castellani, Eutimio. *Catalogo dei Firmani ed altri documenti legali emanati in lingua araba e turca concernenti i santuari le proprietà i diritti della Custodia di Terra Santa conservati nell'Archivio della stessa Custodia in Gerusalemme*. Jerusalem: Franciscan Printing Press, 1922.

———, ed. *Atti del Rev.mo Padre Lorenzo Cozza Custode di Terra Santa*. Vol. 1, part 1: *1709–1715*. Quaracchi: Collegio S. Bonaventura, 1924.

Chardin, Jean. *Voyages du chevalier Chardin, en Perse, et autres lieux de l'Orient*. Edited by L. Langlès. 10 vols. Paris: Le Normant, imprimeur-libraire, 1811.

Colín, Francisco. *Labor Evangélica, ministerios apostólicos de los obreros de la Compañía de Jesús, fundacion, y progressos de su providencia en las Islas Filipinas* (Madrid, 1663), 3 vols. Edited by Pablo Pastells. Barcelona: Henrich, 1900–1902.

Cortes, Adriano de las. *Le voyage en Chine d'Adriano de las Cortes S.J. (1625)*. Translated by Pascale Girard and Juliette Monbeig. Paris: Chandeigne, 2001.

Couplet, Philippe. *Histoire d'une dame chrétienne, par occasion les usages de ces peuples, l'établissement de la Religion, les manières des Missionnaires, & les Exercices de piété des nouveaux Chrétiens sont expliquez*. Paris: Estienne Michalet, 1688.

Danford, Richard K., Robin D. Gill, and Daniel T. Reff, trans. and ed. *The First European Description of Japan, 1585: A Critical English-Language Edition of Striking Contrasts in the Customs of Europe and Japan by Luis Frois, S.J.* London: Routledge, 2014.

Della Valle, Pietro. *Viaggi di Pietro della Valle il Pellegrino descritti da lui medesimo in Lettere familiari all'erudito suo Amico Mario Schipano. Parte seconda: La Persia*. 2 vols. Rome: Biagio Deversin, 1658.

Dos informaciones hechas en Iapón: una de la hazienda que Taycosama, señor del dicho Reyno, mandó tomar de la Nao S. Felipe [. . .], y otra de la muerte de seys religiosos descalzos de S. Francisco. Seville, 1599.

Dyāb, Hanna. *D'Alep à Paris. Les pérégrinations d'un jeune Syrien au temps de Louis XIV*. Translated by Paule Fahmé-Thiéry, Bernard Heyberger, and Jérôme Lentin. Arles: Actes Sud, 2015.

Fleuriau d'Armenonville, Thomas Charles. *Estat présent de l'Arménie tant pour le temporel que pour le spirituel*. Paris: chez la veuve de Jacques Langlois, 1694.

Fortes, Antonio. *Acta definitorii generalis O.C.D. Congregationis S. Eliae*. Vol. 1: *1605–1658*. Rome: Teresianum, 1985.

Francesco da Serino. *Croniche ovvero annali di Terra Santa [. . .]*. Edited by Teodoro Cavallon. 14 vols. Quaracchi: Collegio di S. Bonaventura, 1921–1933.

Fróis, Luís. *Relación del martirio de los veintiséis cristianos crucificados en Nangasaqui el 5 de febrero de 1597*. Edited by Romualdo Galdós. Rome: Tipografía de la Pontificia Universidad Gregoriana, 1935.

———. *Kulturgegensätze Europa-Japan (1585): Tratado em que se contem muito susintae abreviadamente algumas contradições e diferenças de custumes antre a gente de Europa e esta provincia de Japão*. Translated and edited by Josef Franz Schütte. Tokyo: Sophia University, 1955.

———. *Historia de Japam*. Edited by Josef Wicki. 5 vols. Lisbon: Biblioteca Nacional de Lisboa, 1976–1984.

Fryer, John. *A New Account of East India and Persia Being Nine Years Travels, 1672–1681* [London, 1698]. Edited by William Crooke. Vol. 2. London: Hakluyt Society, 1912.

Fucan, Fabian. *Myōtei mondō*. Edited by Katsumi Ide and Arimichi Ebisawa. In *Kirishitan kyōrisho*, edited by Arimichi Ebisawa, Katsumi Ide, and Hisashi Kishino, 287–417. Tokyo: Kyōbunkan, 1993.

Gemelli Careri, Giovanni Francesco. *Giro del mondo del Dottor D. Gio. Francesco Gemelli Careri. Nuova edizione accresciuta, ricorretta, e divisa in nove volumi. Con un indice de' viaggiatori, e loro opere. Tomo secondo contenente le cose piú ragguardevoli vedute nella Persia*. Venice: Sebastiano Coleti, 1719.

Golvers, Nöel ed. *Letters of a Peking Jesuit: The Correspondence of Ferdinand Verbiest, SJ (1623–1688). Revised and Expanded*. Leuven: Ferdinand Verbiest Instituut – KU Leuven, 2017.

Guerreiro, Fernão. *Relação Anual das Coisas que Fizeram os Padres da Companhia de Jesus nas suas Missões do Japão, China... nos anos de 1600 a 1609*. 3 vols. Lisbon and Évora: 1603–1611. Facsimile. Coimbra: Coimbra University Press, 1930.

Gwynne, Paul. *Francesco Benci's, 'Quinque Martyres' (Jesuit Studies): Translation, Edition and Commentary*. Leiden: Brill, 2018.

Horn, Elzear. *Ichonographiae Monumentorum Terrae Sancte, 1724–1744*. Edited by Girolamo Golubovich, OFM. Rome: Typis Sallustianis, 1902.

Hosten, Henry. "*Mongolicae Legationis Commentarius* (António Monserrate)." *Memoirs of the Asiatic Society of Bengal* 3, no. 9 (1914): 513–704.

Idlibī, Nāwufītūs. *Asāqifa al-Rūm al-Malakiyyīn bi-Ḥalab*. Aleppo: Maṭbaʿat al-Aḥsān, 1983.

Isidore de Saint-Joseph and Pierre de Saint-André. *Historia Generalis Fratrum Discalceatorum Ordinis B. Virginis Mariae de Monte Carmelo Congregationis S. Eliae*. 2 vols. Rome: ex Typographia Philippi Mariae Mancini, 1668, 1671.

Juan de Santa María. *Chrónica de la Provincia de San Ioseph de los Descalzos de la Órden de los Menores de nuestro Seráfico Padre San Francisco y de las Provincias y custodias Descalças, que della han salido, y son sus hijas. Parte Primera*. Madrid: Imprenta Real, 1615. *Parte Segunda*. Madrid: Imprenta Real, 1618.

Juan Pobre de Zamora. *Historia de la pérdida y descubrimiento del galeón "San Felipe" de Juan Pobre de Zamora*. Edited by Jesús Martínez Pérez. Ávila: Institución Gran Duque de Alba, Diputación Provincial de Ávila, 1997.

Kaempfer, Engelbert. *Briefe, 1683–1715*. Edited by Detlef Haberland. Munich: Iudicium Verlag, 2001.

Kangxi Renhe xianzhi (康熙) 仁和縣志 (Renhe County local gazetteer), Kangxi edition, 17th century.

Kévorkian, Raymond. "Documents d'archives français sur le Patriarcat arménien de Constantinople (1701–1714)." *Revue des études arméniennes* 19 (1985): 333–371.

Kircher, Athanasius. *China Illustrata. Translated by Charles D. Van Tuyl from the 1667 Original Latin Edition*. Muskogee, OK: Indian University Press – Bacone College, 1987.

Kontemutsusu munji. In *Kirishitanbanshū*. Vol. 1. 369–538. Tenri: Tenri University Press, 1976.

Kōso, Toshiaki, ed. *Sanctos no gosagvueo no vchi nvqigaqi*. Tokyo: Yūshōdō, 2006.

Lemmens, Leonardus, ed. *Acta S. Congregationis de Propaganda Fide pro Terra Sancta*. 2 vols. Quaracchi: Collegio San Bonaventura, 1921–1922.

Li Zhizao 李之藻, ed. *Tianxue chuhan* 天學初函 (First collection of celestial studies) (1626). Taipei: Xuesheng shuju, 1965.

Libois, Charles, ed. *Monumenta Proximi-Orientis*. Vol. 5: *Égypte (1591–1699)*. Rome: Institutum historicum Societatis Iesu, 2002.

———, ed. *Monumenta Proximi-Orientis*. Vol. 6: *Égypte (1700–1773)*. Rome: Institutum historicum Societatis Iesu, 2003.
Loyola, Ignacio de. *Sancti Ignatii de Loyola Constitutiones Societatis Jesu*. Vol. 2: *Textus hispanus*. Rome: Typis Pontificiae Universitatis Gregorianae, 1936.
———. *Écrits*. Edited by Maurice Giuliani. Paris: Desclée de Brouwer, 1991.
Lucena, Afonso de. *Erinnerungen aus der Christenheit von Ōmura. De algumas cousas que ainda se alembra o p[adre] Afonso de Lucena que pertencem à christandade de Ōmura [1578–1614]*. Edited by Josef Franz Schütte. Rome: Institutum Historicum Societatis Iesu, 1972.
Lugo, Juan de. *Disputationes scholasticae et morales de virtute Fidei divinae*. Lyon: Sumpt. Haered. Petri Prost, Philippi Borde et Laurentii Arnauld, 1646.
Manucci, Niccolao. *Storia do Mogor or Mogul India, 1653–1708*. Translated by William Irvine. Vol. 1. London: John Murray, 1907.
Margiotti, Fortunato, ed. *Sinica Franciscana: Relationes et epistolas Fratrum Minorum Hispanorum in Sinis, qui annis 1684–92 missionem ingressi sunt*. Vol. 8, in 2 vols. Rome: [Edizioni Sinica Franciscana], 1975.
Martínez de Ripalda, Juan. *De ente supernaturali disputationes theologicae*. 4 vols. Paris: Apud Victorem Palmé, 1870–1871.
———. *De virtutibus theologicis, sive, de fide, spe et caritate*. 2 vols. Paris: Apud Ludovicum Vivès, 1873.
Martini, Martino. *De bello Tartarico*. Antwerp: Ex Officina Plantiniana Balthasaris Moreti, 1654.
———. *Opera omnia*. Vol. 1: *Lettere e documenti*. Edited by Giuliano Bertuccioli. Trento: Università degli Studi di Trento, 1998.
———. *Opera Omnia*. Vol. 5: *De Bello Tartarico Historia e altri scritti*. Edited by Federico Masini, Luisa M. Paternicò, and Davor Antonucci. Trento: Università degli Studi di Trento, 2013.
Mekhitar of Sebaste. *Lettere del Servo di Dio Abate Mechitar*. Vol. 4: *Lettere e documenti, 1705–1749*. Venice: Casa Editrice Armena, 1980.
Meynard, Thierry, ed. *Confucius Sinarum Philosophus (1687): The First Translation of the Confucian Classics*. Rome: Institutum Historicum Societatis Iesu, 2011.
Monserrat, Antoni de. *Ambaixador a la cort del Gran Mogol: Viatges d'um Jesuïta Català Del segle XVI a l'India, Pakistan, Afganistan, Himalaia*. Edited and translated by Josep Lluis Alay. Lérida: Pagès, 2002.
Montilla, Francisco de. "Memorial." Edited by Lorenzo Pérez. *Archivum Franciscanum Historicum* 15 (1922): 476–507.
Nieuhof, Johan. *Die Gesandtschaft der Ost-Indischen Gesellschaft in den Niederlanden an den Tartarischen Cham und nunmehr auch Sinischen Keiser*. Amsterdam: Moers, 1666.
Obara, Satoru. ed. *Santosu no gosagyō*. Tokyo: Kyōbunkan, 1996.
———. ed. *Kontemutsusu munji*. Tokyo: Kyōbunkan, 2002.
Padberg, John. *The Constitutions of the Society of Jesus and Their Complementary Norms: A Complete English Translation of the Official Latin Text*. Saint Louis, MO: The Institute of Jesuit Sources, 1996.
Pantoja, Diego. *Relatione dell'entrata d'alcuni Padri della Compagnia di Giesu nella China*. Rome: Bartolomeo Zannetti, 1607.
Paulo da Trinidade. *Conquista Espiritual do Oriente*. Introduction and footnotes by F. Félix Lopes. Vol. 1. Lisbon: Centro de Estudos Históricos Ultramarinos, 1961.

Pérez de Chinchón, Bernardo. *Libro Llamado Antialcoran, que quiere dezir contra el [. . .] alcoran de Mahoma, reartido en veynte y seys sermones*. Salamanca: Casa de Juan y Andres Renaut Impresores, 1595.

Pietro Verniero di Montepiloso. *Croniche ovvero annali di Terra Santa*. Edited by Girolamo Golubovich. 5 vols. Quaracchi: Collegio di S. Bonaventura, 1929–1936.

Rabbath, Antoine, ed. *Documents inédits pour servir à l'histoire du christianisme en Orient*. 2 vols. Paris: Picard et fils, 1905–1910.

Rego, António da Silva. *Documentação para a História das Missões do Padroado Português do Oriente*. Vol. 12: *Índia, 1572–1582*. Lisbon: Agência Geral do Ultramar, 1958.

Richard, Francis, ed. *Raphaël du Mans, missionnaire en Perse au XVIIe siècle*. Vol. 1: *Biographie. Correspondance*. Vol. 2: *Estats et Mémoire*. Paris: L'Harmattan, 1995.

Ripa, Matteo. *Matteo Ripa: Giornale (1711–1716)*. Edited by Michele Fatica. Vol. 2. Naples: Istituto Universitario Orientale, 1996.

Roger, Eugène. *La Terre Sainte, ou description topographique très-particulière des saints lieux et de la terre de promission*. Paris: Antoine Bertier, 1646.

Ruiz de Medina, Juan, ed. *Documentos del Japón, 1547–1557*. Rome: Institutum Historicum Societatis Iesu, 1990.

Russell, Alexander. *The Natural History of Aleppo*. Vol. 1: *Description of the City and the Parts Adjacent*. London: GG & J Robinson, 1794.

Schall von Bell, Johann Adam. *Relation historique: Lettres et mémoires d'Adam Schall S. J.* Edited and translated by Henri Bernard and Paul Bornet. Tianjin: Hautes Études, 1942.

Schütte, Josef Franz, ed. *Il cerimoniale per i missionari del Giappone: Advertimentos e avisos acerca dos costumes e catangues de Jappão [. . .] di Alexandro Valignano*. Rome: Edizioni di Storia e Letteratura, 1946.

———, ed. *Textus catalogorum Japoniae aliaeque de persones domibusque Societatis Iesu in Japonia, informationes et relationes 1549–1654*. Rome: Institutum Historicum Societatis Iesu, 1975.

———. *Valignano's Mission Principles for Japan*. Translated by John J. Coyne. 2 vols. St. Louis, MO: The Institute of Jesuit Sources, 1980, 1985.

Seetzen, Ulrich Jasper. *Tagebuch des Aufenthalts in Aleppo 1803–1805*. Hildesheim: Georg Olms Verlag, 2011.

Segneri, Paolo. *Il penitente istruito a ben confessarsi: Operetta spirituale, da cui ciascuno può apprender il modo certo di ritornar in gratia del suo Signore, et di mantenersi*. Venice: Gio Antonio Remondini, 1669.

Semedo, Álvaro. *Historica relatione del Gran Regno della Cina*. Rome: Vitale Mascardi, 1653.

———. *Histoire universelle de la Chine*. Lyon: Hierosme Prost, 1667.

Sicard, Claude. *Œuvres*. Edited by Maurice Martin. 3 vols. Cairo and Paris: Institut français d'Archéologie Orientale, 1982.

Sicardo, Joseph. *Christiandad del Japón, y dilatada persecución que padeció: Memorias sacras de los mártyres de las ilustres religiones de Santo Domingo, San Francisco, Compañia de Jesús; y crecido número de Seglares; y con especialidad, de los Religiosos del Órden de S. Augustín*. Madrid: Francisco Sanz, Impressor del Reyno, 1698.

Silva y Figueroa, García de. *Comentarios de la Embaxada al Rey Xa Abbas de Pérsia (1614–1624)*. Part 2. Edited by Rui Manuel Loureiro, Ana Cristina Costa Gomes, and Vasco Resende. Lisbon: Centro de História de Além-Mar, 2011.

Soto, Domingo de. *De natura et gratia libri tres*. Venice: Apud Floravantem a Prato, 1584.

Sousa, Francisco de. *Oriente conquistado a Jesu Christo pelos Padres da Companhia de Jesus da Provincia de Goa*. Lisbon: na Officina de Valentim da Costa Deslandes, Impressor de Sua Magestade, 1710 [Porto: Lello & Irmão, editors, 1978].

Spence, Jonathan, Janet Chen, Pei-kai Cheng, and Michael Lestz, eds. *The Search for Modern China: A Documentary Collection*, 3rd ed. New York: W. W. Norton & Company, 2013.

Suárez, Francisco. *De gratia*. In *Opera omnia*. Vol. 8. Paris: Apud Ludovicum Vivès, 1857.

———. *De Fide theologica*. In *Opera omnia*. Vol. 12. Paris: Apud Ludovicum Vivès, 1858.

Sweet, Michael J., and Leonard Zwilling. *Mission to Tibet: The Extraordinary Eighteenth-Century Account of Father Ippolito Desideri, S.J.* Boston, MA: Wisdom Publications, 2010.

———. *"More Than the Promised Land": Letters and Relations from Tibet by the Jesuit Missionary António de Andrade (1580–1634)*. Boston, MA: Institute of Jesuit Sources, 2017.

Tello, Francisco. *Relación que don Francisco Tello, governador y capitán general de las Philipinas embió de seys frayles españoles de la órden de San Francisco, que crucificaron los del Japón, este año próximo passado de 1597*. Granada: Sebastian de Mena, 1598.

Trigault, Nicolas. "Lettera Annua della Cina del 1610, Cocino, Maggio 1613." In *Due Lettere Annue Della cina del 1610 e del 1611 scritte al M.R.P. Claudio Acquaviva Generale della Compagnia di Giesu*, 3–66. Milan: Pacifico Pontio & Giovanni Battista Piccaglia, Stampatori Archiepiscopali, 1615.

Valignano, Alessandro. *Il cerimoniale per i missionari del Giappone: Advertimentos e avisos acerca dos costumes e catangues de Jappão: importante documento circa i metodi di adattamento nella missione giapponese del secolo XVI: testo portoghese del manoscritto originale, versione letterale italiana. Nuova edizione anastatica con saggio introduttivo di Michela Catto*. Rome: Edizioni di Storia e Letteratura, 2011.

———. *Les Jésuites au Japon*. Translated by Jacques Bésineau. Paris: Desclée de Brouwer, 1990.

Vega, Andreas de. *De iustificatione doctrina universa libris XV*. Cologne: Apud Geruinum Calenium et Haeredes Quentelios, 1572.

Verbiest, Ferdinand. *Correspondance de Ferdinand Verbiest de la Compagnie de Jésus (1623–1688), Directeur de l'observatoire de Pékin*. Edited by Henri Josson and Léopold Willaert. Brussels: Palais des académies, 1938.

Vitoria, Francisco de. *Relectio de Indis*. Edited by Luciano Pereña. Bari: Levante Editori, 1996.

Wyngaert, Anastasius van den, and Georg Mensaert, eds. *Sinica Franciscana*. Vol. 5: *Relationes et Epistolas D. Fr. Bernardini Della Chiesa O.F.M.* Rome: Collegium S. Antonii, 1954.

Secondary works

Abagian, Mardiros. "La questione della *communicatio in sacris* nel secolo XVIII e la formazione del patriarcato armeno cattolico." *Bazmavep* 139 (1981), 129–182; 141 (1983), 215–232; 146 (1988), 155–172; 147 (1989), 244–258; 148 (1990), 146–161, 413–418; 149 (1991), 461–476; 150 (1992), 202–214.

Ago, Renata. *Carriere e clientele nella Roma barocca*. Rome: Editori Laterza, 1990.
Ahmad, Zahiruddin. "New Light on the Tibet-Ladakh-Mughal War of 1679–84." *East and West* 18 (1968): 340–361.
Ai to shinkō ni ikita Hosokawa Garashiya ten. Tokyo: Mainichi shinbunsha, 1982.
Alam, Muzaffar. "The Culture and Politics of Persian in Precolonial Hindustan." In *Literary Culture in History: Reconstructions From South Asia*, edited by Sheldon Pollock, 131–198. New Delhi: Oxford University Press, 2003.
———. *The Languages of Political Islam in India, 1200–1800*. New Delhi: Permanent Black, 2004.
———. "The Mughals, the Sufi Shaikhs and the Formation of the Akbari Dispensation." In *Expanding Frontiers in South Asian and World History Essays in Honour of John F. Richards*, edited by Richard M. Eaton, Munis D. Faruqui, David Gilmartin, and Sunil Kumar, 124–163. New Delhi: Cambridge University Press, 2013.
Alam, Muzaffar, and Sanjay Subrahmanyam. "Catholics and Muslims in the Court of Jahangir (1608–1611)." In *Writing the Mughal World. Studies on Culture and Politics*, edited by Muzaffar Alam and Sanjay Subrahmanyam, 249–310. New York: Columbia University Press, 2011.
Alden, Dauril. *The Making of an Enterprise: The Society of Jesus in Portugal, its Empire and Beyond, 1540–1750*. Stanford, CA: Stanford University Press, 1996.
Alfonso, Isabel, ed. *The Rural History of Medieval European Societies: Trends and Perspectives*. Turnhout: Brepols, 2007.
Alsteens, Stijn. "A Note on the Young Van Dyck." *Burlington Magazine* 156, no. 1331 (2014): 85–90.
Álvarez Taladriz, José Luis. "Fuentes europeas sobre Murayama Tōan (1562–1619) I. El pleito de Suetsugu Heizō contra Murayama Tōan Antonio según el Padre Matheus de Couros, Provincial de la Compañía de Jesús de Japón." *Tenri Daigaku Gakuhō* 51 (1966): 93–114.
———. "Fuentes europeas sobre Murayama Tōan (1562–1619) II. Murayama Tōan Antonio según Bernardino de Ávila Girón." *Kobe Gaidai Ronsō* 17 (1966): 395–418.
Amaro, Bébio Vieira. "Study on the Christian Facilities in the Port City of Nagasaki." PhD diss., University of Tokyo, 2016.
Amsler, Nadine. *Jesuits and Matriarchs: Domestic Worship in Early Modern China*. Seattle, WA: University of Washington Press, 2018.
Amsler, Nadine, Henrietta Harrison, and Christian Windler, eds. "Transformations of Intercultural Diplomacies: Comparative Views on Asia and Europe (1700 to 1850)," special issue of *The International History Review* 41, no. 5 (2019): 941–1107.
Anesaki, Masaharu. *Kirishitan shūmon no hakugai to senpuku*. Tokyo: Dōbunsha, 1930.
Anonymous. "Une pratique liturgique propre à la Chine: Le Tsikin 祭巾 ou bonnet de messe." *Bulletin catholique de Pékin* 11 (1924): 376–377, 404–406.
Appadurai, Arjun. "Kings, Sects and Temples in South India, 1350–1700 A.D." *Indian Economic Social History Review* 14, no. 1 (1977): 47–73.
———. *Modernity at Large: Cultural Dimensions of Globalization*. Minneapolis, MN: University of Minnesota Press, 1997.
Ardussi, John A. "The Rapprochement Between Bhutan and Tibet Under the Enlightened Rule of Sde-srid XIII Shes-rab-dbang-phyug (r. 1744–63)." *Journal of Bhutan Studies* 1 (1999): 64–83.

———. "Sikkim and Bhutan in the Crosscurrents of Seventeenth and Eighteenth Century Tibetan History." In *Buddhist Himalaya: Studies in Religion, History and Culture*. Vol. 2, edited by Anna Balikci-Denjongpa and Alex McKay, 29–42. Gangtok: Namgyal Institute of Tibetology, 2011.

Arimura, Rie. "The Catholic Architecture of Early Modern Japan: Between Adaptation and Christian Identity." *Japan Review* 27 (2014): 53–76.

———. *Iglesias kirishitan: El arte de lo efímero en las misiones católicas en Japón (1549–1639)*. Mexico: Universidad Iberoamericana, 2017.

Armanios, Febe. *Coptic Christianity in Ottoman Egypt*. New York: Oxford University Press, 2011.

Aslanian, Sebouh. *From the Indian Ocean to the Mediterranean: The Global Trade Networks of Armenian Merchants from New Julfa*. Berkeley, CA: University of California Press, 2011.

Astrain, Antonio. "Bonete de los Hermanos Coadiutores." In *Historia de la Compañía de Jesús en la asistencia de España. Tomo V. Vitelleschi, Carafa, Piccolomini*, 285–300. Madrid: Razón y Fe, 1916.

Axelrod, Paul, and Michelle A. Fuerch. "Portuguese Orientalism and the Making of the Village Communities of Goa." *Ethnohistory* 45, no. 3 (1998): 439–476.

Babaie, Sussan. *Isfahan and its Palaces. Statecraft, Shi'ism and the Architecture of Conviviality in Early Modern Iran*. Edinburgh: Edinburgh University Press, 2008.

Baer, Gabriel. "Village and City in Egypt and Syria." In *The Islamic Middle East, 700–1900*, edited by Abraham Udovitch, 521–546. Princeton, NJ: Darwin Press, 1981.

Bagatti, Beniamino. "L'industria della madreperla a Betlemme." In *Custodia di Terra Santa 1342–1942*, 135–140. Jerusalem: Franciscan Printing Press, 1951.

Bar, Doron. "Rural Monasticism as a Key Element in the Christianization of Byzantine Palestine." *The Harvard Theological Review* 98, no. 1 (2005): 49–65.

Bargiacchi, Enzo Gualtiero. "Ippolito Desideri's First Remarks on Ladakh." In *Mountains, Monasteries, and Mosques: Recent Research on Ladakh and the Western Himalaya*, edited by John Bray and Elena de Rossi Filibeck, 27–43. Rome: Fabrizio Serra, 2009.

Barkan, Ömer L. "Les fondations pieuses comme méthode de peuplement et de colonisation: Les derviches colonisateurs de l'époque des invasions et les couvents (zaviyé)." *Vakiflar Dergisi* 2 (1942): 59–65.

Beatrice, Pier Franco. "La christianisation des campagnes pendant l'Antiquité tardive dans les régions méditerranéennes. Bilan des recherches et questions de méthode." In *La christianisation des campagnes, Actes du colloque du CIHEC*, edited by Marie-Élisabeth Henneau and Jean-Pierre Massaut, 9–35. Brussels and Rome: Institut Historique Belge de Rome, 1996.

Ben-Zaken, Avner. *Cross-Cultural Scientific Exchanges in the Eastern Mediterranean, 1560–1660*. Baltimore, MD: The John Hopkins University Press, 2010.

Bernstein, Gail Lee. "Introduction." In *Recreating Japanese Women, 1600–1945*, edited by Gail Lee Bernstein, 1–14. Berkeley, CA: University of California Press, 1991.

Bettray, Johannes. *Die Akkommodationsmethode des P. Matteo Ricci S.I. in China*. Rome: Universitas Gregoriana, 1955.

Bhabha, Homi K. *The Location of Culture*. New York: Routledge, 1994.

Biermann, Benno. "War Martin Martini chinesischer Mandarin?" *Neue Zeitschrift für Missionswissenschaft* 11 (1955): 221–225.

Binz, Laura E. "Latin Missionaries and Catholics in Constantinople 1650–1760: Between Local Religious Culture and Confessional Determination." PhD diss., European University Institute, 2013.

Bireley, Robert. "Redefining Catholicism: Trent and Beyond." In *The Cambridge History of Christianity*. Vol. 6: *Reform and Expansion*, edited by Ronnie Po-chia Hsia, 145–161. New York: Cambridge University Press, 2007.

Black, Christopher F. *The Italian Inquisition*. New Haven, CT: Yale University Press, 2009.

Blussé, Leonard. "Minnan-jen or Cosmopolitan? The Rise of Cheng Chih-lung alias Nicolas Iquan." In *Development and Decline of Fukien Province in the 17th and 18th Centuries*, edited by Eduard B. Vermeer, 245–264. Leiden: Brill, 1990.

Bontinck, François. *La lutte autour de la liturgie chinoise aux XVIIe et XVIIIe siècles*. Louvain and Paris: Nauwelaerts, 1962.

Boogert, Maurits H. van den. *The Capitulations and the Ottoman Legal System: Consuls, Qadis, and Beratlıs in the Eighteenth Century*. Leiden: Brill, 2005.

Borges, Charles J. *The Economics of the Goa Jesuits, 1542–1759*. New Delhi: Concept Publishing Company, 1994.

Borràs, Antonio. "En torno a la indumentaria de los Jesuitas españoles en los siglos XVI y XVII." *Archivum Historicum Societatis Iesu* 36 (1967): 291–299.

Boudinhon, Auguste, and William Fanning. "Parish." In *The Catholic Encyclopedia*, vol. 11. New York: Robert Appleton Company, 1911. Retrieved from www.newadvent.org/cathen/11499b.htm. Last accessed 12 April 2019.

Bourdon, Léon. *La Compagnie de Jésus et le Japon*. Paris: Centre Calouste Gulbenkian, 1993.

Boxer, Charles Ralph. *The Christian Century in Japan, 1549–1650*. Berkeley, CA: University of California Press, 1951.

———. *The Great Ship from Amacon: Annals of Macao and the Old Japan Trade, 1555–1640*. Lisbon: Centro de Estudos Historicos ultra-marinos, 1959.

———. *Portuguese Merchants and Missionaries in Feudal Japan, 1543–1640*. London: Variorum reprints, 1986.

Brauen, Martin. *Dreamworld Tibet: Western Illusions*. Bangkok: Orchid Press, 2004.

Bray, Francesca. *Technology and Gender: Fabrics of Power in Late Imperial China*. Berkeley, CA: University of California Press, 1997.

Bray, John. "Christian Missionary Enterprise and Tibetan Trade." *Tibet Journal* 39 (2014): 11–37.

Brentjes, Sonja. "The Interests of the Republic of Letters in the Middle East." *Science in Context* 12 (1999): 435–468.

———. "Early Modern Western European Travellers in the Middle East and their Reports about the Sciences." In *Sciences, techniques et instruments dans le monde iranien (X^e – XIXe siècle). Actes du colloque tenu à l'Université de Téhéran, 7–9 juin 1998*, edited by Naṣrallāh Pūrğawādī et al., 435–468. Teheran: Presses universitaires d'Iran, 2004.

———. "The Mathematical Sciences in Safavid Iran: Questions and Perspectives." In *Muslim Cultures in the Indo-Iranian World during the Early-Modern and Modern Periods*, edited by Denis Hermann and Fabrizio Speziale, 325–402. Berlin: Klaus Schwarz Verlag, 2010.

Brockey, Liam Mathew. *Journey to the East: The Jesuit Mission in China, 1579–1724*. Cambridge, MA: Harvard University Press, 2007.

———. *The Visitor: André Palmeiro and the Jesuits in Asia*. Cambridge, MA: Harvard University Press, 2014.

Brook, Timothy. *The Confusions of Pleasure: Commerce and Culture in Ming China*. Berkeley, CA: University of California Press, 1998.

Cammann, Schuyler. "The Development of the Mandarin Square." *Harvard Journal of Asiatic Studies* 8, no. 2 (1944): 71–130.

Cardia, Giulio. *La posizione del de Lugo nella dottrina della universale necessità e possibilità della fede*. Cagliari: F. Trois, 1941.

Castelnau-L'Estoile, Charlotte de. *Les ouvriers d'une vigne stérile: Les jésuites et la conversion des Indiens du Brésil*. Paris: Centre culturel Calouste Gulbenkian, 2000.

Catellani, Andrea. "L'iconographie jésuite de la Chine: Note sémiotique sur quelques series d'images du 17ᵉ siècle." In *Transferts artistiques: Entre Orient et Occident, du 17ᵉ au 21ᵉ siècle*, edited by Paul Servais and Françoise Mirguet, 113–129. Louvain-la-Neuve: Academia-L'Harmattan, 2014.

Catto, Michela. *La Compagnia divisa: Il dissenso nell'Ordine gesuitico tra '500 à '600*. Brescia: Morcelliana, 2009.

Certeau, Michel de. *The Practice of Everyday Life*. Translated by Steven Rendall. Berkeley, CA: University of California Press, 1988.

Champion, Tony, and Graeme Hugo. *New Forms of Urbanization: Beyond the Urban-rural Dichotomy*. Aldershot: Ashgate, 2004.

Chang Pin-tsun. "Chinese Maritime Trade: The Case of Sixteenth-Century Fu-chien (Fukien)." PhD diss., Princeton University, 1983.

Chang Sheng-ching. "Das Porträt von Johann Adam Schall in Athanasius Kirchers *China Illustrata*." In *Western Learning and Christianity in China: The Contribution and Impact of Johann Adam Schall von Bell SJ*. Vol. 2, edited by Roman Malek, 1002–1031. Nettetal: Steyler Verlag, 1998.

Châtellier, Louis. *The Europe of the Devout: The Catholic Reformation and the Formation of a New Society*. Cambridge: Cambridge University Press, 1989.

———. *La religion des pauvres: Les missions rurales en Europe et la formation du catholicisme moderne XVIᵉ-XIXᵉ siècle*. Paris: Aubier, 1993.

[Chick, Herbert]. *A Chronicle of the Carmelites in Persia and the Papal Mission of the XVIIth and XVIIIth Centuries*. 2 vols. London: Eyre & Spottiswoode, 1939.

Christian, William A. *Local Religion in Sixteenth-Century Spain*. Princeton, NJ: Princeton University Press, 1981.

Cieslik, Hubert. "Fabian Fukan den nōto." *Kirishitan bunka kenkyūkai kaihō* 15, no. 3 (December 1972): 244–250.

Clark, Peter. "Introduction." In *The Oxford Handbook of Cities in World History*, edited by Peter Clark, 1–24. Oxford: Oxford University Press, 2013.

Clines, Robert John. "The Society of Jesus and the Early Modern Christian Orient." In *Jesuit Historiography Online*, edited by Robert A. Maryks. BrillOnline Reference Works, 2016. http://dx.doi.org/10.1163/2468-7723_jho_COM_192582.

Clossey, Luke. *Salvation and Globalization in the Early Jesuit Missions*. Cambridge: Cambridge University Press, 2008.

Cogoni, Giovanni. *La dottrina di Francesco Suarez nel problema della salvezza degli infedeli*. Cagliari: Tipografia S. Giuseppe, 1946.

Cohen, Paul Andrew. *China and Christianity: The Missionary Movement and the Growth of Chinese Antiforeignism, 1860–1870*, Cambridge, MA: Harvard University Press, 1963.

Coldiron, Anne B.E. "Translation's Challenge to Critical Categories: Verses from French in the Early English Renaissance." In *Critical Readings in Translation Studies*, edited by Mona Baker, 337–356. New York: Routledge, 2010.

Collani, Claudia von. "Mission and Matrimony." In *Missionary Approaches and Linguistics in Mainland China and Taiwan*, edited by Ku Wei-Ying, 11–31. Leuven: Leuven University Press, 2001.

———. "Lady Candida Xu: A Widow Between Chinese and Christian Ideals." In *Pioneer Chinese Christian Women: Gender, Christianity, and Social Mobility*, edited by Jessie G. Lutz, 224–245. Bethlehem: Lehigh University Press, 2010.

Cooper, Michael. "The Mechanics of the Macao-Nagasaki Silk Trade." *Monumenta Nipponica* 27, no. 4 (1972): 423–433.

Costa, João Paulo Oliveira e. "O Cristianismo no Japão e o Episcopado de D. Luis Cerqueira." PhD diss., Universidade Nova de Lisboa, 1998.

———. "A crise financeira da missão jesuítica do Japão no início do século XVII." In *A companhia de Jesus e a missionação no oriente. Actas do Colóquio Internacional realizado de 21 a 23 de Abril de 1997*, edited by Nuno da Silva Gonçalves, 235–246. Lisbon: Fundação Oriente, 2000.

———. "The *Misericórdias* among Japanese Christian Communities in the 16th and 17th Centuries." *Bulletin of Portuguese/Japanese Studies* 5 (2002): 67–79.

———. "The Brotherhoods (*Confrarias*) and Lay Support for the Early Christian Church in Japan." *Japanese Journal of Religious Studies* 34, no. 1 (2007): 67–84.

———. "Le jésuite Juan Baeza et la communauté chrétienne de Nagasaki pendant la persécution des shoguns Tokugawa." *Histoire, monde et cultures religieuses* 3, no. 11 (2009): 109–130.

Criveller, Gianni. *Preaching Christ in Late Ming China: The Jesuits' Presentation of Christ from Matteo Ricci to Giulio Aleni*. Taipei: Ricci Institute, 1997.

———. "Matteo Ricci's Ascent to Beijing." In *Portrait of a Jesuit: Matteo Ricci*, edited by Cesar Guillén-Nuñez and Gianni Criveller, 39–75. Macao: Macau Ricci Institute, 2010.

Cuevas, Bryan J. "Sorcerer of the Iron Castle: The Life of Blo bzang bstan pa rab rgyas, the First Brag dkar sngags rams pa of A mdo (c. 1647–1726)." *Revue d'Études Tibétaines* 39 (2017): 5–59.

Cushner, Nicholas. *Lords of the Land: Sugar, Wine, and Jesuits Estates of Coastal Peru, 1600–1767*. Albany, NY: State University of New York Press, 1980.

Dabringhaus, Sabine. *Geschichte Chinas 1279–1949*. Munich: Oldenbourg Wissenschaftsverlag, 2006.

De Craon, Constant. "Le projet d'union de 1701 entre les Arméniens catholiques et les Arméniens dissidents d'après la correspondance d'Hyacinthe-François, capucin supérieur de Saint-Louis de Péra." Special issue, *Bazmavep* (1949): 47–67.

Dehergne, Joseph. "La mission de Pékin vers 1700." *Archivum Historicum Societatis Iesu* 22 (1953): 314–338.

———. "Les missions de la Chine du Nord vers 1700." *Archivum Historicum Societatis Iesu* 24 (1955): 251–291.

———. "La Chine centrale vers 1700 I, L'évêché de Nankin." *Archivum Historicum Societatis Iesu* 28 (1959): 289–330.

———. "La Chine centrale vers 1700 II, Les vicariats apostoliques de la côte." *Archivum Historicum Societatis Iesu* 30 (1961): 307–366.

———. "La Chine centrale vers 1700 III, Les vicariats apostoliques de l'intérieur." *Archivum Historicum Societatis Iesu* 36 (1967): 32–71.

———. "La Chine du Sud-Ouest." *Archivum Historicum Societatis Iesu* 45 (1973): 246–287.

———. "La Chine du Sud-Est." *Archivum Historicum Societatis Iesu* 45 (1976): 3–55.

Dekoninck, Ralph. "*Propagatio Imaginum:* The Translated Images of Our Lady of Foy." In *The Nomadic Object: The Challenge of World for Early Modern Religious Art*, edited by Christine Göttler and Mia Mochizuki, 241–269. Leiden: Brill, 2018.

Desmond, William. *Being Between: Conditions of Irish Thought*. Galway: Leabhar Breac, 2008.

Diniz, Sofia. "Jesuit Buildings in China and Japan: A Comparative Study." *Bulletin of Portuguese/Japanese Studies* 3 (2001): 107–128.

Ditchburn, David, and Angus Mackay. *Atlas of Medieval Europe*. New York: Routledge, 2002.

Ditchfield, Simon. "Decentering the Catholic Reformation: Papacy and Peoples in the Early Modern World." *Archiv für Reformationsgeschichte* 101 (2010): 186–208.

Dixon, C. Scott, Dagmar Freist, and Mark Greengrass, eds. *Living with Religious Diversity in Early-Modern Europe*. Farnham: Ashgate, 2009.

Dompnier, Bernard. "Tensions et conflits autour des missions chez les capucins du XVIIe siècle." *Cheiron, Materiali e strumenti di aggiornamento storiografico* 43–44 (2006): 159–184.

Dompnier, Bernard, and Paola Vismara, eds. *Confréries et dévotions dans la catholicité moderne (mi-XVe-début XIXe siècle)*. Rome: École française de Rome, 2008.

Doumani, Beshara B. *Family Life in the Ottoman Mediterranean: A Social History*. New York: Cambridge University Press, 2017.

Dudink, Adrian. "The Sheng-ch'ao tso-p'i (1623) of Hsü Ta-shou." In *Conflict and Accommodation in Early Modern East Asia: Essays in Honour of Erik Zürcher*, edited by Harriet Zurndorfer and Leonard Blussé, 94–140. Leiden: Brill, 1993.

———. "The Holy Mass in Seventeenth- and Eighteenth-Century China: Introduction to and Annotated Translation of *Yu Misa Gongcheng* 與彌撒功程 (1721), Manual for Attending Mass." In *A Lifelong Dedication to the China Mission: Essays Presented in Honor of Father Jeroom Heyndrickx, CICM, on the Occasion of His 75th Birthday and the 25th Anniversary of the F. Verbiest Institute K.U. Leuven*, edited by Sara Lievens and Noël Golvers, 207–326. Leuven: F. Verbiest Institute K.U. Leuven, 2007.

Dudney, Arthur. "Sabk-e Hendi and the Crisis of Authority in Eighteenth-Century Indo-Persian Poetics." *Journal of Persianate Studies* 9, no. 1 (2016): 60–82.

Duindam, Jeroen. *Dynasties: A Global History of Power, 1300–1800*. Cambridge: Cambridge University Press, 2016.

Ebisawa, Arimichi. *Kirishitan nanban bungaku nyūmon*. Tokyo: Kyōbunkan, 1991.

Ebrey, Patricia Buckley. *The Inner Quarters: Marriage and the Lives of Chinese Women in the Sung Period*. Berkeley, CA: University of California Press, 1993.

Ebrey, Patricia Buckley, and James L. Watson, "Introduction." In *Kinship Organization in Late Imperial China 1000–1940*, edited by Patricia Buckley Ebrey and James L. Watson, 1–15. Berkeley, CA: University of California Press, 1986.

Eibach, Joachim. "Das offene Haus: Kommunikative Praxis im sozialen Nahraum der europäischen Frühen Neuzeit." *Zeitschrift für historische Forschung* 38, no. 4 (2011): 621–664.

Eibach, Joachim, and Claudia Opitz-Belakhal. *Zwischen Kulturen: Mittler und Grenzgänger vom 17. bis 19. Jahrhundert*. Hannover: Wehrhahn Verlag 2018.

Elison, George. *Deus Destroyed: The Image of Christianity in Early Modern Japan*. Cambridge, MA: Harvard University Press, 1988.

Emich, Birgit. *Bürokratie und Nepotismus unter Paul V. (1605–1621)*. Stuttgart: Anton Hiersemann, 2001.

Endō, Orie. *A Cultural History of Japanese Women's Language*. Ann Arbor, MI: The Center for Japanese Studies, The University of Michigan, 2006.

Ericson, Joan E. "The Origins of the Concept of 'Women's Literature'." In *The Woman's Hand: Gender and Theory in Japanese Women's Writing*, edited by Paul G. Schalow and Janet A. Walker, 74–116. Stanford, CA: Stanford University Press, 1996.

Fabre, Pierre-Antoine, ed. *Missions religieuses modernes: "Notre lieu est le monde."* Rome: École française de Rome, 2007.

———. "'Entrar con el otro y salir con sigo': nouvelles recherches sur les missions d'évangélisation modernes." *Archives de sciences sociales de religions* 168 (2014): 43–54.

Faini, Marco, and Alessia Meneghin. "Introduction." In *Domestic Devotions in the Early Modern World*, edited by Marco Faini and Alessia Meneghin, 1–29. Leiden: Brill, 2019.

Farge, William J. *The Japanese Translations of the Jesuit Mission Press, 1590–1614: De imitatione Christi and Guía de pecadores*. Lewiston, NY: E. Mellen Press, 2003.

Fattori, Maria Teresa. *Clemente VIII e il Sacro Collegio, 1592–1605: Meccanismi istituzionali e accentramento di governo*. Stuttgart: Anton Hiersemann, 2004.

Flannery, John M. *The Mission of the Portuguese Augustinians to Persia and Beyond (1602–1747)*. Leiden: Brill, 2013.

Flores, Jorge, and António Vasconcelos de Saldanha. *Os Firangis na Chancelaria Mogol: Cópias Portuguesas de documentos de Akbar (1572–1601)*. New Delhi: Portuguese Embassy, 2003.

Flüchter, Antje, ed. *Translating Catechisms, Translating Cultures: The Expansion of Catholicism in the Early Modern World*. Leiden: Brill, 2017.

Forclaz, Bertrand. *Catholiques au défi de la Réforme: La coexistence confessionelle à Utrecht au XVIIe siècle*. Paris: Honoré Champion, 2014.

Forrestal, Alison. *Vincent de Paul, the Lazarist Mission, and French Catholic Reform*. Oxford: Oxford University Press, 1998.

Forrestal, Alison, and Sean Alexander Smith, eds. *The Frontiers of Mission: Perspectives on Early Modern Missionary Catholicism*. Leiden: Brill, 2016.

Forster, Marc R. *The Counter-Reformation in the Villages: Religion and Reform in the Bishopric of Speyer, 1560–1720*. Ithaca, NY: Cornell University Press, 1992.

Frantzman, Seth J., and Ruth Kark. "The Catholic Church in Palestine/Israel: Real Estate in Terra Sancta." *Middle Eastern Studies* 50, no. 3 (2014): 370–396.

Frazee, Charles. *Catholics and Sultans: The Church and the Ottoman Empire 1453–1923*. Cambridge: Cambridge University Press, 1983.

Freedman, Maurice. "Ritual Aspects of Chinese Kinship and Marriage." In *The Study of Chinese Society: Essays by Maurice Freedman*, edited by William Skinner, 273–295. Stanford, CA: Stanford University Press, 1979.

Friedmann, Yohanan. "Dhimma." In *Encyclopaedia of Islam, THREE*, edited by Kate Fleet, Gudrun Krämer, Denis Matringe, John Nawas, and Everett Rowson. Leiden: Brill, 2007. http://dx.doi.org/10.1163/1573-3912_ei3_COM_26005.

Frison, Daniele. "The Office of Procurator through the Letters of Carlo Spinola." *Bulletin of Portuguese/Japanese Studies* 20 (2010): 9–70.

Fukushima, Kunimichi. *Kirishitan shiryō to kokugo kenkyū*, Kasama sōsho 38. Tokyo: Kasama shoin, 1973.

Ganss, George E. "Toward Understanding the Jesuit Brothers' Vocation, Especially as Described in the Papal and Jesuit Documents." *Studies in the Spirituality of Jesuits* 13, no. 3 (1981): 1–63.

Gay, Jean-Pascal. *Jesuit Civil Wars: Theology, Politics and Government under Tirso González (1687–1705)*. Farnham: Ashgate, 2012.

Getcha, Job. "Confession or Spiritual Direction in the Orthodox Church: Some Modern Questions to a Very Ancient Practice." *St. Vladimir's Theological Quarterly* 51, no. 2/3 (2007): 203–220.

Ghobrial, John-Paul. *The Whispers of Cities: Information Flows in Istanbul, London, and Paris in the Age of William Trumbull*. Oxford: Oxford University Press, 2014.

Gil Fernández, Luis. *El imperio luso-español y la Persia safávida*. Vol. 1: *1582–1605*. Vol. 2: *1606–1622*. Madrid: Fundación Universitaria Española, 2006, 2009.

Girard, Aurélien. "Impossible Independence or Necessary Dependency? Missionaries in the Near East, the 'Protection' of the Catholic States and the Roman Arbitrator." In *Papacy, Religious Orders and International Politics in the Sixteenth and Seventeenth Centuries*, edited by Massimo Carlo Giannini, 67–94. Rome: Viella, 2013.

Girard, Émilie, and Felicita Tramontana. "La fabrication des objets de dévotion en Palestine, de l'époque moderne au début du XIXe siècle: le témoignage des maquettes et d'une icône de pèlerin récemment acquis par le MuCEM." *Archives de sciences sociales des religions* 183 (2018): 247–260.

Girard, Pascale. "Les descriptions qui fâchent: La 'Relación' du Jésuite Adriano de las Cortes en Chine (1626) et le déni de la Compagnie." In *L'Empire portugais face aux autres Empires*, ed. by Francisco Bethencourt and Luiz Felipe de Alencastro, 167–184. Paris: Maisonneuve et Larose/Centre culturel Calouste Gulbenkian, 2007.

Golvers, Noël. *François de Rougemont, S.J., Missionary in Ch'ang-shu (Chiang-nan). A Study of the Account Book (1674–1676) and the Eulogium*. Leuven: Leuven University Press, 1999.

———. "Note on the Newly Discovered Portrait of Martini." In *Martino Martini: Man of Dialogue*, edited by Luisa M. Paternicò, Claudia von Collani, and Riccardo Scartezzini, 9–11. Trento: Università di Trento, 2016.

Gommans, Jos, and Ineke Loots. "Arguing with the Heathens: The Further Reformation and the Ethnohistory of Johannes Hoornbeeck (1617–1666)." *Itinerario* 39 (2015): 45–68.

Gonoi, Takashi. *Tokugawa shoki Kirishitan shi kenkyū*. 2nd ed. Tokyo: Yoshikawa Kōbunkan, 1992.

———. *Kirishitan no bunka*. Tokyo: Yoshikawa Kōbunkan, 2012.

———. *Kirishitan shinkōshi no kenkyū*. Tokyo: Yoshikawa Kōbunkan, 2017.

Gonzague, Louis de. "Les anciens missionnaires capuchins de Syrie et leurs écrits apostoliques de langue arabe." *Collectanea Franciscana* 2, no. 2 (1932): 179–207.

Gradeva, Rossitsa. "From the Bottom Up and Back Again until Who Knows When: Church Restoration Procedures in the Ottoman Empire, Seventeenth-Eighteenth Centuries (Preliminary Notes)." In *Political Initiatives "From the Bottom Up" in the Ottoman Empire*, edited by Antonis Anastasopoulos, 135–163. Rethymno: Crete University Press, 2012.

Guasti, Niccolò, ed. *I patrimoni dei gesuiti nell'Italia moderna: una prospettiva comparativa*. Bari: Epiduglia, 2013.

Guillen-Nuñez, César. "The Portrait of Matteo Ricci: A Mirror of Western Religious and Chinese Literati Portrait Painting." *Journal of Jesuit Studies* 1, no. 3 (2014): 443–464.

Halft, Dennis. "Schiitische Polemik gegen das Christentum im safavidischen Iran des 11./17. Jhdts. Sayyid Aḥmad ʿAlawīs *Lawāmiʿ-i rabbānī dar radd-i šubha-yi naṣrānī*." In *Contacts and Controversies between Muslims, Jews and Christians in the Ottoman Empire and Pre-Modern Iran*, edited by Camilla Adang and Sabine Schmidtke, 273–334. Würzburg: Ergon Verlag, 2010.

———. "The Arabic Vulgate in Safavid Persia. Arabic Printing of the Gospels, Catholic Missionaries, and the Rise of Shīʿī Anti-Christian Polemics." PhD diss., Freie Universität Berlin, 2016.

Hall, John Whitney, ed. *The Cambridge History of Japan*. Vol. 4: *Early Modern Japan*. Cambridge: Cambridge University Press, 1991.

Hamilton, Alastair. *The Copts and the West, 1439–1822: The European Discovery of the Egyptian Church*. Oxford: Oxford University Press, 2006.

Harris, George. "The Mission of Matteo Ricci S.J.: A Case Study of an Effort at Guided Cultural Change in China in the Sixteenth Century." *Monumenta Serica* 25 (1966): 1–168.

Harrison, Henrietta. *The Missionary's Curse and Other Tales From a Chinese Catholic Village*. Berkeley: University of California Press, 2013.

Hartmann, Arnulf. *The Augustinians in Seventeenth Century Japan*. New York: Augustinian Historical Institute, 1965.

Hathaway, Jane. *The Politics of Households in Ottoman Egypt*. Cambridge: Cambridge University Press, 1997.

Hauck, Gerhard. *Kultur: Zur Karriere eines sozialwissenschaftlichen Begriffs*. Münster: Westfälisches Dampfboot, 2006.

Hedin, Sven. "Early European Knowledge of Tibet." *Geografiska Annaler* 1 (1919): 290–339.

Heijdra, Martin. "The Socio-Economic Development of Rural China during the Ming." In *The Cambridge History of China*. Vol. 8, part 2: *The Ming Dynasty, 1368–1644*, edited by Denis Twitchett and John K. Fairbank, 417–578. Cambridge: Cambridge University Press, 1998.

Herr, Richard, ed. *Themes in Rural History of the Western World*. Ames: Iowa State University Press, 1993.

Hersche, Peter. *Muße und Verschwendung: Europäische Gesellschaft und Kultur im Barockzeitalter*. 2 vols. Freiburg: Herder Verlag, 2006.

Heyberger, Bernard. "Les chrétiens d'Alep à travers les récits des conversions des missionaires carmes déchaux (1657–1681)." *Mélanges de l'École française de Rome* 100, no. 1 (1988): 461–499.

———. *Les chrétiens du Proche-Orient au temps de la Réforme catholique*. Rome: École française de Rome, 1994.

———. "Terre Sainte et mission au XVIIe siècle." *Dimensioni e problemi della ricerca storica* 2 (1994): 127–153.

———. *Hindiyya (1720–1798), mystique et criminelle*. Paris: Aubier, 2001.

———. "Frontières confessionnelles et conversions chez les chrétiens orientaux (XVIIe-XVIIIe siècles)." In *Conversions Islamiques: Identités religieuses en Islam méditerranéen*, edited by Mercedes García-Arena, 245–258. Paris: Maisonneuve et Larose, 2002.

———. "Individualism and Political Modernity: Devout Catholic Women in Aleppo and Lebanon. Between the Seventeenth and the Nineteenth Centuries." In *Beyond the Exotic: Women's histories in Islamic Societies*, edited by Amira El-Azhary Sonbol, 71–85. New York: Syracuse University Press, 2005.

———. "Morale et confession chez les melkites d'Alep d'après une liste de péchés (fin XVIIe siècle)." In *L'Orient chrétien dans l'empire musulman. Hommage au professeur Gérard Troupeau*, edited by Geneviève Gobillot and Marie-Thérèse Urvoy, 283–306. Paris: Édition de Paris, 2005.

———. "Polemic Dialogues between Christian and Muslims in the Seventeenth Century." In *Cultural Dialogue in South Asia and Beyond*, edited by Corinne Lefèvre and Ines G. Županov, special issue, *Journal of the Economic and Social History of the Orient* 55, no. 2/3 (2012): 495–516.

Heyberger, Bernard, Mercedes García-Arenal, Emanuele Colombo, and Paola Vismara, eds. *L'Islam visto da Occidente: Cultura e religione del Seicento europeo di fronte all'Islam*. Genoa: Marietti, 2009.

Higashibaba, Ikuo. *Christianity in Early Modern Japan: Kirishitan Belief and Practice*. Leiden: Brill, 2001.

Hiiragi, Gen'ichi. "Kaidai." In *Kirishitanbanshū*, Tenri Toshokan zenpon shōso 38, 2 vols. in 3, 1:1–38. Tenri: Tenri University Press, 1976.

Hioki, N. Frances. "Tea Ceremony as a Space for Interreligious Dialogue." In *Exchange* 42 (2013): 125–142.

Hoey, Jack B. III. "Alessandro Valignano and the Restructuring of the Jesuit Mission in Japan, 1579–1582." *Eleutheria* 1, no. 1 (2010): 23–42.

Höfert, Almut. "Gender in Trans-it: Geschlecht und transkulturelle Perspektiven." In *Gender in Trans-it: Transkulturelle und transnationale Perspektiven*, edited by Martina Ineichen, Anna K. Liesch, Anja Rathmann-Lutz, and Simon Wenger, 17–29. Zurich: Chronos, 2009.

Hsia, Ronnie Po-chia. *The World of Catholic Renewal 1540–1770*. Cambridge: Cambridge University Press, 1998.

———. "From Buddhist Garb to Literati Silk: Costume and Identity of the Jesuit Missionary." In *Religious Ceremonials and Images: Power and Social Meaning (1400–1750)*, edited by José Pedro Paiva, 143–154. Coimbra: Palimage, 2002.

———. "Translating Christianity: Counter-Reformation Europe and the Catholic Mission in China, 1580–1780." In *Conversion. Old Worlds and New*, edited by Kenneth Mills and Anthony Grafton, 87–108. Rochester: University of Rochester Press, 2003.

———. *Noble Patronage and Jesuit Missions: Maria Theresia von Fugger-Wellenburg (1690–1762) and Jesuit Missionaries in China and Vietnam*. Rome: Institutum Historicum Societatis Iesu, 2006.

———. "Christian Conversation in Late Ming China: Niccolo Longobardo and Shandong." *The Medieval History Journal* 12, no. 2 (2009): 275–301.

———. "Tianzhu jiao yu Mingmo shehui 天主教與明末社會 (Christianity and late Ming society)." *Lishi yanjiu* 2 (2009): 51–67.

———. *A Jesuit in the Forbidden City: Matteo Ricci, 1552–1610*. Oxford: Oxford University Press, 2010.

———. "Convergence and Conversion: The Virgin Mary and Mazu as Maritime Patroness in Late Imperial China." *Urbana University Journal, Nova Series* 68, no. 2 (2015): 149–172.

———. "Christianity and Empire: The Catholic Mission in Late Imperial China." *Studies in Church History* 54 (2018): 208–224.

———. ed. *A Companion to Early Modern Catholic Global Missions*. Leiden: Brill, 2018.

———. "Imperial China and the Christian Mission." In *A Companion to Early Modern Catholic Global Missions*, edited by Ronnie Po-chia Hsia, 344–364. Leiden: Brill, 2018.

Huang Yilong. *Liang tou she: Ming mo Qing chu de diyitai Tianzhu jiaotu*. 兩頭蛇: 明末清初的第一代天主教徒 (The two-headed snake: The first generation of

Chinese Christians in the seventeenth century). Xinzhu: Guoli Qinghua daxue chubanshe, 2005.

Huber, Toni. "Pushing South: Tibetan Economic and Political Activities in the Far Eastern Himalaya, ca. 1900–1950." In *Buddhist Himalaya: Studies in Religion, History and Culture*. Vol. 1, edited by Anna Balikci-Denjongpa and Alex McKay, 259–276. Gangtok: Namgyal Institute of Tibetology, 2011.

Hur, Nam-lin. *Death and Social Order in Tokugawa Japan: Buddhism, Anti-Christianity, and the Danka System*. Cambridge, MA: Harvard University Press, 2007.

Ide, Katsumi. *Kirishitan shisōshi kenkyū josetsu: Nihonjin no Kirisutokyō juyō*. Tokyo: Perikansha, 1995.

Ikas, Karin, and Gerhard Wagner, eds. *Communicating in the Third Space*. New York: Routledge, 2009.

Imbruglia, Girolamo. *The Jesuit Missions in Paraguay and a Cultural History of Utopia (1568–1789)*. Leiden: Brill, 2017.

Inalcik, Halil. *The Middle East and the Balkans under the Ottoman Empire: Essays on Economy and Society*. Bloomington, IN: Indiana University Press, 1993.

Iskandar Bēg Munshī. *History of ʿAbbas the Great* (Tārīk̲-e ʿĀlamārā-ye ʿAbbāsī). Translated by Roger M. Savory. 3 vols. Boulder, CO: Westview Press, 1978 (vols. 1 and 2), New York: Bibliotheca Persica, 1986 (vol. 3).

Jami, Catherine, Peter Engelfriet, and Gregory Blue, eds. *Statecraft and Intellectual Renewal in Late Ming China: The Cross-cultural Synthesis of Xu Guangqi (1562–1633)*. Leiden: Brill, 2001.

Jensen, Lionel. *Manufacturing Confucianism: Chinese Traditions and Universal Civilization*. Durham, NC: Duke University Press, 1997.

Jericó Bermejo, Ignacio. "Domingo Báñez: Teología de la infidelidad en los paganos y herejes (1584)." *Revista Augustiniana* 41 (2000): 7–479.

Jiang, Wei. "Missionary Rivalries in the Far East, 16th–17th c." PhD diss., University of London, 2017.

Jinpa, Nawang. "Why Did Tibet and Ladakh Clash in the 17th Century? Rethinking the Background to the 'Mongol War' in Ngari (1679–1684)." *Tibet Journal* 40 (2015): 113–150.

Jordan, Joseph. "Le P. Jacques Gachoud, jésuite fribourgeois (1657–1726)." *Zeitschrift für schweizerische Kirchengeschichte* 54 (1960): 282–302; 55 (1961): 1–20, 168–190, 288–308.

Joseph, Sabrina. *Islamic Law on Peasant Usufruct in Ottoman Syria: 17th to Early 19th Century*. Leiden: Brill, 2012.

Kaneko, Sachiko, Hiroko Kuroda, Noriko Sugano, and Akiko Yoshie, eds. *Nihon joseishi daijiten*. Tokyo: Yoshikawa kōbunkan, 2008.

Kaplan, Benjamin J. *Divided by Faith: Religious Conflict and the Practice of Toleration in Early Modern Europe*. Cambridge, MA: Harvard University Press, 2007.

Kapstein, Matthew T. *The Tibetans*. Oxford: Blackwell Publishing, 2006.

Kark, Ruth, and Michal Oren-Nordheim. *Jerusalem and Environs: Quarters, Neighborhoods, Villages*. Detroit, MI: Wayne State University Press, 2001.

Kataoka, Rumiko. *Kirishitan jidai no joshi shūdōkai: Miyako no bikunitachi*, Kirishitan kenkyū series 14. Tokyo: Kirishitan bunka kenkyūkai, 1976.

———. "Fundação e organização da Misericordia de Nagasáqui." *Oceanos* 35, no. 35 (1998): 111–120.

Kataoka, Yakichi. *Nihon Kirishitan junkyōshi*. Tokyo: Jiji tsūshinsha, 1979.

Kawahara, Atsushi, and Shunʿichi Ikegami, eds. *Yōroppa chūkinsei no kyōdaikai*. Tokyo: Tokyo University Press, 2014.

Kawamura, Shinzō. "Communities, Christendom and a Unified Regime in Early Modern Japan." In *Christianity and Cultures: Japan and China in Comparison, 1543–1644*, edited by M. Antoni Üçerler, 151–166. Rome: Institutum Historicum Societatis Iesu, 2009.

Khalilieh, Hasan. "Amān." In *Encyclopaedia of Islam, THREE*, edited by Kate Fleet, Gudrun Krämer, Denis Matringe, John Nawas, and Everett Rowson. Leiden: Brill, 2007. http://dx.doi.org/10.1163/1573-3912_ei3_SIM_0048.

Kirsch, Johann Peter. "Council of Trent." In *The Catholic Encyclopedia*, vol. 15. New York: Robert Appleton Company, 1912. Retrieved from www.newadvent.org/cathen/15030c.htm. Last accessed 9 January 2019.

Knost, Stefan. *Die Organisation des religiösen Raums in Aleppo: Die Rolle der islamischen Stiftungen (auqāf) in der Gesellschaft einer Provinzhauptstadt des Osmanischen Reiches an der Wende zum 19. Jahrhundert*. Beirut: Orient-Institut, 2009.

Ko, Dorothy, JaHyun Kim Haboush, and Joan R. Piggott. "Introduction." In *Women in Confucian Cultures in Premodern China, Korea and Japan*, edited by Dorothy Ko, JaHyun Kim Haboush, and Joan R. Piggott, 1–24. Berkeley, CA: University of California, 2003.

Koch, Ludwig, ed. *Jesuiten-Lexikon: Die Gesellschaft Jesu einst und jetzt*. 3 vols. Leuven and Heverlee: Verlag der Bibliothek SJ, 1962.

Kolovos, Elias. "*Monasteries* in the *Rural* Society and Economy of the *Greek* Lands under the Ottomans: A Historiographical Appraisal." In *Ottoman Rural Societies and Economies, Halcyon Days in Crete VII: A Symposium Held in Rethymno 13–15 January 2012*, edited by Elias Kolovos, 165–172. Rethymno: Crete University Press, 2015.

Kornicki, Peter. *The Book in Japan: A Cultural History from the Beginnings to the Nineteenth Century*. Honolulu: Univ. of Hawai'i, 2001.

Kōso, Toshiaki, ed. *Sanctos no gosagvueo no vchi nvqigaqi*. Kirishitanban seisen. Tokyo: Yūshōdō, 2006.

Kouamé, Nathalie. "L'État des Tokugawa et la religion: Intransigeance et tolérance religieuses dans le Japon moderne (XVIe–XIXe siècles)." *Archives de sciences sociales des religions* 137 (2007): 107–123. https://doi.org/10.4000/assr.4328.

Krahl, Joseph. *China Missions in Crisis: Bishop Laimbeckhoven and His Times 1738–1787*. Rome: Gregorian University Press, 1964.

Kümin, Beat, and Felicita Tramontana. *Catholicism Decentralized: Local Religion in the Early Modern Periphery* (forthcoming).

Lapidus, Ira Marvin. *Muslim Cities in the Later Middle Ages*. Cambridge: Cambridge University Press, 1984.

Lederle, Julia. *Mission und Ökonomie der Jesuiten in Indien: Intermediäres Handeln am Beispiel der Malabar-Provinz im 18. Jahrhundert*. Wiesbaden: Harrassowitz Verlag, 2009.

Lee, Rosemary Virginia. "A Printing Press for Shah ʿAbbas: Science, Learning, and Evangelization in the Near East, 1600–1650." PhD diss., University of Virginia, 2013.

Levy, Evonne. "Jesuit Identity, Identifiable Jesuits? Jesuit Dress in Theory and in Image." In *Le monde est une peinture: Jesuitische Identität und die Rolle der Bilder*, edited by Elisabeth Oy-Marra, Volker R. Remmert, and Kristina Müller-Bongard, 127–152. Berlin: Akademie Verlag, 2011.

Li Sher-shiueh. *Yishu: Mingmo yesuhui fanyi wenxuelun* 譯述: 明末耶穌會翻譯文學論 (Transwriting: Translated literature and Late Ming Jesuits). Hong Kong: Xianggang zhongwen daxue chubanshe, 2012.

Li Sher-shiueh, and Thierry Meynard, eds. *Jesuit Chreia in Late Ming China: Two Studies with an Annotated Translation of Alfonso Vagnone's Illustrations of the Grand Dao*. Bern: Peter Lang, 2013.

Lieberman, Victor. *Strange Parallels: Southeast Asia in Global Context, c.800–1800*. New York: Cambridge University Press, 2009.

Lin Xiaoping. "Seeing the Place: The Virgin Mary in a Chinese Lady's Inner Chamber." In *Early Modern Catholicism: Essays in Honour of John W. O'Malley, S.J.*, edited by Kathleen M. Comerford and Hilmar M. Pabel, 183–210. Toronto: University of Toronto Press, 2001.

Lippiello, Tiziana, and Roman Malek, eds. *"Scholar from the West": Giulio Aleni S.J. (1582–1649) and the Dialogue between Christianity and China*. Nettetal: Steyler, 1992.

Logan, Anne-Marie, and Liam M. Brockey. "Nicolas Trigault, SJ: A Portrait by Peter Paul Rubens." *Metropolitan Museum Journal* 38 (2003): 157–167.

Lombardi, Riccardo. *La salvezza di chi non ha fede*. Rome: Edizioni La Civiltà Cattolica, 1943.

Lopez, Donald S. *Prisoners of Shangri-La: Tibetan Buddhism and the West*. Chicago, IL: University of Chicago Press, 1998.

López Gay, Jesús. *La liturgia en la misión del Japón del siglo XVI*. Roma: Libreria dell'Universita Gregoriana, 1970.

———. "Father Francesco Pasio (1554–1612) and His Ideas about the Sacerdotal Training of the Japanese." *Bulletin of Portuguese/Japanese Studies* 3 (2001): 27–42.

Leung Yuen-sang 梁元生 [Liang Yuansheng], *Bianyuan yu zhijian* 邊緣與之間 (The margin and what is in-between). Hong Kong: Sanlian, 2008 (reprint Shanghai, Fudan daxue chubanshe, 2010).

Luria, Keith. *Sacred Boundaries: Religious Coexistence and Conflict in Early-Modern France*. Washington: The Catholic University of America Press, 2005.

Lutz, Jessie, ed. *Pioneer Chinese Christian Women: Gender, Christianity, and Social Mobility*. Bethlehem: Lehigh University Press, 2010.

MacLagen, Edward. *The Jesuits and the Great Mogul*. London: Burns Oates & Washbourne Ltd., 1932.

Magnino, Leo. *Pontificia Nipponica*. Roma: Officium Libri Catholici, 1947.

Maifreda, Germano. *I denari dell'inquisitore: Affari e giustizia di fede nell'Italia moderna*. Turin: Giulio Einaudi, 2014.

Malatesta, Edward, and Francis Rouleau. "The 'Excommunication' of Ferdinand Verbiest." In *Ferdinand Verbiest (1623–1688): Jesuit Missionary, Scientist, Engineer and Diplomat*, edited by John Witek, 485–494. Nettetal: Steyler Verlag, 1994.

Maldavsky, Aliocha. *Vocaciones inciertas: Misión y misioneros en la provincia jesuita del Perú en los siglos XVI y XVII*. Seville: Consejo superior de investigaciones científicas / Lima, Instituto francés de estudios andinos, 2012.

———. "Giving for the Mission: The *Encomenderos* and Christian Space in the Andes of the Late Sixteenth Century." In *Space and Conversion in Global Perspective*, edited by Wietse de Boer, Aliocha Maldavsky, Giuseppe Marcocci, and Ilaria Pavan, 260–284. Leiden: Brill, 2014.

Mann, Susan. *Precious Records: Women in China's Long Eighteenth Century*. Stanford, CA: Stanford University Press, 1997.

Marcocci, Giuseppe, Wietse de Boer, Aliocha Maldavsky, and Ilaria Pavan, eds. *Space and Conversion in Global Perspective*. Leiden: Brill, 2014.

Marcus, Abraham. *The Middle East on the Eve of Modernity: Aleppo in the Eighteenth Century*. New York: Columbia University Press, 1989.

Marino, Brigitte. "Le 'Quartier des Chrétiens' (*Maḥallat al-Naṣârâ*) de Damas au milieu du XVIIIe siècle (1150–1170/1737–1757)." *Revue des mondes musulmans et de la Méditerranée* 107–110 (2012): 323–351.

Massey, Doreen B. "A Global Sense of Place." *Marxism Today* 38 (1991): 24–29.

Masters, Bruce. *Christians and Jews in the Ottoman Arab World*. Cambridge: Cambridge University Press, 2001.

Matthee, Rudi. "Negotiating across cultures: The Dutch Van Leene mission to the Iranian court of Šāh Sulaymān, 1689–1692." *Eurasian Studies* 3 (2004): 35–63.

———. "The Politics of Protection. Iberian Missionaries in Safavid Iran Under Shāh ʿAbbās I (1587–1629)." In *Contacts and Controversies between Muslims, Jews and Christians in the Ottoman Empire and Pre-Modern Iran*, edited by Camilla Adang and Sabine Schmidtke, 245–271. Würzburg: Ergon Verlag, 2010.

———. *Persia in Crisis. Safavid Decline and the Fall of Isfahan*. London: I. B. Tauris, 2012.

Mayeur-Jaouen, Catherine. "Les familles au Moyen-Orient moderne et contemporain (XVIIe – XXIe siècle)." In *La famille en Islam d'après les sources arabes*, edited by Mohammed H. Benkheira, Avner Giladi, Catherine Mayeur-Jaouen, and Jacqueline Sublet, 391–489. Paris: Les Indes Savantes, 2013.

McLaren, Anne E. "Women's Work and Ritual Space in China." In *Chinese Women – Living and Working*, edited by Anne E. McLaren, 169–187. London: Routledge, 2004.

Méndez Fernández, Benito. *El problema de la salvación de "los infieles" en Francisco de Vitoria*. Rome: Iglesia Nacional Española, 1993.

Menegon, Eugenio. *Un solo cielo: Giulio Aleni S.J. (1582–1649). Geografia, arte, scienze, religione dall'Europa alla Cina*. Brescia: Grafo, 1994.

———. "I movimenti di Martino Martini nel Fujian (1646) in alcuni documenti inediti." *Studi Trentini di Scienze Storiche. Supplemento: Studi su Martino Martini* 73, Sezione Prima (1998): 629–640.

———. "Popular or Local? Historiographical Shifts in the Study of Christianity in Late Imperial China." In *Dongxi jiaoliushi de xinju: Yi jidu zongjiao wei zhongxin* 東西交流史的新局: 以基督宗教為中心 (New developments of the history of exchange between East and West: Focusing on Christianity), edited by Ku Wei-ying 古偉瀛, 247–307. Taipei: Taiwan daxue chuban zhongxin, 2005.

———. "Deliver Us from Evil: Confession and Salvation in Seventeenth- and Eighteenth-Century Chinese Catholicism." In *Forgive Us Our Sins: Confession in Late Ming and Early Qing China*, edited by Nicolas Standaert and Ad Dudink, 9–101. Nettetal: Steyler Verlag, 2006.

———. *Ancestors, Virgins, and Friars: Christianity as a Local Religion in Late Imperial China*. Cambridge, MA: Harvard University Press, 2009.

Menniti Ippolito, Antonio. *1664. Un anno della Chiesa universale: Saggio sull'italianità del papato in età moderna*. Rome: Viella, 2011.

Meriwether, Margaret L. *The Kin Who Count: Family and Society in Ottoman Aleppo 1770–1840*. Austin, TX: University of Texas Press, 1999.

Mitchell, Colin P. *The Practice of Politics in Safavid Iran: Power, Religion and Rhetoric*. London: I. B. Tauris Publishers, 2009.

Miyamoto, Kenji. "Nagasaki Santo Domingo kyōkai no fukugen ni tsuite – Kinsei Nihon kenchiku no ishō ni okeru seiō shuhōno kenkyū 15." *Kokusai bunka kenkyū* 8 (2004): 59–66.

Mochizuki, Mia M. "Sacred Art in an Age of Mechanical Reproduction: The *Salus Populi Romani* Madonna in the World." In *Sacred and Profane in Early Modern*

World, edited by Kayo Hirokawa, 129–143. Kyoto: Kyoto University/Nakanishi Printing Ltd., 2016.

Mohanty, Chandra Talpade. "Under Western Eyes: Feminist Scholarship and Colonial Struggle." In *Third World Women and the Politics of Feminism*, edited by Chanrda Talpade Mohanty, Ann Russo, and Lourdes Torres, 51–80. Bloomington, IN: Indiana University Press, 1991.

Mohasseb Saliba, Sabine. *Les monastères doubles du Liban, entre Rome et l'Empire ottoman XVIIe–XIXe siècle*. Paris: Presses de l'Université du Saint-Esprit de Kaslik, 2008.

Morali, Ilaria. "Gratia et infidelitas: F. de Toledo S.J. e F. Suarez S.J. Maestri del Collegio Romano e la questione della *salus infidelium* al tempo delle grandi missioni gesuitiche," *Studia missionalia* 55 (2006): 99–150.

Moran, Joseph Francis. *The Japanese and the Jesuits: Alessandro Valignano in Sixteenth-Century Japan*. London: Routledge, 1993.

Mörner, Magnus. *The Political and Economic Activities of the Jesuits in the La Plata Region, the Hapsburg Era*. Stockholm: Petherson, 1953.

Morris, V. Dixon. "The City of Sakai and Urban Autonomy." In *Warlords, Artists, and Commoners: Japan in the Sixteenth Century*, edited by George Elison and Bardwell L. Smith, 23–54. Honolulu, HI: University of Hawai'i, 1987.

Mostaccio, Silvia. "Spiritual Exercises: Obedience, Conscience, Conquest." In *The Oxford Handbook of the Jesuits*, edited by Ines G. Županov. New York: Oxford University Press, 2018. http://doi.org/10.1093/oxfordhb/9780190639631.013.4.

Muchnik, Natalia. *De paroles et de gestes: Constructions marranes en terre d'Inquisition*. Paris: Éditions de l'EHESS, 2014.

Muller, Jeffrey. "The Jesuit Strategy of Accommodation." In *Jesuit Image Theory*, edited by Wietse de Boer, Karl Enenkel, and Walter Melion, 461–492. Leiden: Brill, 2016.

Mundy, Martha, and Richard Saumarez Smith. *Governing Property, Making the Modern State: Law, Administration and Production in Ottoman Syria*. London: I. B. Tauris, 2007.

Mungello, Daniel E. *Curious Land: Jesuit Accommodation and the Origins of Sinology*. Stuttgart: Franz Steiner Verlag, 1985.

Muñoz, Honorio. *Los Dominicos españoles en Japón (siglo XVII)*. Madrid: Raycar, 1965.

Nagasaki kyōiku iinkai. *Nagasakishi Sakuramachi shōgakkō shinsetsu ni tomonau maizō bunkazai hakkutsu chōsa hōkokusho*. Nagasaki: Nagasaki kyōiku iinkai, 2003.

Necipoğlu, Gülru. *Architecture, Ceremonial, and Power: The Topkapi Palace in the Fifteenth and Sixteenth Centuries*. New York: The Architectural History Foundation and Cambridge, MA: MIT Press, 1991.

Negro, Sandra, and Manuel Marzal, eds. *Esclavitud, economía y evangelización: las haciendas jesuitas en la América virreinal*. Lima: Pontifica universidad católica del Perú, 2005.

Norris, Jacob. "Exporting the Holy Land: Artisans and Merchant Migrants in Ottoman-Era Bethlehem." *Mashriq & Mahjar* 2 (2013): 14–40.

———. "Dragomans, Tattooists, Artisans: Palestinian Christians and their Encounters with Catholic Europe in the 17th and 18th Centuries." *Journal of Global History* 14, no. 1 (2019): 68–86.

Nurikhan, Minas. *Il servo di Dio abate Mechitar*. Rome: 1914.

Obara, Satoru. "Kaisetsu kaidai." In *Santosu no gosagyō*, edited by Satoshi Obara. Kirishitan kenkyū 33, 383–411. Tokyo: Kyōbunkan, 1996.

Oesterle, Jenny. "Missionaries as Cultural Brokers at the Fatimid Court in Cairo." In *Cultural Brokers at Mediterranean Courts in the Middle Ages*, edited by Marc von der Höh, Nikolas Jaspert, and Jenny Rahel Oesterle, 63–72. Paderborn: Wilhelm Fink Verlag, 2013.

Ó hAnnracháin, Tadhg. *Catholic Europe, 1592–1648. Centre and Peripheries*. Oxford: Oxford University Press, 2015.

Olle, Manel. *La invención de China: Percepciones y estrategias filipinas respecto a China durante el siglo XVI*. Wiesbaden: Harrassowitz, 2000.

O'Malley, John W. *The First Jesuits*. London: Harvard University Press, 1993.

The Oxford English Dictionary, Second Edition. Oxford: Clarendon, 1989.

Pacheco, Diego. "The Founding of the Port of Nagasaki and Its Cession to the Society of Jesus." *Monumenta Nipponica* 25, no. 3/4 (1970): 303–323.

———. "Iglesias de Nagasaki durante el 'Siglo Cristiano', 1568–1620." *Boletín de la Asociación Española de Orientalistas* 13 (1977): 49–70.

Paramore, Kiri. *Japanese Confucianism: A Cultural History*. Cambridge: Cambridge University Press, 2016.

Park, Chris C. *Sacred Worlds: An Introduction to Geography and Religion*. London: Routledge, 1994.

Pattenden, Miles. *Electing the Pope in Early Modern Italy, 1450–1700*. Oxford: Oxford University Press, 2017.

Pavone, Sabina. "Dentro e fuori la Compagnia di Gesù: Claude Visdelou tra riti cinesi e riti malabarici." In *Los jesuitas: Religión, política y educación (siglos XVI – XVIII)*, edited by José Martínez Millán, Henar Pizarro Llorente, and Esther Jiménez Pablo, 943–960. Madrid: Universidad Pontificia Comillas, 2012.

———. "Spie, mandarini, bramini: i gesuiti e i loro travestimenti." *Il capitale culturale. Studies on the Value of Cultural Heritage* 7 (2013): 227–247.

Peri, Oded. "The Christian Population of Jerusalem." *The Journal of the Economic and Social History of the Orient* 39, no. 4 (1996): 398–421.

———. *Christianity under Islam in Jerusalem: The Question of the Holy Sites in Early Ottoman Times*. Leiden: Brill, 2001.

Perrone, Lorenzo. "Monasticism as a Factor of Religious Interaction in the Holy Land during the Byzantine Period." In *Sharing the Sacred: Religious Contacts and Conflicts in the Holy Land, First – Fifteenth Centuries CE*, edited by Arieh Kofsky and Guy Stroumsa, 67–98. Jerusalem: Yad Ben-Zvi Press, 1998.

Petech, Luciano. *I missionari italiani nel Tibet e nel Nepal*. 7 vols. Rome: Libreria dello Stato, 1954–56.

———. *The Kingdom of Ladakh, c. 950–1842 A.D.* Rome: Istituto italiano per il Medio ed Estremo Oriente, 1977.

———. "The Tibetan-Ladakhi-Moghul War (1679–1683)." In Luciano Petech, *Selected Papers on Asian History*, 19–44. Rome: Istituto italiano per il Medio ed Estremo Oriente, 1990.

Peterson, Willard. "What to Wear? Observation and Participation by Jesuit Missionaries in Late Ming Society." In *Implicit Understandings: Observing, Reporting, and Reflecting on the Encounters Between Europeans and Other Peoples in the Early Modern Era*, edited by Stuart B. Schwartz, 403–421. Cambridge: Cambridge University Press, 1994.

Pfister, Louis. *Notices biographiques et bibliographiques sur les jésuites de l'ancienne mission de Chine 1552–1773*. Shanghai: Imprimerie de la Mission catholique, 1932.

Philipp, Thomas. *Acre: The Rise and Fall of a Palestinian City, 1730–1831*. New York: Columbia University Press, 2001.

Philippi, Dieter. *Sammlung Philippi: Kopfbedeckungen in Glaube, Religion und Spiritualität*. Leipzig: St. Benno Verlag, 2009.

Piemontese, Angelo Michele. "I due ambasciatori in Persia ricevuti da Papa Paolo V al Quirinale." *Miscellanea Bibliotecae Apostolicae Vaticanae* 12 (2005): 357–425.

Pierre, Benoist. *Le Père Joseph: L'Éminence grise de Richelieu*. Paris: Perrin, 2007.

Pih, Irene. *Le P. Gabriel de Magalhães: Un jesuite portugais en Chine au XVIIe siècle*. Paris: Fundação Calouste Gulbenkian – Centro Cultural Português, 1979.

Pissurlenkar, Panduronga S.S. *Regimentos das Fortalezas da Índia*. Goa: Tipografia Rangel, 1951.

Pizzorusso, Giovanni. *Roma nei Caraibi: L'organizzazione delle missioni cattoliche nelle Antille e in Guyana (1635–1675)*. Rome: École française de Rome, 1995.

———. "La Congregazione 'de Propaganda Fide' e gli ordini religiosi: Conflittualità nel mondo delle missioni del XVII secolo." In *Religione, conflittualità e cultura*, edited by Massimo Carlo Giannini, special issue, *Cheiron* 43/44 (2005): 197–240.

———. *Governare le missioni, conoscere il mondo nel XVII secolo: La Congregazione pontificia de Propaganda Fide*. Viterbo: Edizioni Sette città, 2018.

Prodi, Paolo. *Il sovrano pontefice: Un corpo e due anime. La monarchia papale nella prima età moderna*. Bologna: Il Mulino, 1982.

———. "Il 'sovrano pontefice'." In *La Chiesa e il potere politico dal Medioevo all'età contemporanea*, edited by Giorgio Chittolini and Giovanni Miccoli, 195–216. Turin: Giulio Einaudi, 1986.

———. "Europe in the Age of Reformations: The Modern State and Confessionalization." In *The Protestant Reformation in a Context of Global History. Religious Reforms and World Civilizations*, edited by Heinz Schilling and Silvana Seidel Menchi, 49–68. Bologna: il Mulino, 2017.

Prosperi, Adriano. "L'Europa cristiana e il mondo: Alle origine dell'idea di missione." *Dimensioni e problemi della ricerca storica* 2 (1992): 189–220.

———. "Diari femminili e discernimento degli spiriti: le mistiche della prima età moderna in Italia." *Dimensioni e Problemi della ricercha storica* 2 (1994): 77–103.

Ramos, Martin Nogueira. "Religion et identité villageoise dans les communautés de chrétiens cachés et catholiques de Kyûshû (XIXe siècle)." *Cipango*, no. 21 (2014). https://journals.openedition.org/cipango/2300.

Raymond, André. *Grandes villes arabes à l'époque ottomane*. Paris: Sindbad, 1985.

Reinhard, Wolfgang. *Papstfinanz und Nepotismus unter Paul V. (1605–1621): Studien und Quellen zur Struktur und zu quantitativen Aspekten des päpstlichen Herrschaftssystems*. 2 vols. Stuttgart: Anton Hiersemann, 1974.

———. *Ausgewählte Abhandlungen*. Berlin: Duncker & Humblot, 1997.

———. *Paul V. Borghese (1605–1621): Mikropolitische Papstgeschichte*. Stuttgart: Anton Hiersemann, 2009.

Reinhardt, Volker. *Kardinal Scipione Borghese (1605–1633): Vermögen, Finanzen und sozialer Aufstieg eines Papstnepoten*. Tübingen: Max Niemeyer Verlag, 1984.

Rezavi, Syed Ali Nadeem. "Religious Disputations and Imperial Ideology: The Purpose and Location of Akbar's Ibadatkhana." *Studies in History* 24, no. 2 (2008): 195–209.

Ribeiro, Madalena. "The Christian Nobility of Kyushu: a Perusal of Jesuit Sources." *Bulletin of Portuguese/Japanese Studies* 13 (2006): 45–64.

Ribeiro, Vítor. *Bispos portugueses e Jesuitas no Japão: Cartas de D. Luiz Cerqueira*. Lisbon: Academia das Ciências, 1936.

Richard, Francis. "Catholicisme et Islam chiite au 'Grand Siècle:' Autour de quelques documents concernant les Missions catholiques en Perse au XVIIe siècle." *Euntes docete. Commentaria Urbaniana* 33 (1980): 339–403.

———. "Un Augustin portugais renégat, apologiste de l'Islam chiite au début du XVIIIe siècle." *Moyen Orient & Océan Indien XVIe – XIXe* 1 (1984): 73–85.

Richardson, Hugh. "Armenians and Indians in Tibet." *Journal of the Tibet Society* 1 (1981): 63–67.

Robinson, Rowena. "Cuncolim: Weaving a Tale of Resistance." *Economic and Political Weekly* 32, no. 7 (February 1997): 334–340.

Rocca, Giancarlo, ed. *La sostanza dell'effimero: Gli abiti degli ordini religiosi in Occidente*. Rome: Edizioni Paoline, 2000.

Rodrigues, Helena. "Local Sources of Funding for the Japanese Mission." *Bulletin of Portuguese/Japanese Studies* 7 (2003): 115–137.

Romano, Antonella. *Impressions de Chine: l'Europe et l'englobement du monde (XVIe-XVIIe siècle)*. Paris: Fayard, 2016.

Roper, Lindal. *The Holy Household: Women and Morals in Reformation Augsburg*. Oxford: Clarendon Press, 1989.

Rosaldo, Michelle Z. "The Use and Abuse of Anthropology: Reflections on Feminism and Cross-Cultural Understanding." *Signs* 5, no. 3 (1980): 389–417.

Rosenlee, Li-Hsiang Lisa. *Confucianism and Women: A Philosophical Interpretation*. Albany, NY: State University of New York Press, 2006.

Rosenwein, Barbara H. *Emotional Communities in the Early Middle Ages*. Ithaca, NY: Cornell University Press, 2006.

Rothman, Natalie E. *Brokering Empire: Trans-Imperial Subjects Between Venice and Istanbul*. Ithaca, NY: Cornell University Press, 2012.

Rozbicki, Michal Jan, and George O. Ndege, eds. *Cross-Cultural History and the Domestication of Otherness*. Basingstoke: Palgrave Macmillan, 2012.

Ruch, Barbara. "Woman to Woman: *Kumano bikuni* Proselytizers in Medieval and Early Modern Japan." In *Engendering Faith: Women and Buddhism in Premodern Japan*, edited by Barbara Ruch, 567–575. Ann Arbor, MI: Center for Japanese Studies, University of Michigan, 2002.

Ruiu, Adina. "Missionaries and French Subjects: The Jesuits in the Ottoman Empire." In *A Companion to the Early Modern Catholic Global Missions*, edited by Ronnie Po-chia Hsia, 181–204. Leiden: Brill, 2018.

Ruiz de Medina, Juan G. *Iezusu kaishi to Kirishitan fukyō*. Tokyo: Iwata shoin, 2003.

Sabean, David Warren, Simon Teuscher, and Jon Mathieu, eds. *Kinship in Europe: Approaches to Long-Term Development (1300–1900)*. New York: Berghahn, 2007.

Sakamoto, Mitsuru, ed. *Nanban byōbu shūsei*. Tokyo: Chūōkōron bijutsu shuppan, 2008.

Sanfilippo, Matteo. "Travestimento o tradimento? I missionari cattolici in Cina nei secoli XVI e XVII." *Miscellanea di storia delle esplorazioni* 21 (1996): 113–123.

———. "L'abito fa il missionario? Scelte di abbigliamento, strategie di adattamento e interventi romani nelle missioni ad haereticos e ad gentes tra XVI e XX secolo." *Mélanges de l'École française de Rome. Italie et Méditerranée* 109, no. 2 (1997): 601–620.

———. "Adattamento e travestimento: l'abito religioso nelle missioni." In *La sostanza dell'effimero. Gli abiti degli ordini religiosi in Occidente*, edited by Giancarlo Rocca, 113–118. Rome: Edizioni Paoline, 2000.

Santus, Cesare. "La *communicatio in sacris* con gli 'scismatici' orientali in età moderna." *Mélanges de l'École française de Rome-Italie et Méditerranée modernes et contemporaines* 126, no. 2 (2014): 325–340.

———. "La comunità armena di Costantinopoli all'inizio del XVIII secolo: Scontri e tentativi di accordi interconfessionali (XVIII sec.)." *Rassegna degli Armenisti italiani* 17 (2016): 51–59.

———. "Conflicting Views. Catholic Missionaries in Ottoman Cities between Accommodation and Latinization." In this volume.

———. *Trasgressioni necessarie: "Communicatio in sacris", coesistenza e conflitti tra le comunità cristiane orientali (Levante e Impero ottomano, XVII-XVIII secolo).* Rome: École française de Rome, 2019.

Schilling, Doroteo, and Fidel de Legarza. "Relación del Reino de Nippon por Bernardino de Ávila Girón." *Archivo Iberoamericano* 38 (1935): 103–130.

Schmidt-Voges, Inken. "Das Haus in der Vormoderne." In *Das Haus in der Geschichte Europas: Ein Handbuch*, edited by Joachim Eibach and Inken Schmidt-Voges, 1–18. Berlin: Walter de Gruyter, 2015.

Schurhammer, Georg. *Orientalia.* Rome: Institutum Historicum Societatis Iesu / Lisbon: Centro de Estudios Históricos Ultramarinos, 1963.

Schweiger, Peter. "The Long Arm of the Fifth Dalai Lama: Influence and Power of the Fifth Dalai Lama in Southeast Tibet." In *Buddhist Himalaya: Studies in Religion, History and Culture.* Vol. 1, edited by Anna Balikci-Denjongpa and Alex McKay, 239–257. Gangtok: Namgyal Institute of Tibetology, 2011.

Sekiguchi, Hiroko. "The Patriarchal Family Paradigm in Eighth-Century Japan." In *Women in Confucian Cultures in Premodern China, Korea and Japan*, edited by Dorothy Ko, JaHyun Kim Haboush, and Joan R. Piggott, 27–46. Berkeley, CA: University of California, 2003.

Shirane, Haruo, ed. *Traditional Japanese Literature: An Anthology, Beginnings to 1600, Translations from the Asian Classics.* New York: Columbia University Press, 2007.

Sidler, Daniel. *Heiligkeit aushandeln: Katholische Reform und lokale Glaubenspraxis in der Eidgenossenschaft.* Frankfurt a. M.: Campus Verlag, 2017.

Siebenhüner, Kim. *Bigamie und Inquisition in Italien 1600–1700.* Paderborn: Ferdinand Schöningh, 2006.

Signorotto, Gianvittorio, and Maria Antonietta Visceglia, eds. *Court and Politics in Papal Rome, 1492–1700.* Cambridge: Cambridge University Press, 2002.

Simmonds, Gemma. "Women Jesuits." In *The Cambridge Companion to the Jesuits*, edited by Thomas Worcester, 120–135. Cambridge: Cambridge University Press, 2008.

Singer, Amy. *Palestinian Peasants and Ottoman Officials.* Cambridge: Cambridge University Press, 1994.

———. "Transcrire les frontières de village." In *Lucette Valensi à l'œuvre: Une histoire anthropologique de l'Islam méditerranéen*, edited by François Pouillon, 133–143. Paris: Éditions Bouchène, 2002.

Skinner, G. William. "Cities and Local Hierarchy of Local Systems." In *The City in Late Imperial China*, edited by G. William Skinner, 275–351. Stanford: Stanford University Press, 1977.

———. "Regional Urbanization in Nineteenth-Century China." In *The City in Late Imperial China*, edited by G. William Skinner, 211–249. Stanford: Stanford University Press, 1977.

Smith, Henry D. II. "The History of the Book in Edo and Paris." In *Edo and Paris: Urban Life and the State in the Early Modern Era*, edited by James L. McClain, John M. Merriman, and Kaoru Ugawa, 332–352. New York: Cornell University, 1994.

Soalheiro, Bruna. "Política e retórica: estratégias de conversão nas missões jesuítas do Mogol, Tibete e Bengala (XVI-XVIII)." Unpublished PhD, USP/EHESS, 2014.

Souza, Teotónio R. de. "Why Cuncolim Martyrs." In *Jesuits in India in Historical Perspective*, edited by Teotónio R. de Souza and Charles J. Borges, 37–47. Macao: Instituto Cultural de Macao and Xavier Center of Historical Research, 1992.

Spence, Jonathan. *The Question of Hu*. New York: Faber and Faber, 1989.

———. "The Paris Years of Arcadio Huang." In *Chinese Roundabout: Essays in History and Culture*, edited by Jonathan Spence, 11–24. New York: Norton, 1992.

Standaert, Nicolas. "Jesuit Corporate Culture as Shaped by the Chinese." In *The Jesuits. Cultures, Sciences, and the Arts, 1540–1773*, edited by John W. O'Malley, Gauvin Alexander Bailey, Steven J. Harris, and T. Frank Kennedy, 352–363. Toronto: University of Toronto Press, 1999.

———. "The Jesuits Did NOT Manufacture "Confucianism" (Review Article on Lionel Jensen, The Manufacturing of Confucianism, Durham, NC, Duke University Press, 1997)." In *East Asian Science, Technology and Medicine* 16 (1999): 115–132.

———. "The Creation of Christian Communities." In *Handbook of Christianity in China*. Vol. 1: *635–1800*, edited by Nicolas Standaert, 534–543. Leiden: Brill, 2001.

———. ed. *Handbook of Christianity in China*. Vol. 1: *635–1800*. Leiden: Brill, 2001.

———. "Numbers of Missionaries." In *Handbook of Christianity in China*. Vol. 1: *635–1800*, edited by Nicolas Standaert, 300–308. Leiden: Brill, 2001.

———. *The Interweaving of Rituals: Funerals in the Cultural Exchange Between China and Europe*. Seattle, WA: University of Washington Press, 2008.

———. "Don't Mind the Gap: Sinology as an Art of In-Betweenness." *Philosophy Compass* 10, no. 2 (2015): 91–103.

———. "Attention à l'écart: l'art de l'entre-deux." In *Michel de Certeau: Le voyage de l'œuvre*, edited by Luce Giard, 207–231. Paris: Facultés jésuites de Paris, 2017.

Steensgaard, Niels. *The Asian Trade Revolution of the Seventeenth Century: The East India Companies and the Decline of the Caravan Trade*. Chicago, IL: University of Chicago Press, 1974.

Strumia, Alberto. *Che cos'è una religione: La concezione di Tommaso d'Aquino di fronte alle domande odierne*. Siena: Edizioni Cantagalli, 2006.

Struve, Lynn A. *Voices from the Ming-Qing Cataclysm: China in Tiger's Jaws*. New Haven, CT: Yale University Press, 1993.

———. "The Southern Ming, 1644–1662." In *The Cambridge History of China*. Vol. 8, part 2: *The Ming Dynasty, 1368–1644*, edited by Denis Twitchett and John K. Fairbank, 641–725. Cambridge: Cambridge University Press, 1998.

Sweet, Michael J. "Gleanings from the Account Book 1: New Light on Some Episodes of His Life in Tibet." *Buddhist-Christian Studies* 38 (2018): 119–123.

Swierenga, Robert P. "The New Rural History: Defining the Parameters." *Great Plains Quarterly* 1, no. 4 (1981): 211–223.

Talbot, Cynthia. "Temples, Donors, and Gifts: Patterns of Patronage in Thirteenth-Century South India." *The Journal of Asian Studies* 50, no. 2 (May 1991): 308–340.

Tamburello, Adolfo, Antoni Üçerler, and Maria Di Russo, eds. *Alessandro Valignano, uomo del Rinascimento: ponte tra Oriente e Occidente*. Rome: Institutum Historicum Societatis Iesu, 2008.

Tawtal, Ferdinand. *Wathā'iq tārikhiyya 'an Ḥalab*. Beirut: Al-Maṭba'at al-Kāthūlīkiyya, 1958.

Teng, Jinhua Emma. "The West as a Kingdom of Women: Woman and Occidentalism in Wang Tao's Tales of Travel." In *Traditions of East Asian Travel*, edited by Joshua A. Fogel, 97–124. London: Berghahn Books, 2006.

ter Haar, Barend J. *The White Lotus Teachings in Chinese Religious History*. Leiden: Brill, 1992.

Theiss, Janet M. *Disgraceful Matters: The Politics of Chastity in Eighteenth-Century China*. Berkeley, CA: University of California Press, 2004.

Thomas, David. *Christian Doctrines in Islamic Theology*. Leiden: Brill, 2008.

Thomas, David, and Alex Mallett, eds. *Christian-Muslim Relations: A Bibliographical History*. Vol. 4: *1200–1350*. Leiden: Brill, 2012.

Todeschini, Giacomo. *Il prezzo della salvezza: Lessici medievali del pensiero economico*. Rome: Carocci, 1994.

Tonomura, Hitomi. "Sexual Violence Against Women: Legal and Extralegal Treatment in Premodern Warrior Societies." In *Women and Class in Japanese History*, edited by Hitomi Tonomura, Anne Walthall, and Haruko Wakita, 135–152. Ann Arbor, MI: University of Michigan, 1999.

Tramontana, Felicita. "La corte islamica e gli abitanti cristiani del distretto di Gerusalemme (secolo XVII)." *Società e Storia* 138 (2012): 791–806.

———. *Passage of Birth: Conversion in Palestinian Villages*. Wiesbaden: Harrassowitz, 2014.

Tronu, Carla. "Sacred Space and Ritual in Early Modern Japan: The Christian Community of Nagasaki (1569–1643)." PhD diss., University of London, 2012.

———. "The Rivalry between the Society of Jesus and the Mendicant Orders in Early Modern Nagasaki." *Agora: Journal of the International Centre for Regional Studies* 12 (2015): 25–39.

Truschke, Audrey. *Culture of Encounter: Sanskrit at the Mughal Court*. New York: Columbia University Press, 2016.

Tsakiris, Vasileios. *Die gedruckten griechischen Beichtbücher zur Zeit der Türkenherrschaft: Ihr kirchenpolitischer Entstehungszusammenhang und ihre Quellen*. Berlin: de Gruyter, 2009.

Turley, Steven E. *Franciscan Spirituality and Mission in New Spain, 1524–1599. Conflict Beneath the Sycamore Tree (Luke 19:1–10)*. Aldershot: Ashgate, 2014.

Tymoczko, Maria. "Ideology and the Position of the Translator: In What Sense is a Translator 'In Between'?" In *Critical Readings in Translation Studies*, edited by Mona Baker, 213–228. New York: Routledge, 2010.

Üçerler, M. Antoni J. "The Jesuit Enterprise in Japan (1573–1580)." In *The Mercurian Project: Forming Jesuit Culture, 1573–1580*, edited by Thomas M. McCoog, 831–875. Rome: Institutum Historicum Societatis Iesu: Institute of Jesuit Sources, 2004.

———. "The Jesuit Enterprise in Sixteenth- and Seventeenth-Century Japan." In *The Cambridge Companion to the Jesuits*, edited by Thomas Worcester, 153–168. Cambridge: Cambridge University Press, 2008.

Uno, Kathleen S. "Women and Changes in the Household Division of Labor." In *Recreating Japanese Women, 1600–1945*, edited by Gail Lee Bernstein, 17–41. Berkeley, CA: University of California Press, 1991.

Urdañoz, Teofilo. "La necesidad de la fe explícita para salvarse según los teólogos de la Escuela Salmantina." *Ciencia Tomista* 31 (1940): 529–537.

Urquiola, Alberto Tiburcio. "Convert Literature, Interreligious Polemics, and the 'Signs of Prophethood' Genre in Late Safavid Iran (1694–1722): The Work of ʿAlī Qulī Jadīd al-Islām (d. circa 1722)." PhD diss., McGill University (Montreal), 2014.

———. "Muslim-Christian polemics and scriptural translation in Safavid Iran: ʿAli-Qoli Jadid al-Eslām and his interlocutors." *Iranian Studies* 50 (2017): 247–269.

Valensi, Lucette. "Inter-Communal Relations and Changes in Religious Affiliation in the Middle East (Seventeenth to Nineteenth Centuries)." *Comparative Studies in Society and History* 39 (1997): 251–269.

Vande Walle, Willy. "Ferdinand Verbiest and the Chinese Bureaucracy." In *Ferdinand Verbiest (1623–1688): Jesuit Missionary, Scientist, Engineer and Diplomat*, edited by John Witek, 495–515. Nettetal: Steyler Verlag, 1994.

Vareschi, Severino. "Martino Martini S.I. e il decreto del Sant'Ufficio nella Questione dei riti cinesi (1655–56)." *Archivum Historicum Societatis Iesu* 63 (1994): 209–260.

Väth, Alfons. *Johann Adam Schall von Bell S.J., Missionar in China, kaiserlicher Astronom und Ratgeber am Hofe von Peking, 1592–1666*. Nettetal: Steyler Verlag 1991 (1933).

Vatin, Nicolas, and Elisabeth Zachariadou. "Le monastère de Saint-Jean à Patmos et son environnement rural." In *Ottoman Rural Societies and Economics, Halcyon Days in Crete VII: A Symposium Held in Rethymno, 13–15 January 2012*, edited by Elias Kolovos, 173–194. Rethymno: Crete University Press, 2015.

Verdeil, Chantal. *La mission jésuite du Mont-Liban et de Syrie (1830–1864)*. Paris: Les Indes Savantes, 2011.

Vermeer, E. B., ed. *Development and Decline of Fukien Province in the 17th and 18th Centuries*. Leiden: Brill, 1990.

Vermote, Frederick. "The Role of Urban Real Estate in Jesuit Finances and Networks between Europe and China, 1612–1778." PhD diss., University of British Columbia, 2013.

———. "Finances of the Missions." In *A Companion to Early Modern Catholic Global Missions*, edited by Ronnie Po-chia Hsia, 367–400. Leiden: Brill, 2018.

Visceglia, Maria Antonietta. *Morte e elezione del papa: Norme, riti e conflitti. L'Età moderna*. Rome: Viella, 2013.

Vitali, Roberto. *The Dge lugs pa in Gu ge and the Western Himalaya (Early 15th – Late 17th Century)*. Dharamshala: Amnye Machen Institute, 2012.

Vries, Wilhelm de. "*Communicatio in Sacris*: An Historical Study of the Problem of Liturgical Services in Common with Eastern Christians Separated from Rome." *Concilium* 4 (1965): 18–40.

Vu Thanh, Hélène. "'Il nous faut acquérir de l'autorité sur les Japonais': le problème de l'adaptation de la hiérarchie jésuite aux conditions religieuses et sociales japonaises." *Revue d'histoire ecclésiastique* 106, no. 3/4 (2011): 471–496.

———. "Between Accommodation and Intransigence: Jesuit Missionaries and Japanese Funeral Rites (16th–17th Centuries)." *Journal of the LUCAS Graduate Conference* 2 (2014). http://hdl.handle.net/1887/23303.

———. "Les liens complexes entre missionnaires et marchands ibériques: deux modèles de présence au Japon (1543–1639)." *Le Verger*, no. 5 (2014). www.cornucopia16.com/a-le-verger-revue-en-ligne/.

———. *Devenir japonais. La mission jésuite au Japon (1549–1614)*. Paris: Presses de l'Université Paris-Sorbonne, 2016.

———. "Un équilibre impossible: financer la mission jésuite du Japon, entre Europe et Asie (1579–1614)." *Revue d'Histoire Moderne et Contemporaine*, 63, no. 3 (2016): 7–30.

Wakita, Haruko. "The Medieval Household and Gender Roles within the Imperial Family, Nobility, Merchants and Commoners." Translated by Gary P. Leupp. In *Women and Class in Japanese History*, edited by Hitomi Tonomura, Anne Walthall, and Haruko Wakita, 81–97. Ann Arbor, MI: University of Michigan, 1999.

———. *Women in Medieval Japan: Motherhood, Household Management and Sexuality*. Translated by Alison Tokita. Clayton, Australia: Monash University Press and Tokyo: University of Tokyo Press, 2006.

Ward, Haruko Nawata. "Jesuits, Too: Jesuits, Women Catechists and Jezebels in Christian-Century Japan." In *The Jesuits: Cultures, Sciences, and the Arts, 1540–1773*, vol. 2, edited by John W. O'Malley, Gauvin Alexander Bailey, Steven J. Harris, and T. Frank Kennedy, 638–657. Toronto: University of Toronto Press, 2006.

———. "Jesuit Encounters with Confucianism in Early Modern Japan." *Sixteenth Century Journal* 40, no. 4 (2009): 1045–1068.

———. *Women Religious Leaders in Japan's Christian Century, 1549–1650*. Farnham: Ashgate, 2009.

———. "Women and Kirishitanban Literature: Translation, Gender and Theology in Early Modern Japan." *Early Modern Women: An Interdisciplinary Journal* 7 (2012): 271–281.

———. "Images of the Incarnation in the Jesuit Japan Mission's Kirishitanban Story of Virgin Martyr St. Catherine of Alexandria." In *Image and Incarnation: The Early Modern Doctrine of the Pictorial Image*, edited by Walter S. Melion and Lee Palmer Wandel, 489–509. Leiden: Brill Publishing, 2015.

———. "Women Apostles in Early Modern Japan, 1549–1650." In *Devout Laywomen in the Early Modern World*, edited by Alison Weber, 312–330. Abingdon: Routledge, 2016.

Wassilowsky, Günther. *Die Konklavenreform Gregors XV. (1621/22): Wertekonflikte, symbolische Inszenierung und Verfahrenswandel im posttridentinischen Papsttum*. Stuttgart: Anton Hiersemann, 2010.

Wei-chung, Cheng. *War, Trade and Piracy in the China Seas 1622–1683*. Leiden: Brill, 2013.

Wilkinson, Endymion Porter. *Chinese History: A New Manual*. Second revised printing. Cambridge, MA: Harvard University Asia Center, 2013.

Willeke, Bernward. *Kirishitan jidai ni okeru Furanshisukokai no katsudō*. Sapporo: Kōmeisha, 1994.

Windler, Christian. "Ambiguous Belongings: How Catholic Missionaries in Persia and the Roman Curia Dealt with *Communicatio in Sacris*." In *A Companion to Early Modern Catholic Global Missions*, edited by Ronnie Po-chia Hsia, 205–234. Leiden: Brill, 2018.

———. *Missionare in Persien: Kulturelle Diversität und Normenkonkurrenz im globalen Katholizismus (17.–18. Jahrhundert)*. Cologne: Böhlau Verlag, 2018.

Winter, Michael. *Egyptian Society Under Ottoman Rule, 1517–1798*. London: Routledge, 1992.

Wong, Roy Bin. *China Transformed: Historical Change and the Limits of European Experience*. Ithaca, NY: Cornell University Press, 1997.

Xavier, Ângela Barreto. *A Invenção de Goa*. Lisbon: Instituto de Ciências Sociais da Universidade de Lisboa, 2008.

———. "Power, Religion and Violence in Sixteenth-Century Goa." *Portuguese Literary and Cultural Studies* 17/18 (2010): 27–50.

Xavier, Ângela Barreto, and Ines G. Županov. *Catholic Orientalism: Portuguese Empire, Indian Knowledge*. New Delhi: Oxford University Press, 2015.

Yajima, Yutaka. *Bungo no kuni Kirishitan ruizokuchō no kenkyū*. Tokyo: Musashino shobō, 1976.

Yamazaki, Shinji. *Nagasaki Kirishitanshi – Fukō Kirisuto kyōkai no kawara*. Tokyo: Yūzankaku, 2015.

Yang C[hing] K[un]. *Religion in Chinese Society: A Study of Contemporary Functions of Religion and Some of Their Historical Factors*. Berkeley, CA: University of California Press, 1961.

Yoshida, Kazuhiko. "The Enlightenment of the Dragon King's Daughter in the Lotus Sutra." Translated by Margaret H. Childs. In *Engendering Faith: Women and Buddhism in Premodern Japan*, edited by Barbara Ruch, 297–324. Ann Arbor, MI: Center for Japanese Studies, University of Michigan, 2002.

Zampol D'Ortia, Linda. "Purple Silk and Black Cotton: Francisco Abral and the Negotiation of Jesuit Attire in Japan (1570–73)." In *Exploring Jesuit Distinctiveness: Interdisciplinary Perspectives on Ways of Proceeding Within the Society of Jesus*, edited by Robert Aleksander Maryks, 137–155. Leiden: Brill, 2016.

Ze'evi, Dror. *An Ottoman Century: The District of Jerusalem in the 1600s*. New York: SUNY Press, 1996.

Zekiyan, Boghos Levon. "Armenians and the Vatican during the Eighteenth and Nineteenth Centuries: Mekhitar and the Armenian Catholic Patriarchate: The Challenge of Mechitarian Ecumenism and Latin-Roman Loyalty." *Het Christelijk Oosten* 52, no. 3/4 (2000): 251–267.

Zhang Xianqing. *Guanfu, zongzu yu Tianzhujiao: Ming-Qing shiqi Fu'an xiangcun jiaohui de lishi xushi* 官府、宗族与天主教：17–19 世纪福安乡村教会的历史叙事 (The official, the lineage and Catholicism: The history of the village church in Fu'an County, seventeenth to nineteenth centuries). Beijing: Zhonghua shuju, 2009.

Zhou Yiqun. "The Hearth and the Temple: Mapping Female Religiosity in Late Imperial China, 1550–1900." *Late Imperial China* 24, no. 2 (2003): 109–155.

Županov, Ines G. *Disputed Mission. Jesuit Experiments and Brahmanical Knowledge in Seventeenth-century India*. New York: Oxford University Press, 1999.

———. *Missionary Tropics: The Catholic Frontier in India (16th–17th Centuries)*. Ann Arbor, MI: University of Michigan Press, 2005.

———. "'The Wheel of Torments': Mobility and Redemption in Portuguese Colonial India (16th century)." In *Cultural Mobility*, edited by Stephen Greenblatt, Ines G. Županov, Reinhard Meyer-Kalkus, Heike Paul, Pál Myíri, and Friederike Pannewick, 24–74. Cambridge: Cambridge University Press, 2009.

Županov, Ines G., and Pierre Antoine Fabre, eds. *The Rites Controversies in the Early Modern World*. Leiden: Brill, 2018.

Zürcher, Erik. "The Jesuit Mission in Fujian in Late Ming Times: Levels of Response." In *Development and Decline of Fukien Province in the 17th and 18th Centuries*, edited by Eduard B. Vermeer, 417–457. Leiden: Brill, 1990.

———. "Jesuit Accommodation and the Chinese Cultural Imperative." In *The Chinese Rites Controversy: Its History and Meaning*, edited by David E. Mungello, 31–64. Nettetal: Steyler Verlag, 1994.

———. "Confucian and Christian Religiosity in Late Ming China." *Catholic Historical Review* 83, no. 4 (1997): 614–653.

———. ed. *Kouduo richao. Li Jiubiao's Diary of Admonitions: A Late Ming Christian Journal*. 2 vols. Nettetal: Steyler Verlag, 2007.

Zwilling, Leonard. "Gleanings from the Account Book 2: The Teacher, the Servant, and the Cook." *Buddhist-Christian Studies* 38 (2018): 139–146.

Zwyssig, Philipp. *Täler voller Wunder: Eine katholische Verflechtungsgeschichte der Drei Bünde und des Veltlins (17. und 18. Jahrhundert)*. Affalterbach: Didymos Verlag, 2018.

Index

Note: Page numbers in *italic* indicate a figure on the corresponding page. **Bold** page numbers indicate a chart. An "n" following a page number indicates a note on that page.

Made in the USA
Las Vegas, NV
29 October 2024

759da7e3-87aa-444a-8ad7-feb981611303R01